Crosslinguistic Influence in L3 Acquisition

This book explores crosslinguistic influence in third language acquisition, drawing insights from a study of young bilingual secondary school students in Germany to unpack the importance of different variables in the acquisition and use of English as an additional language.

Lorenz draws on data from a learner corpus of written and spoken picture descriptions toward analyzing sources of crosslinguistic influence in L3 acquisition in bilingual heritage speakers with unbalanced proficiency in heritage versus majority languages as compared with their monolingual German peers. This unique approach allows for a clearer understanding of the extent of influence of access to heritage languages, the impact of being a "balanced" vs. "unbalanced" bilingual speaker, and the importance of extra-linguistic variables, such as age, gender, socio-economic status, and type of school. The final two chapters highlight practical considerations for the English language classroom and the implications of the study for future directions for research on third language acquisition.

With its detailed overview of L2 and L3 acquisition and contribution toward ongoing debates on the advantages of being bilingual and multilingual, this book will be of interest to students and scholars in applied linguistics, foreign language acquisition, foreign language teaching, and learner corpus research.

Eliane Lorenz is a senior researcher and lecturer (Akademische Rätin a. Z.) in the English Linguistics section of the Department of English, at Justus Liebig University Giessen, Germany. Prior to this, she held a post-doctoral fellowship in English linguistics and multilingualism at the Department of Teacher Education at the Norwegian University of Science and Technology (NTNU), as part of the project 'The Acquisition of English in the Multilingual Classroom' (AcEngMulCla). In 2019, she completed her PhD in English Linguistics at the University of Hamburg.

Routledge Studies in Applied Linguistics

Contexts of Co-Constructed Discourse
Interaction, Pragmatics, and Second Language Applications
Edited by Lori Czerwionka, Rachel Showstack, and Judith Liskin-Gasparro

Second Language Prosody and Computer Modeling
Okim Kang, David O. Johnson, Alyssa Kermad

Reconsidering Context in Language Assessment
Transdisciplinary Perspectives, Social Theories, and Validity
Janna Fox and Natasha Artemeva

Evaluation Across Newspaper Genres
Hard News Stories, Editorials and Feature Articles
Jonathan Ngai

Understanding Variability in Second Language Acquisition, Bilingualism, and Cognition
A Multi-layered Perspective
Edited by Kristin Kersten and Adam Winsler

Crosslinguistic Influence in L3 Acquisition
Bilingual Heritage Speakers in Germany
Eliane Lorenz

Bilingual Writers and Corpus Analysis
Edited by David M. Palfreyman and Nizar Habash

Reflexivity in Applied Linguistics
Opportunities, Challenges, and Suggestions
Edited by Sal Consoli and Sara Ganassin

For more information about this series, please visit: www.routledge.com/Routledge-Studies-in-Applied-Linguistics/book-series/RSAL

Crosslinguistic Influence in L3 Acquisition
Bilingual Heritage Speakers in Germany

Eliane Lorenz

NEW YORK AND LONDON

First published 2023
by Routledge
605 Third Avenue, New York, NY 10158

and by Routledge
4 Park Square, Milton Park, Abingdon, Oxon, OX14 4RN

Routledge is an imprint of the Taylor & Francis Group, an informa business

© 2023 Eliane Lorenz

The right of Eliane Lorenz to be identified as author of this work has been asserted in accordance with sections 77 and 78 of the Copyright, Designs and Patents Act 1988.

All rights reserved. No part of this book may be reprinted or reproduced or utilised in any form or by any electronic, mechanical, or other means, now known or hereafter invented, including photocopying and recording, or in any information storage or retrieval system, without permission in writing from the publishers.

Trademark notice: Product or corporate names may be trademarks or registered trademarks, and are used only for identification and explanation without intent to infringe.

Library of Congress Cataloging-in-Publication Data
Names: Lorenz, Eliane, author.
Title: Crosslinguistic influence in L3 acquisition : bilingual heritage speakers in Germany / Eliane Lorenz.
Description: New York, NY : Routledge, 2023. |
Series: Routledge studies in applied linguistics |
Includes bibliographical references and index. |
Identifiers: LCCN 2022021964 (print) | LCCN 2022021965 (ebook) |
ISBN 9780367681210 (hardback) | ISBN 9781003134336 (ebook)
Subjects: LCSH: Multilingualism–Germany. | Second language acquisition. | English language–Study and teaching (Secondary)–Germany.
Classification: LCC P115.5.G3 L67 2023 (print) | LCC P115.5.G3 (ebook) |
DDC 306.44/60943–dc23/eng/20220801
LC record available at https://lccn.loc.gov/2022021964
LC ebook record available at https://lccn.loc.gov/2022021965

ISBN: 978-0-367-68121-0 (hbk)
ISBN: 978-0-367-68122-7 (pbk)
ISBN: 978-1-003-13433-6 (ebk)

DOI: 10.4324/9781003134336

Typeset in Sabon
by Newgen Publishing UK

Contents

List of figures ix
List of tables x
Acknowledgments xii
List of abbreviations xiii

1 **Introduction** 1
  1.1 Background and motivation 1
  1.2 Setting the scene: second and third language acquisition 3
    1.2.1 Language acquisition 3
    1.2.2 Second versus third language acquisition 5
    1.2.3 Third language learners 6
    1.2.4 Transfer versus crosslinguistic influence 7
    1.2.5 Advantages 9
  1.3 Research questions 10
  1.4 Structure of the book 11

2 **Acquisition of English in Germany** 17
  2.1 The role of English in Germany 17
  2.2 Heterogeneous and diverse foreign language classrooms 20
  2.3 Monolingual versus multilingual teaching reality in Germany and beyond 22
  2.4 Summary 25

3 **Previous and current research on language acquisition** 31
  3.1 Terminology 31
    3.1.1 L1, L2, L3 31
    3.1.2 Minority/heritage language 32
    3.1.3 Majority/dominant language 32
    3.1.4 Bilingual heritage speakers 33
    3.1.5 Learning versus acquiring 33
  3.2 Third versus second language acquisition 33
    3.2.1 Emergence of the field 34
    3.2.2 Crosslinguistic influence in third language acquisition 35
    3.2.3 Evaluation 41

3.3 Bilingualism and heritage speakers 43
3.4 Third language acquisition of heritage bilinguals 46
3.5 Metalinguistic awareness 52
3.6 Bilingual advantages or effects 54
3.7 Summary 57

4 Tense and aspect 68
4.1 General properties of tense, aspect, aktionsart 68
    4.1.1 Tense 68
    4.1.2 Aspect 69
    4.1.3 Aktionsart 70
4.2 Tense and aspect marking in English 72
4.3 Tense and aspect marking in German 76
4.4 Tense and aspect marking in Russian 79
4.5 Tense and aspect marking in Turkish 84
4.6 Tense and aspect marking in Vietnamese 88
4.7 Similarities and differences in tense and aspect marking 91

5 Acquisition of tense and aspect 97
5.1 Acquisition of tense and aspect by native speakers of English 97
5.2 Acquisition of tense and aspect by non-native speakers of English 98
    5.2.1 General comments 98
    5.2.2 The English progressive aspect 100
5.3 Specific foreign language learners of English 101
    5.3.1 German learners of English 101
    5.3.2 Russian learners of English 103
    5.3.3 Turkish learners of English 105
    5.3.4 Vietnamese learners of English 106
5.4 Summary 109

6 English learner corpus based on written and spoken stories 114
6.1 Research design and data collection 114
    6.1.1 Written task 114
    6.1.2 Oral task 116
    6.1.3 Questionnaire 117
6.2 Corpus data coding scheme 118
6.3 Profile of participants 124
    6.3.1 General 124
    6.3.2 Background variables 125
6.4 Research objectives and predictions 131

7 Use of tense and aspect of monolinguals versus bilinguals 140
7.1 *Frequency overview (written component of the learner corpus)* 140
    7.1.1 Text composition (sentences, words, verbs) 140
    7.1.2 Subject-verb agreement 142
    7.1.3 Copula verb *be* 146
    7.1.4 Formal correctness and target-like meaning of verbs 148
7.2 *Progressive aspect (written component of the learner corpus)* 150
7.3 *Present versus past time reference (written component of the learner corpus)* 152
7.4 *Written versus spoken production* 154
    7.4.1 Frequency overview: written texts versus oral recordings 155
    7.4.2 Subject-verb agreement 157
    7.4.3 Copula verb *be* 158
    7.4.4 Formal correctness and target-like meaning of verbs 161
    7.4.5 Use of tenses and the progressive aspect 163
7.5 *Summary* 165

8 Use of tense and aspect versus social variables 169
8.1 *Formal correctness and target-like meaning of verbs* 169
    8.1.1 Formal correctness 169
    8.1.2 Target-like meaning 174
    8.1.3 Subject-verb agreement 177
8.2 *Progressive aspect* 181
    8.2.1 Formal correctness 181
    8.2.2 Target-like meaning 182
8.3 *Present versus past time reference* 183
8.4 *Written versus spoken production* 184
    8.4.1 Formal correctness 185
    8.4.2 Target-like meaning 190
    8.4.3 Subject-verb agreement 195
8.5 *Limitations* 197
8.6 *Summary* 198

9 Crosslinguistic influence in heritage speakers' L3 production 202
9.1 *Crosslinguistic influence in third language acquisition* 202
9.2 *Language dominance* 207
9.3 *Influence of (social) background variables* 209
    9.3.1 Type of school 209
    9.3.2 Socio-economic status 210
    9.3.3 Number of books per household 211
    9.3.4 Age 212
    9.3.5 Language task assessment: written versus spoken 213

       9.3.6 Age of onset of acquiring German 214
       9.3.7 Attitudes toward learning English 215
  9.4 *Shortcomings and limitations* 216

10 Bi-/multilingual advantages of heritage speakers   223
  10.1 *Advantages in foreign language acquisition?* 223
  10.2 *Metalinguistic awareness* 226
  10.3 *Learning environment in the English classroom in Germany* 228
  10.4 *Implications for foreign language education* 231

11 Conclusion and outlook   239
  11.1 *Summary of findings* 239
  11.2 *Future directions of further research* 244

Index   249

Figures

1.1	Transfer in second language acquisition	8
1.2	Transfer possibilities with three languages	9
1.3	Transfer in third language acquisition: focus of the current study	9
4.1	Continuum of analytic and inflectional tense and aspect marking	92
6.1	Picture story *Gut gemeint...* ('Good intentions...')	115
6.2	Potential patterns of crosslinguistic influence	133
7.1	Pearson's correlations between number of words written and spoken per language group	157
8.1	Effects plots binary logistic regression of correct form of verbs	172
8.2	Effects plots binary logistic regression of target-like meaning of verbs	176
8.3	Conditional inference tree of third person singular –s 'present' versus 'missing'	179
8.4	Conditional inference tree of formally correct and incorrect progressives	182
8.5	Conditional inference tree of main tense used in the written story ('present' versus 'other')	184
8.6	Effects plots binary logistic regression of correct form of verbs in the spoken and written data	189
8.7	Effects plots binary logistic regression of target-like meaning of verbs in the spoken and written data	194
8.8	Conditional inference tree of third person singular –s 'present' versus 'missing' in the spoken and written data	196

Tables

4.1	Simplified summary of tense and aspect properties	93
6.1	Descriptive overview (sum, mean, standard deviation) of participants and social variables	126
7.1	Frequency overview: absolute numbers, mean values (with standard deviations in parenthesis), normalized mean values per 100 words (with standard deviations in parenthesis) of sentences, words, and verbs per text	142
7.2	Affixal and suppletive SVA: absolute frequencies and percentages	144
7.3	Absolute frequencies and percentages of required and missing copula verbs	147
7.4	Absolute frequencies and proportions (with standard deviations in parenthesis) of formally (in)correct verbs and (non-)target-like meaning of verbs per learner group	149
7.5	Overview of formal correctness and target-like usage of the progressive aspect, absence of auxiliary verb	151
7.6	Overview of tenses (absolute frequencies and percentages)	153
7.7	Frequency overview of written and spoken component of the learner corpus; absolute numbers and means (with standard deviations in parenthesis)	156
7.8	Affixal and suppletive SVA: absolute frequencies and percentages of spoken and percentages of written corpus component	159
7.9	Absolute frequencies and percentages of required and missing copula verbs of spoken and percentages of written corpus component	160
7.10	Absolute frequencies and proportions (with standard deviations in parenthesis) of formally (in)correct verbs and (non-)target-like meaning of spoken and proportions of written corpus component	162
7.11	Overview of tenses in the oral recordings and written texts (absolute frequencies and percentages)	164
8.1	Binary logistic regression of formal correctness of verbs (predicting 'true')	171

8.2	Binary logistic regression of target-like meaning of verbs (predicting 'true')	175
8.3	Binary logistic regression of formal correctness of verbs (predicting 'true') in the spoken and written data	187
8.4	Binary logistic regression of target-like meaning of verbs (predicting 'true') in the spoken and written data	192

Acknowledgments

This book is a heavily revised and shortened version of my PhD thesis, which I completed in 2019. A few words of acknowledgment are in order to give credit to all those who supported me on this truly long and exciting journey.

First and foremost, my utmost gratitude goes to Peter Siemund. His never-ending excitement, inspiration, confidence, and complete trust, even after I had officially stopped working for him, was what kept me going. In addition, I would like to thank my dear colleagues and fellow PhD students at the universities of Hamburg, Trondheim, and Giessen for their support, stimulating conversations, and encouragement, and in particular Barbara Ann Güldenring for meticulously reading and commenting on the manuscript.

Most of the data were collected within the LiMA-Cluster at the University of Hamburg (Linguistic Diversity Management in Urban Areas, 2009–2013) and the financial support of the Hamburg Behörde für Wissenschaft und Forschung is gratefully acknowledged. Furthermore, I was fortunate to have access to language learners and to have additional help from talented students, extremely constructive and accessible native speakers, as well as wonderful English teachers in Hamburg and Hanoi. I would also like to thank the *Übersee-Club e.V.*, and most importantly Ingrid Harré-Eichmann, for the generous grant which allowed me to travel to Hanoi, Vietnam, to collect the missing data. I further express my gratitude to the Institute of English and American studies at the University of Hamburg, the Department of Teacher Education at the Norwegian University of Science and Technology (NTNU) in Trondheim, as well as the Department of English at Justus Liebig University Giessen for excellent working conditions.

Apart from my academic life, there is of course a large support system behind the scenes: family, friends, and sports partners. Their presence in my life is invaluable! And to be honest: practicing (kick)boxing in Hamburg, Trondheim, and Giessen ensured my well-being.

Finally, I would like to thank Stefan Ebert, my supporting pillar and person I can always go to. Thank you for understanding my commitment and craziness! Thank you for being there for me. This book is dedicated to you!

Abbreviations

Ø	zero
1PL	first person plural
1SG	first person singular
2PL	second person plural
2SG	second person singular
3PL	third person plural
3rd sg –s	third person singular –s morpheme
3SG	third person singular
ABL	ablative
ACC	accusative
AoO	age of onset of acquiring German
AOR	aorist
AUX	auxiliary
BNC	British National Corpus
CEFR	Common European Framework of Reference for Languages
CEM	Cumulative Enhancement Model
CL	(nominal) classifier
CLI	crosslinguistic influence
COCA	Corpus of Contemporary American English
COND	conditional
COP	copula
DAT	dative
DEF.ART	definite article
EFL	English as a foreign language
ELF	English as a Lingua Franca
E-LiPS	English LiMA panel study
ENG	English; English native speaker(s)
ENL	English as a native language
ESL	English as a second language
F	feminine
FUT	future
GER	German monolingual(s)

GM	generalizing modality
GY	*Gymnasium* (university-bound secondary school track)
HISEI	socio-economic status, operationalized via the Highest International Socio-Economic Index of Occupational Status
INF	infinitive
INS	instrumental
INT	interrogative
IPFV	imperfective
ISEI	International Socio-Economic Index of Occupational Status
KMK	Kultusministerkonferenz (Standing conference of the ministers of education and cultural affairs of the federal states of Germany)
L1	first language
L2	second language
L3	third language
LiMA	Linguistic Diversity Management in Urban Areas
LiPS	LiMA panel study
LOC	locative
LPM	Linguistic Proximity Model
M	masculine
MEZ	Mehrsprachigkeitsentwicklung im Zeitverlauf ('Multilingual development: A longitudinal perspective')
N	absolute frequency
NA	not applicable/not available (unknown information)
NC	noun compound
NEG	negation, negative
NMLZ	nominalization
no.	number
p.c.	private conversation
PL	plural
POS	positive
POSS	possession
PRF	perfective
PROG	progressive
PROSP	prospective
PRS	(simple) present tense
PST	(simple) past tense
PTCP	participle
RN	relator noun
RUS	Russian monolingual(s)
RUS-GER	Russian-German bilingual(s)
s	spoken
sd	standard deviation

List of abbreviations xv

SES	socio-economic status
SVA	subject-verb agreement
TPM	Typological Primacy Model
TTR	type-token-ratio
TUR	Turkish monolingual(s)
TUR-GER	Turkish-German bilingual(s)
V	verb
VIET	Vietnamese monolingual(s)
VIET-GER	Vietnamese-German bilingual(s)
Vs	verbs
w	written

1 Introduction

1.1 Background and motivation

> "Human beings are remarkable language learners who can easily learn and master several languages throughout their lives."
>
> (De Angelis 2007: 1)

As is illustrated in this quotation, humans are capable of learning and handling multiple languages concurrently. Thus, the human brain has the potential and the capacity to learn more than one or two languages – evidently with ease – as is emphasized by the two words *remarkable* and *easily*. De Angelis (2007: 1) further insists that learning and speaking several languages is a commonplace accomplishment that many people will ultimately achieve. Although humans are such impressive language learners, this process itself is not easy or simple but highly complex and multifaceted (Quay and Montanari 2019). In an increasingly multilingual society (Aronin 2005; Aronin and Hufeisen 2009; De Angelis 2007; Montanari and Quay 2019), it is becoming more and more relevant to know how learning language after language works and how these languages interfere with and influence each other. The significance of this issue can be understood when following Hammarberg, who refers to *multilingualism* as "the normal state of linguistic competence" (2010: 92) or the "default form of human language competence" (2010: 101; see also Hammarberg 2018). Thus, it is, in a multifaceted form, "a typical aspect of everyday life for most of the world's population" (Quay and Montanari 2019: 1).

The notion of multilingualism has been defined in various ways. For the purpose of the current study, Franceschini (2009: 33–34) provides a suitable and precise definition of multilingualism that illustrates what can be found in many areas of the world:

> The term/concept of multilingualism is to be understood as the capacity of societies, institutions, groups and individuals to engage on a regular basis in space and time with more than one language in everyday life. Multilingualism is a product of the fundamental human

DOI: 10.4324/9781003134336-1

ability to communicate in a number of languages. Operational distinctions may then be drawn between social, institutional, discursive and individual multilingualism. The term multilingualism is used to designate a phenomenon embedded in the cultural habits of a specific group, which are characterised by significant inter and intracultural sensitivity.

To put this definition into context and to provide some facts about language diversity, let us take a look at how many languages there are on earth. It is difficult to provide a precise answer to this question as the number is not stable, nor are there clear classification boundaries between languages or dialects (Pereltsvaig 2017: 12). Velupillai (2013: 44) speaks of approximately 7,000 living languages. The *Ethnologue* reports that there are 7,117 living languages in the world (Eberhard, Simons, and Fennig 2020), whereas Pereltsvaig (2017: 12) is more cautious and assumes that there are between 6,500 and 7,000 languages. Moreover, the *Ethnologue* provides a list with 249 countries and regions based on the statistics of the United Nations Statistics Division but also enumerates the number of languages that are spoken in each area (Simons and Fennig 2018). Not only the native languages (here, referred to as "established languages") are given, but the number of immigrant languages is specified as well (Simons and Fennig 2018). It is striking that there are only four areas (British Indian Ocean Territory; North Korea; Saint Helena, Ascension, and Tristan da Cunha; Saint Pierre and Miquelon) where the *Ethnologue* presents only one language. Those areas are, however, rather small and accordingly only involve a limited number of speakers. The other extreme case is Papua New Guinea with 841 languages, followed by Indonesia (710 languages) and Nigeria (524 languages) (Eberhard, Simons, and Fennig 2020). When observing these numbers, one realizes that most countries and regions are multilingual, either because of several established languages or one official language and numerous immigrant languages.

This rough overview demonstrates the linguistic diversity and complexity present in most areas of the world, characterized by official or national languages and other languages, sometimes classified as "regional minority languages" and "immigrant minority languages" (Extra and Gorter 2001: 2; Romaine 2008). In the European context, the former were established mostly during state-formation in the nineteenth century and represent the languages that did not gain official status in the newly created states (Extra and Gorter 2001: 2). The latter, however, appeared and stabilized as a consequence of large-scale migration processes (Extra and Gorter 2001: 3; Extra and Yağmur 2004). Let us have an initial look at Germany (which will be extended in Chapter 2). Although it officially counts as a monolingual country, this does not imply that in Germany, we only find monolingual German speakers. Quite the opposite is true. There are, for instance, regional minority languages such as North Frisian,

Saterfrisian, or Sorbian (Extra and Gorter 2001: 10) and numerous immigrant languages like Russian, Turkish, or Arabic (Barthelheimer, Hufeisen, and Montanari 2019: 52), both of which are widely spoken, in addition to foreign languages studied in educational contexts (more about the acquisition of English in Germany in Chapter 2).

Increasing globalization and migration movements have considerable influence on the awareness of (multiple) language acquisition and the need for mastering foreign languages. As previously discussed, most societies are multilingual. The same applies to their inhabitants. Thus, most humans are not monolingual, and a task for contemporary societies is to foster foreign language acquisition (Cook 2016a: 1). Cook lists reasons for potentially positive results that are attributed to knowing more than one language. It may result in

> getting a job; a chance to get educated; the ability to take a fuller part in the life of one's own country or the opportunity to emigrate to another; an expansion of one's literary and cultural horizons; the expression of one's political opinions or religious beliefs; the chance to talk to people on a foreign holiday. A second language affects people's careers and possible futures, their lives and their very identities. In a world where more people probably speak two languages than one, the acquisition and use of second languages are vital to the everyday lives of millions …
> (Cook 2016a: 1)

Cook here uses the plural "second languages." Hence, he does not limit this to the one language that a person acquires after having acquired the native language, but he refers to *foreign languages* in general, i.e., languages that are not considered one's native tongue. For a long time, non-native language acquisition was not further distinguished (regardless of whether this was the first or the second foreign language) but only seen as different than the acquisition of a *native language* (Rothman, González Alonso and Puig-Mayenco 2019: 1). This understanding, however, has changed and scholars have started to specifically differentiate between second (L2) and third (L3) language acquisition.

1.2 Setting the scene: second and third language acquisition

1.2.1 Language acquisition

Before contrasting L2 and L3 acquisition, let us first have a look at a definition of *language acquisition*. Language acquisition in general "describes[s] the process whereby children become speakers of their native language (first-language acquisition) or children or adults become speakers of a second language (second-language acquisition)" (Parodi 2010: 287). This precisely shows that we differentiate between the acquisition of the *first language* (or in other words the *native language*) and a *second language* (or *non-native language*). Following Parodi (2010: 296), a clear distinction needs to be drawn between *first* (L1) and *second language* (L2) *acquisition*, because (nearly) everyone achieves complete competence in their first language, as opposed to the level of competence in the second language, which in most cases does not reach the level of native speakers. Some argue that the specific capacity to learn a language changes over time and that it is not available to adults anymore (Parodi 2010: 288–290). There remains a lack of understanding as to how the process of children acquiring the first language relates and compares to second language acquisition. Ellis (2015: 5) defines second language acquisition as an even more complex process than first language acquisition: it follows first language acquisition and could involve any age (from very young learners, shortly after the onset of acquiring the first language, up to old age), the learners are often cognitively (more) mature and may have other potential learning strategies at their disposal, and the acquisition contexts can be much more diverse. Diverse learning contexts refer, on the one hand, to the common distinction between second language acquisition and foreign language acquisition, and, on the other hand, to a variety of learning environments and situations such as obligatory acquisition in a school context, optional acquisition as an adult, and so on.

Let us briefly disambiguate the difference between *second* and *foreign language acquisition*. We usually refer to second language acquisition when we talk about the acquisition of another language in a context where this particular language is the majority or one of the major languages (Ellis 2015: 6). One example would be a child with a Russian heritage background who moves with his or her parents to Germany at the age of three and starts to learn German from that moment onwards. Foreign language acquisition, however, describes the process of acquiring another language, typically via formal instruction, that is not one of the majority languages in the country (Ellis 2015: 6). A possible context could be the following: the acquisition of French or Spanish in school by students who grow up in Germany. In general, when referring to the area of second language acquisition, normally both learning contexts are included (Ellis 2015: 6). Ellis explains that this is due to the fact that "we cannot take it for granted that the process of acquiring a second language is different in these different contexts" (Ellis 2015: 6).[1]

Third language acquisition, even though it shares many properties with second language acquisition (Cenoz 2003: 71), presents another type of language acquisition and should therefore be distinguished from second language acquisition (Rothman 2011, 2013). Cenoz defines it as "the acquisition of a non-native language by learners who have previously acquired or are acquiring two other languages" (2003: 71). She uses a broad definition in that she includes *simultaneous* and *consecutive acquisition* of the first two languages. Hence, *early bilingualism* (i.e., growing up with and being exposed to two languages from birth onward), *late bilingualism* (i.e., growing up with one language and acquiring a second language later), and *adult bilingualism* could all be starting conditions of third language acquisition (more about bilingualism and related concepts in Chapter 3). Strictly speaking, this definition allows for second language learners and foreign language learners, relating to the concepts that have just been described.

1.2.2 Second versus third language acquisition

During the past decades, researchers have shown that L3 acquisition is not just another form of foreign language acquisition, but that L2 acquisition (the acquisition of a first foreign language) and L3 acquisition (the acquisition of an additional foreign language) need to be studied as two separate (yet related) phenomena (among others Cabrelli Amaro, Flynn, and Rothman 2012; Cenoz and Jessner 2001; Cenoz, Hufeisen, and Jessner 2001; De Angelis 2007; de Bot and Jaensch 2015). Aronin (2019: 11) argues that bilingualism and multilingualism are characterized by "systemic differences." Thus, there should be an observable difference between L2 and L3 acquisition.

One such difference, and this is the key issue pursued in the current study, may manifest in the source of *crosslinguistic influence*. It is crucial to determine the source of crosslinguistic influence in third language acquisition, as there are two potential sources available. To start off, let us consider Hermas (2015: 588) who precisely states what is of concern here:

> Unlike first-language (L1) acquisition where there is no source of linguistic transfer and L2A [second language acquisition] where the only source available is the L1, L3A [third language acquisition] provides two languages at a time, the L1 and the L2. One research question this study considers is which of the two linguistic systems conditions morphosyntactic transfer in the early stages of the L3.

Hermas raises an important controversy, namely which of the two previously acquired languages affects the acquisition of the L3. Hermas is of course not the first or the only one to ask this question, but he is exemplary for numerous scholars of a widely researched area in (applied) linguistics. In addition, he specifically points to morphosyntax. Nevertheless, it should be clear that studies concentrating on crosslinguistic influence in third language acquisition are not limited to this grammatical area, but many other transfer phenomena are analyzed (a variety of them are discussed in Chapter 3). What Hermas (2015) argues is that L3 acquisition is special in comparison to L1 and L2 acquisition, because it allows us to understand not only how one language influences the acquisition process of another language (as is the case in second language acquisition), but it looks at a more complex and entangled situation.

Rothman is even more upfront than Hermas and claims that "the study of (adult) multilingualism provides an unparalleled opportunity to begin to properly contextualize and thus understand the dynamic role that previous linguistic knowledge plays in the acquisition process" (2011: 107). He not only limits the study of language acquisition to third language acquisition, but also stresses the dynamic character of previous linguistic knowledge. It is not an either/or relationship, i.e., either L1 or L2 influence, but a dynamic model that might be prone to change over time, with varying competences in L1 and L2. At the same time, he acknowledges that there is still a long way to go because he insists that we are only beginning to understand the underlying concepts (Rothman 2011: 123; Rothman 2013: 243).

Even though there are various studies about second, third, and additional language acquisition (see Chapter 3), the fundamental issues in third language acquisition remain unclear: (i) which of the two previously acquired linguistic systems influences the third language; (ii) to what extent do they influence the third language; or (iii) how does the interaction between these two systems influence the third language. We seem to know a lot about both first and second language acquisition (see, for example, Clark 2009 and Lust and Foley 2004 on L1 acquisition; Gass and Mackey 2012 and Slabakova 2016 on L2 acquisition), but studies in third language acquisition produce differing and conflicting results, especially in terms of crosslinguistic influence, which can partly be traced back to the diverse groups of learners that are analyzed (for instance adult versus child language acquisition, or early versus late bilingualism).

1.2.3 Third language learners

It follows quite naturally that one does not find a homogeneous group of *third language learners*, because the language biography of the individual learners could vary drastically. Again, globalization and current developments in our world are two of the reasons for this. Hoffmann differentiates between five different groups of *trilinguals* (2001: 3):

(1) Trilingual children who are brought up with two languages which are different from the one spoken in the wider community;
(2) Children who grow up in a bilingual community and whose home language (either that of one or both parents) is different from the community languages;
(3) Third language learners, that is, bilinguals who acquire a third language in the school context;
(4) Bilinguals who have become trilingual through immigration; and
(5) Members of trilingual communities.

In addition to this classification, it becomes even more complicated when the different types of bilingual speakers that have previously been outlined (i.e., early versus late bilinguals, adult bilinguals) are included (see also Chapter 3).

For the study of language acquisition this means that one cannot simply talk about third language learners but that different groups of third language learners need to be analyzed in order to fully understand how the previously acquired languages interact with each other and how they influence the acquisition process of the third language. Yet, most studies that focus on third language learners analyze adult learners, particularly learners that acquired their L2 rather late (see Hopp et al. 2018 for an overview). There is still a lack of systematic studies that target child L3 learners, even though, especially during the past years, research focusing on child L3 acquisition has fundamentally changed. There are some recent studies, such as Westergaard et al. (2017), Hopp (2019), Hopp et al. (2019), and Siemund and Lechner (2015), to name but a few, that investigate child L3 acquisition and they furthermore focus on a specific type of bilingual speaker, namely *heritage speakers* (more details in Section 3.4).

Not only the type of L3 learner but also the specific domain investigated produces different results (Hopp et al. 2018; Westergaard et al. 2017). All grammatical domains, for example phonetics and phonology, vocabulary, or morphosyntax, need to be studied, because previous studies have found crucial differences that suggest that the interactions between the languages are not uniform in all areas. One domain that has so far not been analyzed thoroughly is the area of tense and aspect. Hence, the aim of this study is to fill this gap by analyzing monolingual children who acquire English as their second language and bilingual children who acquire English as an additional language in school. This research sets out to investigate how these monolingual and bilingual participants use different tenses and how they use aspectual marking when writing an English text and when producing an oral picture description. The phenomenon that is being investigated is *transfer*, sometimes used synonymously with *crosslinguistic influence*, hence the influence from the previously acquired languages.

1.2.4 Transfer versus crosslinguistic influence

A general and broad definition of *transfer* is given by Rothman, who proposes that transfer "refers to influence from previous linguistic knowledge on the development and/or performance of a target non-native language" (2013: 223). He specifies this by stating that transfer is about transposing grammatical features, hence "functional features and associated functional categories," from the previously learned language or languages to the language currently being acquired (Rothman 2013: 224). In a more recent publication, Rothman, González Alonso, and Puig-Mayenco (2019) draw a distinction between transfer and *crosslinguistic influence* (or cross-language effects). They situate transfer at the representational level, i.e., they argue that "linguistic transfer refers to reduplication of a representation from previously acquired linguistic representations, as an initial hypothesis for a given domain" (Rothman, González Alonso, and Puig-Mayenco 2019: 24). In this sense, linguistic transfer is more than a one-time non-target language use, but it manifests for a longer time as it has truly affected the representation of a specific category. They contrast this with crosslinguistic influence, which is in their understanding "the interaction between two, three, or more languages that are part of a speaker's linguistic competence" (Rothman, González Alonso, and Puig-Mayenco 2019: 24). Crosslinguistic influence is not located at the representational level but belongs to the processing of particular items. Therefore, it encompasses all types of non-target language production (also one-time uses) caused by the previously acquired language(s) like lexical transfer or the use of a false cognate (Rothman et al. 2019: 25–26).

Although this division may be useful (however, see Westergaard 2021; Wrembel 2021 for the opposite view), it is not possible to clearly distinguish between these two concepts in the present study as the type of data does not qualify to make a claim about whether the representation in the L3 has been truly affected (transfer) or whether the observed non-target language use belongs to the processing of a specific item or property (crosslinguistic influence). Therefore, crosslinguistic influence and transfer will be used synonymously, without referring to this difference explained in Rothman, González Alonso, and Puig-Mayenco (2019) but in the understanding of a more general term, covering both concepts (more about crosslinguistic influence in Section 3.2.2).

Hence, the current study considers the grammatical domain of *tense* and *aspect* and compares how far the previously learned languages influence the acquisition and use of English. This is possible because the participants of the current study have a different linguistic repertoire available which should allow for finding transfer differences. In second language acquisition, transfer typically happens from the first language to the second language. It is, however, not limited to a one-way process but transfer can also occur from the second language to the first language (Figure 1.1), which results in a possible reciprocal interference (Siemund 2022).

If there is an interaction of more than two languages, for instance three languages as in third language acquisition, possible transfer processes

Figure 1.1 Transfer in second language acquisition.

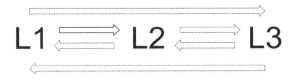

Figure 1.2 Transfer possibilities with three languages.

Figure 1.3 Transfer in third language acquisition: focus of the current study.

augment, i.e., transfer is likely to occur between all three languages (Figure 1.2) (see also Lorenz 2019; Siemund 2022). Berthele and Vanhove (2020: 550) state quite clearly that "bi- and multilinguals' languages influence each other" which "is one of the tenets of contemporary scholarly work in our field."

Yet, the extent and the exact characteristics of transfer between the languages are not entirely clear (Siemund 2022), and still remain to be analyzed. Therefore, a dotted line is used to visualize the potential transfer directions between the three languages. An exception is the arrow from the L1 to the L2. Here, a continuous line is used because there is no doubt that the L1 influences the L2 (Schwartz and Sprouse 1996). For the current study, however, only two of the six directions are of interest, namely transfer from the first to the third and from the second to the third language (see the full black arrows in Figure 1.3).

1.2.5 Advantages

Finally, there is another possible difference between second and third language learners that has to do with the notion of *advantages*. There are numerous studies that investigate whether bilinguals have an advantage over monolinguals in further foreign language acquisition or not (see, for example, Cenoz 2003, 2013). Here, advantages are not to be understood as positive effects on executive function or control (as addressed in Bialystok 2001; Bialystok, Craik, and Luk 2012). Instead, what is meant are *linguistic advantages* in terms of a more target-like performance in a foreign language. Since bilinguals have previous knowledge of two languages, this enlarged linguistic repertoire could potentially influence the acquisition of further languages. Furthermore, having access to two languages instead of one may result in an enhanced competence or set of skills, sometimes referred to as *multi-competence* (Cook 2016b), *metalinguistic awareness* (Jessner 2006, 2008), or *M-effect* (Allgäuer-Hackl and Jessner 2019). This topic of potential bilingual benefits in additional language acquisition will be elaborated on in Section 3.6 (see also Section 10.1).

1.3 Research questions

The current study investigates the differences between second and third language learners of English. The participants included are monolingual German school-aged learners of English and their bilingual peers (Russian-German, Turkish-German, Vietnamese-German), in addition to monolingual Russian, Turkish, and Vietnamese monolingual learners of English. The aim is to explore the role of crosslinguistic influence from the heritage language (Russian, Turkish, or Vietnamese) and/or the language of the environment (German) when acquiring a third language (English) in comparison to monolingual (German, Russian, Turkish, and Vietnamese) learners of English. The central question involves finding out how crosslinguistic influence affects the acquisition of the foreign language, more specifically the use of tense and aspect in a written and oral production task.

One note of caution is in order here: it is almost impossible to look at the acquisition process in natural surroundings, especially with such a large group as examined in this study. Hence, strictly speaking, it is not the acquisition process that is being observed but the *performance outcome*. Foote explains that "production data do not allow us to observe the acquisition of functional categories" (2009: 92). Yet, what can be observed is the outcome, which is the result of language instruction and its realization. The performance of the participants will be measured by analyzing written English texts and oral recordings.

Thus, the study investigates how far the two previously acquired languages influence the acquisition of the third or additional language and how this output in the L3 differs from the output in the L2 as a consequence of second language acquisition. The focus lies on the use of tense and aspect based on written texts produced. This is supplemented by and compared to oral recordings. First, the language production of the different groups is compared. In a second step, additional background information such as language biography, age, type of school, and socioeconomic status is considered to complement the linguistic analysis. The following research questions are addressed throughout the succeeding sections and answered in the discussion.

(1) Are there general differences (i.e., text length) and are there grammatical differences concerning the use of tense and aspect in the

texts produced by monolingual learners of English and bilingual learners of English?
(2) How do the different native languages influence the acquisition and use of tense and aspect in English?
(3) Are both the heritage language (Russian, Turkish, or Vietnamese) and the language of the environment (German) sources of (positive or negative) crosslinguistic influence for the acquisition of English as an additional foreign language?
(4) Can a similar development of each language group (both monolinguals and bilinguals) be identified over time, i.e., an improvement in their English skills with increasing age?
(5) How do the type of school, age of onset of acquiring German, or additional background variables affect the results?
(6) How does the concept of metalinguistic awareness relate to the dataset? Is there a visible linguistic (dis)advantage of the bilingual learners over the monolingual learners of English?
(7) Is there a difference between written and oral production in the use of tense and aspect in English?

1.4 Structure of the book

This book addresses two highly debated topics, namely crosslinguistic influence in (second and) third language acquisition and bi- or multilingual advantages in further language acquisition. Both topics are approached from a theoretical perspective and are ultimately empirically investigated by analyzing a written and a spoken learner corpus which was collected from monolingual and bilingual learners of English. The study is based on a population of bilinguals that can be frequently encountered in countries such as Germany or other Western European countries: unbalanced bilingual heritage speakers. The book exclusively focuses on the German context, with references to the Russian, Turkish, and Vietnamese contexts. The data is based on two different age cohorts to approximate a developmental perspective. A triangular, cross-sectional design makes it possible to compare different monolingual and bilingual learners of English.

The theoretical part of the book consists of five chapters. Chapter 1, the main introduction into the topic, is meant to guide the reader in what is presented in the subsequent parts. It offers a general introduction into bi- and multilingualism in addition to foreign language acquisition. These concepts will be taken up and extended throughout the book. Chapter 2 focuses on the acquisition of English in Germany (with some occasional references to other contexts such as Norway or the Netherlands, whenever parallels appear useful) and narrows down the specific focal point of the study. It presents the contextual setting of the study, i.e., how the foreign language English is taught and studied in German secondary schools and how mono- and bilingual learners of English grow up in Germany. Thereafter, in Chapter 3, the most important concepts and theories that are relevant for the motivation of this study as well as the understanding of the empirical analysis are introduced and discussed in great detail. It covers topics such as multilingualism, first versus second versus third language acquisition, third language acquisition of heritage bilinguals, different types of bilingual speakers with a special focus on heritage bilinguals, metalinguistic awareness, and bilingual advantages. Chapter 4 is dedicated to the introduction of the grammatical area of tense and aspect. First, on a general level and without being language specific, tense, aspect, and *aktionsart* are explained. In a second step, the relevant languages, i.e., English, German, Russian, Turkish, and Vietnamese, are addressed individually and the respective tense and aspect systems are discussed and supported with specific examples. Finally, from a typological and contrastive linguistic perspective, similarities and differences across the languages are presented. Chapter 5, the final chapter of the theoretical part, discusses native and non-native acquisition of tense and aspect. First, a survey of the research concerning how tense and aspect is acquired by native speakers of English is given, followed by a general section discussing non-native acquisition of tense and aspect. The next subsections outline, parallel to Chapter 4, studies for each of the relevant languages individually, i.e., how different learners of English (i.e., with a German, Russian, Turkish, or Vietnamese background) acquire tense and aspect.

The second part of the book contains the empirical analysis and is divided into six chapters. A brief description of the project, the data collection, as well as data coding is followed by a close analysis of the participants and their background variables (Chapter 6). The subsequent two chapters make up the results part of this book and investigate the written and oral learner data of the mono- and bilingual participants. In Chapter 7, the linguistic analysis, the use of tense and aspect across the different learner groups is compared, exclusively based on language group membership and age cohort. In Chapter 8, the sociolinguistic analysis is presented, i.e., the former analysis is extended and supplemented by the previously introduced social background variables. Linguistic and extra-linguistic data are combined to unravel crosslinguistic influence and advantages in foreign language acquisition from numerous perspectives, which ultimately allows for a highly differentiated picture. The following discussion part is also divided into two chapters. Chapter 9 discusses crosslinguistic influence in this specific group of unbalanced bilingual heritage speakers who grow up in Germany and relates the current findings back to what was introduced and reviewed in the theoretical part (Chapters 2 to 5). In addition, it includes one section discussing some shortcomings and limitations of the present study. In Chapter 10, the focus is slightly narrower and takes up the question of whether there is a bi-/multilingual advantage in further foreign language acquisition when bilinguals are compared with their monolingual peers. It additionally comments on the learning environment in foreign language classrooms and offers some implications for foreign language education. The further research potential of the points raised in the two discussion chapters is taken up in Chapter 11 to offer an outlook for future studies. Moreover, this last chapter also provides a concise conclusion of the entire study.

Note

1 This, of course, is a controversial claim. However, it will not be looked at in detail and its validity will not be questioned. It is not of concern for the current study, because the participants that are being looked at are either simultaneous learners of the first and the second language or second language learners that are acquiring the majority language of the community.

References

Allgäuer-Hackl, E. and U. Jessner. 2019. Cross-linguistic interaction and multilingual awareness. In *Multidisciplinary perspectives on multilingualism: The fundamentals*, ed. S. Montanari and S. Quay, 325–349. Boston/Berlin: De Gruyter Mouton.

Aronin, L. 2005. Theoretical perspectives of trilingual education. *International Journal of the Sociology of Language* 2005:7–22.

Aronin, L. 2019. What is multilingualism? In *Twelve lectures on multilingualism*, ed. D. Singleton and L. Aronin, 3–34. Bristol: Multilingual Matters.

Aronin, L. and B. Hufeisen. 2009. On the genesis and development of L3 research, multilingualism and multiple language acquisition. In *The exploration of multilingualism*, ed. L. Aronin and B. Hufeisen, 1–9. Amsterdam: Benjamins.

Barthelheimer, L., B. Hufeisen, and S. Montanari. 2019. Multilingualism in Europe. In *Multidisciplinary perspectives on multilingualism: The fundamentals*, ed. S. Montanari and S. Quay, 51–75. Boston/Berlin: De Gruyter Mouton.

Berthele, R. and J. Vanhove. 2020. What would disprove interdependence? Lessons learned from a study on biliteracy in Portuguese heritage language speakers in Switzerland. *International Journal of Bilingual Education and Bilingualism* 23:550–566.

Bialystok, E. 2001. *Bilingualism in development: Language, literacy, and cognition*. Cambridge: Cambridge University Press.

Bialystok, E., F. I. M. Craik, and G. Luk. 2012. Bilingualism: Consequences for mind and brain. *Trends in Cognitive Sciences* 16:240–250.

Cabrelli Amaro, J., S. Flynn, and J. Rothman (eds.). 2012. *Third language acquisition in adulthood*. Amsterdam: Benjamins.

Cenoz, J. 2003. The additive effect of bilingualism on third language acquisition: A review. *International Journal of Bilingualism* 7:71–87.

Cenoz, J. 2013. The influence of bilingualism on third language acquisition: Focus on multilingualism. *Language Teaching* 46:71–86.

Cenoz, J, B. Hufeisen, and U. Jessner (eds.). 2001. *Cross-linguistic influence in third language acquisition: Psycholinguistic perspectives*. Clevedon: Multilingual Matters.

Cenoz, J. and U. Jessner (eds.). 2001. *English in Europe: The acquisition of a third language.* Clevedon: Multilingual Matters.

Clark, E. V. 2009. *First language acquisition.* 2nd edn. Cambridge: Cambridge University Press.

Cook, V. 2016a. *Second language learning and language teaching.* London/New York: Routledge.

Cook, V. 2016b. Premises of multi-competence. In *The Cambridge handbook of linguistic multi-competence*, ed. V. Cook, and Li Wei, 1–25. Cambridge: Cambridge University Press.

De Angelis, G. 2007. *Third or additional language acquisition.* Clevedon: Multilingual Matters.

de Bot, K. and C. Jaensch. 2015. What is special about L3 processing? *Bilingualism: Language and Cognition* 18:130–144.

Eberhard, D. M., G. F. Simons, and C. D. Fennig (eds.). 2020. *Ethnologue: Languages of the world.* 23rd edn. Dallas, TX: SIL International. www.ethnologue.com.

Ellis, R. 2015. *Understanding second language acquisition.* 2nd edn. Oxford: Oxford University Press.

Extra, G. and D. Gorter. 2001. Comparative perspectives on regional and immigrant minority languages in multicultural Europe. In *The other languages of Europe: Demographic, sociolinguistic and educational perspectives*, ed. G. Extra and D. Gorter, 1–41. Clevedon: Multilingual Matters.

Extra, G. and K. Yağmur (eds.). 2004. *Urban multilingualism in Europe: Immigrant minority languages at home and school.* Clevedon: Multilingual Matters.

Foote, R. 2009. Transfer in L3 acquisition: The role of typology. In *Third language acquisition and universal grammar*, ed. I. Leung, 89–114. Clevedon: Multilingual Matters.

Franceschini, R. 2009. The genesis and development of research in multilingualism: Perspectives for future research. In *The exploration of multilingualism*, ed. L. Aronin and B. Hufeisen, 27–62. Amsterdam: Benjamins.

Gass, S. M. and A. Mackey (eds.). 2012. *The Routledge handbook of second language acquisition.* New York: Routledge.

Hammarberg, B. 2010. The languages of the multilingual: Some conceptual and terminological issues. *International Review of Applied Linguistics in Language Teaching* 48:91–104.

Hammarberg, B. 2018. L3, the tertiary language. In *Foreign language education in multilingual classrooms*, ed. A. Bonnet and P. Siemund, 127–150. Amsterdam: Benjamins.

Hermas, A. 2015. The categorization of the relative complementizer phrase in third-language English: A feature re-assembly account. *International Journal of Bilingualism* 19:587–607.

Hoffmann, C. 2001. Towards a description of trilingual competence. *International Journal of Bilingualism* 5:1–17.

Hopp, H. 2019. Cross-linguistic influence in the child third language acquisition of grammar: Sentence comprehension and production among Turkish-German and German learners of English. *International Journal of Bilingualism* 23:567–583.

Hopp, H., T. Kieseier, M. Vogelbacher, and D. Thoma. 2018. L1 effects in the early L3 acquisition of vocabulary and grammar. In *Foreign language education in multilingual classrooms*, ed. A. Bonnet and P. Siemund, 305–330. Amsterdam: Benjamins.

Hopp, H., M. Vogelbacher, T. Kieseier, and D. Thoma. 2019. Bilingual advantages in early foreign language learning: Effects of the minority and the majority language. *Learning and Instruction* 61:99–110.

Jessner, U. 2006. *Linguistic awareness in multilinguals: English as a third language*. Edinburgh: Edinburgh University Press.

Jessner, U. 2008. A DST model of multilingualism and the role of metalinguistic awareness. *Modern Language Journal* 2:270–283.

Lorenz, E. 2019. Analysis of verb phrases and the progressive aspect in a learner corpus of L2 and L3 learners of English. In *Widening the scope of learner corpus research: Selected papers from the 4th Learner Corpus Research Conference*, ed. A. Abel, A. Glaznieks, V. Lyding, and L. Nicholas, 253–287. Louvain-la-Neuve: Presses Universitaires de Louvain.

Lust, B. C. and C. Foley (eds.). 2004. *First language acquisition: The essential readings*. Malden, MA: Blackwell.

Montanari, S. and S. Quay (eds.). 2019. *Multidisciplinary perspectives on multilingualism: The fundamentals*. Boston/Berlin: De Gruyter Mouton.

Parodi, T. 2010. Language acquisition. In *The Routledge linguistics encyclopedia*, 3rd edn, ed. K. Malmkjaer, 287–297. London/New York: Routledge.

Pereltsvaig, A. 2017. *Languages of the world: An introduction*. Cambridge: Cambridge University Press.

Quay, S. and S. Montanari. 2019. Multilingualism from multidisciplinary perspectives: Introduction and overview. In *Multidisciplinary perspectives on multilingualism: The fundamentals*, ed. S. Montanari and S. Quay, 1–4. Boston/Berlin: De Gruyter Mouton.

Romaine, S. 2008. The bilingual and multilingual community. In *The handbook of bilingualism*, ed. T. K. Bhatia and W. C. Ritchie, 385–405. Malden, MA: Blackwell.

Rothman, J. 2011. L3 syntactic transfer selectivity and typological determinacy: The typological primacy model. *Second Language Research* 27:107–127.

Rothman, J. 2013. Cognitive economy, non-redundancy and typological primacy in L3 acquisition: Evidence from initial stages of L3 Romance. In *Romance languages and linguistic theory 2011: Selected papers from 'Going Romance' Utrecht 2011*, ed. S. Baauw, F. Drijkoningen, L. Meroni, and M. Pinto, 217–248. Amsterdam: Benjamins.

Rothman, J., J. González Alonso, and E. Puig-Mayenco. 2019. *Third language acquisition and linguistic transfer*. Cambridge: Cambridge University Press.

Schwartz, B. D. and R. A. Sprouse. 1996. L2 cognitive states and the full transfer/full access model. *Second Language Research* 12:40–72.

Siemund, P. 2022. Englisch als weitere Sprache im Kontext herkunftsbedingter Mehrsprachigkeit. In *Sprachentwicklung im Kontext von Mehrsprachigkeit: Hypothesen, Methoden, Forschungsperspektiven*, ed. J. Duarte, I. Gogolin, T. Klinger, B. Schnoor, and M. Trebbels, 193–210. Wiesbaden: Springer.

Siemund, P. and S. Lechner. 2015. Transfer effects in the acquisition of English as an additional language by bilingual children in Germany. In *Transfer effects in multilingual language development*, ed. H. Peukert, 147–160. Amsterdam: Benjamins.

Simons, G. F. and C. D. Fennig (eds.). 2018. *Ethnologue: Languages of the world*. 21st edn. Dallas, TX: SIL International. www.ethnologue.com

Slabakova, R. 2016. *Second language acquisition*. Oxford: Oxford University Press.

Velupillai, V. 2013. *An introduction to linguistic typology*. Amsterdam: Benjamins.

Westergaard, M. 2021. Microvariation in multilingual situations: The importance of property-by-property acquisition. *Second Language Research* 37:379–407.

Westergaard, M., N. Mitrofanova, R. Mykhaylyk, and Y. Rodina. 2017. Crosslinguistic influence in the acquisition of a third language: The linguistic proximity model. *International Journal of Bilingualism* 21:666–682.

Wrembel, M. 2021. Multilingual acquisition property by property: A view from a wider perspective. *Second Language Research* 37:441–447.

2 Acquisition of English in Germany

2.1 The role of English in Germany

Arguably, English plays a substantial role for everyone in the world (Mair 2020; Schneider 2017). This general influential status is underlined in de Swaan's (2001, 2010) "Global Language System," where English is classified as the *hyper-central language* (i.e., at the top of his hierarchy) of all the languages in the world. It serves the function of global communication and thus enables people from different countries with varying (native) languages to interact. Most importantly, it possesses the highest economic and social capital (Siemund 2018: 134). One can understand this in a literal sense, meaning that investing in English, for instance, via studying it as a foreign language, has the potential to turn into a financial asset in the long run, as it may open doors for more job opportunities (de Swaan 2010), to name just one possible benefit (see also Norton 2018 on identity and language investment on a broader scale).

In scrutinizing Germany, one needs to recognize that apart from German, English is undoubtedly the second most important language in this country (see Hickey 2020a). It is associated with extremely high prestige (Mair 2020: 26; Stefanowitsch 2002: 73), and it has increasingly gained importance, especially after World War II. Whereas prior to World War II, regular use of English was largely confined to a restricted part of the population and for most people it was merely a foreign language studied at school, it could now be considered an actively used "global lingua franca" and not just one of the many foreign languages present in Germany (Mair 2020: 19). Hilgendorf (2007: 135) further corroborates this phenomenon by explaining that English can now be found in many domains, such as politics, academia, media, as well as education, and that an ever-growing part of the German population uses English frequently, perhaps even daily. This means that English is no longer an exclusive part of the elite social sphere (i.e., academia or economy), but rather it has an important standing in non-elite spheres such as modern culture and tourism, and it serves as a tool for communication between German speakers and foreigners (Mair 2020: 27; see also Fuller 2020). In addition, the Council of Europe endorses an L1+2 policy, which means that each

DOI: 10.4324/9781003134336-2

EU member state should support the learning of two further languages in addition to one's native language, with English typically being one of them (Bartelheimer, Hufeisen, and Montanari 2019: 61).

Even though English can now, in the twenty-first century, be described as an important and frequently used language among speakers in Germany, these rather general claims need further substantiation. Mollin (2020: 32) maps out a useful classification of English users (although certainly not uncontroversial, see, for example, Bruthiaux 2003), based on three prominent systems, which all use a tripartite model. The earliest, introduced by Strang (1970), separates English users into *A-speakers* (native speakers), *B-speakers* (non-native speakers but early learners of English), and *C-speakers* (foreign language users). Quirk et al. (1985) essentially follow the same hierarchical scheme but focus on the language itself instead of the speakers. They distinguish the use of English as a *native*, *second*, or *foreign language* (ENL, ESL, and EFL, respectively). This same viewpoint is applied in Kachru's (1985) model of World Englishes, where he distinguishes three concentric circles: the *inner circle* (which represents the L1 varieties), the *outer circle* (which represents the English as a second language varieties), and the *expanding circle* (which represents the English as a foreign language varieties).[1]

The question that arises is how the use of English in Germany should be classified from the national perspective (see also Kautzsch 2014). Hilgendorf (2007) clearly questions the previously assigned status of an expanding circle variety, stresses the changing dynamicity in this country, and argues for a shift from a foreign to an additional language. Nevertheless, she leaves open whether the expanding or the outer circle would represent the correct categorization. In addition, Mair (2020) also puts forward the idea that English does not have the status of a foreign language anymore. However, he does not use the terms second or additional language but refers to it as a "global lingua franca" (Mair 2020: 19; see also Fuller 2020: 167). Moreover, Siemund (2018: 154) describes a shift in-progress from a foreign language to a second language, which would place Germany in a transition space between the expanding and the outer circle. He further suggests that in the Scandinavian countries as well as in the Netherlands, English has already reached the status of a second language (Siemund 2018: 154).

Mollin (2020) tries to find evidence for such claims and uses data from the Eurobarometer (2001, 2012, 2017). She compares Germany within the European context and reports that the figures in the Eurobarometer (2012) show that "only 56% of German respondents consider themselves to be fluent enough to conduct a conversation in English, compared to a stunning 90% of Dutch or even 70% of Finnish speakers" (Mollin 2020: 37). What is more, Mollin (2020: 39) reports that only approximately 22 percent of those Germans who participated in this survey indicated that they use English regularly. For Danish and Dutch respondents, she documents 58 percent and 55 percent, respectively (Mollin 2020: 40).

In a direct comparison between the Netherlands and Germany, Mollin (2020: 45–46) argues that English in the Netherlands may in fact be in a phase between a second and a foreign language (see also Edwards 2016), whereas in Germany, English functions mainly as a lingua franca and is not typically used as a communicative language among speakers of German (see also Edwards and Fuchs 2020: 269–270). In sum, Mollin (2020) partly agrees with Siemund (2018) in that English in Germany has a different status than in the Scandinavian countries as well as the Netherlands, and she overall argues that "the entrenchment of English in German society seems to be smaller than previous accounts have implied" (Mollin 2020: 40; see also Kautzsch 2014; Davydova 2020), at least from a national perspective. Nevertheless, Mollin (2020: 41) concedes that a limitation of the Eurobarometer data is that it does not allow for a comparison between different age groups. A more fine-grained analysis of different generations of speakers would be needed to predict and project future developments (see also Gerritsen 2017).

This last point, namely that it matters which age group is considered, is crucial and of special importance for the current study. Clearly, Germany (or any other country for that matter) should not be understood as a uniform entity. Different subgroups, most importantly "young, educated, urban, and internationally mobile elites," may indeed use English more frequently and proficiently than the average citizen (Mollin 2020: 48). Fuller (2020: 167) confirms that high proficiency in English is specifically linked to being highly educated or having an "elite status." Crucially, Mollin (2020) argues that these highly proficient and frequent users of English are rather the exception and not necessarily representative of the majority population in Germany. However, since English is now being introduced early on in schools, this may in fact change into a broader phenomenon in the future (Kautzsch 2014: 222). Furthermore, Fuller (2020: 169) suggests that being proficient in English may also be part of a German identity. Yet, this should equally be seen as something specifically restricted to the younger generations in urban areas (see also Davydova 2020: 690, 699).

Since a differentiated perspective is imperative, a final discussion of school-aged children is offered, as this cohort will be the focus of the current study. Even though Mollin (2020) reports a higher affinity for English of Danes in comparison to Germans, the situation appears quite comparable when examining school-aged children in these two countries. Spellerberg (2016) provides some valuable insights from Denmark that are transferrable to the German context. Overall, she contends that for some Danes, English may be undergoing a change in status from a former foreign language to a second language (Spellerberg 2016: 21). However, for the largest part of the population, English may still be considered a foreign language, despite being introduced as a school subject in year one (Spellerberg 2016: 21). She provides support from a study where she found that secondary-school-aged children (age 14–16) barely used English outside of the classroom (Spellerberg 2016: 26). When considering a different age group, such as university-aged participants in their late teens or early twenties, this observation might have been different, as this cohort would more likely have additional contact with English outside of the foreign language classroom via media sources such as the internet or through traveling (see, for instance, Davydova 2020 and Erling 2002, who argue this for German university students). In sum, Spellerberg (2016) maps out that Danish secondary school students are not regularly exposed to English apart from the foreign language classroom input.

The status quo in Germany seems to be similar to what Spellerberg (2016) observed in her study. As previously indicated, there appears to be an ongoing change of the status of English within Germany, i.e., it is gaining in importance and prestige. Also, in addition to English being taught as a foreign language in school, there are other sources of English input, for example via TV, radio, social media, and the internet in general, which are enjoying more and more popularity. However, this does not equally apply to all age groups. Specifically, the main contact with English for the participants of the current study, i.e., secondary school students at the ages of 12 and 16, is via instruction at school and additional English input outside of the classroom is supposedly quite rare. What this means is that especially for younger, school-aged children, English is currently mainly the function of what is learned in school (see also Davydova 2020: 692). Since English plays such an important role as a school subject, the following two sections focus specifically on the classroom context and the English-as-a-foreign-language teaching reality in Germany.

2.2 Heterogeneous and diverse foreign language classrooms

As pointed out in Chapter 1, multilingualism is also on the rise in Germany, a country characterized by language diversity (see Fuller 2020; Gogolin et al. 2013; Li Wei 2008; Meyer 2008; Montrul 2016) even though it is officially considered a monolingual country (Bartelheimer, Hufeisen, and Montanari 2019; Cantone 2020). In particular, Fuller (2020: 165) claims that "Germany, and especially its capital city, Berlin, is a multilingual space, with many languages visible and audible in everyday life."[2] There are manifold environmental, economic, cultural, and socio-political factors that have led to an acceleration in immigration figures. This became relevant because of the increasing numbers of foreign workers who came to Germany after World War II.[3] The resulting societal changes affected and still affect both primary and secondary schools (Schroedler and Fischer 2020: 50).

Hamburg, the second largest city in Germany by population, will serve as an example for Germany's multilingual and multicultural reality. In 2014, over 43 percent of children and young adults had an immigrant background (Pohlan and Albrecht 2015).[4] In 2015, almost half of all people below the age of 18 were first, second, or third generation immigrants[5] (Statistisches Amt für Hamburg und Schleswig-Holstein 2016). This number reached 52 percent by the end of 2018 (Statistisches Amt für Hamburg und Schleswig-Holstein 2020). Because immigration is ongoing, this figure may even be higher today. Among the most important immigrant or home countries listed are Turkey, Russia, other countries once part of the former Soviet Union, as well as Poland (Statistisches Amt für Hamburg und Schleswig-Holstein 2020), but this certainly does not reflect the multicultural and diverse reality currently present in Hamburg, or Germany in general. In 2018, all continents were indexed as regions of origin of people currently residing in Germany (Bundesamt für Migration und Flüchtlinge 2020). This gives us an idea of how complex and heterogeneous the situation in Hamburg, and Germany in general, is.

Having an immigrant background, however, does not necessarily imply that this person speaks the language of the country of origin, i.e., the *heritage language*[6] (Cantone 2020). Gogolin (2002: 130) critically acknowledges that "data on nationality or citizenship gives us only very weak pointers to linguistic and cultural diversity." Often, while the parents were born in the foreign country, the child was born and raised in Germany without acquiring the language of their parents.[7] Other children grow up in Germany, learn German, and go to German schools, and use, in addition to German, their heritage language at home with their family or with their peers in or outside of school. Therefore, these heritage speakers make up a heterogeneous group with diverse cultural backgrounds and whose language competences vary on a continuum from little to no proficiency in the heritage language to frequent use and (near-)native proficiency (see also Montrul 2016; Polinsky 2018; more information in Chapter 3).

Immigration as well as the demands of globalization force many people into mastering several languages. These two developments combine to create a complex situation: it is often the case that monolinguals, bilinguals, and also multilinguals, acquire foreign languages together in mixed groups (see Schauer 2019; compare Schwarzl and Vetter 2019 for a similar observation in Austria). This is especially relevant in secondary schools: monolingual German students learn English as their first foreign language together with bilingual or multilingual children, for whom English is considered an additional language (Bonnet and Siemund 2018; Gogolin et al. 2013). Even without regarding the linguistic upbringing of the children, the situation in schools is already heterogeneous. Children from all kinds of socio-economic backgrounds live in the same urban district (Pohlan and Albrecht 2015), attend the same school, or share classes. Hence, the foreign language classroom includes a heterogeneous student population, which, depending on the level of ethnic diversity in the respective region, may include students coming from different cultures who speak various languages (see also Duarte and Gogolin

2013). Teachers now face the challenge of creating an adequate learning environment for everyone (see also Chapter 10). They are expected to encourage and support the individual needs of every student.

Bausch (2016) closely analyzed modern German society with an explicit focus on learners in schools. He states that the situation can be described as "komplexe individuell gelebte, lebensweltliche sowie kollektiv-gesellschaftliche Mehrsprachigkeitsrealitäten"[8] (Bausch 2016: 289). He adds that this should lead to a change in the school system by introducing more provision for multilingual perspectives in didactics (Bausch 2016: 289–290) (see also Burwitz-Melzer et al. 2016 on foreign language teaching in Germany and other German-speaking countries).[9] The German education system, however, still follows a mainly monolingual syllabus (Bergmann 2017; Jakisch 2015a, 2015b) despite the reality of multilingual classes, and it is becoming increasingly apparent that this diverse classroom situation clashes with the established educational framework. This is further examined in the following section.

2.3 Monolingual versus multilingual teaching reality in Germany and beyond

As the previous discussion has shown, the global language English occupies a priority position in Germany with respect to foreign language education (Davydova 2020: 691), even though it does not have an official status (Erling 2002; see also Crystal 2012: 4–5). It is typically the first foreign language taught in school (Siemund, Davydova, and Maier 2012: 245). After briefly pointing out some details about school education in general, this chapter focuses on English teaching in Germany.

In Germany, education policy is regulated autonomously in the individual federal states. This justifies the differences that will be pointed out here. Overall, compulsory education lasts for nine or ten years for all children (Kultusministerkonferenz (KMK) 2019: 24). Primary education typically starts at the age of six and covers the school years one to four (except for the federal states Berlin and Brandenburg, where primary education continues until year six) (KMK 2019: 25). Secondary education is divided into several types of school and the decision as to which school a child should attend is normally based on the teacher's assessment in accordance with the opinion of parent(s) or caretaker(s) (KMK 2019: 25–26). Traditionally, there is a choice between *Hauptschule* (up to school year 9), *Realschule* (up to school year 10), or *Gymnasium* (up to school year 12 or 13) and this decision usually paves the way for any future career track, i.e., occupational training for the former two versus university degree for the latter (KMK 2019: 26; for more details, see KMK 2019: 105–150).[10]

Whereas English teaching used to begin in school year five, since 2006/ 2007, English has been established as a foreign language subject from year one or year three onwards (occasionally, French is also already taught in primary schools) (Demircioglu 2010: 491; KMK 2019: 112; see also Böttger 2010). Nevertheless, English classes in primary schools crucially differ from those in secondary education, as initially, the focus lies on imparting a communicative competence and on teaching simple vocabulary (KMK 2019: 112). Later on, during secondary schooling, reading, writing, listening, oral production, as well as grammar are taught, which essentially cover the necessary skills as defined in the Common European Framework of Reference for Languages (CEFR). The target variety in schools is mainly British English (Hickey 2020b: 208).

Although education in general as well as teacher training more specifically are independently structured and governed in the federal states, there seems to be a rather similar teacher education standard all over Germany (Cantone 2020: 107; Gogolin 2002: 133). What is largely, or perhaps even entirely, missing is systematic instruction for future teachers on how to include multilingualism in the classroom (Cantone 2020). This results, according to Gogolin (1994, 2002), in a monolingual and monocultural ideology among teachers. This "monolingual habitus" (Gogolin 2002; see also Gogolin 1994) is rooted in long-standing traditions of teacher education and teaching practices, which have ultimately manifested as a largely monolingual foreign language teaching approach with strictly separated subjects and languages (Jakisch 2015a: 4).

As a consequence, such teaching approaches, which are specifically designed for monolingual students, disregard the heterogeneity of the German foreign language classroom (see Bonnet and Siemund 2018), even though researchers have pleaded for a change of the monolingual habitus for a while now (Jakisch 2015a: 4) in order to accommodate the needs of the heterogeneous student body. As discussed in the previous section, for some students, English is the second language they acquire, whereas for others, it is their third or additional language. Therefore, the instruction of English (and other foreign languages) in schools would benefit from including strategies that incorporate and promote, in addition to the German perspective, other (foreign) languages and their grammatical systems as well. This seems necessary in order to create a profitable learning environment for both monolingual German students and speakers of other languages, i.e., heritage speakers who grow up in Germany but use one or more additional languages at home. Previous linguistic knowledge of the students could be activated in order to transfer this information to other contexts and languages. Yet, the educational system specifically fosters what Fuller (2020: 177) calls "elite bilingualism" – this means that it is not the heritage language that is valued, encouraged, and supported, but it attends to children who already know German and study a foreign language, mostly English. Moreover, Norton (2018: 245) raises an important point, namely that

> the extent to which teachers are able to recognize the value of the linguistic or cultural capital learners bring to the classroom – their

prior knowledge, home literacies, and mother tongues – will impact the extent to which learners will invest in the language and literacy practices of their classrooms.

Furthermore, Siemund (2023: chapter 4) critically assesses that traditional foreign language practices fail to include the student's linguistically and culturally diverse backgrounds and thus, these largely monolingual beliefs and teaching principles discriminate against multilingual students. In a nutshell, German monolingual students hold a beneficial position and enjoy comparably favorable learning conditions, whereas other students may experience a detrimental learning environment.

It appears that there is a discrepancy between theory and practice, specifically between positive attitudes toward multilingual teaching approaches on the one hand, and the application of such, on the other hand (Martinez 2015: 14; see also Jakisch 2015b). Martinez (2015: 9) stresses the importance of a paradigm shift and argues for the development of a multilingual competence instead of teaching foreign languages exclusively as separate identities. This certainly finds support in the understanding that the languages in the minds of multilinguals are interconnected and not simply the sum of each individual language (Cook and Li Wei 2016). Martinez (2015: 11–12) exemplifies a number of strategies of how language awareness via foreign language teaching in school can be enhanced. Most importantly, she mentions the inclusion of heritage languages and the systematic connection of the different language repertoires of the individual students (Martinez 2015: 11; see also Brevik, Rindal, and Beiler 2020 for a topical and differentiated discussion of mono-, bi-, and multilingual teaching approaches in the English language classroom in Norway). Nevertheless, such a "Gesamtsprachencurriculum"[11] seems to be difficult, or perhaps even impossible to realize and constitutes a challenge for teachers (Martinez 2015: 12; see also Hufeisen 2011). Yet, initial evidence based on recent intervention studies which specifically included *pedagogical translanguaging*[12] approaches (Cenoz and Gorter 2020) in the foreign language classroom (for Germany, see Hopp et al. 2020; for Spain – Basque Autonomous Country – see Leonet, Cenoz and Gorter 2020; for Norway, see Breivik, Rindal, and Beiler 2020) appear to be promising new directions in language acquisition research (see also Schwarzl and Vetter 2019 who applied pedagogical translanguaging in the Austrian context in a number of different school subjects). Crucially, Hopp et al. (2020: 158) found that including multilingual activities in the English language classroom contributed to an enhanced performance in English not only by multilingual but also monolingual German students.[13] Thus, reducing the amount of in-class English input was not at the expense of English development but arguably equipped all students equally well with new learning strategies which they could apply successfully. This line of argumentation will be taken up again in Chapter 10.

2.4 Summary

This chapter provided a short contextualization of the present situation in Germany with respect to the status of English, the acquisition of the foreign language English in linguistically diverse classrooms, as well as the foreign language teaching approach in secondary education. It emphasized the ubiquitous status of English in this country. Yet, at the same time, it underlined that schools, and thus teachers, play a particularly important role. It was argued that for secondary school students, the main English exposure arguably takes place in the foreign language classroom. It is therefore essential to create a learning environment that serves all learners, i.e., both monolingually as well as bilingually raised students. However, the predominantly monolingual habitus which characterizes the current educational focus in foreign language teaching in Germany largely neglects the heterogeneous classroom realities.

Notes

1 For two further, more recent models of World Englishes that go beyond a tripartite classification, see Schneider (2003) and Mair (2013). See also Schneider (2017) for a topical overview.
2 Note that Fuller (2020) mainly describes Berlin, which is, as claimed elsewhere (see, for example, Heyd and Schneider 2020), distinctly different from the rest of Germany.
3 Numbers have also increased with the influx of refugees since 2015 and are likely to be affected by the political developments in Eastern Europe that started in early 2022.
4 According to *PISA Germany* (OECD 2010) and Statistisches Amt für Hamburg und Schleswig-Holstein (2016), a student is defined as having an immigrant background if both parents and the student him- or herself were born in a foreign country, if both parents were born in a foreign country but the student was born in Germany, or if at least one parent was born in a foreign country. Citizenship is not a decisive criterion, i.e., a person can have German citizenship but still belong to the group considered to have an immigrant background (Reiss et al. 2016).
5 First generation immigrants were born in a foreign country, second generation immigrants were born in Germany but have parents born in another country, and third generation immigrants have parents who were born in Germany to parents from a foreign country (i.e., the grandparents are first generation immigrants) (see also Reiss et al. 2016).
6 See Bono and Melo-Pfeifer (2020: 1) for different terms referring to this language, such as "mother tongue, *langue d'origine*, home language, … second language, or foreign language."
7 To complicate things further, the parents themselves may also come from two different foreign countries and bring two separate languages into the home.
8 "Complex, individually lived experiences and collective-social multilingualism" (my translation).

9 Interestingly, the opposite development can be observed in other contexts, as many African and Asian countries reverted to English-only from bilingual schemes. For an overview, see Siemund (2023: chapter 5).
10 This brief overview can at best be understood as a simplification of the German education system. Interested readers are referred to the entire publication of the Kultusministerkonferenz (KMK) (2019), Surkamp and Viebrock (2018), or material from the *Deutscher Bildungsserver* (www.bildungsserver.de).
11 'Global language curriculum or concept' (my translation).
12 Pedagogical translanguaging refers to "the use of different languages for input and output or to other planned strategies based on the use of students' resources from the whole linguistic repertoire" (Cenoz 2017: 194). It takes place in the (foreign language) classroom and presents a planned teacher action (see also Cenoz and Gorter 2021).
13 One could perhaps argue that everything that enhances *metalinguistic awareness* is useful (Peter Siemund, p.c.; see also the discussion about metalinguistic awareness in Section 3.5).

References

Bartelheimer, L., B. Hufeisen, and S. Montanari. 2019. Multilingualism in Europe. In *Multidisciplinary perspectives on multilingualism: The fundamentals*, ed. S. Montanari and S. Quay, 51–75. Boston/Berlin: De Gruyter Mouton.

Bausch, K.-R. 2016. Formen von Zwei- und Mehrsprachigkeit. In *Handbuch Fremdsprachenunterricht*, ed. E. Burwitz-Melzer, G. Mehlhorn, C. Riemer, K.-R. Bausch, and H.-J. Krumm, 285–290. Tübingen: Narr Francke Attempto Verlag.

Bergmann, A. 2017. Curricula für mehrsprachige Klassen: Bildungspolitische Rahmenbedingungen und didaktische Prinzipien. Paper presented at Conference *Biliteralität zwischen Mündlichkeit und Schriftlichkeit*, March 24–25, 2017. University of Hamburg.

Bonnet, A. and P. Siemund (eds.). 2018. *Foreign language education in multilingual classrooms*. Amsterdam: Benjamins.

Bono, M. and S. Melo-Pfeifer. 2020. English and heritage languages from a multilingual perspective: Challenges and possibilities for integration. In *English as a foreign language: Perspectives on teaching, multilingualism and interculturalism*, ed. F. Anastassiou and G. Andreou, 1–19. Newcastle-upon-Tyne: Cambridge Scholars Publishing.

Böttger, H. 2010. *Englisch lernen in der Grundschule*. 2nd edn. Bad Heilbrunn: Verlag Julius Klinkhardt.

Breivik, L. M., U. E. Rindal, and I. R. Beiler. 2020. Language use in English lessons: Monolingual, bilingual and multilingual approaches. In *Teaching English in Norwegian classrooms: From research to practice*, ed. L. M. Breivik and U. E. Rindal, 92–116. Oslo: Universitetsforlaget.

Bruthiaux, P. 2003. Squaring the circles: Issues in modeling English worldwide. *International Journal of Applied Linguistics* 13:159–179.

Bundesamt für Migration und Flüchtlinge. 2020. *Migrationsbericht der Bundesregierung: Migrationsbericht 2018*. Berlin: Bundesministerium des Inneren, für Bau und Heimat. www.bamf.de/SharedDocs/Anlagen/DE/Forschung/Migrationsberichte/migrationsbericht-2018.pdf?__blob=publicationFile&v=15 (accessed April 4, 2022).

Burwitz-Melzer, E., G. Mehlhorn, C. Riemer, K.-R. Bausch, and H.-J. Krumm (eds.). 2016. *Handbuch Fremdsprachenunterricht*. Tübingen: Narr Francke Attempto Verlag.

Cantone, K. F. 2020. Immigrant minority language maintenance in Europe: Focusing on language education policy and teacher-training. *International Multilingual Research Journal* 14:100–113.

Cenoz, J. 2017. Translanguaging in school context: International perspectives. *Journal of Language, Identity and Education* 16:193–198.

Cenoz, J. and D. Gorter. 2020. Teaching English through pedagogical translanguaging. *World Englishes* 39:300–311.

Cenoz, J. and D. Gorter. 2021. *Pedagogical translanguaging*. Cambridge: Cambridge University Press.

Cook, V. and Li Wei (eds.). 2016. *The Cambridge handbook of linguistic multi-competence*. Cambridge: Cambridge University Press.

Crystal, D. 2012. *English as a global language*. 2nd edn. Cambridge: Cambridge University Press.

Davydova, J. 2020. English in Germany: Evidence from domains of use and attitudes. *Russian Journal of Linguistics* 24:687–702.

de Swaan, A. 2001. *Words of the world: The global language system*. Cambridge: Polity Press.

de Swaan, A. 2010. Language systems. In *The handbook of language and globalization*, ed. N. Coupland, 56–76. Malden, MA: Backwell.

Demircioglu, J. 2010. Zur Vorverlegung des Fremdsprachenunterrichts am Beispiel des Englischunterrichts in der Grundschule: Evaluative Argumente. *Bildung und Erziehung* 63:489–504.

Duarte, J. and I. Gogolin (eds.). 2013. *Linguistic superdiversity in urban areas: Research approaches*. Amsterdam: Benjamins.

Edwards, A. 2016. *English in the Netherlands: Functions, forms and attitudes*. Amsterdam: Benjamins.

Edwards, A. and R. Fuchs. 2020. Varieties of English in the Netherlands and Germany. In *English in the German-speaking world*, ed. R. Hickey, 267–293. Cambridge: Cambridge University Press.

Erling, E. J. 2002. 'I learn English since ten years': The global English debate and the German university classroom. *English Today* 18:8–13.

Eurobarometer. 2001. *Standard Eurobarometer 54*. Brussels: Commission of the European Communities. https://data.europa.eu/euodp/en/data/dataset/S1406_54_1_ST54 (accessed April 4, 2022).

Eurobarometer. 2012. *Special Eurobarometer 386*. Brussels: Commission of the European Communities. https://data.europa.eu/euodp/data/dataset/S1049_77_1_EBS386 (accessed April 4, 2022).

Eurobarometer. 2017. *Standard Eurobarometer 87*. Brussels: Commission of the European Communities. https://data.europa.eu/euodp/en/data/dataset/S2142_87_3_STD87_ENG (accessed April 4, 2022).

Fuller, J. M. 2020. English in the German-speaking world: Immigration and integration. In *English in the German-speaking world*, ed. R. Hickey, 165–184. Cambridge: Cambridge University Press.

Gerritsen, M. 2017. English in the EU: Unity through diversity. *World Englishes* 36:339–342.

Gogolin, I. 1994. *Der monolinguale Habitus der multilingualen Schule*. Münster: Waxmann.

Gogolin, I. 2002. Linguistic and cultural diversity in Europe: A challenge for educational research and practice. *European Educational Research Journal* 1:123–138.

Gogolin, I., P. Siemund, M. Schulz, and J. Davydova. 2013. Multilingualism, language contact, and urban areas: An introduction. In *Multilingualism and language contact in urban areas: Acquisition, identities, space, education*, ed. P. Siemund and I. Gogolin, 1–15. Amsterdam: Benjamins.

Heyd, T. and B. Schneider. 2020. Anglophone practices in Berlin: From historical evidence to transnational communities. In *English in the German-speaking world*, ed. R. Hickey, 143–164. Cambridge: Cambridge University Press.

Hickey, R. (ed.). 2020a. *English in the German-speaking world*. Cambridge: Cambridge University Press.

Hickey, R. 2020b. Persistent features in the English of German speakers. In *English in the German-speaking world*, ed. R. Hickey, 208–228. Cambridge: Cambridge University Press.

Hilgendorf, S. K. 2007. English in Germany: Contact, spread and attitudes. *World Englishes* 26:131–148.

Hopp, H., J. Jakisch, S. Sturm, C. Becker, and D. Thoma. 2020. Integrating multilingualism into the early foreign language classroom: Empirical and teaching perspectives. *International Multilingual Research Journal* 14:146–162.

Hufeisen, B. 2011. Gesamtsprachencurriculum: Weitere Überlegungen zu einem prototypischen Modell. In *'Vieles ist sehr ähnlich': Individuelle und gesellschaftliche Mehrsprachigkeit als Bildungsaufgabe*, ed. R. S. Baur and B. Hufeisen, 265–282. Baltmannsweiler: Schneider Verlag Hohengehren.

Jakisch, J. 2015a. Zur Einführung in den Themenschwerpunkt. *Fremdsprachen Lehren und Lernen (FLuL)* 44:3–6.

Jakisch, J. 2015b. Mehrsprachigkeitsförderung über die 1. Fremdsprache: Der Beitrag des Faches Englisch. *Fremdsprachen Lehren und Lernen (FLuL)* 44: 20–33.

Kachru, B. B. 1985. Standards, codification and sociolinguistic realism: The English language in the outer circle. In *English in the world: Teaching and learning the language and literatures*, ed. R. Quirk and H. Widdowson, 11–30. Cambridge: Cambridge University Press.

Kautzsch, A. 2014. English in Germany: Spreading bilingualism, retreating exonormative orientation and incipient nativization? In *The evolution of Englishes: The dynamic model and beyond*, ed. S. Buschfeld, T. Hoffmann, M. Huber, and A. Kautzsch, 203–227. Amsterdam: Benjamins.

Kultusministerkonferenz (KMK). 2019. *Das Bildungswesen in der Bundesrepublik Deutschland 2016/2017*. www.kmk.org/fileadmin/Dateien/pdf/Eurydice/Bildungswesen-dt-pdfs/dossier_de_ebook.pdf (accessed April 4, 2022).

Leonet, O., J. Cenoz, and D. Gorter. 2020. Developing morphological awareness across languages: Translanguaging pedagogies in third language acquisition. *Language Awareness* 29:41–59.

Li Wei. 2008. Research perspectives on bilingualism and multilingualism. In *Research methods in bilingualism and multilingualism*, ed. Li Wei and M. G. Moyer, 3–17. Malden, MA: Blackwell.

Mair, C. 2013. The world system of Englishes: Accounting for the transnational importance of mobile and mediated vernaculars. *English World-Wide* 34:253–278.

Mair, C. 2020. English in the German-speaking world: An inevitable presence. In *English in the German-speaking world*, ed. R. Hickey, 13–30. Cambridge: Cambridge University Press.
Martinez, H. 2015. Mehrsprachigkeitsdidaktik: Aufgaben, Potenziale und Herausforderungen. *Fremdsprachen Lehren und Lernen (FLuL)* 44:7–19.
Meyer, B. 2008. *Nutzung der Mehrsprachigkeit von Menschen mit Migrationshintergrund: Berufsfelder mit besonderem Potential. Expertise für das Bundesamt für Migration und Flüchtlinge*. Hamburg: Universität Hamburg.
Mollin, S. 2020. English in Germany and the European context. In *English in the German-speaking world*, ed. R. Hickey, 31–52. Cambridge: Cambridge University Press.
Montrul, S. 2016. *The acquisition of heritage languages*. Cambridge: Cambridge University Press.
Norton, B. 2018. Identity and investment in multilingual classrooms. In *Foreign language education in multilingual classrooms*, ed. A. Bonnet and P. Siemund, 237–252. Amsterdam: Benjamins.
OECD. 2010. *PISA 2009 at a Glance*. OECD Publishing. http://dx.doi.org/10.1787/9789264095298-en (accessed April 4, 2022).
Pohlan, J. and M. Albrecht. 2015. *Sozialmonitoring Integrierte Stadtteilentwicklung: Bericht 2014*. Hamburg: Freie und Hansestadt Hamburg. www.hamburg.de/contentblob/4596628/3146eccd0cc179a290ad5f17bb721d2d/data/sozialmonitoring-bericht-2014.pdf (accessed April 4, 2022).
Polinsky, M. 2018. *Heritage languages and their speakers*. Cambridge: Cambridge University Press.
Quirk, R., S. Greenbaum, G. Leech, and J. Svartvik. 1985. *A comprehensive grammar of the English language*. London/New York: Longman.
Reiss, K., C. Sälzer, A. Schiepe-Tiska, E. Klieme, and O. Köller (eds.). 2016. *PISA 2015: Eine Studie zwischen Kontinuität und Innovation*. Münster/New York: Waxmann.
Schauer, G. A. 2019. *Teaching and learning English in the primary school: Interlanguage pragmatics in the EFL context*. Cham: Springer.
Schneider, E. W. 2003. The dynamics of New English: From identity construction to dialect birth. *Language* 79:233–281.
Schneider, E. W. 2017. Models of English in the world. In *The Oxford handbook of world Englishes*, ed. J. Klemola, M. Filppula, and D. Sharma, 35–57. Oxford: Oxford University Press.
Schroedler, T. and N. Fischer. 2020. The role of beliefs in teacher professionalisation for multilingual classroom settings. *European Journal of Applied Linguistics* 8:49–72.
Schwarzl, L. and E. Vetter. 2019. Translanguaging and plurilingual texts as a resource in superdiverse classrooms. *Cahiers de L'Ilob* 10:229–248.
Siemund, P. 2018. Modeling world Englishes from a cross-linguistic perspective. In *Modeling world Englishes: Assessing the interplay of emancipation and globalization of ESL varieties*, ed. S. C. Deshors, 133–162. Amsterdam: Benjamins.
Siemund, P. 2023. *Multilingual development: English in a global context*. Cambridge: Cambridge University Press.
Siemund, P., J. Davydova, and G. Maier. 2012. *The amazing world of Englishes: A practical introduction*. Berlin: De Gruyter Mouton.

Spellerberg, S. M. 2016. Metalinguistic awareness and academic achievement in a linguistically diverse school setting: A study of lower secondary pupils in Denmark. *International Journal of Multilingualism* 13:19–39.

Statistisches Amt für Hamburg und Schleswig-Holstein (Statistikamt Nord). 2016. *Bevölkerung mit Migrationshintergrund in den Hamburger Stadtteilen Ende 2015*. www.statistik-nord.de/fileadmin/Dokumente/Statistik_informiert_SPEZIAL/SI_SPEZIAL_I_2016_komplett.pdf (accessed April 4, 2022).

Statistisches Amt für Hamburg und Schleswig-Holstein (Statistikamt Nord). 2020. *Statistisches Jahrbuch Hamburg 2019/2020*. www.statistik-nord.de/fileadmin/Dokumente/Jahrb%C3%BCcher/Hamburg/JB19HH_Gesamt.pdf (accessed April 4, 2022).

Stefanowitsch, A. 2002. Nice to *miet* you: Bilingual puns and the status of English in Germany. *Intercultural Communication Studies* 11:67–84.

Strang, B. M. H. 1970. *A history of English*. London: Methuen.

Surkamp, C. and B. Viebrock (eds.). 2018. *Teaching English as a foreign language: An introduction*. Stuttgart: J. B. Metzler.

3 Previous and current research on language acquisition

3.1 Terminology

First, it is imperative to introduce some terms and concepts to set the scene for the present chapter and beyond. There are numerous terminological inconsistencies (De Angelis 2007: 8) prevailing in the field of third language acquisition. To provide a basis for the current contexts, a number of definitions and explanations are given.

3.1.1 L1, L2, L3

In theory, the labels *L1*, *L2*, and *L3* appear relatively straightforward. The L1 would be the first language, i.e., the native language a person acquires, followed by the L2 and subsequently the L3. However, Hammarberg argued that "it will often be neither meaningful nor even possible to order a multilingual's languages along a linear time scale" (2010: 93). Some people acquire two languages simultaneously, which would then, in principle, result in two L1s. If an additional language is then subsequently acquired, the question arises if this language should be labeled L2 or L3 instead. In addition, such a linear ordering usually implies highest proficiency in the L1 (i.e., the native language) and decreasing competences in the consecutive languages (i.e., higher proficiency in the L2 in comparison with the L3, etc.). Yet, as Jessner, Megens, and Graus (2016: 194) remarked, "dominance (in terms of proficiency or frequency of use) and/or the 'emotional weight' given to a certain language do/does not necessarily correspond to the chronological order of acquisition." In such situations, the labels L1, L2, or L3 could be misleading.

Arguably, in some contexts, L1, L2, and L3 are useful descriptors. If a person is raised with one language (L1), acquires a foreign language in school (L2), and subsequently learns another foreign language during university education (L3), the labels can indeed be applied. Yet, in other constellations, it is difficult or impossible to rightly assign these labels to a multilingual person. This is particularly relevant in the present study. Therefore, the choice of terminology will not rely on the labels L1, L2, or

L3 once the current study is presented, but makes use of majority/dominant language and minority/heritage language instead. However, when the different transfer models are presented in Section 3.2, or whenever research referred to makes use of this classification, the labels L1, L2, and L3 will be used.

3.1.2 Minority/heritage language

A *minority* or *heritage language* is understood as the language of origin of immigrants. Typically, it is confined to the home context, used for communication within the family (Meisel 2014; Montrul 2016). Whereas for those migrating to another country at a relatively late age the heritage language could still remain the dominant language, i.e., the language they are most proficient in, this may be quite different for children or young adults (who may either be born in the new country or have migrated at a young age). Even though the heritage language is typically the first language the children are in contact with (either before or simultaneously with the official language of the new speech community), there is often a proficiency shift visible, mostly after entering school in the new country (see, for example, Franceschini 2016; Grosjean and Beyers-Heinlein 2018; Montrul 2016). This means that over time, these speakers become more fluent in the language of the speech community in comparison to the heritage language.[1] In other words, these bilinguals become *unbalanced bilinguals*. This unbalanced language proficiency is a frequent characteristic of heritage bilinguals or heritage speakers (see Montrul 2016, Montrul and Polinsky 2021 for comprehensive accounts of heritage speakers and heritage languages). This means that instead of being equally (or nearly equally) proficient in their two languages, heritage bilinguals are typically less proficient in the heritage language. Often, heritage languages are naturally acquired without support via formal education. Heritage language tuition is largely optional.

3.1.3 Majority/dominant language

The *majority* or *dominant language* is the language a bilingual speaker is most proficient in because it is most often activated during everyday life situations (Hopp 2019; Montrul 2016). In the contexts of heritage bilinguals, as outlined above, it is the language spoken by the speech community of the (new) country of residence (Meisel 2014; Montrul 2016), which may or may not be the L1. This means that the dominant language is another language than the family or heritage language that is spoken in many homes of immigrants. Moreover, it is the language of instruction used during school education, which means that in addition to being orally exposed to this language, speakers are also formally trained in it.

3.1.4 Bilingual heritage speakers

A *bilingual heritage speaker* is one specific type of a bilingual person, growing up with two different languages (see Section 3.3 for a more detailed account of bilingualism and different kinds of bilinguals). As indicated above, the status of the two languages of heritage speakers is shaped by frequency of use. Typically, the official language of the speech community is most frequently used and activated, which results in heritage bilinguals being dominant and more comfortable in this language. On the contrary, due to limited use of the heritage language, they are frequently less proficient in the other language of their linguistic repertoire (Hopp 2019; Montrul 2016). Due to globalization and high rates of mobility, growing up as a bilingual heritage speaker is therefore a phenomenon that is rather frequently encountered in countries such as Germany (see again Chapter 2).

3.1.5 Learning versus acquiring

Krashen (1981) differentiated between *acquisition* on the one hand, and *learning* on the other. In his understanding, the former refers to the natural process of language acquisition, i.e., through communication in natural settings (as opposed to explicit language instruction) (Krashen 1981: 1). It is typically the L1 that falls into this category. Language learning, however, happens in contexts of formal language instruction, such as in (foreign) language classrooms (Krashen 1981: 1). Other scholars (for example Ellis 1994; Odlin 1989) use these terms interchangeably. Ellis (1994: 14) remarked that particularly due to globalization, categorizing learners into one or the other category may be problematic; there may perhaps be phases where one process dominates, but other phases that are characteristic of the other process. In the current study, both terms will be used as synonyms without implying any differences.

3.2 Third versus second language acquisition

This section focusses on *second* and *third* (or *additional*) *language acquisition*. Third language acquisition is presented as considerably different from second language acquisition, which justifies the research area of third language acquisition as a field on its own. It follows the idea that third language acquisition cannot, or rather should not, be put on a level with second language acquisition. In addition, this chapter examines and summarizes predominant theories and proposed models of crosslinguistic influence in third language acquisition. It concludes with an evaluation of the individual theories and models and puts the diverse, and at times contradictory findings, into perspective by highlighting, among others, the status of the previously acquired languages.

3.2.1 Emergence of the field

In the second half of the twentieth century, particularly during the 1960s, first studies with second language learners were brought forward and the research field of second language acquisition was established as an area in its own right (Ellis 1994; Saville-Troike 2012). It clearly distinguishes itself from the acquisition of the first language, because learners of a second language have "already one language present in their minds" (Cook 2016a: 17).

In the early years of this new research strand, many scholars agreed that it was not necessary to differentiate between the second language and further foreign languages as "the process underlying the acquisition of all non-native languages is essentially the same" (De Angelis 2007: 4). Thus, at first, the term *second language* was a cover term for the acquisition of any language other than the *native language* (Ellis 1994: 11). Later, Klein (1995) pointed out that bilingual or multilingual learners may use "their previous nonnative linguistic knowledge to aid in learning a new language" (Klein 1995: 423). Thus, the context may be different for bi- or multilinguals when compared to learners of their first non-native language and claims made for second language acquisition might not necessarily hold for third or additional language acquisition.

In the following years, several scholars investigated multilingual behavior and found crucial differences between second language and third or additional language acquisition (see, for example, De Angelis 2007). The understanding shifted towards an agreement "that a general theory of non-native language acquisition cannot be based on L2 learner behavior alone" (De Angelis 2007: 4). Moreover, third or additional language acquisition may as such be even more complex than second language acquisition, due to the diversity that is covered by the terms *bilingualism* and *multilingualism*. Third and additional languages are acquired in multifaceted settings and at various ages. Furthermore, complexity augmentation is also due to the increased sources of crosslinguistic influence. Unlike in second language acquisition, where transfer happens between the L1 and the L2, there are two potential sources for crosslinguistic influence in third language acquisition in addition to possible crosslinguistic influence across all three languages (Cenoz 2001: 8; Jarvis and Pavlenko 2008: 21–22; Jessner 2008: 271; Peukert 2015: 4–5). It seems plausible that the knowledge and competences a language learner has gained throughout the process of learning a foreign language play a crucial and possibly also helpful role in further language learning processes (De Angelis 2007: 7).

However, the extent to which the individual languages interact with each other is still a matter of debate. The following section zooms in on numerous studies investigating third language acquisition and presents evidence for different language acquisition models. Before diving into this topical overview, a few more words about crosslinguistic influence are indispensable.

3.2.2 Crosslinguistic influence in third language acquisition

3.2.2.1 Defining crosslinguistic influence

Crosslinguistic influence, defined as "the interplay between earlier and later acquired languages" (Sharwood Smith and Kellerman 1986: 1), is sometimes used synonymously with terms such as *transfer*[2] or *interference* (Odlin 2013: 1; but see Rothman, González Alonso, and E. Puig-Mayenco 2019 who differentiate transfer and crosslinguistic influence). However, crosslinguistic influence is often understood as the more neutral term covering a larger variety of phenomena (Cook 2016b; Sharwood Smith and Kellerman 1986), including both *positive/facilitative* and *negative/non-facilitative transfer*. In addition, it is not limited to the L1 influencing the L2 but allows influence in the opposite direction as well (see, for example, Pavlenko and Jarvis 2002). In the current context, this goes beyond the influence between two languages but extends to three languages and thus describes the interplay of languages in the minds of bi- or multilingual speakers (Gabrys-Barker 2012; Cenoz, Hufeisen, and Jessner 2001). Moreover, even though a neutral and broad perspective is taken in the current study, both crosslinguistic influence as well as transfer will be used to refer to the same overall concept (see again Section 1.2.4).

3.2.2.2 Transfer scenarios in third language acquisition

In theory, based on the linguistic background, there are four different transfer scenarios that could explain crosslinguistic influence in third language acquisition (Lorenz et al. 2019: 1411). Potentially, it could be that (i) none of the two previously acquired languages influences the third language; (ii) crosslinguistic influence comes exclusively from the first language; (iii) it is the second language that influences the third language; or (iv) both the L1 and the L2 influence the L3.

In the following, these transfer scenarios will be looked at in turn, except for (i), i.e., no transfer from the background languages. The reason is that research in second language acquisition (i.e., the process of acquiring a first foreign language) has shown that the L1 influences the L2. Evidence comes, for instance, from Schwartz and Sprouse (1994) who argued for the *Full Transfer/Full Access Model*, and from Håkansson, Pienemann and Sayheli (2002) who presented evidence in favor of the *Processability Theory*. The former predicts that all syntactic characteristics available in the L1 will be fully transferred to the L2. The latter limits transfer to structures that are "processable within the developing L2" (Håkansson, Pienemann and Sayheli 2002: 269). Thus, it seems plausible that there must be at least some influence coming from the other languages in the speakers' minds when acquiring an additional foreign language, because even though third language acquisition differs from second language acquisition, the two processes are not fundamentally different. Slabakova and García Mayo (2017: 82) rightly pointed out "that L3/Ln acquisition is essentially language acquisition; that is, we can expect all the factors affecting L1 and L2 acquisition to continue to play significant roles in L3/Ln acquisition" (see also Rothman 2015).

3.2.2.3 Influence from the L1

Na Ranong and Leung (2009) presented evidence that the L1 plays a privileged role in L3 acquisition. This is based on a study examining native speakers of Thai who learned English as their first foreign language during childhood and started to learn Chinese as an L3 during their university education. Na Ranong and Leung (2009) investigated the use of (null) objects in Chinese, Thai, and English. They compared these L3 learners of Chinese with L2 learners of Chinese and found the L1 to be the only source of crosslinguistic influence among both groups. Moreover, Hermas (2014), who investigated L3 learners of English with L1 Arabic and L2 French, also argued for transfer from the L1 in the initial stages of L3 acquisition. Based on an acceptability judgment task and a preference test, Hermas (2014) identified negative transfer effects from the L1 Arabic and no positive influence from the L2 French.

3.2.2.4 Influence from the L2

Yet, opposing evidence comes from studies arguing for L2 instead of L1 influence. One such study is Dewaele (1998) who analyzed two groups of learners, namely L1 Dutch, L2 French speakers, and L1 Dutch, L2 English, L3 French speakers. He investigated French oral production focusing on non-target-like lexemes (Dewaele 1998: 477). He found that for the L3 French learners, it was not the L1 Dutch but the L2 English that was activated in L3 production (Dewaele 1998: 488). Additional support comes from Bardel and Falk who claimed that "syntactic structures are more easily transferred from L2 than from L1" (2007: 459) because the L1 is implicitly learned, whereas the L2 is explicitly learned (Bardel and Falk 2012). Therefore, Bardel and Falk argued for "the so-called L2 status factor" (2007: 460) and extended what had already been argued for in a case study by Williams and Hammarberg in 1998 (see also Hammarberg 2009). In their study on negation placement comparing L3 learners of Dutch and Swedish with various L1s and L2s, Bardel and Falk (2007) found support for crosslinguistic influence from the L2. They put forward the hypothesis of the *L2 Status Factor*, which assigns a special role to the L2 in L3 acquisition causing the L1 to be inaccessible (Bardel and Falk 2007; see also Bardel and Falk 2012; Hammarberg 2009). In Falk and

Bardel (2011), it was again the L2 that predominantly influenced the L3 German when testing the placement of object pronouns. Rothman and Cabrelli Amaro (2010) also presented data that can be explained with the L2 Status Factor. They compared five groups of learners (L1 English; L1 English, L2 French; L1 English, L2 Italian; L1 English, L2 Spanish, L3 French; L1 English, L2 Spanish, L3 Italian) and the differences they found across the groups matched the propositions made by the L2 Status Factor (Rothman and Cabrelli Amaro 2010).[3]

3.2.2.5 Influence from the L1 and the L2
Unlike the previously introduced transfer scenarios, Flynn, Foley, and Vinnitskaya (2004) argued against the preferential role of the L1 or the L2, suggesting that all previously acquired languages influence the subsequently acquired language. They compared the use of relative clauses of L1 Kazakh, L2 Russian learners of English with L2 learners of English (L1 Japanese and L1 Spanish background). Based on their results, they argued that not only the L1 but also the L2 influenced the acquisition process of English, thus "language acquisition is accumulative, i.e., the prior language can be neutral or enhance subsequent language acquisition" (Flynn, Foley, and Vinnitskaya 2004: 14). This means that in their *Cumulative Enhancement Model*, Flynn, Foley, and Vinnitskaya (2004) proposed combined crosslinguistic influence, with the exclusion of negative or non-facilitative transfer. In sum, the influence of the L1 and the L2 is exclusively positive or remains neutral in third language acquisition.

More support for L1 and L2 influence comes from Hermas (2015) who analyzed L1 Arabic, L2 French learners of L3 English (pre-intermediate and advanced English learners). The use of relative clauses of the L3 learners was compared to the performance of native speakers of English and L1 French speakers. Hermas (2015) also concluded that third language acquisition is a cumulative process, which in part supported the premises presented in the Cumulative Enhancement Model (Flynn, Foley, and Vinnitskaya 2004). Yet, in addition to facilitative transfer, Hermas (2015) identified non-facilitative transfer from Arabic in the pre-intermediate English learners. In that, these findings only partly supported Flynn, Foley, and Vinnitskaya's (2004) Cumulative Enhancement Model and did not exclude negative transfer.

3.2.2.6 Other factors influencing crosslinguistic influence in third language acquisition
In addition, several recent studies in the area of L3 acquisition have convincingly demonstrated that the choice of the source language in L3 acquisition does not only depend on the order of acquisition (see Puig-Mayenco, Gonzáles Alonso, and Rothman 2020 for an overview), as was previously assumed. Instead, additional (non)linguistic variables play a

tremendous role and are perhaps even more influential than the order of acquisition. For example, similarity based on typology or rather perceived typology/psychotypology (Kellerman 1983; Rothman 2011) between the languages at stake seems to greatly affect the source of crosslinguistic influence.

3.2.2.7 Transfer based on typological similarity

Rothman (2011) investigated two groups of L3 learners, namely L1 Italian, L2 English, L3 Spanish and L1 English, L2 Spanish, L3 Portuguese, focusing on adjective placement. He did not identify statistically significant differences between the groups. For both L3 learners, it was the Romance language (either the L1 or the L2) that was transferred. This finding was not in line with the L2 Status Factor proposed by Bardel and Falk (2007) (see also Williams and Hammarberg 1998; Hammarberg 2009). Even though this might be understood as support for the Cumulative Enhancement Model (Flynn, Foley, and Vinnitskaya 2004), Rothman (2011) did not exclude non-facilitative influence (similarly to what Hermas 2015 suggested). Therefore, he proposed "a modification of the CEM [Cumulative Enhancement Model]" (Rothman 2011: 121) and argued for crosslinguistic influence from either the L1 or the L2, depending on *typological proximity* (actual or perceived) to the third language (see also García Mayo and Slabakova 2015). In addition, Rothman (2011) explicitly included transfer as either facilitative or non-facilitative. This *Typological Primacy Model* makes propositions for the initial state of transfer (Rothman 2011). An updated version of the Typological Primacy Model was presented in Rothman (2013). In this study, Rothman specifically argued that recognition of structural proximity is essentially guided by the principle of economy, i.e., to be maximally efficient in learning a new language. The language – either the L1 or L2 – that is perceived as structurally more similar to the target language (the L3) is selected as the source of transfer and transferred completely (Rothman 2013: 236). Thus, property-by-property transfer is excluded (see Section 3.2.2.8 below). Instead, the Typological Primacy Model (Rothman 2013: 242) predicts holistic transfer.[4] Notably, Cabrelli et al. (2020) presented additional evidence supporting full transfer and the core ideas of the Typological Primacy Model. Beyond this, however, they also demonstrated that from a developmental perspective, i.e., after the initial stages of L3 acquisition, it makes a difference whether the typologically similar language is the L1 or the L2 (Cabrelli et al. 2020). Based on L1 English, L2 Spanish and L1 Spanish, L2 English learners of Brazilian Portuguese, they observed that "an L1 Spanish/L2 English speaker acquiring L3 BP [Brazilian Portuguese] will require more input/ experience in the L3 to override the L1 Spanish system than an L1 English/L2 Spanish speaker will" (Cabrelli et al. 2020: 26), which means that "learners who transfer their L2 converge on an L3 target faster than learners that transfer their L1" (Cabrelli et al. 2020: 29).

3.2.2.8 Transfer based on linguistic proximity

This notion of *property-by-property* versus *holistic transfer* is addressed in Westergaard, Mitrofanova, Mykhaylyk, and Rodina's (2017) *Linguistic Proximity Model* (see also Westergaard 2021b). The main claims of this model are that "general typological proximity is the decisive factor" but that "similarity of abstract linguistic properties is the main cause of CLI [crosslinguistic influence] from previously learned languages" (Westergaard et al. 2017: 670). In addition, they also argued against exclusively positive transfer from the previously acquired languages but allowed for facilitative and non-facilitative transfer (Westergaard et al. 2017: 676). This means, it is not the order in which the languages of one's linguistic repertoire were acquired that drives crosslinguistic influence, but the specific similarities between the languages (Westergaard et al. 2017: 670). These claims were based on a study investigating Norwegian-Russian bilinguals, Russian monolinguals, as well as Norwegian monolinguals and their performance in an English grammaticality judgment task assessing adverb-verb-placement and subject-auxiliary inversion. Westergaard et al. (2017) identified positive influence from Russian (adverb-verb-placement) and negative transfer from Norwegian (verb second status) in the responses of the L3 English learners. What they showed was that the Russian monolinguals outperformed the other groups with respect to adverb placement, and that the Norwegian monolingual students performed lowest (the opposite was true for subject-auxiliary inversion). In both conditions, the bilinguals' performance was in-between, due to facilitative and non-facilitative crosslinguistic influence from Russian and Norwegian (Westergaard et al. 2017: 676). This means that all languages in the learners' repertoires are active throughout the process of learning a new language (see also Jensen et al. 2021, Kolb, Mitrofanova, and Westergaard 2022, and Wrembel 2021 for further support of the Linguistic Proximity Model).

Being active, however, does not necessarily imply that everything from both languages will be transferred. Instead, Westergaard (2021a: 389) introduced the *Full Transfer Potential*, which means that "anything may transfer" but does not inevitably have to (see also Westergaard 2021a: 394). With this proposition, it is perfectly plausible that for some grammatical features, one of the two previously acquired languages is the main (or perhaps even only) source of transfer (Westergaard 2021a: 394). The driving factor is similarity on a structural level, but this structural similarity is likely to be influenced by typological or lexical similarity (Westergaard 2021a). Moreover, the order of acquisition does not play a role in the Linguistic Proximity Model, which makes it applicable in contexts where the L1 and L2 are not clearly distinguishable (Westergaard 2021a; see Section 3.4 below).

Similarly, Slabakova (2017) presented the *Scalpel Model* that also argues for property-by-property or selective transfer based on (perceived) typological similarity and against the privileged role of the L1 or the L2 in L3 acquisition. She also disagreed with the assumptions of the Cumulative Enhancement Model (Flynn, Foley, and Vinnitskaya 2004) that transfer can never be detrimental and argued against wholesale transfer as proposed by the Typological Primacy Model (Rothman 2011, 2015). Slabakova (2017) further outlined that additional factors have an impact on the acquisition process, such as frequency of the phenomenon under investigation and the availability of positive or negative evidence. She used the metaphor of a scalpel by explaining that it precisely dissects specific properties, yet there are "factors that can lead the scalpel away from precision" (Slabakova 2017: 662). It can therefore be expected that some grammatical features are more easily transferred than others. In a sense, Slabakova (2017) extended Westergaard et al.'s (2017) Linguistic Proximity Model by advocating that language acquisition in multilingual contexts is complex as well as dynamic and by admitting that additional individual variables need to be considered to fully understand these processes (see also Slabakova and García Mayo 2015; Slabakova 2021). Nevertheless, the Scalpel Model remains relatively unspecific and Slabakova (2017: 662) admitted that "refinements of any proposed model are possible and welcome, especially in the face of new evidence. The search for the definitive L3 acquisition account continues."

3.2.2.9 *Transfer from the dominant language*

One last proposition for transfer in third language acquisition to be discussed in the current section comes from a study by Fallah and Jabbari (2018). The authors considered school-aged bilinguals (Mazandarani and Persian) who grew up in Iran and studied English as a foreign language in school (Fallah and Jabbari 2018: 201–202). Three groups of bilinguals were investigated to control for order of acquisition and frequency of use: group A (L1 Mazandarani, L2 Persian; L1 is the dominant language), group B (L1 Mazandarani, L2 Persian; L2 is the dominant language), and group C (L1 Persian, L2 Mazandarani; L1 is the dominant language) (Fallah and Jabbari 2018: 203). Based on a grammaticality judgment task and an element rearrangement task focusing on the placement of attributive adjectives, Fallah and Jabbari (2018) showed that crosslinguistic influence came from the dominant language, irrespective of order of acquisition (see also Fallah, Jabbari, and Fazilatfar 2016). With this, they presented counter evidence for the earlier introduced models that argued for L1, L2, or cumulative enhancement in third language acquisition. Moreover, the Typological Primacy Model cannot be supported because Mazandarani and Persian are not typologically related to English. Similarly, this study argued against the Linguistic Proximity Model or the Scalpel Model, as transfer did not seem to be selective but could be traced back to only one language, namely the dominant language.

3.2.2.10 Conclusion

This section provided a comprehensive overview of studies investigating crosslinguistic influence in third language acquisition. Clearly, the findings and corresponding models are crucially different and make contrary predictions. The next section offers an evaluation of the aforementioned studies and tries to explain why the findings are so diverse.

3.2.3 Evaluation

The preceding discussion has shown how lively the debate about crosslinguistic influence in third language acquisition still is. In the following, some explanations for the – at first sight – contradictory results of the previously introduced studies are offered (for additional comprehensive meta-analyses, see Puig-Mayenco, Gonzáles Alonso, and Rothman 2020; Rothman, Gonzáles Alonso, and Puig-Mayenco 2019).

First, the number of participants included in the above-mentioned studies differs quite drastically and is at times relatively low (e.g., 9 L3 learners in Bardel and Falk 2007; 14 L3 learners in Hermas 2014; 26 L3 learners in Hermas 2015; 27 L3 learners in Rothman 2011; 22 L3 learners in Westergaard et al. 2017). The question arises to what extent results based on studies with relatively few participants can be generalized to third language acquisition in general.

Furthermore, in several studies, only one grammatical phenomenon was investigated (for example negation in Bardel and Falk 2007; relative clauses in Flynn, Foley, and Vinnitskaya 2004 and Hermas 2015; interpretation and use of pre- and post-nominal adjectives in Rothman 2011). Siemund, Schröter, and Rahbari (2018: 384) rightly criticize that "the examination of one particular phenomenon is usually taken to be sufficient to allow for far-reaching generalizations." Investigating more than one feature is particularly relevant since the Linguistic Proximity Model (Westergaard et al. 2017) specifically argues for selective transfer that needs to be justified with more than one grammatical feature. However, time and money constraints as well as simply the difficulty of finding suitable L3 learners (see Hermas 2014: 11) certainly limit the number of participants as well as phenomena that can be included in studies investigating third language acquisition.

A further possible confounding factor is the age of the L3 learners. Whereas most of the studies rely on adults, typically university students (see, for example, Bardel and Falk 2007; Cabrelli et al. 2020; Dewaele 1998; Flynn, Foley, and Vinnitskaya 2004; Hermas 2015; Na Ranong and

Leung 2009), there are other studies whose participants are adolescents or children attending secondary or primary schools (Fallah and Jabbari 2018; Fallah, Jabbari, and Fazilatfar 2016; Flynn, Foley, and Vinnitskaya 2004; Jensen et al. 2021; Kolb, Mitrofanova, and Westergaard 2022). It is crucial to distinguish between adult and child language learners, since, for example, motivation or the specific learning environments may impact the acquisition of a third language (see Ellis 2015 and Richards and Sampson 2014 on adults versus children in second language acquisition).

In addition, differences regarding the findings of L3 studies are to be expected if one considers initial, intermediate, or advanced stages of the third language. Some studies explicitly limit their findings to the initial stages/initial state[5] of L3 acquisition (Hermas 2014; Fallah and Jabbari 2018) and may thus not apply to more advanced third language learners. Yet, some of the studies cited above present findings based on at least (pre-)intermediate third language learners (Hermas 2015; Jensen et al. 2021; Kolb, Mitrofanova, and Westergaard 2022; Rothman 2011; Westergaard et al. 2017), meaning that these learners had several years of exposure to the third language (via formal education in school), or compare early L3 learners with advanced learners (Cabrelli et al. 2020). In addition, Slabakova (2017) suggests that L3 studies should go beyond the initial stages of learning an L3 and focus on developmental processes.

Another confounding factor is the language combination considered in each study (see also Puig-Mayenco, Gonzáles Alonso, and Rothman 2020: 59–60). Some studies include language pairings so that the L3 is typologically related to either the L1 or the L2 (Italian/English/Spanish and English/Spanish/Brazilian Portuguese in Cabrelli et al. 2020 and Rothman 2011; Norwegian/Russian/English in Jensen et al. 2021 and Westergaard et al. 2017; Russian/German/English in Kolb, Mitrofanova, and Westergaard 2022; Dutch/French/English in Dewaele 1998). Other studies, however, include typologically unrelated languages (Mazandarani/Persian/English in Fallah and Jabbari 2018 and Fallah, Jabbari, and Fazilatfar 2016; Thai/English/Chinese in Na Ranong and Leung 2009; Arabic/French/English in Hermas 2014; Kazakh/Russian/English in Flynn, Foley, and Vinnitskaya 2004) or at least language combinations where the L3 differs typologically from both the L1 and the L2 (but the L1 and L2 are part of the same language family, e.g., Dutch/English/French in Dewaele 1998). One note of caution: even though English (Germanic language) and French (Romance language) belong to different language families, these two languages share a number of cognates due to historical reasons (Dewaele 1998: 477) and may thus be perceived as (typologically) related by language learners. The aspect of typological relatedness is particularly crucial since the Typological Primacy Model (Rothman 2011, 2015) makes explicit predictions based on (perceived) relatedness of the languages present in the speakers' repertoires.

Moreover, the previously presented studies differ with respect to the types of bilingual learner investigated. The majority base their findings on adult L3 learners who were monolingually raised and acquired their first foreign language in school (see, for example, Bardel and Falk 2007; Cabrelli et al. 2020; Flynn, Foley, and Vinnitskaya 2004; Na Ranong and Leung 2009; Rothman 2011). In such contexts, differentiating between the native language (L1) and two subsequently learned foreign languages (L2 and L3) seems to be relatively straightforward. Other studies consider bilinguals who acquired both of their languages naturally during childhood and study their first foreign language (i.e., the L3) in school (Fallah and Jabbari 2018; Fallah, Jabbari, and Fazilatfar 2016). The participants in Westergaard et al.'s (2017) study, however, are heritage bilinguals, who grew up with a heritage language and the language of the speech community in addition to studying a foreign language in school. In these latter contexts, the L1 and L2 may not be clearly distinguishable (they may both count as native languages, see Wiese et al. 2022) and seem to have a different status than the L1 and L2 of the former studies (see, for example, Dewaele 1998; Hopp 2019). This means that for some of the studies, it may be difficult or strictly speaking impossible to prove or disprove L1 transfer (Na Ranong and Leung 2009; Hermas 2014) or the L2 Status Factor (Bardel and Falk 2007).

Particularly this latter point – the type of bilingual speaker considered – is of importance. That the type of learner has an impact on third language acquisition and therefore crosslinguistic influence has been acknowledged (Cenoz 2003). There are different types of third language learner and a clear distinction as to which type is considered in a study is imperative. The L3 models introduced and discussed above were largely based on adult L3 learners with a clear distinction between the previously acquired L1 and L2. Increasingly, however, other third language learners are being investigated. This can be shown with a number of recent studies, many of which are located in Germany, that investigate third language acquisition of heritage bilinguals (see Kupisch, Snape, and Stangen 2013). The following two sections first provide some more detailed background information about bilingualism in general and more specifically about heritage speakers, and then zoom into third language acquisition in such heritage contexts, arguably a field in its own right.

3.3 Bilingualism and heritage speakers

This section deals with the conception and definition of *bilingualism* and the concept of a *heritage speaker*, a special type of a *bilingual speaker*. The previous sections indicated that there are different kinds of bilinguals. Yet, what has so far not been explicitly provided is a definition of bilingualism.

Defining *bilingualism* should include two languages – simply based on the Latin-based prefix *bi-* that means 'two'. Yet, the details remain somewhat unclear. There are various definitions that one can find, ranging from a relatively broad to an extremely narrow perspective (see Berthele

2021: 84 for an overview of definitions). An example of the former is a definition provided by Butler and Hakuta (2006: 114–115) who consider bilinguals "individuals or groups of people who obtain the knowledge and use of more than one language." In this understanding, bilingualism is seemingly not limited to knowledge of two languages. Bloomfield (1984: 57) instead defines bilingualism in a narrower sense and argues that a bilingual speaker needs to have "native-like control of two languages." There are several issues with both definitions. What exactly is meant by "knowledge" – does knowing some (individual) words of a language in addition to being fluent in another already count for being considered a bilingual in Butler and Hakuta's (2006) understanding? Moreover, even more difficult to account for is "native-like control" – how can it be measured? It certainly implies perfect language skills – but what does this exactly mean?

Peal and Lambert (1962) introduced the idea of a *balanced bilingual*, i.e., someone who is equally fluent in both languages (Duarte 2011: 25). With this addition, it already becomes clear that there must be more than just one type of a bilingual speaker. Thus, instead of viewing bilingualism as a categorical variable, one could understand it as a continuum, ranging between monolingualism (proficiency in one language) and bilingualism (perfectly balanced/equal proficiency in two languages) (Bonfieni 2018; Leivada et al. 2021) or as a spectrum of experiences (DeLuca et al. 2019). On an assumed continuum there are many different stages between the two extreme points, such as one strong language and merely receptive skills in the other, for example.

Berthele (2021: 86) proposes one additional dimension to the gradient concept of bilingualism. In addition to *proficiency* in the two languages (from skewed to balanced), Berthele (2021) adds *language status* as a second dimension. Language status ranges from style/register, to dialect, to language. Bilingualism may not only be limited to some proficiency in two languages but includes dialects and different registers as well. He further elaborates that within this classification, there are more or less prototypical representatives. The most prototypical or idealized case, according to his scheme, is someone who, just as Bloomfield (1984) proposed, has "native-like control of 2 'proper' languages" (Berthele 2021: 86). A "regular bilingual" would be dominant in one language and non-dominant in the other, and a "limiting case" would be someone who masters one and has only limited skills in the other language (Berthele 2021: 86).[6]

Another classification of different types of bilinguals is offered in Franceschini (2016). Here, the focus is on age of acquisition and the social context in which the two languages are being acquired (see also Butler and Hakuta 2006; Duarte 2011).[7]

    i. *Simultaneous* bilinguals. These grew up in a bilingual environment; since birth they had contact with persons in their close environment who regularly interacted with the child in two languages.

ii. *Covert simultaneous* bilinguals. These were born into a monolingual family whose language differed from the one spoken in the surrounding context. While having only little and irregular direct interactive contact with this second extra-familial language, they were nonetheless exposed to it since birth, leading to a 'passive' competence that was later on activated by an increase in input and direct interaction.
iii. *Sequential* bilinguals (age of L2 acquisition, 1–5 years): these subjects were born into a monolingual family speaking the language of their surrounding environment. Because of the emigration of their family to a country in which a different language was spoken, they acquired their L2 between the ages of one and five years.
iv. *Late* multilinguals. These subjects were born in a monolingual family speaking the language of their surrounding environment. These subjects learned their first foreign language at school, i.e. at the age of nine years or older.

(Franceschini 2016: 103)

What is, however, absent from Franceschini's (2016) typology is the proficiency level of the two languages, resulting from these different acquisition patterns. Nevertheless, this typology as well as the understanding of bilingualism as a continuum and Berthele's (2021) two-dimensional conceptualization can lead us back to the earlier introduced distinction of majority/dominant language and minority/heritage language, i.e., the two languages of bilingual heritage speakers. In that, heritage speakers are, just like balanced bilinguals, one specific type of a bilingual speaker. Pascual y Cabo and Rothman (2012: 450) define a heritage speaker as a "bilingual who has acquired a family language (the heritage language, HL) and a majority societal language naturalistically in early childhood" (see also Montrul 2016: 16–17). As indicated in Section 3.1, the statuses of the two languages of a bilingual heritage speaker are shaped by frequency of usage and proficiency: heritage speakers are typically dominant in the majority language (Hopp 2019; Montrul 2016). The proficiency of the heritage language can range from barely any skills (for instance receptive skills only) to very high skills (Montrul 2016: 44) in all four language domains as defined in Macnamara's (1967) matrix of language skills or in the seven domains of the Common European Framework of Reference for Languages (CEFR).[8] Moreover, some heritage bilinguals acquire the heritage language first and the majority language second, and others acquire both heritage and majority language simultaneously. So even within the subtype of heritage bilingual we find heterogeneity and should rather speak of a continuum instead of a categorical variable.

Arguably, the concept of language dominance is difficult to define and may relate to language proficiency or frequency of language use (Grosjean and Byers-Heinlein 2018; see also Hamann, Rinke, and Genevska-Hanke 2019). Moreover, the status of the two languages can change over time: the dominant language during childhood may be the less dominant language during adulthood (Grosjean and Byers-Heinlein 2018: 10). A change often happens with the entry of school in the new country of residence as the majority language is typically the language of instruction and replaces the heritage language in terms of frequency of use.

As the previous discussion should have shown, there are numerous types of third language learners who differ, among other factors, in the status of their previously acquired languages. Thus, heritage bilinguals have a different starting position when learning a third language in comparison to adult third language learners who grew up with one language and acquired their second language during school. Since most third language acquisition models discussed in Section 3.2.2 are based on the latter type of learner, they may not necessarily be true for heritage bilinguals. In the following section, several (recent) studies that investigated the acquisition of a third language among heritage speakers are introduced and discussed.

3.4 Third language acquisition of heritage bilinguals

All studies reviewed in this section are located in Germany and investigate the acquisition of English by primary or secondary school students. The majority of these (Lechner 2016; Lechner and Siemund 2014b; Siemund and Lechner 2015; Siemund, Schröter, and Rahbari 2018) were part of the E-LiPS (English LiMA Panel Study) project situated at the University of Hamburg. E-LiPS, a subproject of the Linguistic Diversity Management in Urban Areas (LiMA) Panel Study (LiPS), was conducted between 2009 and 2013 and directed by Peter Siemund and Ingrid Gogolin. The overriding goal was to document the linguistic development of bilingual schoolchildren. The E-LiPS subproject was specifically concerned with the development of the foreign language English (for more information about E-LiPS see Chapter 6). One study (Lorenz et al. 2019) presents findings from the follow-up and more comprehensive, longitudinal MEZ (Mehrsprachigkeitsentwicklung im Zeitverlauf / Multilingual development: a longitudinal perspective) project, conducted between 2014 and 2019 also at the University of Hamburg (Gogolin et al. 2017). This multidisciplinary endeavor set out to investigate the language development of more than 2,000 secondary school students in Germany over a period of 2.5 years (see also Klinger, Brandt, and Dittmers 2022). Studies stemming from these two projects are in a sense highly specialized as they include unbalanced bilingual heritage speakers growing up in Germany (see Gogolin 2021; Lorenz et al. 2020). This, however, allows for a relatively straightforward comparison of the language learners. The remaining studies (Hopp 2019; Lloyd-Smith, Gyllstad, and Kupisch 2017; Lloyd-Smith et al. 2018) also include heritage bilinguals growing up in Germany which make them equally relevant and comparable. All studies will be evaluated with respect to the earlier introduced L3 acquisition models.

Based on a small-scale study, Lechner and Siemund (2014b) investigated 20 16-year-old learners of English, separated into four different language groups with five students each (Russian-German, Turkish-German, Vietnamese-German, German monolingual). All bilinguals acquired Russian, Turkish, or Vietnamese first, and German as their second language. They focused on two grammatical areas, namely subject-verb agreement and tense and aspect marking, and included language-external factors (gender, age of onset of acquiring German, socio-economic status, type of school). With respect to subject-verb agreement or tense and aspect marking, they found no differences across the groups and the most frequent non-target-like occurrence for all learners was the omission of the third person singular –*s* morpheme (Lechner and Siemund 2014b). No differences between the learner groups would in principle argue for exclusive crosslinguistic influence from German, the majority language of all students. In relation to the L3 transfer scenarios introduced in Section 3.2.2, one could understand this as support for the L2 Status Factor (Bardel and Falk 2007), considering German is the chronologically second language the bilinguals acquired (but see an explanation for the inapplicability of this model below). In addition, German is typologically related to English, which supports Rothman's (2011, 2015) Typological Primacy Model. Lechner and Siemund (2014b) also calculated attainment scores for each student and the Turkish-German and Vietnamese-German bilinguals were found to be on the lower end. When additionally factoring in the language-external variables, Lechner and Siemund (2014b) found effects of socio-economic status and school type. They reported that lower attainment scores were found among those students with a lower socio-economic status and that most of the students who had higher attainment scores attended a higher academic school type (yet the latter was not true for all students and some notable exceptions remained).

Instead of only relying on one age cohort, Siemund and Lechner (2015) assessed 12- and 16-year-old German monolinguals as well as Russian-German and Vietnamese-German bilinguals (ten students per group) based on written English production. Among the younger participants, they found the two bilingual groups to outperform the monolingual German participants with respect to target-like use of verbs (subject-verb agreement); most importantly, the Vietnamese-German students performed comparably best. Siemund and Lechner (2015: 156) argued that particularly for the Vietnamese-German bilinguals, "higher typological proximity between English and Vietnamese in this particular domain of grammar" may be the explanation for the relatively target-like performance. This seems to be in line with Westergaard et al.'s (2017) claims in the Linguistic Proximity Model. Even though English and German are typologically related, English uses only few inflectional endings and may thus be more like the isolating language Vietnamese. The same observations, however, can neither be made for the 16-year-old cohort nor when analyzing article usage (Siemund and Lechner 2015).

With respect to article usage, Siemund and Lechner (2015) reported that transfer appeared to come from the majority language German in the bilingual groups, just as in the monolingual German groups. Notably, Vietnamese and Russian do not have a comparable article paradigm; yet the bilingual students seemed to be able to profit from German and no negative transfer from either Russian or Vietnamese could be observed. Again, this could be understood as support for property-by-property transfer as argued in the Linguistic Proximity Model (Westergaard et al. 2017), even though in 2015, when Siemund and Lechner's study was published, the Linguistic Proximity Model had not yet been proposed.

Another study investigating subject-verb agreement which is equally based on the E-LiPS dataset is Lechner (2016). She controlled for high versus low socio-economic status, included two age cohorts (12- and 16-year-old students) and compared monolingual German students with three bilingual groups (Russian-German, Turkish-German, Vietnamese-German). In addition to subject-verb agreement, she also calculated a task accomplishment score. Even though Lechner (2016) found no statistically significant differences across the groups – which she attributed to the low number of participants included in the study – she observed some interesting trends. Two of the bilingual groups, i.e., the 12-year-old Russian- and Vietnamese-German bilinguals, appeared to have comparably higher accomplishment scores than their peers. This trend, however, could not be replicated among the older cohorts. This may be interpreted as a bilingual advantage of the younger students. However, it did not apply to the Turkish-German bilinguals, and it seemed to have leveled out among the older participants (see Section 3.6 for a more thorough discussion of bilingual advantages or effects). Lechner (2016) further argued that particularly the Russian-German bilinguals had comparably high literacy skills in their heritage language. This may be positively related to a potential advantage in further foreign language acquisition and may explain why an equally high performance of the Turkish-German participants could not be found (as they had lower literacy skills in Turkish) (see also Usanova 2019 on *biliteracy* and *biscriptuality*). Finally, the fact that none of the differences was statistically significant may not only be due to the low number of participants (five students per group), but it may also be explained by the typological similarity between German and English which makes crosslinguistic influence from German more likely (Lechner 2016). The L2 Status Factor (Bardel and Falk 2007) may in principle also apply. However, Lechner (2016) highlighted that German, the second language of the bilinguals and at the same time their dominant language, is hardly comparable to a formally learned foreign language as discussed in Bardel and Falk (2007). This cast some doubt on the applicability of the L2 Status Factor in heritage bilingual contexts.

In a more comprehensive study, relying on both spoken as well as written data with more participants ($n = 172$), Siemund, Schröter, and Rahbari (2018) analyzed the use of demonstrative pronouns (determinative, subordinating, and identifying uses) in the same groups of participants as described above (see Lechner 2016). Strikingly, Siemund, Schröter, and Rahbari (2018) identified differences across the four language groups. One such discrepancy concerned the use of "demonstrative pronouns in the function of simple personal pronouns" which only occurred in the spoken data of the Russian-German bilinguals and represents a feature of Russian (Siemund, Schröter, and Rahbari 2018: 399). Thus, crosslinguistic influence from Russian appears plausible. With respect to the earlier introduced L3 models, the Cumulative Enhancement Model (Flynn, Foley, and Vinnitskaya 2004) needs to be rejected, as this observation is a case of negative transfer. Also, the L2 Status Factor (Bardel and Falk 2007) is not supported, as this is transfer from Russian, i.e., the first language of the students. However, L1 transfer in general is also difficult to argue, as only among one of the three bilingual groups was transfer from the heritage language found. Moreover, transfer was only observed with respect to that one particular use of demonstratives, which seems to support the Linguistic Proximity Model (Westergaard et al. 2017). The linguistic property of one grammatical feature is transferred, despite the overall typological similarity between German and English.

The English learners investigated in Hopp's (2019) study are slightly younger. He compared Turkish-German bilinguals (n = 31) with German monolinguals (n = 31) at primary school level (school years three and four). Hopp (2019) employed a sentence repetition and a picture story retelling task and assessed word order as well as subject and article usage. For some of the features, English patterns with German (verb-complement order, subject and article usage), whereas for the others, English differs from German, but also from Turkish (verb and adverb placement). Crucially, Hopp (2019) did not find differences between the two groups, which he interpreted as crosslinguistic influence exclusively from German (i.e., no transfer from Turkish in the bilingual group could be verified). Even though German is technically the L2 of the bilinguals, it may be more applicable to regard it as an early acquired second language having the same status as a first language (Hopp 2019). Hopp (2019) further explained that the heritage language Turkish is the weaker language, and that German, the language of instruction in school as well as the language of the larger speech community, is their dominant language. Because of this language constellation, the bilingual English learners relied on their stronger (German) and not their weaker language (Turkish) and thus performed comparably to the German monolingual learners (Hopp 2019). With this finding, Hopp (2019) specifically argued against all previously proposed L3 acquisition models but claimed that in such heritage contexts, it is the dominant language that is being transferred. Finally, Hopp (2019) admitted that, strictly speaking, language dominance and typological similarity could not be unequivocally distinguished, as both apply to German. Therefore, in this particular setting it is the typologically related and dominant language that acts as the source of crosslinguistic influence in L3 English acquisition.

Further support for (mainly) dominant language transfer comes from Lorenz et al. (2019). In this study, three different learner groups were considered (German monolinguals, Russian-German and Turkish-German bilinguals) and their performance in an English word order test was compared. Based on pronominal object placement, both facilitative and non-facilitative transfer from all background languages was found. In addition, the age of the participants as well as frequency of occurrence were identified as influential factors determining the outcome of the word order test (Lorenz et al. 2019). Nevertheless, it was German that displayed the strongest influence on the English production data of the monolingual and bilingual participants. These findings could be interpreted as support for the Linguistic Proximity Model (Westergaard et al. 2017) as well as the Scalpel Model (Slabakova 2017). In addition, German is again the typologically closest language to English and at the same time the dominant language, which further supports Rothman's (2011, 2015) Typological Primacy Model (even though the claims in this model exclusively relate to the initial stages of foreign language acquisition) as well as Hopp's (2019) proposal of dominant language transfer.

Different from the other studies reviewed so far, Lloyd-Smith, Gyllstad, and Kupisch (2017) investigated phonological crosslinguistic influence and focused on global accent in English (= phonological proficiency) among German-Turkish heritage bilinguals and German as well as Turkish monolinguals. In addition, they investigated older learners (age range between 20 and 42) instead of school-aged children. Like Lorenz et al. (2019), they made mixed observations and concluded that it was mainly German, the majority language, that was being transferred. In principle, when native English speakers rated the English learners, the German monolingual and German-Turkish bilingual speakers were rated almost identically, meaning that with respect to "perceived accent strength in English, no significant difference existed between the bilinguals and the L1 German control group" (Lloyd-Smith, Gyllstad, and Kupisch 2017: 146). They additionally noticed that when the raters were to assign L1 membership to the English speech samples of the L1 German and the bilingual learners, they straightforwardly recognized L1 German speakers, but categorized the bilinguals as either German, Turkish, English, or speakers of another language. Lloyd-Smith, Gyllstad, and Kupisch (2017) identified a relationship between higher phonological proficiency in Turkish and a resulting L1 classification as Turkish or another language (but not German). All in all, they argued that transfer may be selective, as was proposed by the Cumulative Enhancement Model (Flynn, Foley, and Vinnitskaya 2004), but that it mainly came from German. It may be noteworthy to point out that at the time of this publication, the Linguistic Proximity Model (Westergaard et al. 2017) had most likely not yet been published and the authors might have come to a different conclusion if it had been. Given the results presented in Lloyd-Smith, Gyllstad, and Kupisch (2017), it appears likely that selective transfer, which – according to their findings – resulted in an accent difficult to assign to either L1 German or L1 Turkish, may represent supportive evidence for the Linguistic Proximity Model. Finally, they admitted that they could not test the L2 Status Factor (Bardel and Falk 2007) based on their data set because of the status of the two languages of the bilinguals (i.e., both acquired naturalistically during early childhood). In addition, they could only implicitly test the Typological Primacy Model (Rothman 2011, 2015), as they did not investigate initial state foreign language learners, but they concluded that their findings may be in line with the Typological Primacy Model "if we assume transfer from German, the typologically closest language, by default, unless proficiency in another language is so strong that structure-based transfer will be overridden by proficiency-induced transfer" (Lloyd-Smith, Gyllstad, and Kupisch 2017: 159; for similar results based on German-Italian heritage bilinguals see Lloyd-Smith 2021).

In a different approach, this time investigating syntactic crosslinguistic influence, Lloyd-Smith et al. (2018) analyzed embedded *wh*-questions in the foreign language English based on an acceptability judgment task. Embedded *wh*-questions in English share similarities with both German and Italian. In English and German, the subject follows the *wh*-element in embedded contexts, whereas subject-verb inversion is found in Italian. Moreover, in English and Italian, the verb precedes the object, whereas in German, the verb follows the object (Lloyd-Smith et al. 2018: 438–439). The monolingual and bilingual participants were again young adults. Moreover, the heritage bilinguals were separated into two groups, i.e., simultaneous Italian-German bilinguals and successive Italian-German bilinguals (the latter acquired German around the age of three to six) (Lloyd-Smith et al. 2018). Regardless of group membership, all bilinguals were dominant in German. The results obtained from the English acceptability judgment task indicated that transfer occurred selectively, both from German and Italian. Importantly, Lloyd-Smith et al. (2018) stated that "exclusive CLI [crosslinguistic influence] from German can be ruled out." Furthermore, they observed that higher (or lower) proficiency in Italian was no indicator for more (or less) transfer from Italian (Lloyd-Smith et al. 2018). With their findings, they argued against dominant transfer from German (see Hopp 2019) but provided some support for Westergaard et al.'s (2017) Linguistic Proximity Model.

To summarize, a number of different L3 studies – all investigating heritage bilinguals, either school-aged or in their early twenties – were reviewed. Crucially, some studies observed differences between the monolingual foreign language learners and their bilingual peers. However, these findings appeared to be marginal or relatively minor and became smaller over time with increasing age (Lloyd-Smith, Gyllstad, and Kupisch 2017; Lloyd-Smith et al. 2018; Lorenz et al. 2019; Siemund and Lechner 2015;

Siemund, Schröter, and Rahbari 2018). What these studies additionally have in common is that transfer mainly came from the dominant language German. A more extreme perspective was presented in the remaining studies (Hopp 2019; Lechner 2016; Lechner and Siemund 2014b), where the authors argued for exclusive transfer from the majority language German (and the exclusion of transfer from the heritage language). The former perspective is in line with Westergaard et al.'s (2017) Linguistic Proximity Model or Slabakova's (2017) Scalpel Model, whereas the latter, i.e., transfer from the dominant language, has not yet been formulated as an explicit model (but see again Fallah and Jabbari 2018). Moreover, it needs to be pointed out that typological similarity may be an additional factor intensifying crosslinguistic influence (Hopp 2019; Rothman 2011, 2015). Lastly, a number of additional linguistic and extra-linguistic variables, including socio-economic status, cognitive ability, or literacy skills, have been occasionally pointed out to further impact the acquisition of a third language, which highlights the complexity of this research area (see again Slabakova 2017; see also Lorenz et al. 2022). Among these, heightened metalinguistic awareness is said to positively influence further foreign language acquisition. This is the topic of the following section.

3.5 Metalinguistic awareness

According to Bono (2011) (meta)linguistic awareness has received much attention in third language acquisition research as it is the core component that distinguishes multilingual from monolingual speakers. This finds support in Jessner (2006: 42) who defined *metalinguistic awareness* as

> the ability to focus attention on language as an object in itself or to think abstractly about language and, consequently, to play with or manipulate language. A multilingual certainly makes more use of this ability than a monolingual. One might even state that linguistic objectivation is the multilingual's most characteristic cognitive ability.

Similarly, Malakoff (1992: 518) stated that metalinguistic awareness is "the ability to think flexibly and abstractly about language" which "allows the individual to step back from the comprehension or production of an utterance in order to consider the linguistic form and structure underlying the meaning of the utterance." Thus, metalinguistic awareness can be understood as structural knowledge about language, which is not limited to the understanding of the meaning of an utterance or language use in general but goes beyond.

Jessner (2006) further specified that bi- and multilingual speakers have access to increased structural knowledge because they have theoretical insights into more than just one language. Hence, this enlarged linguistic system is what divides bilinguals or multilinguals and monolinguals, and it is claimed to cause the development of skills and competences that further influence foreign language acquisition (Jessner 1999, 2008).

As such, metalinguistic awareness can be assumed to be part of the so-called *multilingualism factor*, or *M-factor* (Jessner 2006, 2008). M-factor refers to language skills and language aptitude of multilingual learners that develop because of increased language contact within one speaker (Jessner 2006: 56; Jessner 2008: 275; see also Allgäuer-Hackl and Jessner 2019). Such enlarged language contact due to access to more than one language leads, according to Jessner (2006: 35), to "an enhanced level of metalinguistic awareness and metacognitive strategies." This concept is comparable to what Cook (2016c) and Franceschini (2016) label *multi-competence*. Multi-competence is "the overall system of a mind or a community that uses more than one language" (Cook 2016c: 2) and it is not just the availability of more than one language. More precisely, Franceschini (2016: 105) used the expression "third quality" and added that this is "a quality that represents more than the sum of its parts." She further continued that all the linguistic competences learners experience throughout their lives add to their linguistic repertoires and turn them into "flexible speakers" (Franceschini 2016: 106). This also includes the awareness of such competences and the theoretical knowledge about linguistic systems and may either be a conscious or an unconscious potential (Franceschini 2016).

Yet, this quality is not something that only bi- or multilingual speakers possess. Quite the opposite: monolingual speakers can also be flexible or multi-competent speakers of one language, meaning that the one language can be used variably depending on the social or communicative context (Franceschini 2016: 106). Jessner (2008) equally argued that monolingual speakers have metalinguistic awareness. This, however, is necessarily tied to one language which in turn makes the metalinguistic awareness that bi- or multilinguals possess higher than that of monolinguals, at least in terms of volume. This understanding is shared by Cenoz (2013) who also maintained that the previous learning experience of two different linguistic systems augments the level of metalinguistic awareness in bilinguals. Differently put, the more languages you learn, the more strategies or techniques about language learning in general you acquire as well (Cenoz 2013: 76). Thus, in addition to being able to communicate in two different linguistic systems, bilinguals may have further theoretical knowledge, both about learning (foreign) languages as well as about language in an abstract sense. Such heightened metalinguistic awareness may in turn become an advantage for bilinguals leading to higher success rates in additional (foreign) language learning (Cook 2016a; Jessner 2008; but see Spellerberg 2016). This assumed advantage in further foreign language acquisition is the topic of the following section (for more information about metalinguistic or multilingual awareness see Jessner 2006; Jessner and Allgäuer-Hackl 2020).

3.6 Bilingual advantages or effects

Bilinguals and multilinguals have a larger linguistic repertoire than monolinguals since they have access to two or more languages instead of just one. This augmented linguistic repertoire may be helpful in further (foreign) language acquisition, visible in the often-cited popular folk wisdom "the more languages a person knows, the easier it becomes to acquire an additional language" (Cenoz 2013: 74). The reason for this assumption is certain *advantages* or *effects* associated with bi- and multilingualism (Leivada et al. 2021). Advantages or effects may play out in different domains, of which two are surveyed below.

Particularly in recent years, numerous studies investigated the effects of bilingualism on cognitive functions, more specifically executive function or control, and found bilinguals to outperform monolinguals (Bialystok 2001, 2018; Bialystok, Craik, and Luk 2012). Moving away from viewing bilingualism as something negative (see, for example, Harris 1948; Saer 1923), this new research strand seeks to find proof of positive effects of bilingualism, particularly related to cognition. Bialystok (2018: 284) argued that the "explanation for why bilingual language use should have an effect on cognitive processing follows from substantial behavioral and neuroimaging evidence showing that both languages in the bilingual mind are jointly activated during language use" (see also Kroll et al. 2015). Since the two languages in a bilingual's brain are constantly activated, selected, and inhibited, it is said to affect the system of executive function in the frontal lobe, which in turn leads to a better or faster performance in tasks involving executive function (Bialystok 2018). Tasks typically used to demonstrate this bilingual superiority are the Flanker task, Simon task, or Stroop task[9] (Leivada et al. 2021). In addition, bi- or multilinguals have been shown to exhibit greater cognitive reserve which is said to delay age-related brain degeneration such as dementia (Adesope et al. 2010; Bialystok, Craik, and Luk 2012). However, more recent studies cast some doubt on these assumed bi- or multilingual advantages by returning either mixed or even null results (see, for example, Antón et al. 2014; de Bruin, Treccani, and Della Sala 2014; Duñabeitia and Carreiras 2015; Lehtonen et al. 2018; Paap, Johnson, and Sawi 2016). Therefore, Leivada et al. (2021: 208) refer to this as the "phantom-like appearance of bilingual effects on cognition" spelling out that such effects are dynamic and that sometimes positive effects can be measured, whereas sometimes they cannot. In another, more recent study, Bialystok and Craik (2022) convincingly argue that this has to do with the specific demands within each task. Beyond just comparing different tasks, future research would need to manipulate each task to test varying levels of difficulty. Under certain conditions bilinguals show performance differences when compared to monolinguals; yet these may only feature among the more demanding conditions and less so among the easier conditions within one specific task (Bialystok and Craik 2022: 16). In turn, this means that "research moving forward will inevitably be more complex than previous studies that have relied largely on categorically different groups of individuals performing simple tasks" (Bialystok and Craik 2022: 17).

Another field where bi- or multilingual advantages are explicitly investigated is the learning of third or additional languages (see, for example, Aronin and Jessner 2015; Cenoz 2013; Jessner 2006). As with advantages related to executive function or control, some studies find advantages (Agustín-Llach 2019; Cenoz and Valencia 1994; Sanz 2000; Maluch et al. 2015; see also Cenoz 2003), whereas other do not (Hopp 2019; Lechner and Siemund 2014a; Lorenz, Toprak-Yildiz, and Siemund 2022; Maurer et al. 2021; Şahingöz 2014; Steinlen and Piske 2013) or even present mixed results (Lorenz, Toprak, and Siemund 2021; Maluch and Kempert 2019; Maluch, Neumann, and Kempert 2016; Siemund and Lechner 2015). A closer look at these selected studies may disentangle their contradictory findings.

Noticeably, the first three studies are located in officially bilingual regions in Spain, namely in the Basque Autonomous Country (Agustín-Llach 2019; Cenoz and Valencia 1994) and Catalonia (Sanz 2000). Cenoz and Valencia (1994) investigated speaking, listening, reading, writing, and vocabulary knowledge among Spanish-Basque and Spanish learners of English and found an advantage for the bilingual learners of English. Sanz (2000) examined Catalan-Spanish bilinguals and Spanish monolinguals and identified better performance in English of the former group. In Agustín-Llach's (2019) study, equally based on Basque-Spanish and Spanish learners of English, an advantage of the bilinguals could also be attested. It needs to be mentioned that both languages, Basque and Catalan respectively, have a relatively high social standing in these areas and children receive formal education in school in both languages. This means that this is a special social environment, which may in fact add to the results (Cenoz and Valencia 1994: 197–198) and the authors were careful about extending their findings to other contexts (Sanz 2000: 38; for further studies documenting positive effects of bilingualism see, for example, Lasagabaster 1998, 2001; Safont Jordà 2003; Sagasta Errasti 2003). In a different setting, located in Germany, Maluch et al. (2015) also reported positive effects of bilingualism on the acquisition of English; yet they also noticed some variation across the different bilingual groups.

Contrary to these rather positive results, supporting the idea of bilingual advantages in further foreign language acquisition, there are several studies, most of which are located in Germany and involve heritage bilinguals, that found no advantages or rather no differences between monolingual and bilingual learners of English. One such study, located in the German-speaking part of Switzerland, investigated the performance in English after one year of English tuition in primary school (Maurer et al. 2021). Even after controlling for social background variables, i.e., intelligence (IQ) and socio-economic status, no bilingual advantage could be attested, but a comparable performance in English was found. Similarly, Steinlen and Piske (2013) did not find differences with respect to English proficiency (grammar, vocabulary, and reading) in monolingual German children and bilingual heritage speakers who attended a primary school following a bilingual immersion program (approximately 50 percent of exposure to English and German). Further evidence can be found in a study by Lechner and Siemund (2014a). They also could not attest a bi- or multilingual advantage for 16-year-old learners of English, which means that the bilingual heritage speakers investigated did not outperform their monolingual peers in English (Lechner and Siemund 2014a). More evidence comes from Hopp (2019) who compared monolingual German learners of English with Turkish-German bilingual learners attending primary schools in Germany. No difference between these two groups in their English performance was attested (Hopp 2019). Moreover, Lorenz, Toprak-Yildiz, and Siemund (2022) assessed monolingual German and Russian- or Turkish-German bilingual secondary school students and found the groups to be highly similar with respect to predicting their English proficiency. Slightly different are the observations made by Şahingöz (2014). She observed differences in English between German monolingual students and their bilingual peers. Precisely, Şahingöz identified less target-like word order in the bilingual data, which clearly challenges the idea of a bilingual advantage.

In addition to either identifying bilingual advantages in further foreign language acquisition or not finding such advantages, there are also some studies that report mixed results. Lorenz, Hasai, and Siemund (2021), for instance, investigated lexical transfer in short English texts among two groups of bilingual (Russian-German, Turkish-German) and German monolingual secondary school students. They expected the bilinguals to have an advantage in English, visible in lower lexical transfer instances in their written English performance when compared to the German monolingual English learners. However, what they found instead was a comparable better performance of the Turkish-German bilinguals and a lower performance of the Russian-German bilinguals. Whereas for the former, one could argue for a bilingual advantage, this was not true for the latter. Correspondingly, Maluch and Kempert (2019) also presented nuanced results for the different bilingual groups they investigated. Only the simultaneous bilinguals outperformed the monolingual students in English (achievement in listening and reading), but no advantage was found for the sequential bilinguals (see also Hesse, Göbel, and Hartig 2008; Göbel, Rauch, and Vieluf 2011). Maluch and Kempert (2019) argued that the advantages of the simultaneous bilinguals could be explained by their relatively high skills in both of their languages. In another study, Maluch, Neumann, and Kempert (2016: 115) reported "significant advantages in L3 achievement" among the younger participants (school year six). However, two years later, among the same students (school year eight), they identified dissimilarities with respect to the different bilingual groups they investigated, and advantages were only found among those bilingual students who mainly used the majority language German at home (Maluch, Neumann, and Kempert 2016). Thus, a general bilingual advantage was not visible in their data. Similar age constraints were also found in a study by Siemund and Lechner (2015). They also attested a bilingual advantage among 12-year-old English learners, yet not among their 16-year-old peers (Siemund and Lechner 2015; see also Lechner 2016). The older bilingual students performed similarly in English to the monolingual German students.

The diverse findings with respect to possible bilingual advantages in further foreign language acquisition have shown that one cannot easily generalize. It needs to be acknowledged that "language acquisition is a complex phenomenon that is also influenced by many other factors" (Cenoz 2013: 77). Hence, among some bilingual individuals, advantages or positive effects can be attested, whereas bilinguals in other contexts or with a different social or linguistic background may not profit from their bilingual experience in further foreign language acquisition to the same extent. Most importantly, cognitive skills or socio-economic status appear to impact the acquisition of foreign languages (Lorenz, Toprak-Yildiz, and Siemund 2022; Maurer et al. 2021). Moreover, it is once again the type of bilingualism that explains some of the differences pointed out above. In Section 3.3, bilingualism was introduced as a gradable variable. Yet, Titone et al. (2017) remark that in many studies, bilinguals are typically assumed to represent a homogeneous group all leading to the same advantages. In fact, "bilingual experience is not homogeneous [but] it comprises a host of individual differences" (Titone et al. 2017: 283). This finds support in Maluch, Neumann, and Kempert (2016: 112) who address the "enormous heterogeneity in linguistic profiles" of immigrant bilinguals. Keeping in mind these crucial differences among bilinguals, the diverse findings presented above are not that surprising anymore. Thus, one can say that a host of individual features are co-dependent and influence or shape further foreign language acquisition, which in turn affects the existence, or not, of advantages.

3.7 Summary

Chapter 3 dealt with previous and more recent research on language acquisition and provided a general overview of the current state of the field. Most importantly, different models of third language acquisition explaining crosslinguistic influence were presented. These models make contradictory predictions, and this controversy may be due to the specific grammatical phenomenon investigated, the language combinations included, or – most importantly – the different third language learners considered (Puig-Mayenco, Gonzáles Alonso, and Rothman 2020). The category bilingualism has been established as a gradable instead of a categorical variable, comprising different types of bilingual speaker. One such type is bilingual heritage speakers, usually characterized by unbalanced proficiencies of their two languages. However, even heritage bilingualism should be understood as a gradable phenomenon. A number of recent studies analyzing third language acquisition of this type of bilingual were presented. Suggestive evidence with respect to an important or dominant function of the majority language was established. Yet, the role of the heritage as well as the majority language of these speakers in further foreign language acquisition remains unclear and numerous inconsistencies remain. Finally, additional aspects influencing third language acquisition were discussed, namely metalinguistic awareness as well as the general idea of bilingual advantages. Due to extended language learning experiences, metalinguistic awareness is said to be heightened in bi- or multilingual speakers as compared to monolinguals, which may ultimately lead to an assumed advantage in further foreign language acquisition. Yet, once again, evidence remains inconclusive, and a diverse picture was presented.

The following Chapter 4 introduces the grammatical area which will be the basis of the current investigation.

Notes

1 Note that this does not imply any negative judgment (see Bayram et al. 2021).
2 Odlin (1989: 27) offered a definition of transfer, namely that "Transfer is the influence resulting from similarities and differences between the target language and any other language that has been previously (and perhaps imperfectly) acquired." This understanding seems to limit influence from an earlier acquired language to a later or subsequent acquired language.
3 Due to the language combinations investigated in Rothman and Cabrelli Amaro (2010), the authors argued that another explanation for the results may be possible, namely *psychotypological* or *typological similarity*. This line of argumentation will be introduced further below.
4 This view finds support in language contact research, where this idea of holistic transfer is called 'systemic transfer' (for further information see, for example, Bao 2005, 2012; Bao and Lye 2005).
5 Initial stages and initial state are sometimes used synonymously, yet Rothman (2015) explicitly differentiates these two concepts. Initial state goes back to Schwartz and Sprouse (1996) and second language acquisition and refers to the onset of L2 acquisition. Initial stages, however, could be defined as "the period in which structurally driven wholesale transfer from the L1 or the L2 takes place" (González Alonso and Rothman 2017: 688). In other words, it is the time between first exposure to the L3 and the time when the learner of the new language has already had some (limited) learning experience (Westergaard et al. 2017: 669).
6 Note that Berthele (2021) does not stop here. He suggests that one could add more dimensions, such as age of onset, language usage, or attitudes to create an even more adequate, multidimensional representation of bilingualism (Berthele 2021: 88).

7 Another distinction made by Cenoz (2013) differentiates *active bilinguals*, on the one hand, and *foreign language users*, on the other hand. Active bilinguals use both languages regularly during their everyday lives and foreign language users have acquired the second language in an institutional setting and may not have many opportunities to use this language outside of the foreign language classroom (Cenoz 2013: 78–79). This latter type seems to overlap with what Franceschini (2016) labels a *late multilingual*.
8 Macnamara (1967: 59) distinguishes between speaking, writing, listening, and reading proficiency. The CEFR differentiates oral comprehension, reading comprehension, oral interaction, written interaction, oral production, written production, and mediation (e.g., mediating a text) (Council of Europe 2020).
9 The designs of the Flanker, Stroop, and Simon tasks measure inhibition. Participants are presented with congruent and incongruent conditions and are asked to respond to a specific target while ignoring competing cues, i.e., distractors interfering with the target response (Bialystok 2018; Hilchey and Klein 2011).

References

Adesope, O.O., T. Lavin, T. Thompson, and C. Ungerleider. 2010. A systematic review and meta-analysis of the cognitive correlates of bilingualism. *Review of Educational Research* 80:207–245.

Agustín-Llach, M. d. P. 2019. The impact of bilingualism on the acquisition of an additional language: Evidence from lexical knowledge, lexical fluency, and (lexical) cross-linguistic influence. *International Journal of Bilingualism* 23:888–900.

Allgäuer-Hackl, E. and U. Jessner. 2019. Cross-linguistic interaction and multilingual awareness. In *Multidisciplinary perspectives on multilingualism*, ed. S. Montanari and S. Quay, 325–349. Boston/Berlin: De Gruyter Mouton.

Antón, E., J. A. Duñabeitia, A. Estévez, J. A. Hernández, A. Castillo, L. J. Fuentes, D. J. Davidson, and M. Carreiras. 2014. Is there a bilingual advantage in the ANT task? Evidence from children. *Frontiers in Psychology* 5: Article 398. doi: 10.3389/fpsyg.2014.00398

Aronin, L. and U. Jessner. 2015. Understanding current multilingualism: What can the butterfly tell us? In *The multilingual challenge: Cross-disciplinary perspective*, ed. U. Jessner and C. Kramsch, 271–292. Berlin/Boston: De Gruyter Mouton.

Bao, Z. 2005. The aspectual system of Singapore English and the systemic substratist explanation. *Journal of Linguistics* 41:237–267.

Bao, Z. 2012. Substratum transfer targets grammatical system. *Journal of Linguistics* 48:479–482.

Bao, Z. and H. M. Lye. 2005. Systemic transfer, topic prominence, and the bare conditional in Singapore English. *Journal of Pidgin and Creole Languages* 20:269–291.

Bardel, C. and Y. Falk. 2007. The role of the second language in third language acquisition: The case of Germanic syntax. *Second Language Research* 23:459–484.

Bardel, C. and Y. Falk. 2012. The L2 status factor and the declarative/procedural distinction. In *Third language acquisition in adulthood*, ed. J. Cabrelli Amaro, S. Flynn, and J. Rothman, 61–78. Amsterdam: Benjamins.

Bayram, F., M. Kubota, A. Luque, D. Pascual y Cabo, and J. Rothman. 2021. You can't fix what is not broken: Contextualizing the imbalance of perceptions about heritage language bilingualism. *Frontiers in Education* 6:628311.

Berthele, R. 2021. The extraordinary ordinary: Re-engineering multilingualism as a natural category. *Language Learning* 71:80–120.

Bialystok, E. 2001. *Bilingualism in development: Language, literacy, and cognition.* Cambridge: Cambridge University Press.

Bialystok, E. 2018. Bilingualism and executive function: What's the connection? In *Bilingual cognition and language: The state of the science across its subfields,* ed. D. Miller, F. Bayram, J. Rothman, and L. Serratrice, 283–305. Amsterdam: Benjamins.

Bialystok, E. and F. I. M. Craik. 2022. How does bilingualism modify cognitive function? Attention to the mechanism. Psychonomic Bulletin & Review. https://doi.org/10.3758/s13423-022-02057-5

Bialystok, E., F. I. M. Craik, and G. Luk. 2012. Bilingualism: Consequences for mind and brain. *Trends in Cognitive Sciences* 16:240–250.

Bloomfield, L. 1984. *Language.* Chicago: University of Chicago Press.

Bonfieni, M. 2018. *The bilingual continuum: Mutual effects of language and cognition.* PhD diss., University of Edinburgh. http://hdl.handle.net/1842/31365

Bono, M. 2011. Crosslinguistic interaction and metalinguistic awareness in third language acquisition. In *New trends in crosslinguistic influence and multilingualism research,* ed. G. De Angelis and J.-M. Dewaele, 25–52. Clevedon: Multilingual Matters.

Butler, Y. G. and K. Hakuta. 2006. Bilingualism and second language acquisition. In *The handbook of bilingualism,* ed. T. K. Bhatia, and W. C. Ritchie, 114–145. Malden, MA: Blackwell.

Cabrelli, J., M. Iverson, D. Giancaspro, and B. Halloran González. 2020. The roles of L1 Spanish versus L2 Spanish in L3 Portuguese morphosyntactic development. In *Linguistic approaches to Portuguese as an additional language,* ed. K. V. Molsing, C. Becker Lopes Perna, and A. M. Tramunt Ibaños, 11–33. Amsterdam: Benjamins.

Cenoz, J. 2001. The effect of linguistic distance, L2 status and age on crosslinguistic influence in third language acquisition. In *Cross-linguistic influence in third language acquisition: Psycholinguistic perspectives,* ed. J. Cenoz, B. Hufeisen, and U. Jessner, 8–20. Clevedon: Multilingual Matters.

Cenoz, J. 2003. The additive effect of bilingualism on third language acquisition: A review. *International Journal of Bilingualism* 7:71–87.

Cenoz, J. 2013. The influence of bilingualism on third language acquisition: Focus on multilingualism. *Language Teaching* 46:71–86.

Cenoz, J., B. Hufeisen, and U. Jessner (eds.). 2001. *Cross-linguistic influence in third language acquisition: Psycholinguistic perspectives.* Clevedon: Multilingual Matters.

Cenoz, J. and J. Valencia. 1994. Additive trilingualism: Evidence from the Basque Country. *Applied Psycholinguistics* 15:195–207.

Cook, V. 2016a. *Second language learning and language teaching.* London/New York: Routledge.

Cook, V. 2016b. Transfer and the relationship between the languages of multicompetence. In *Crosslinguistic influence in second language acquisition,* ed. R. Alonso Alonso, 24–37. Bristol: Multilingual Matters.

Cook, V. 2016c. Premises of multi-competence. In *The Cambridge handbook of linguistic multi-competence*, ed. V. Cook and Li Wei, 1–25. Cambridge: Cambridge University Press.
Council of Europe. 2020. *Common European framework of reference for languages: Learning, teaching, assessment – Companion volume*. Strasbourg: Council of Europe Publishing. www.coe.int/lang-cefr (accessed April 4, 2022).
De Angelis, G. 2007. *Third or additional language acquisition*. Clevedon: Multilingual Matters.
de Bruin, A., B. Treccani, and S. Della Sala. 2014. Cognitive advantage in bilingualism: An example of publication bias? *Psychological Science* 26:99–107.
DeLuca, V., J. Rothman, E. Bialystok, and C. Pliatsikas. 2019. Redefining bilingualism as a spectrum of experiences that differentially affects brain structure and function. *Proceedings of the National Academy of Sciences of the United States of America* 116:7565–7574.
Dewaele, J.-M. 1998. Lexical inventions: French interlanguage as L2 versus L3. *Applied Linguistics* 19:471–490.
Duarte, J. 2011. *Bilingual language proficiency: A comparative study*. Münster: Waxmann.
Duñabeitia, A. and M. Carreiras. 2015. The bilingual advantage: Acta est fabula? *Cortex* 73:371–372.
Ellis, R. 1994. *The study of second language acquisition*. Oxford: Oxford University Press.
Ellis, R. 2015. *Understanding second language acquisition*. 2nd edn. Oxford: Oxford University Press.
Falk, Y. and C. Bardel. 2011. Object pronouns in German L3 syntax: Evidence for the L2 status factor. *Second Language Research* 27:59–82.
Fallah, N. and A. A. Jabbari. 2018. L3 acquisition of English attributive adjectives: Dominant language of communication matters for syntactic cross-linguistic influence. *Linguistic Approaches to Bilingualism* 8:193–216.
Fallah, N., A. A. Jabbari, and A. M. Fazilatfar. 2016. Source(s) of syntactic cross-linguistic influence (CLI): The case of L3 acquisition of English possessives by Mazandarani-Persian bilinguals. *Second Language Research* 32:225–245.
Flynn, S., C. Foley, and I. Vinnitskaya. 2004. The cumulative-enhancement model for language acquisition: Comparing adult's and children's patterns of development in first, second and third language acquisition of relative clauses. *International Journal of Multilingualism* 1:3–16.
Franceschini, R. 2016. Multilingualism research. In *The Cambridge handbook of linguistic multi-competence*, ed. V. Cook and Li Wei, 97–124. Cambridge: Cambridge University Press.
Gabrys-Barker, D. 2012. *Cross-linguistic influences in multilingual language acquisition*. Berlin/Heidelberg: Springer.
García Mayo, M. d. P. and R. Slabakova. 2015. Object drop in L3 acquisition. *International Journal of Bilingualism* 19:483–498.
Göbel, K., D. Rauch, and S. Vieluf. 2011. Leistungsbedingungen und Leistungsergebnisse von Schülerinnen und Schülern Türkischer, Russischer und Polnischer Herkunftssprachen. *Zeitschrift für Interkulturellen Fremdsprachenunterricht* 16:50–65.
Gogolin, I. 2021. Multilingualism: A threat to public education or a resource in public education? European histories and realities. *European Educational Research Journal* 20:297–310.

Gogolin, I., T. Klinger, M. Lagemann, and B. Schnoor, in collaboration with C. Gabriel, M. Knigge, M. Krause, and P. Siemund. 2017. *Indikation, Konzeption und Untersuchungsdesign des Projekts Mehrsprachigkeitsentwicklung im Zeitverlauf (MEZ)*. MEZ Arbeitspapier Nr. 1. Hamburg (University of Hamburg). www.pedocs.de/frontdoor.php?source_opus=14825 (accessed April 4, 2022).

González Alonso, J. and J. Rothman. 2017. Coming of age in L3 initial stages transfer models: Deriving developmental predictions and looking towards the future. *International Journal of Bilingualism* 21:683–697.

Grosjean, F. and K. Byers-Heinlein. 2018. Bilingual adults and children: A short introduction. In *The listening bilingual: Speech perception, comprehension, and bilingualism*, ed. F. Grosjean and K. Byers-Heinlein, 4–24. Hoboken, NJ: Wiley-Blackwell.

Håkansson, G., M. Pienemann, and S. Sayheli. 2002. Transfer and typological proximity in the context of second language processing. *Second Language Research* 18:250–273.

Hamann, C., E. Rinke, and D. Genevska-Hanke (eds.). 2019. *Bilingualism: The role of dominance*. Lausanne: Frontiers.

Hammarberg, B. (ed.). 2009. *Processes in third language acquisition*. Edinburgh: Edinburgh University Press.

Hammarberg, B. 2010. The languages of the multilingual: Some conceptual and terminological issues. *International Review of Applied Linguistics in Language Teaching* 48:91–104.

Harris, C. W. 1948. An exploration of language skill patterns. *Journal of Educational Psychology* 39:321–336.

Hermas, A. 2014. Multilingual transfer: L1 morphosyntax in L3 English. *International Journal of Language Studies* 8:1–24.

Hermas, A. 2015. The categorization of the relative complementizer phrase in third-language English: A feature re-assembly account. *International Journal of Bilingualism* 19:587–607.

Hesse, H.-G., K. Göbel, and J. Hartig. 2008. Sprachliche Kompetenzen von mehrsprachigen Jugendlichen und Jugendlichen nicht-deutscher Erstsprache. In *Unterricht und Kompetenzerwerb in Deutsch und Englisch: Ergebnisse der DESI-Studie*, ed. DESI Konsortium, 208–230. Weinheim: Beltz.

Hilchey, M. D. and R. M. Klein. 2011. Are there bilingual advantage on non-linguistic interference tasks? Implications for the plasticity of executive control processes. *Psychonomic Bulletin & Review* 18:625–658.

Hopp, H. 2019. Cross-linguistic influence in the child third language acquisition of grammar: Sentence comprehension and production among Turkish-German and German learners of English. *International Journal of Bilingualism* 23:567–583.

Jarvis, S. and A. Pavlenko. 2008. *Crosslinguistic influence in language and cognition*. London: Routledge.

Jensen, I. N., N. Mitrofanova, M. Anderssen, Y. Rodina, R. Slabakova, and M. Westergaard. 2021. Crosslinguistic influence in L3 acquisition across linguistic modules. *International Journal of Multilingualism*. https://doi.org/10.1080/14790718.2021.1985127

Jessner, U. 1999. Metalinguistic awareness in multilinguals: Cognitive aspects of third language learning. *Language Awareness* 8:201–209.

Jessner, U. 2006. *Linguistic awareness in multilinguals: English as a third language*. Edinburgh: Edinburgh University Press.
Jessner, U. 2008. A DST model of multilingualism and the role of metalinguistic awareness. *Modern Language Journal* 92:270–283.
Jessner, U. and E. Allgäuer-Hackl. 2020. Multilingual awareness and metacognition in multilingually diverse classrooms. *Journal of Multilingual Theories and Practices* 1:66–88.
Jessner, U., M. Megens, and S. Graus. 2016. Crosslinguistic influence in third language acquisition. In *Crosslinguistic influence in second language acquisition*, ed. R. Alonso Alonso, 193–214. Bristol: Multilingual Matters.
Kellerman, E. 1983. Now you see it, now you don't. In *Language transfer in language learning*, ed. S. Gass and L. Selinker, 112–134. Rowley, MA: Newbury House.
Klein, E. C. 1995. Second versus third language acquisition: Is there a difference? *Language Learning* 45:419–465.
Klinger, T., H. Brandt, and T. Dittmers. 2022. The making of MEZ – multilingual development: A longitudinal perspective. Study design and methods. In *Language development in diverse settings: Interdisziplinäre Ergebnisse aus dem Projekt Mehrsprachigkeitsentwicklung im Zeitverlauf (MEZ)*, ed. H. Brandt, M. Krause, and I. Usanova. Westport, CT: Springer. https://link.springer.com/book/9783658356491
Kolb, N., N. Mitrofanova, and M. Westergaard. 2022. Cross-linguistic influence in child L3 English: An empirical study on Russian-German heritage bilinguals. *International Journal of Bilingualism* 26: 476–501.
Krashen, S. D. 1981. *Second language acquisition and second language learning*. Oxford: Pergamon Press.
Kroll, J. F., P. E. Dussias, K. Bice, and L. Perrotti. 2015. Bilingualism, mind, and brain. *Annual Review of Linguistics* 1:377–394.
Kupisch, T., N. Snape, and I. Stangen. 2013. Foreign language acquisition in heritage speakers: The acquisition of articles in L3-English by German-Turkish bilinguals. In *Linguistic superdiversity in urban areas*, ed. J. Duarte and I. Gogolin, 99–121. Amsterdam: Benjamins.
Lasagabaster, D. 1998. Learning English as an L3. *ITL Review of Applied Linguistics* 121–122:51–84.
Lasagabaster, D. 2001. The effect of knowledge about the L1 on foreign language skills and grammar. *International Journal of Bilingual Education and Bilingualism* 4:310–331.
Lechner, S. 2016. Literale Fähigkeiten als Ressource beim Erwerb von Fremdsprachen in mehrsprachigen Kontexten. In *Mehrsprachigkeit als Ressource in der Schriftlichkeit*, ed. P. Rosenberg and C. Schröder, 113–131. Berlin: De Gruyter Mouton.
Lechner, S. and P. Siemund. 2014a. Double threshold in bi- and multilingual contexts: Preconditions for higher academic attainment in English as an additional language. *Frontiers in Psychology* 5:1–8.
Lechner, S. and P. Siemund. 2014b. The role of language external factors in the acquisition of English as an additional language by bilingual children in Germany. In *Language contacts at the crossroads of disciplines*, ed. H. Paulasto, L. Meriläinen, H. Riionheimo, and M. Kok, 319–345. Newcastle-upon-Tyne: Cambridge Scholars Publishing.

Lehtonen, M., A. Soveri, A. Laine, J. Järvenpää, A. de Bruin, and J. Antfolk. 2018. Is bilingualism associated with enhanced executive functioning in adults? A meta-analytic review. *Psychological Bulletin* 144:394–425.

Leivada, E., M. Westergaard, J. A. Duñabeitia, and J. Rothman. 2021. On the phantom-like appearance of bilingualism effects on neurocognition: (How) should we proceed? *Bilingualism: Language and Cognition* 24:197–210.

LiMA, Linguistic Diversity Management in Urban Areas – LiPS, LiMA Panel Study. 2009–2013. *Projektkoordination LiPS: Prof. Dr. Dr. h. c. Ingrid Gogolin;* ©*LiMA-LiPS 2013*. Hamburg: LiMA.

Lloyd-Smith, A. 2021. Perceived foreign accent in L3 English: The effects of heritage language use. *International Journal of Multilingualism*. https://doi.org/10.1080/14790718.2021.1957899

Lloyd-Smith, A., H. Gyllstad, and T. Kupisch. 2017. Transfer into L3 English: Global accent in German-dominant heritage speakers of Turkish. *Linguistic Approaches to Bilingualism* 2:131–162.

Lloyd-Smith, A., H. Gyllstad, T. Kupisch, and S. Quaglia. 2018. Heritage language proficiency does not predict syntactic CLI into L3 English. *International Journal of Bilingual Education and Bilingualism* 24:435–451.

Lorenz, E., R. J. Bonnie, K. Feindt, S. Rahbari, and P. Siemund. 2019. Cross-linguistic influence in unbalanced bilingual heritage speakers on subsequent language acquisition: Evidence from pronominal object placement in ditransitive clauses. *International Journal of Bilingualism* 23:1410–1430.

Lorenz, E., K. Feindt, S. Rahbari, and P. Siemund. 2022. The influence of extra-linguistic variables on cross-linguistic influence – case studies of bilingual heritage speakers. In *Language development in diverse settings: Interdisziplinäre Ergebnisse aus dem Projekt Mehrsprachigkeitsentwicklung im Zeitverlauf (MEZ)*, ed. H. Brandt, M. Krause, and I. Usanova, 305–338. Westport, CT: Springer.

Lorenz, E., Y. Hasai, and P. Siemund. 2021. Multilingual lexical transfer challenges monolingual educational norms: Not quite! *Multilingua* 40:791–813.

Lorenz, E., S. Rahbari, U. Schackow, and P. Siemund. 2020. Does bilingualism correlate with or predict higher proficiency in L3 English? A contrastive study of monolingual and bilingual learners. *Journal of Multilingual Theories and Practices* 1:185–217.

Lorenz, E., T. E. Toprak, and P. Siemund. 2021. English L3 acquisition in heritage contexts: Modelling a path through the bilingualism controversy. *Poznan Studies in Contemporary Linguistics* 57:273–298.

Lorenz, E., T. E. Toprak-Yildiz, and P. Siemund. 2022. Why are they so similar? The interplay of linguistic and extra-linguistic variables in monolingual and bilingual learners of English. *Pedagogical Linguistics*. https://doi.org/10.1075/pl.21016.lor

Macnamara, J. 1967. The bilingual's linguistic performance – A psychological overview. *Journal of Social Issues* 23:58–77.

Malakoff, M. E. 1992. Translation ability: A natural bilingual and metalinguistic skill. In *Cognitive processing in bilinguals*, ed. R. J. Harris, 515–530. Amsterdam: North-Holland.

Maluch, J. T. and S. Kempert. 2019. Bilingual profiles and third language learning: The effects of the manner of learning, sequence of bilingual acquisition, and language use practices. *International Journal of Bilingual Education and Bilingualism* 22:870–882.

Maluch, J. T., S. Kempert, M. Neumann, and P. Stanat. 2015. The effect of speaking a minority language at home on foreign language learning. *Learning and Instruction* 36:76–85.

Maluch, J. T., M. Neumann, and S. Kempert. 2016. Bilingualism as a resource for foreign language learning of language minority students? Empirical evidence from a longitudinal study during primary and secondary school in Germany. *Language and Individual Differences* 51:111–118.

Maurer, U., L. B. Jost, S. E. Pfenninger, and A. K. Eberhard-Moscicka. 2021. Effects of German reading skills and bilingualism on early learning of English as a foreign language in primary school children. *Reading and Writing* 34:2673–2689.

Meisel, J. M. 2014. Heritage language learners: Incomplete acquisition of grammar in early childhood. In *Perspectives in the study of Spanish language variation: Papers in honor of Carmen Silva-Corvalán*, ed. A. Enrique-Arias, M. J. Gutiérrez, A. Landa, and F. Ocampo, 435–464. Santiago de Compostela: Verba/Anexa.

MEZ — Mehrsprachigkeitsentwicklung im Zeitverlauf. 2014–2019. Projektkoordination: Prof. Dr. Dr. h. c. Ingrid Gogolin, Universität Hamburg; © MEZ 2017.

Montrul, S. 2016. *The acquisition of heritage languages*. Cambridge: Cambridge University Press.

Montrul, S. and M. Polinsky (eds.). 2021. *The Cambridge handbook of heritage languages and linguistics*. Cambridge: Cambridge University Press.

Na Ranong, S. and I. Leung. 2009. Null objects in L1 Thai-L2 English-L3 Chinese: An empiricist take on a theoretical problem. In *Third language acquisition and universal grammar*, ed. I. Leung, 162–191. Bristol: Multilingual Matters.

Odlin, T. 1989. *Language transfer: Cross-linguistic influence in language learning*. Cambridge: Cambridge University Press.

Odlin, T. 2013. Crosslinguistic influence in second language acquisition. In *The encyclopedia of applied linguistics*, ed. C. A. Chapelle. Chichester, West Sussex, UK: Wiley-Blackwell. https://doi.org/10.1002/9781405198431.wbeal0292

Paap, K., H. Johnson, and O. Sawi. 2016. Should the search for bilingual advantages in executive functioning continue? *Cortex* 74:305–314.

Pascual y Cabo, D. and J. Rothman. 2012. The (il)logical problem of heritage speaker bilingualism and incomplete acquisition. *Applied Linguistics* 33:450–455.

Pavlenko, A. and S. Jarvis. 2002. Bidirectional transfer. *Applied Linguistics* 23:190–214.

Peal, E. and W. Lambert. 1962. The relation of bilingualism to intelligence. *Psychological Monographs: General and Applied* 76:1–23.

Peukert, H. 2015. Transfer effects in multilingual language development. In *Transfer effects in multilingual language development*, ed. H. Peukert, 1–17. Amsterdam: Benjamins.

Puig-Mayenco, E., J. Gonzáles Alonso, and J. Rothman. 2020. A systematic review of transfer studies in third language acquisition. *Second Language Research* 36:31–64.

Richards, J. C. and G. P. Sampson. 2014. The study of learner English. In *Error analysis: Perspectives on second language acquisition*, ed. J. C. Richards, 3–18. New York: Routledge.

Rothman, J. 2011. L3 syntactic transfer selectivity and typological determinacy: The typological primacy model. *Second Language Research* 27:107–127.
Rothman, J. 2013. Cognitive economy, non-redundancy and typological primacy in L3 acquisition: Evidence from initial stages of L3 Romance. In *Romance languages and linguistic theory 2011: Selected papers from 'Going Romance' Utrecht 2011*, ed. S. Baauw, F. Drijkoningen, L. Meroni, and M. Pinto, 217–248. Amsterdam: Benjamins.
Rothman, J. 2015. Linguistic and cognitive motivations for the typological primacy model (TPM) or third language (L3) transfer: Timing of acquisition and proficiency considered. *Bilingualism: Language and Cognition* 18:179–190.
Rothman, J. and J. Cabrelli Amaro. 2010. What variables condition syntactic transfer? A look at the L3 initial state. *Second Language Research* 26:189–218.
Rothman, J., J. González Alonso, and E. Puig-Mayenco. 2019. *Third language acquisition and linguistic transfer*. Cambridge: Cambridge University Press.
Saer, D. J. 1923. The effect of bilingualism on intelligence. *British Journal of Psychology* 14:25–38.
Safont Jordà, M. P. 2003. Metapragmatic awareness and pragmatic production of third language learners of English: A focus on request acts realizations. *International Journal of Bilingualism* 7:43–69.
Sagasta Errasti, M. P. 2003. Acquiring writing skills in a third language: The positive effects of bilingualism. *International Journal of Bilingualism* 7:27–42.
Şahingöz, Y. 2014. *Schulische Mehrsprachigkeit bei türkisch-deutsch bilingualen Schülern: Eine Analyse von transferinduzierten Wortstellungsmustern*. PhD diss., University of Hamburg. http://ediss.sub.uni-hamburg.de/volltexte/2018/9128
Sanz, C. 2000. Bilingual education enhances third language acquisition: Evidence from Catalonia. *Applied Psycholinguistics* 21:23–44.
Saville-Troike, M. 2012. *Introducing second language acquisition*. Cambridge: Cambridge Univesity Press.
Schwartz, B. D. and R. A. Sprouse. 1994. Word order and nominative case in nonnative language acquisition: A longitudinal study of (L1 Turkish) German interlanguage. In *Language acquisition studies in generative grammar*, ed. T. Hoekstra and B. D. Schwartz, 317–365. Amsterdam: Benjamins.
Schwartz, B. D. and R. A. Sprouse. 1996. L2 cognitive states and the full transfer/full access model. *Second Language Research* 12:40–72.
Sharwood Smith, M. and E. Kellerman. 1986. Crosslinguistic influence in second language acquisition: An introduction. In *Crosslinguistic influence in second language acquisition*, ed. E. Kellerman and M. Sharwood Smith, 1–9. New York: Pergamon Press.
Siemund, P. and S. Lechner. 2015. Transfer effects in the acquisition of English as an additional language by bilingual children in Germany. In *Transfer effects in multilingual language development*, ed. H. Peukert, 147–160. Amsterdam: Benjamins.
Siemund, P., S. Schröter, and S. Rahbari. 2018. Learning English demonstrative pronouns on bilingual substrate: Evidence from German heritage speakers of Russian, Turkish, and Vietnamese. In *Foreign language education in multilingual classrooms*, ed. A. Bonnet and P. Siemund, 381–405. Amsterdam: Benjamins.

Slabakova, R. 2017. The scalpel model of third language acquisition. *International Journal of Bilingualism* 21:651–665.
Slabakova, R. 2021. Does full transfer endure in L3A? *Linguistic Approaches to Bilingualism* 11:96–102.
Slabakova, R. and M. d. P. García Mayo. 2015. The L3 syntax-discourse interface. *Bilingualism: Language and Cognition* 18:208–226.
Slabakova, R. and M. d. P. García Mayo. 2017. Testing the current models of third language acquisition. In *L3 syntactic transfer: Models, new developments and implications*, ed. T. Angelovska and A. Hahn, 63–84. Amsterdam: Benjamins.
Spellerberg, S. M. 2016. Metalinguistic awareness and academic achievement in a linguistically diverse school setting: A study of lower secondary pupils in Denmark. *International Journal of Multilingualism* 13:19–39.
Steinlen, A. K. and T. Piske. 2013. Academic achievement of children with and without migration backgrounds in an immersion primary school: A pilot study. *Zeitschrift für Anglistik und Amerikanistik* 61:215–244.
Titone, D., J. Gullifer, S. Subramaniapillai, N. Rajah, and S. Baum. 2017. History-inspired reflections on the bilingual advantages hypothesis. In *Growing old with two languages: Effects of bilingualism on cognitive aging*, ed. M. Sullivan and E. Bialystok, 265–295. Amsterdam: Benjamins.
Usanova, I. 2019. *Biscriptuality: Writing skills among German-Russian adolescents*. Amsterdam: Benjamins.
Westergaard, M. 2021a. Microvariation in multilingual situations: The importance of property-by-property acquisition. *Second Language Research* 37:379–407.
Westergaard, M. 2021b. The plausibility of wholesale vs property-by-property transfer in L3 acquisition. *Linguistic Approaches to Bilingualism* 11:103–108.
Westergaard, M., N. Mitrofanova, R. Mykhaylyk, and Y. Rodina. 2017. Crosslinguistic influence in the acquisition of a third language: The linguistic proximity model. *International Journal of Bilingualism* 21:666–682.
Wiese, H., A. Alexiadou, S. Allen, O. Bunk, N. Gagarina, K. Iefremenko, M. Martynova, T. Pashkova, V. Rizou, C. Schroeder, A. Shadrova, L. Szucsich, R. Tracy, W. Tsehaye, S. Zerbian, and Y. Zuban. 2022. Heritage speakers as part of the native language continuum. *Frontiers in Psychology* 12:717973.
Williams, S. and B. Hammarberg. 1998. Language switches in L3 production: Implications of a polyglot speaking model. *Applied Linguistics* 19:295–333.
Wrembel, M. 2021. Multilingual acquisition property by property: A view from a wider perspective. *Second Language Research* 37:441–447.

4 Tense and aspect

4.1 General properties of tense, aspect, *aktionsart*

The following sections can only provide a rough overview of *tense*, *aspect*, and *aktionsart*. Owing to the fact that these are not simple or straightforward concepts, it is not possible to cover every detail. Therefore, interested readers are, whenever applicable, referred to additional literature.

4.1.1 Tense

One of the most influential works discussing *tense* was written by Comrie (1985). He visualizes time in the form of a horizontal line on which every situation happening in real life can be located[1] (Comrie 1985: 2). The present moment is situated in the center of that line, with the past reaching to the left and the future reaching to the right side. Languages differ in how individual points or longer-lasting situations are represented on this line. Some languages may lack grammatical devices for expressing time reference and hence, they do not possess grammatical tense (Comrie 1985: 4). Yet, it would be incorrect to claim that there are individuals or cultures that have no concept of time or that lack the ability to express time as this is rather a matter of how tense is encoded (Comrie 1985: 3). Thus, there is a distinction between the concept of tense and the concept of time. Tense refers to the form, typically a specific verb form. By contrast, time can be defined as the resulting function or meaning (that may or may not be expressed with a tensed form). Hence, tense concerns the grammaticalized convention with which specific temporal relations or periods of time are expressed (see also Klein 1994 for another discussion of time and tense).

Comrie maintains that languages differ along two parameters when expressing time or time relations, i.e., "the degree of accuracy of temporal location" and "the way in which situations are located in time" (1985: 7). On the one hand, there are lexical items (single lexical items, such as *now*, *yesterday*; or composite expressions, such as *ten hours later*, *three days ago*), and, on the other hand, there are grammatical forms (for instance inflectional affixes attached to the verb) (Comrie 1985: 8). The

DOI: 10.4324/9781003134336-4

respective significance or frequency of either or both strategies differs in each language (Comrie 1985: 7). A language that has grammatical categories to express location in time is said to possess tense distinctions. The following two examples show this non-past- and past-distinction in English.

(1) They **look** at the sky.
(2) They **looked** at the sky.

Sentence (1) refers to a habitual, non-past situation and the verb is in the present tense. However, sentence (2) refers to a situation that happened before the moment of utterance and is not (at least not necessarily) true in the present moment anymore. It lies in the past. The structure and the lexical items are identical in both sentences; the only formal difference between sentence (1) and sentence (2) is the ending *–ed* attached to the verb *look* in the second sentence.

Languages that do not possess grammatical tense distinctions express time reference lexically (Comrie 1985: 51), for instance with adverbials, such as *yesterday* or *tomorrow*, or with larger phrases, for example *a week ago*, *in five days*. Burmese would be an example of a tenseless language that is nevertheless able to communicate temporal distinctions (Comrie 1985: 50–53).

(3) They **looked** at the sky **yesterday**.

Moreover, languages that draw temporal distinctions via grammatical categories are not automatically limited to only using these grammatical categories. Sentence (3) includes (in addition to the past ending) an adverbial (*yesterday*) to further specify the location of the situation in time. Both sentences, with or without the adverbial – compare (2) and (3) – express past time reference. The only difference is that the latter sentence is more specific than the former. It is also common for no adverbial to be present because the context or aforementioned adverbials are still valid in the current utterance.

4.1.2 Aspect

The category of *aspect* represents "different ways of viewing the internal temporal constituency of a situation" (Comrie 1976: 3). Instead of locating a situation in time as with tense, the inner structure of a situation is expressed with aspectual marking. Thus, the viewpoint of the situation changes: the focus is now on the property of the situation, regardless of whether it happened in the past or whether it is yet to happen. One can view a situation, be it an action, an event, or a process, as something that is complete, ongoing, forthcoming, etc. (Klein 1994: 16). Relevant parameters here are *completeness* or *boundedness* (Siemund 2013). These form the two contrasting distinctions, namely *perfective meaning* (completeness) and *imperfective meaning* (boundedness), that exist as grammatical categories in some languages (Comrie 1976: 7; Klein 1994: 16). More specifically, perfective means that a situation is regarded as complete, i.e., the "situation [is] viewed in its entirety" (Comrie 1976: 12). Imperfectivity, on the contrary, regards it as incomplete (Comrie 1976: 24). In some languages, imperfectivity is an individual category; in other languages, imperfectivity is further subdivided into habitual and continuous situations (Comrie 1976: 24). *Habituality* describes a situation that typically stretches over an extended period, i.e., is repeated, which means that it can be protracted, or it stands for a situation that can be iterated for a long period (Comrie 1976: 30). To understand the meaning of the category *continuousness*, Comrie uses the former concept of habituation to negatively define it "as imperfectivity that is not habituality" (1976: 26). On that account, it refers to a homogeneous situation that is durative. The following opposition, *progressive* versus *non-progressive* as subcategories of continuousness, will be more thoroughly discussed in Section 4.2. English, for instance, makes an obligatory distinction between these two categories, meaning that each finite verb form must be in either the progressive or non-progressive form (Comrie 1976: 33). In other languages (German would be an example here, see Section 4.3), this distinction is optional, which means that a non-progressive form does not necessarily imply a non-progressive meaning, but a progressive interpretation is also possible (Comrie 1976: 33).

There are languages that use grammaticalized forms to differentiate between different aspectual meanings, and there are other languages that do not have grammaticalized forms (Comrie 1976: 8). Nevertheless, it would be inadequate to reason that languages without grammaticalized aspectual forms cannot express the same aspectual distinctions as languages that mark aspect grammatically (similar to what was said about tense). The specific form to express this meaning difference may simply vary from verb to verb, and from situation to situation (Comrie 1976: 8).

4.1.3 Aktionsart

The use and the meaning of both tense and aspect are connected to and depend on the inherent meaning of the verb (Huddleston and Pullum 2002: 118). This is called *aktionsart* or *lexical aspect*. Siemund explains that "Grammatical aspect such as the progressive ... heavily interacts with the temporal properties inherent in the meaning of the verb and its arguments" (2013: 136–137). This goes back to Vendler (1957) who categorizes verbs into four different groups, namely *states*, *achievements*, *activities*, and *accomplishments* (see also Huddleston and Pullum 2002; Klein 1994; Rothstein 2004). Following Vendler's (1957: 147) classification, *states* can be defined as situations that have a duration for a (long) period of time. Sentences (4) and (5) are examples of states but note that their duration is quite different.

(4) *She is a student.*
(5) *Germany is a country in Europe.*

Achievements belong to the larger category of dynamic occurrences and are by definition punctual. This means that they occur instantaneously, as a single moment (Vendler 1957: 147), in opposition to processes that take longer and are thus durative and not punctual. Sentence (6) is an example of an achievement.

(6) *She reached the bus.*

There are two types of processes: activities and accomplishments. *Activities* are situations that extend homogeneously over a variable period of time, which means that "any part of the process is of the same nature as the whole" (Vendler 1957: 146). The latter part of the description, the homogeneous nature of activities, is what differentiates activities from accomplishments. *Accomplishments* are also durative, but they have a logical and necessary endpoint toward which they proceed (Vendler 1957: 146). Huddleston and Pullum (2002: 120) use the terms *telic* and *atelic* to emphasize the difference between activities and accomplishments. Activities are said to be atelic, i.e., they have no natural or inherent endpoint. Accomplishments, however, are telic because the endpoint is by definition given. Moreover, verbs can change from one situation type to another in combination with complements, such as objects (Huddleston and Pullum 2002: 120).

(7) *He walked in the park.*
(8) *He walked to school.*

The verb *walk* is, without any further additions, an activity verb (Huddleston and Pullum 2002: 120). This meaning is expressed in (7). The object *in the park* does not change this meaning, it only specifies where the action takes place. In contrast (8) expresses the meaning of an accomplishment, because the prepositional phrase *to school* defines the endpoint of this situation. Once the destination is reached, the situation will be over.

There are several restrictions as to which situation type can occur in which tense or with which aspectual marking. To name just one example, Vendler (1957: 148) proposes that states cannot co-occur with progressive tenses (the term progressive tense refers, according to the former discussion, to a combination of tense and aspect). More on the use of progressive aspect with stative verbs is discussed in the next section.

4.2 Tense and aspect marking in English

English belongs to the West-Germanic branch of the Indo-European language family (Baugh and Cable 2002; van Gelderen 2006). Yet structurally, morphologically, and lexically, English does not behave as a typical Germanic language since Present-Day English displays heavy influence from multiple languages of other language families (Miller 2012: 236). One salient feature is the simplification and loss of inflectional endings (Baugh and Cable 2002: 13). This means that most tense and aspect distinctions are marked analytically, i.e., with auxiliaries that are preposed to the main verb (Huddleston and Pullum 2002: 115). There is only one tense opposition that is marked inflectionally, namely that between non-past and simple past (Huddleston and Pullum 2002: 115). Morphological distinctions suggest that English does not possess a three-way opposition between present, past, and future, as "English has no future form of the verb in addition to present and past forms" (Quirk et al. 1985: 176; see also König and Gast 2018: 82). From this perspective, there is no future tense in English, because future time reference is expressed periphrastically with auxiliary forms in combination with lexical verbs (König and Gast 2018: 82). Along this line, there are also no complex past tenses, because all past tense forms are combinations of the auxiliary verb or perfect marker *have* in addition to a past participle form (König and Gast 2018: 82). Nevertheless, for the purpose of the subsequent contrastive analysis, König and Gast (2018) and their inventory of six English tenses are taken as a point of reference. This classification is adopted because (i) in German, there are parallel tenses and this facilitates a direct comparison (see Section 4.3); (ii) even if there are no dedicated forms but only combinations in English, they nevertheless express a unique meaning different than the simple present or simple past; and (iii) because this classification is commonly used in English language classrooms in Germany for didactic purposes (König and Gast 2018: 83).

Thus, the six tenses distinguished here, as proposed by König and Gast (2018: 83), are: (i) simple present (*I look at a fish*); (ii) simple past (*I looked at a fish*); (iii) future (*I will look at a fish*); (iv) present perfect (*I have looked at a fish*); (v) past perfect (*I had looked at a fish*); and (vi) future perfect (*I will have looked at a fish*).

The *simple present* is normally used for present time reference, such as situations located at or around the moment of utterance, regularly occurring situations, scheduled situations, or habits. Notice that future time reference is only possible for scheduled events (König and Gast 2018: 85). With stative verbs, the simple present form can be used to make timeless statements, which are generally true and not located at a specific moment in time (Quirk et al. 1985: 179). Moreover, it can also refer to the past in the historic present (a situation or story told from the perspective of an eyewitness), or it can be used in fictional narratives (an invented story that happened in the past) (Quirk et al. 1985: 181–183). The simple present could also be considered a habitual aspect (see Binnick 2005). For all these uses, the verb appears in the *plain form* (alternatively called *base form*). The only exception is the third person singular, which is marked with the inflectional ending *–s* (Quirk et al. 1985: 97). This means that in the simple present tense, there is person and number agreement in the third person singular (Quirk et al. 1985: 149). The verb *be* is an exception showing distinct person forms in the present singular, but only one form in the plural not further distinguished according to person. Examples (9) to (12) represent a selection of simple present tense uses.

(9) *Today **is** Friday!* [Present time reference]
(10) *We **go** to kickboxing five times a week.* [Regularly occurring situation, habit]
(11) *Water **boils** at 100°C.* [Timeless statement]
(12) *It was really crazy. I was standing there, and then suddenly, this person **comes** and **looks** at me as if ...* [Historic past]

The *simple past* locates a situation anterior to the moment of utterance (Huddleston and Pullum 2002: 137). This means that the situation lies completely in the past. This tense is formed with the preterit form of the verb. Regular verbs form the preterit with *–ed*, whereas irregular verbs have a unique preterit form that cannot be derived from the base form but needs to be learned individually for every verb (Swan 2005: 282–285). Typically, simple past tense verb forms combine with adverbials of time that refer to the past. Examples are *yesterday*, *last week*, *a year ago*, etc. See the use of an irregular (13) and regular (14) past tense sentence with adverbials present.

(13) ***Last weekend**, I **went** blueberry picking in the forest.*
(14) ***An hour ago**, I **talked** to my colleague.*

Although there is strictly speaking no future tense in English, there are several strategies to express *future time reference*. The most basic form of referring to a future event consists of using *will*, or less frequently *shall*, and the base form of a lexical verb (König and Gast 2018: 85). Frequently, the *will*-future is used to express some kind of consequence used in *if*-clauses (König and Gast 2018: 86). The second most frequent future marker is a form of *be going to* in combination with the base form of a lexical verb (König and Gast 2018: 85). These two strategies to express future time reference differ in meaning. The *will*-future has a predictive meaning. The *going-to*-future also predicts, but it indicates intention of future fulfillment or is based on some kind of (outside) evidence (König and Gast 2018: 85). The present progressive form can also refer to the future, conveying the meaning of future plans or arrangements that have already been made (König and Gast 2018: 86). Finally, the use of the auxiliaries *will* or *shall* plus the progressive form is another (relatively infrequent) way of expressing future time reference. It can, for instance, be a more cautious way of indicating that a situation is not planned but the necessary consequence of another action (König and Gast 2018: 86). Quirk et al. (1985: 216) interpret these cases as "Future as a matter of course," i.e., as something that was going to happen anyway, see (18). In addition, adverbials that express future time reference, such as *later today*, *tomorrow*, *next year*, etc., very often co-occur with these forms of future time reference. Sentences (15) to (18) contextualize the different uses.

(15) *I will finish in time!* [Hidden condition: If I stick to my schedule.]
(16) *I am going to study tonight.* [Intention]
(17) *She is flying to Hanoi later this week.* [Arrangements have already been made.]
(18) *You can come with us. We will be driving to Jena anyway.* [Consequence / 'Future as a matter of course']

The *present perfect* is used for situations that started in the past and are still relevant at the moment of utterance. Thus, they extend to the present moment or could even include it (König and Gast 2018: 89). It is formed with the simple present form of *have* and the past participle of a lexical verb. König and Gast (2018: 90–91) differentiate between four different uses of the present perfect that heavily interact with *aktionsart*. The *universal use*, which refers to states or habits that reach up to the present moment, is formed with state or activity verbs. The *existential use* is restricted to bounded events that are situated in the past but not definitely located in time. The *resultative perfect* occurs with achievement and accomplishment verbs indicating a change with current relevance. The *hot-news perfect* introduces a yet unknown event in the recent past. (19) to (22) represent typical examples of each type.

(19) *I have lived in Trondheim for nearly 11 months now.* [Universal use]
(20) *I have been to Røros once.* [Existential use]
(21) *Someone has stolen my bicycle.* [Resultative use]
(22) *They have declared Germany a red country.* (The Norwegian government in August 2020, because of rising cases of Corona infections.) [Hot-news perfect]

Only adverbials that include the present moment can combine with the present perfect. Examples could be *this week*, *so far*, *until now*, and *today*. Adverbs that are used in combination with the simple past (with a definite point in the past) typically do not qualify for use with the present perfect (König and Gast 2018: 89).

The *past perfect* refers to situations that are located anterior to a past context, which means that these are cases of double anteriority (Huddleston and Pullum 2002: 140), see example (23).[2]

(23) *I had given up on the stolen bicycle before I received the good news that someone found it.*

Following this description of the different tenses, the category of aspect will be briefly discussed. English possesses a fully grammaticalized opposition of simple (or non-progressive) versus progressive aspect (König and Gast 2018). The *progressive aspect* describes "activities or events that are in progress [...] or are about to take place in the near future" (Biber et al. 2000: 470). It combines with all tenses available in English. A typical example of a progressive sentence is (24), taken from König and Gast (2018: 93).

(24) *Charles is working.*

This sentence stands in direct opposition to its simple form *Charles works*. The former expresses a situation where Charles is right now in the middle of performing an action (i.e., work), whereas the simple aspect in the present tense can be classified as habitual, i.e., the general property of Charles of having a job. However, the progressive and the simple form are not (always) interchangeable (Comrie 1976: 33) since they express different meanings. The progressive adds dynamicity, duration, and ongoingness to the so-called basic meaning expressed in simple tenses.

In addition, the *aktionsart* of the verb interacts with the progressive aspect. According to Biber et al. (2000: 471), the progressive aspect can only be used with verbs expressing activities or describing events, so-called dynamic verbs like *dance, march, bring, laugh, play, work*, etc. Using Vendler's (1957) classification, activities and accomplishments typically combine with the progressive, but achievements and states are less likely to be used with the progressive aspect. Biber et al. (2000) present verbs that only rarely occur in the progressive aspect. Some examples are *agree, believe, know, want,* and *appreciate* (Biber et al. 2000: 472; see also Huddleston and Pullum 2002: 119; Smith 1983: 482). These belong to the group of mental/attitudinal state verbs. Swan (2005: 457) even provides a list of common non-progressive verbs, which are *believe, doubt, feel, hate, imagine, know, (dis)like, love, prefer, realize, recognize, remember, see, suppose, think, understand, want,* and *wish*.

It can thus be said that the use of the progressive with dynamic verbs that describe events and actions is particularly frequent. However, this grammatical structure seems to be spreading to state verbs, too (Aarts, Close, and Wallis 2010: 162), and this use could be considered a recent

76 *Tense and aspect*

innovation (like the *I am loving it* campaign of a major fast-food corporation). It is not widely dispersed (Kranich 2010: 251) and only a small number of state verbs are infrequently used in the progressive aspect as an addition to the more or less restricted, standard use of the present progressive (see also Hirtle and Bégin 1991; Hundt 2004). Kranich (2010: 192) argues that most of these uses can be interpreted as "a state of limited duration," i.e., as something temporary. Furthermore, Mair (2006: 92) points out that such uses can carry rhetorical meaning in that they purposefully convey a specific effect. Moreover, the progressive is used significantly more often in speech than in written English (Aarts, Close, and Wallis 2010: 158), and it is also more frequently used in informal registers than in formal registers (Axelsson and Hahn 2001: 12; Hundt 2004: 61; Kranich 2010: 251). See Section 5.2.2 for more information about the English progressive aspect.

For more details on tense and aspect in English, see Biber et al. (2000), Huddleston and Pullum (2002), Quirk et al. (1985), and Swan (2005).

4.3 Tense and aspect marking in German

German belongs to the Germanic branch of the Indo-European language family and shares numerous grammatical categories with English. Yet, in many respects, German differs from English because both languages developed differently due to their specific historical situation (for an overview, see Baugh and Cable 2002; Chambers and Wilkie 2014; Hogg and Denison 2008; see also König and Gast 2018 for a detailed comparison of German and English). Whereas German belongs to the group of fusional or inflecting languages, English is developing into an isolating or analytic language (König and Gast 2018: 315; Iggesen 2013; Siemund 2004; Velupillai 2013: 96).

In comparison to English, German has preserved many inflectional endings (König and Gast 2018: 69) and marks person, number, tense, and mood on the verb (Hentschel 2010: 378; König and Gast 2018: 69). The different forms of the verb *spielen* ('play') show person and number marking for the present tense: *ich spiele* 'I play', *du spielst* 'you play', *er/sie/es spielt* 'he/she/it plays', *wir spielen* 'we play', *ihr spielt* 'you play', *sie spielen* 'they play'.

Even though there is a considerable formal overlap between German and English tense formation (König and Gast 2018: 83), the meaning and use of these two systems substantially differ. In German, the present tense refers to non-past situations, i.e., to the present moment ((25) and (26)), to currently ongoing situations (27), or it expresses future time reference (28) (Hentschel 2010: 27; König and Gast 2018: 92). Notice that in English, the present perfect is used in (26), a progressive form in (27), and a future form in (28) as opposed to simple present uses (see again Section 4.2 for the use of the simple present in English).

(25) Ich **trinke** morgens Tee.
    1SG drink.PRS.1SG morning tea
    'I drink tea in the morning.'

(26) Ich **wohne** seit zwei Jahren in Trondheim.
    1SG live.PRS.1SG for two year.PL in Trondheim
    'I have lived in Trondheim for two years.'

(27) Es **schneit.**
    3SG snow.PRS.3SG.
    'It is snowing.'

(28) Morgen **gehe** ich ins Fitnessstudio.
    tomorrow go.PRS.1SG 1SG into gym
    'Tomorrow, I will go to the gym.'

The present tense is the default tense that is used to refer to the future (König and Gast 2018: 84). Another way of referring to prospective situations is the use of the future marker *werden*, an auxiliary verb, and the plain form of the main verb (König and Gast 2018: 84). Therefore (28) could also be expressed by using this form (*Futur I*), as shown in (29). See König and Gast (2018: 84) for further explanations.

(29) Morgen **werde** ich ins Fitnessstudio **gehen.**
    tomorrow will.PRS.1SG 1SG into gym go.INF
    'Tomorrow, I will go to the gym.'

The simple past (*Präteritum*) is used to refer to situations in the past, without implying how long this situation has lasted, and to tell stories (Hentschel 2010: 273). In spoken discourse, however, the present perfect (*Perfekt*) is favored, whereas in written texts, the simple past is more frequently used (Hentschel 2010: 40–41). Examples (30) and (31) refer to a completed situation in the past, with the former being more common in writing and the latter in spoken discourse.

(30) Ich **schlief** den ganzen Tag.
    1SG sleep.PST.1SG DEF.ART.ACC whole day
    'I slept the whole day.'

(31) Ich **habe** den ganzen Tag **geschlafen.**
    1sg have.PRS.1SG DEF.ART.ACC whole day sleep.PTCP
    'I slept the whole day.'

In addition, the German present perfect combines with past tense adverbials such as *gestern* ('yesterday') or *letzte Woche* ('last week'). This is called the narrative use (König and Gast 2018: 87) and both present perfect and simple past can be used interchangeably[3] (representing different levels of formality). Another use of the present perfect is the resultative use that indicates recent change, and here, the simple past cannot be used (König and Gast 2018: 87–88). This use is comparable in English and in German (see (32), taken from König and Gast 2018: 92).

(32) *Jemand   hat   mein   Auto   gestohlen.*
     someone have.PRS.3SG my   car   steal.PTCP
     'Someone has stolen my car.'

The use of the resultative perfect also extends to future situations (König and Gast 2018: 87). An example is (33). In English, we would have to use the future perfect, which is also possible in German, see (34), but the future perfect (*Futur II*) expresses less certainty than the same situation expressed with a perfect form.

(33) *Nächstes   Jahr   **habe**   ich   meine   Dissertation   fertig*
     next   year   have.PRS.1SG   1SG   my   thesis   finish
     geschrieben.
     write.PTCP
     'Next year, I will have finished my thesis.'

(34) *Nächstes   Jahr   **werde**   ich   meine   Dissertation   fertig*
     next   year   will.PRS.1SG   1SG   my   thesis   finish
     geschrieben haben.
     write.PTCP have.INF
     'Next year, I will have finished my thesis.'

In contrast to English, German uses two auxiliary verbs, *sein* ('be') or *haben* ('have'), to form the present perfect (Hentschel 2010: 233).[4] Another difference to English is that the auxiliary verb invariably appears in second position of the sentence, and that the participle form is the last constituent of the sentence (Hentschel 2010: 254; König and Gast 2018: 92).

Moreover, the past perfect (*Plusquamperfekt*) and the future perfect share formal features with English and are used in comparable contexts. The past perfect refers to a situation in the past that happened before another reference point in the past, see (35) (Hentschel 2010: 250). It is formed with the auxiliary verbs *sein* ('be') or *haben* ('have') in the simple past form plus the past participle (Hentschel 2010: 250–251).

(35) *Als   sie   nach   Hause   kam,   hatte   er*
     when   3SG.F   to   home   come.PST.3SG have.PST.3SG   3SG.M
     *schon   **gekocht.***
     already cook.PTCP
     'When she came home, he had already prepared the meal.'

The future perfect expresses a future result (Hentschel 2010: 92). It is a complex tense that consists of three verbal forms (see (36), taken from König and Gast 2018: 92). For further information, see Hentschel (2010: 91–96).

(36) *Ich* **werde** *das bis morgen* **erledigt haben.**
1SG will.PRS.1SG DEF.ART until tomorrow do.PTCP have.INF
'I will have done this by tomorrow.'

Furthermore, in German, there is no grammaticalized form that signifies an aspectual distinction such as the progressive aspect (Hentschel 2010: 40; König and Gast 2018: 92–93). This, however, does not mean that German cannot express what is conveyed with the progressive aspect in English. Instead, there are several lexical items that correspond to it (König and Gast 2018: 92–93). (37) to (40), possible translations of (24) from above (*Charles is working*), taken from König and Gast (2018: 93), demonstrate how flexible German is, and how many different (optional) structures are available to express ongoing situations.

(37) *Karl arbeitet gerade.*
Karl work.PRS.3SG now

(38) *Karl ist am Arbeiten.*
Karl be.PRS.3SG at work.NMLZ

(39) *Karl ist beim Arbeiten.*
Karl be.PRS.3SG by work.NMLZ

(40) *Karl ist arbeiten.*
Karl be.PRS.3SG work.INF

One might argue that there are indications of grammaticalization in German, considering there are constructions that are particularly common and serve as progressive markers in some contexts and with certain (intransitive) verbs. This is particularly prominent in southern German varieties or in regions close to the Netherlands (Hentschel 2010: 40; see König and Gast 2018: 94 for a more detailed discussion). Nevertheless, the status of the progressive aspect in English is currently undeniably different from German.

4.4 Tense and aspect marking in Russian

Russian, like English and German, belongs to the Indo-European language family, but is part of the Slavonic branch and uses the Cyrillic script (Comrie 2011: 329). Additionally, Russian is a fusional language (König and Gast 2018; Iggesen 2013) and is classified as "strongly suffixing" (Dryer 2013a, 2013b). Therefore, tense and aspect are predominantly marked with affixes (Wade 2011: 240).

In contrast to the sections before, aspect is here discussed first, because "The Russian verb system is dominated by the concept of aspect" (Wade

2011: 268). Essentially, Russian possesses verb pairs. The simple form of a verb is either the imperfective part of the pair, and with a prefix, the verb is turned into the perfective counterpart; or the verb stem is perfective and by adding a suffix it changes into an imperfective verb (Comrie 2011: 340–341; but see Lehmann 2013: 258 for exceptions). Examples of perfective-imperfective verb pairs are shown in (41), taken from Comrie (2011: 340) and Lehmann (2013: 258). The variant on the left is the imperfective verb form with its perfective counterpart on the right side.

(41) *pisát'* – *napisát'* 'to write'
     čitát' – *pročitát'* 'to read'
     zakryvát' – *zakrýt'* 'to close'
     rešát' – *rešít'* 'to decide'

Earlier, it was explained that aspect is a way of considering or "viewing the internal temporal constituency of a situation" (Comrie 1976: 3). The imperfective aspect portrays situations as incomplete (Comrie 1976: 24) and it is usually used for ongoing or habitual situations or to provide background information of a particular event (Comrie 2011: 341). Generally, it is the unmarked aspect in Russian and it "may denote anything but explicit boundary selection" (Sonnenhauser 2004: 249). It combines with all tenses, i.e., situations in the past, present, and future (Wade 2011: 273), but in the present tense, the imperfective aspect is the only aspect that can be used since the perfective aspect has future time reference in the present tense (Wade 2011: 267, 295). See examples (42) to (44), taken from Wade (2011: 273). (42) refers to an ongoing situation at the present moment and (43) in the future. Example (44) refers to a repeated situation in the past. For more explanations, see Wade (2011: 267, 295–320).

(42) On **účit** urók.
     3SG.M learn.3SG.PRS.IPFV lesson
     'He is learning the lesson.'

(43) On **búdet** **účit'** urók.
     3SG.M be.3SG.FUT.IPFV learn.INF.IPFV lesson
     'He will be learning the lesson.'

(44) Oná **platíla** reguljárno.
     3SG.F pay.3SG.PST.IPFV regularly
     'She paid regularly.'

The perfective aspect, on the contrary, views a situation as a complete whole and portrays a situation or event in its entirety (Comrie 1976: 12). In Russian, the perfective aspect is the marked aspectual form, because the boundaries of the event are clearly included in the topic time, i.e., the situation is conveyed as temporally bounded (Sonnenhauser 2004: 249). Furthermore, if the focus is not on the process but rather on the result, the perfective aspect is also used, even if there is common agreement that it must have taken a while to produce this result, meaning that an ongoing situation is automatically implied (Wade 2011: 273–274).

(45) Oná   pročitála   knígu.
     3SG.F   read.3SG.PST.PRF   book
     'She has read the book.' (Now you can read it; i.e., it has current relevance.)

(46) Oná   zaplátit   za   èlektríčestvo.
     3SG.F   pay.3SG.PRS.PRF   for   electricity
     'She will pay the electricity.' (The account will be settled.)

(47) Oná   prigotóvila   úžin.
     3SG.F   cook.3SG.PST.PRF   dinner
     'She cooked the dinner.' (The focus is on the finished product and not on the process.)

(45) and (46) report single actions, the former about a past situation, and the latter about the future. Example (47) is what Wade (2011: 273) explains to be a "culmination of a process," i.e., the focus is on the result of an extended process. Hence, situations that are expressed with the perfective form of a verb are not necessarily short or instantaneous but can clearly refer to durative actions. Yet, the focus lies on the completion.

As already indicated, aspect co-occurs with tense. More precisely, the imperfective aspect occurs in present, past, and future situations, whereas the perfective aspect is used in past situations and has future time reference in the present tense. In addition, there is an obligatory choice between imperfective and perfective aspect. There is some overlap to the progressive aspect in English, as English also requires a definite choice between simple or progressive aspect (see Section 4.2). Imperfectives in the present tense tend to express ongoing processes (Comrie 1976: 63), which corresponds to the English progressive aspect (see (48), taken from Wade 2011: 267).

(48) Ja   pišú   pis'mó.
     1SG   write.1.SG.PRS.IPFV letter
     'I am writing a letter.'

In the past tense, ongoing situations are expressed with the imperfective aspect in Russian and the progressive aspect in English, and completed actions are expressed with the perfective aspect in Russian and with a non-progressive form in English. However, for repeated actions in the past, Russian uses the imperfective aspect, whereas in English, a non-progressive form is used (see (49), taken from Wade 2011: 299).

(49) On   zvoníl   nam po večerám.
     3SG.M   ring.3SG.PST.IPFV   us   by evening
     'He used to ring us in the evenings.'

With respect to tense, there is a binary distinction between non-past and past. In the non-past, person and number distinctions are marked inflectionally on the verb (Comrie 2011: 340), either following the first (*-e-*) or the second (*-i/ja-*) conjugation (Wade 2011: 241). For instance, *ja čitáju* 'I read', *ty čitáeš* 'you read', and *oní čitájut* 'they read', are examples of a verb using the first conjugation (Comrie 2011: 340).

In the past tense, however, verbs do not conjugate for person and number but for gender and number (see Comrie 2011: 340 for examples), since today's verb forms are participles that have lost the auxiliary (Comrie 2011: 342). Furthermore, Russian has lost all other (periphrastic) past tenses, which makes the simple past the only past tense in Russian (Comrie 2011: 342).

However, there are two periphrastic tenses in Russian, the *conditional form* and the *imperfective future* (Comrie 2011: 341). The *conditional* is formed with the past tense form of the verb and the clitic *by* either before or after the verb (Wade 2011: 333). Consider example (50), a conditional form in the perfective aspect. For further uses and more examples, see Wade (2011: 341).

(50) Ja   pošël   by.
     1SG   go.SG.M.PRF   COND
     'I would go.'

The *imperfective future*, or compound future, consists of a form of the verb *byt'* ('be') and the imperfective infinitive form (Comrie 2011: 341; Wade 2011: 266). There is another future tense, the *perfective future*, which is not formed periphrastically but this tense is formed by conjugating a perfective verb (Wade 2011: 267). Compare the following example sentences (adapted from Wade 2011: 266–267).

(51) Ja   búdu   otdychát'.
     1SG   be.1SG.FUT   rest.INF.IPFV
     'I will rest.'

(52) Ja   napišú   pis'mó.
     1SG   write.1SG.PRS.PRF   letter
     'I will write a letter.'

Moreover, the verb *byt'*, which is similar in meaning to the English copula verb *be*, behaves quite differently in Russian than in English, because there is generally no copula use in Russian. In addition, in many contexts, for example in the present tense, it is not expressed (Wade 2011: 257).

Therefore, there are no equivalents for the English expressions *it is* or *there is/are* (Wade 2011: 257). What we find instead is either no verb (see sentences (53) and (54)), a dash – this may be used for emphasis or in definitions (see (55) and (56)), an impersonal expression without a subject (57), the verb *est'* for questions and in positive answers (58), or when the desired meaning is 'to exist' (59). For more information, see Wade (2011: 257–259).

(53) *Ja   stúdent.*
     1SG   student
     'I am a student.'

(54) *On   némec.*
     3SG.M   German
     'He is German.'

(55) *Ja málen'kij, a   on   – net.*
     1SG small   and 3SG.M   not
     'I am small and he is not.'

(56) *Berlín – stolíca Germánii.*
     Berlin   capital Germany
     'Berlin is the capital of Germany.'

(57) *Chólodno.*
     cold.3SG
     'It is cold.'

(58) *Jábloki   ést'?   /   Ést'!*
     apple.PL exist.INF   /   exist.INF
     'Are there any apples? / Yes, there are.'

(59) ***Ést'***   *takíe   ljúdi,   kotórye ljúbjat   lingvístiku.*
     exist.INF   such   people   who   love.3PL.PRS linguistics
     'There are people who love linguistics.'

Nevertheless, in the past tense, the copula verb *byt'* ('be') is used. Compare the present tense sentence (53) with its past tense version in (60).

(60) *Ja **byl**   stúdent.*
     1SG be.M.PST.IPFV   student
     'I was a student.'

For more detailed information on the use of tense and aspect in Russian, see Comrie (2011) and Wade (2011).

4.5 Tense and aspect marking in Turkish

Turkish belongs to the Turkic languages and is classified as an agglutinating language (Göksel and Kerslake 2005: viii; Jendraschek 2011: 246; Taylan 2001: vii). As in Russian, temporal and aspectual information is expressed by adding affixes to the verb (Cinque 2001: 47–55). This means that the Turkish verb "can host a series of grammatical morphemes" (Taylan 2001: vii). More precisely, we largely find suffixes, mostly with a "one-to-one relationship between morpheme and function" (Kornfilt 2011: 628).

Turkish distinguishes between past and non-past. Both present and future are expressed with a zero marker, i.e., the absence of the past marker, whereas the past tense is characterized by verbal suffixes (*-DI* and *-mIş*) and a copular marker (*-(y)DI*) that attach to the verb stem (Göksel and Kerslake 2005: 284–286). The past with *-DI* corresponds to the simple past and the present perfect in English, and it is used to report events a speaker has experienced or witnessed him- or herself (Lewis 1967: 127–128). In other words, it locates an event prior to the moment of utterance. The opposite is true for the past formed with the suffix *-mIş*. This can be considered a relative past because it can locate an event before any point of reference and not just the moment of utterance (Göksel and Kerslake 2005: 285). In addition, Lewis explains that it can be used to "convey that the information given is based on hearsay, less often that it is based on inference" (1967: 122). This means that *-mIş* is an *evidentiality marker* (Slobin 2016: 109–110; Slobin and Aksu 1982; see also Aikhenvald 2004). See examples (61) and (62) (adapted from Göksel and Kerslake 2005: 285), but notice that in English both a simple past and a present perfect reading would be possible.

(61) *Ev-i   sat-tı-nız   mı?*
     house-ACC sell-PST-2PL INT
     'Did you sell/have you sold the house?'

(62) *Kerem'in   babası   ona biraz para   **ver-miş**.*
     Kerem-2SG father   him some money give-PST
     'Apparently, Kerem's father gave/has given him some money.'

Furthermore, in morphologically rich languages like Turkish, it is common to find vowel harmony. This means that the exact realization of suffixes depends on the features of the preceding vowel. An example of such a verbal suffix with different realizations is the past tense marker. The suffix *-ti* is used for verbs that end in an unrounded front vowel and a consonant that is voiceless, for example *git-ti* (the past of the English verb *go*). The suffix *-di* attaches to a verb that ends with an unrounded front vowel and a consonant that is voiced, for example *gel-di* (past tense of *come*) (Bickel and Nichols 2013).

To demonstrate *zero marking* (= present tense) as opposed to past tense marking, observe the non-verbal predicates in (63) and (64) (taken from Jendraschek 2011: 247, 250).

(63) *Bodrum'-da-∅-yım* / *Bodrum'-da-ydı-m*
 Bodrum-LOC-PRS-1SG / Bodrum-LOC-PST-1SG
 'I'm in Bodrum. / I was in Bodrum.'

(64) *Hasta-∅-yım.* / *Hasta-ydı-m.*
 sick-PRS-1SG / sick.PST-1SG
 'I am sick. / I was sick.'

In addition, Göksel and Kerslake (2005: 287) also list a future tense marker *-(y)AcAK*. Jendraschek (2011: 256), however, claims that it is not a future tense but rather the combination of present tense and the prospective aspect. Both interpretations are given here, as a future tense in (65) (adapted from Göksel and Kerslake 2005: 287) and as a combination of present tense and prospective aspect in (66) (adapted from Jendraschek 2011: 257). In the former, the suffix *-acak* is regarded as the future marker, in the latter as the marker of the prospective with a zero marker for present tense.

(65) *Herkes bu roman-a* **bayıl-acak.**
 Everyone this novel-DAT love-FUT
 'Everyone will like this novel.'

(66) *Hakan yarın ev-de* **ol-acak-∅-∅.**
 Hakan tomorrow house-LOC be-PROSP-PRS-3SG
 'Hakan will be at home tomorrow.'

Furthermore, aspectual information is also expressed by adding suffixes to the verb (Cinque 2001: 47–55; Taylan 2001: vii). Göksel and Kerslake (2005) differentiate perfective and imperfective aspect (but see Jendraschek 2011 for a different approach). *Perfective aspect* refers to completed situations, i.e., the starting and endpoint are included, and *imperfective aspect* expresses incompleteness and refers to situations that are ongoing (Göksel and Kerslake 2005: 288). This is mainly relevant for past tenses. In addition, the imperfective aspect can be further subdivided into progressive (either a state or dynamic event) and habitual (recurrent situations), and this equally applies to non-past and past situations (Göksel and Kerslake 2005: 289). There are two imperfective markers that express progressive and habitual situations, i.e., *–(I)yor* and *–mAktA* (Göksel and Kerslake 2005: 289).[5] The difference between the two markers is mainly stylistic. The former (*–(I)yor*) is more common in spoken conversation, because it is less formal. The latter (*–mAktA*) is relatively formal but can, under specific circumstances, occur in informal speech as well (Göksel and Kerslake 2005: 289). According to Lewis (1967: 112), there is a meaning difference between these two, in that *–mAktA* can only be used for actions that are in progress but not for situations that are anticipated. Examples (67) to (71), taken from Göksel and Kerslake (2005: 288–289), are illustrations of this aspectual difference between perfective and imperfective aspect.

(67) Geçen hafta her gün iki saat **çalış-tı-m**.
last week each day two hour work-PRF-1SG
'Last week, I worked for two hours every day.'

(68) Şu an-da ne **yap-ıyor-sunuz?**
this moment-LOC what do-IPFV-2PL
'What are you doing at the moment?'

(69) Yemek **yi-yor-uz**.
meal eat-IPFV-1PL
'We're having dinner.'

(70) Bugün aile yapı-sı hız-la **değiş-mekte-dir**.
today family structure-NC speed-INS change-IPFV-GM
'Today, the structure of the family is changing rapidly.'

(71) Sen Ömer'-i ben-den daha iyi **tanı-yor-sun**.
2SG Ömer-ACC 1SG-ABL more well know-IPFV-2SG
'You know Ömer better than me.'

Furthermore, there is the *aorist* (or *dispositive aspect* in Jendraschek 2011) which could be interpreted as another aspectual category (Göksel and Kerslake 2005: 295). It is comparable to the imperfective aspect, but it expresses a universal or general statement, whereas the imperfect aspect reflects the personal experience of the speaker (Göksel and Kerslake 2005: 295). The aorist is expressed with the suffix forms *-(A/I)r/-mAz* in verbal sentences (Göksel and Kerslake 2005: 290), see (72) and (73), taken from Göksel and Kerslake (2005: 295). Note that *-(A/I)r* is used for positive and *-mAz* for negative statements.

(72) İki, iki daha dört **ed-er**.
two two more four make-POS.AOR
'Two and two make four.'

(73) Para mutluluk **getir-mez**.
money happiness bring-NEG.AOR
'Money doesn't bring happiness.' [Generally accepted truth]

(74) *Para   mutluluk   **getir-mi-yor.***
money   happiness   bring-NEG-IPFV
'Money doesn't bring happiness.' [Personal assessment of the speaker]

The difference between the imperfective aspect and the aorist becomes apparent in examples (73) and (74). The same English translation is offered, yet the former sentence (aorist) is understood as a general (negative) truth, and the latter is a personal judgment of the speaker, indicated by the imperfective form (see Göksel and Kerslake 2005: 295–297 for more information).

Moreover, there are copular markers in form of suffixes (i.e., *-(y)DI* (past copula), *-(y)mIş* (evidential copula), and *-(y)sA* (conditional copula)), as bound stem *i-*, and *ol-* (Göksel and Kerslake 2005: 73, 79). The suffix markers attach to the verb stem, and *i-* is now an obsolescent form that is only rarely used (for more information, see Göksel and Kerslake 2005: 79). What is crucial, however, is that the marker *-(y)DI* is not expressed in the present tense. Thus, there appear only the suffixed personal pronouns, but no equivalent to the English copula verb *be* (Lewis 1967: 96), as can be seen in examples (75) and (76), taken from Lewis (1967: 98), as well as (77) and (78) taken from Göksel and Kerslake (2005: 110).

(75) *evde-yim,   evde-sin,   evde-∅,   evde-y-iz,   evde-siniz,*
at home-1SG   at home-2SG   at home-3SG   at home-1PL   at home-2PL
evde-ler
at home-3PL
'I am/you are/he/she/it is/we are/you are/they are at home'

(76) *hazır-ım,   hazır-sın,   hazır-∅,   hazır-ız,   hazır- sınız,*
ready-1SG   ready-2SG   ready-3SG   ready-1PL   ready-2PL
hazır-lar
ready-3PL
'I am/you are/he/she/it is/we are/you are/they are ready'

(77) *Bugün   çok   yorgun-um.*
today   very   tired-1SG
'I am very tired today.'

(78) *Çok   güzel-siniz.*
very   pretty-2PL
'You are very pretty.'

The absence in the present tense and presence in the past tense are demonstrated in (79) and (80). They nicely contrast with the last copula form that was mentioned, i.e., *ol-*, which is used for all other tense and aspect distinctions, such as future situations in the past (81).

88 *Tense and aspect*

(79) *Necla öğretmen.*
Necla teacher
'Necla is a teacher.'

(80) *Necla öğretmen-**di**.*
Necla teacher-PST.COP
'Necla was a teacher.'

(81) *Necla öğretmen ol-acak-tı.*
Necla teacher be-FUT-PST.COP
'Necla was going to be a teacher.'

With this short and by no means exhaustive summary, Turkish was presented as a language that heavily relies on tense and especially aspectual distinctions which are attached to the verb stem as suffixes. For more detailed information, see Göksel and Kerslake (2005), Jendraschek (2011), and Kornfilt (2011).

4.6 Tense and aspect marking in Vietnamese

The final language to be discussed is Vietnamese. It belongs to the Mon-Khmer language group within the family of the Austro-Asiatic languages (Nguyễn 2011: 777). It is an isolating language (Ngô 2001: 10), meaning that it does not have inflectional endings. Instead, the form of the word is (more or less) fixed, because "Grammatical relationships are expressed not by changing the internal structure of the words … but by the use of auxiliary words and word order" (Ngô 2001: 10). Another distinct feature of Vietnamese is that it possesses tones that affect the meaning of the word (Nguyễn 1997: 25–26).

Due to the absence of morphological cues, syntactic and lexico-syntactic criteria play an important role in distinguishing word classes and in deriving meaning (Nguyễn 2011: 786–792). The situational and linguistic context establish time reference and not the verb itself, as Vietnamese verbs are timeless (Thompson 1965: 217–218). Thus, temporal distinctions can be derived from the context, which means that an explicit tense marker is not needed and can be omitted (Ngô 2001: 17; Tang 2007: 17). Consider example (82) (taken from Nguyễn 1997: 17). The past tense marker *đã* is not necessary, and in fact, it is usually left out. It would be considered unnatural if expressed, because *sáng nay* ('this morning') already indicates that it refers to the (recent) past (see also Ngô 2001: 17).

(82) ***Sáng** **nay** tôi **uống** hai tách cà-phê.*
morning this 1SG drink two cup coffee
'I drank two cups of coffee this morning.'

Nevertheless, the verb *uống* ('drink') could in principle mean *drink*, *drank*, or *drinking* (Nguyễn 1997: 17), depending on the situation. The same applies to markers indicating aspectual distinctions. They can also be omitted if the context allows a non-ambiguous interpretation. For instance, if temporal adverbials, which frequently appear sentence initially, are present (such as *chiều mai* 'tomorrow afternoon', *bây giờ* 'now', *tuần sau* 'next week', or *hôm qua* 'yesterday'), a separate tense or aspect marker is normally not present (Nguyễn 1997: 153–155).

Despite these rather simplified rules, there are several grammatical markers in the form of individual words that explicitly express tense and aspect distinctions (Ngô 2001: 17). The following sentences, representing variations of the first person singular pronoun and the verb *nói* ('speak, talk'), exemplify the use of five tense and aspect markers and the modality marker *phải* ('must').

(83) *Tôi* **nói** *rất* *nhiều.*
 1SG speak very a lot
 'I talk a lot.'

(84) *Tôi* **đang** *nói* *rất* *nhiều.*
 1SG PROG speak very a lot
 'I am talking a lot.'

(85) *Tôi* **đang** **phải** *nói* *rất* *nhiều.*
 1SG PROG must speak very a lot
 'I must be talking a lot.'

(86) *Tôi* **mới** *nói* *rất* *nhiều.*[6]
 1SG PST speak very a lot
 'I have just talked a lot.'

(87) *Tôi* **đã** *nói* *rất* *nhiều.*
 1SG PST speak very a lot
 'I spoke a lot.'

(88) *Tôi* **sắp** *nói* *rất* *nhiều.*
 1SG FUT speak
 'I am about to talk a lot.'

(89) *Tôi* **sẽ** *nói* *rất* *nhiều.*
 1SG FUT speak
 'I will talk a lot.'

There are several past tense markers, for example *mới/vừa/vừa mới* and *đã*. One variant of the former is used to refer to the recent past, and the latter is the standard past tense marker (Nguyễn 1997: 186;

90 *Tense and aspect*

Thompson 1965: 206, 209, 268). Similarly, the two future markers *sắp* and *sẽ* express recent or immediate future (*sắp*) and general future (*sẽ*) (Nguyễn 1997: 186; Thompson 1965: 206, 209, 268). They are classified as particles, auxiliaries, or adverbs (Nguyễn 1997: 87) and function as a verbal modifier (see also Thompson 1965: 217–222).

In addition, the marker *đang* differentiates states from processes, but it is also optional (Hanske 2013: 190). See the following two sentences (90) and (91) (taken from Hanske 2013: 190).

(90) **Quyển sách **đang ở** trên kệ sách.*
 CL book PROG be.at RN shelf
 Intended: 'The book is on the shelf.'

(91) *Chị ấy **đang cắt** bánh mì trên đĩa.*
 3SG.F PROG cut bread RN plate
 'She is cutting the bread on a plate.'

Whereas sentence (90) is ungrammatical in Vietnamese (as would be the use of the progressive aspect in English), sentence (91) is perfectly acceptable with the progressive marker *đang* as it expresses a current, ongoing situation. *Đang* may also appear with stative verbs, but then in the meaning of a state that is only temporary, see example (92) (taken from Hanske 2013: 190). This use is again largely parallel to what we find in English, with the exception that in Vietnamese, the form of the verb remains the same in both contexts (whereas in English, the ending *-ing* is added to the main verb).

(92) *Chị ấy **đang ở** nhà.*
 3SG.F PROG be.at house
 'She is staying at home.'

The auxiliary *có* has a similar distribution to the English auxiliary verb *do* (Thompson 1965: 216). It can be used in affirmative sentences where it emphasizes the verb that follows, it often occurs in negative sentences, and it can be used in questions (Thompson 1965: 216). Two such uses are demonstrated with examples (93) and (94) (see Thompson 1965: 216 for further explanations and examples).

(93) *Hôm qua tôi có đi săn.*
 yesterday 1SG AUX go hunt
 'Yesterday I did go hunting.'

(94) *Tôi không có đi.*[7]
 1SG NEG AUX go
 'I'm not going.'

Furthermore, Vietnamese has a copula verb *là* which appears before a noun (just as in English), but not before adjectives or numerals. To understand this difference, see examples (95) to (98) (taken from Ngô 2001: 18).

(95) *Tên   tôi   là   John.*
     name 1SG   COP John
     'I am John.'

(96) *Anh ấy   là   bạn   tôi.*
     3SG.M   COP   friend 1SG
     'He is my friend.'

(97) *Bộ phim   ấy   ∅   hay.*
     movie   that   good
     'The movie is good.'

(98) *Tôi   ∅   18   tuổi.*
     1SG   18   year old
     'I am 18 years old.'

In Vietnamese, the use of *là* in (97) and (98) would be ungrammatical. This is a clear difference to English, as in all four sentences, a form of *be* is required to form a grammatical English sentence.

For further readings that include a more detailed account of tense and aspect in Vietnamese see Nguyễn (1997) and Thompson (1965).

4.7 Similarities and differences in tense and aspect marking

Similarities and differences across or between languages can, essentially, be investigated from both a typological as well as contrastive linguistic perspective. *Linguistic typology* considers "structural differences" (Siemund 2013: 13) by comparing different languages, usually a relatively large number, to establish systemic patterns (Velupillai 2013: 15). *Contrastive linguistics*, or *contrastive analysis*, could be understood as a special or more limited case of linguistic typology (Gast 2013: 155), as it "investigates the differences between pairs (or small sets) of languages against the background of similarities and with the purpose of providing input to applied disciplines such as foreign language teaching and translation studies" (Gast 2013: 153). It is the purpose of this section to provide a short (and simplified) comparison of the grammatical features discussed in the previous sections.

The first point of comparison pertains to *morphological typology*. Vietnamese, as an isolating language, does not use inflectional endings to mark tense and aspect, but these distinctions are expressed with separate markers in the form of individual words or simply with time adverbials. In this language, tense or aspect markers are not obligatory and may

92 Tense and aspect

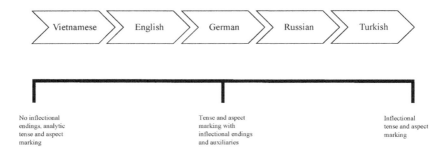

Figure 4.1 Continuum of analytic and inflectional tense and aspect marking.

be omitted. This is a clear contrast to the other languages of interest here. German and Russian are fusional languages and Turkish is an agglutinating language. Interestingly, English, formerly also classified as a fusional language, has gradually been developing into an isolating language. Moreover, English and German were presented as largely relying on auxiliaries, while Russian and Turkish mainly use inflectional suffixes to mark tense and aspectual distinctions. Therefore, Vietnamese could be located at one end of a continuum (no inflectional endings) and Turkish at the other end (almost exclusively inflectional endings) (see Figure 4.1). English, German, and Russian are lined up next to each other, ranging from some inflectional endings and many auxiliary verb uses (English), to more inflectional endings plus use of auxiliary verbs (German), to even more inflectional endings and fewer auxiliary verb uses (Russian). This classification corresponds to Greenberg's (1960) morphological typology of languages and his synthetic index (see also Siemund 2004: 192).

Furthermore, English and German both belong to the Indo-European languages. This genetic relatedness explains why there is a considerable formal overlap between these two languages with respect to the six tenses available in both languages (König and Gast 2018). Nevertheless, there are clear functional differences. This is, for instance, visible when comparing the use of the simple present. In German, it can be used in situations that have started in the past and extend to the present moment. In English, however, the present perfect is required in these contexts.

Russian, Turkish, and Vietnamese are genetically further apart from English (and German). This is reflected in a number of differences. Russian, for instance, has only one past tense form, whereas in English, there is the simple past, in addition to the present and past perfect. Turkish possesses two past tense markers to refer to events located prior to the moment of speaking, either for known events, or to refer to events from hearsay. In English, the simple past or the present perfect can be used for both markers. In Vietnamese, there are specific past tense (to distinguish between common past and recent past) and future tense markers (to refer to near future events and future events that are further away). Yet, tense markers are not obligatory in Vietnamese. One feature shared by all five languages is the use of adverbials. They are context dependent and add specific information but are optional.

Moreover, English differentiates between non-progressive and progressive aspect. This grammatical differentiation is absent in German. Russian and Turkish, however, rely on aspect marking and there are also aspectual markers in Vietnamese. Russian, for instance, differentiates between imperfective and perfective aspect. In some situations, the Russian imperfective aspect overlaps with the use of the progressive aspect in English. In Turkish, a subcategory of the imperfective aspect, which is used for progressive situations, is comparable to the use of the English progressive. Yet, the two imperfective markers are not only used for ongoing and incomplete situations, but also for states. This is a crucial difference to English, as the progressive aspect typically does not combine with stative verbs. Furthermore, the grammatical marker that expresses progressiveness in Vietnamese is not obligatory but can be omitted and it can also occur with stative verbs in currently ongoing situations. Even though there are differences between the progressive uses in Russian, Turkish, and Vietnamese in comparison to English, they share, on a conceptual level, the grammatical feature aspect, which is (arguably) absent in German.

The copula verb *be*, used comparably similarly in English and German, is absent in numerous contexts in Russian, Turkish, and Vietnamese. In Russian and in Turkish, for example, the copula verb is not used in the present tense. In Vietnamese, there is no copula verb before adjectives or numerals.

Finally, Table 4.1 summarizes the main points, although it somewhat simplifies the properties of English, on the one hand, and the respective similarities and differences of German, Russian, Turkish, and Vietnamese,

Table 4.1 Simplified summary of tense and aspect properties

Feature	English	German	Russian	Turkish	Vietnamese
Morphological tense distinctions	✓	✓	✓	✓	✗
Adverbials to indicate tense distinctions	✓	✓	✓	✓	✓
Grammaticalized aspect	✓	✗	✓	✓	(✓)
Auxiliary verbs	✓	✓	✗	(✓)	(✓)
Copula verb *be*	✓	✓	(✓)	(✓)	(✓)
Predominantly affixes to mark tense and aspect	(✓)	(✓)	✓	✓	✗
Predominantly analytic tense and aspect marking	✓	(✓)	(✓)	✗	✓

on the other hand. Evidently, there is a (partial) overlap for some features, especially between English and German, and there are clear differences for others. To what extent these language specific features affect the acquisition of English as a foreign language will be discussed in the following chapter.

Notes

1 In opposition to this view, there are cultures in which time is conceptualized in a cyclic form. Nevertheless, see Comrie (1985: 3–4) for a detailed explanation of why his universal representation is still adequate in these contexts.
2 In this study, the present perfect and past perfect are regarded as tenses and not as aspect. This is not entirely uncontroversial (see, for instance, Radden and Dirven 2007: 206) as some consider the present perfect as a form of aspect (Klein 1994; Quirk et al. 1985). Following König and Gast (2018: 92), English is treated as a language that only has one aspectual contrast, namely progressive aspect versus non-progressive aspect.
3 In these contexts, only the simple past tense could be used in English.
4 The choice between these two auxiliary verbs depends on syntactic and semantic properties of the verb (see Hentschel 2010: 233–237).
5 Note that the specific form of the suffix depends on the preceding vowel or consonant following vowel harmony rules (see Göksel and Kerslake 2005: 21–25; Jendraschek 2011: 251–253).
6 Here, any of the three recent past tense markers, i.e., *mới/vừa/vừa mới*, could be used with similar meaning and function (Tran Thi Minh, p.c.).
7 This sentence represents a spoken utterance in Southern Vietnamese rather than the Northern dialect (Ngo Thi Diem Hang, p.c.). In addition, it can also be uttered without the auxiliary *có*, as in *Tôi không đi* (see Thompson 1965: 216).

References

Aarts, B., J. Close, and S. Wallis. 2010. Recent changes in the use of the progressive construction in English. In *Distinctions in English grammar: Offered to Renaat Declerck*, ed. B. Cappelle and N. Wada, 148–168. Tokyo: Kaitakusha.
Aikhenvald, A. Y. 2004. *Evidentiality*. Oxford: Oxford University Press.
Axelsson, M. W. and A. Hahn. 2001. The use of the progressive in Swedish and German advanced learner English: A Corpus-based study. *ICAME Journal* 25:5–30.
Baugh, A. C. and T. Cable. 2002. *A history of the English language*. 5th edn. London: Routledge.
Biber, D., S. Johannson, G. Leech, S. Conrad and E. Finegan. 2000. *Longman grammar of spoken and written English*. Harlow, UK: Longman.
Bickel, B. and J. Nichols. 2013. Fusion of selected inflectional formatives. In *The world atlas of language structures online*, ed. M. S. Dryer and M. Haspelmath. Leipzig: Max Planck Institute for Evolutionary Anthropology. http://wals.info/chapter/20 (accessed April 4, 2022).
Binnick, R. I. 2005. The markers of habitual aspect in English. *Journal of English Linguistics* 33:339–369.

Chambers, W. W. and J. R. Wilkie. 2014. *A short history of the German language.* New York: Routledge.
Cinque, G. 2001. A note on mood, modality, tense and aspect affixes in Turkish. In *The verb in Turkish*, ed. E. E. Taylan, 47–60. Amsterdam: Benjamins.
Comrie, B. 1976. *Aspect.* Cambridge: Cambridge University Press.
Comrie, B. 1985. *Tense.* Cambridge: Cambridge University Press.
Comrie, B. 2011. Russian. In *The world's major languages*, ed. B. Comrie, 329–347. London: Routledge.
Dryer, M. S. 2013a. Position of tense-aspect affixes. In *The world atlas of language structures online*, ed. M. S. Dryer and M. Haspelmath. Leipzig: Max Planck Institute for Evolutionary Anthropology. http://wals.info/chapter/69 (accessed April 4, 2022).
Dryer, M. S. 2013b. Prefixing vs. suffixing in inflectional morphology. In *The world atlas of language structures online*, ed. M. S. Dryer and M. Haspelmath. Leipzig: Max Planck Institute for Evolutionary Anthropology. http://wals.info/chapter/26 (accessed April 4, 2022).
Gast, V. 2013. Contrastive analysis. In *Routledge encyclopedia of language teaching and learning*, ed. M. Byram and A. Hu, 153–158. London/New York: Routledge.
Göksel, A. and C. Kerslake. 2005. *Turkish: A comprehensive grammar.* London/New York: Routledge.
Greenberg, J. H. 1960. A quantitative approach to the morphological typology of language. *International Journal of American Linguistics* 26:178–194.
Hanske, T. 2013. Serial verbs and change of location constructions in Vietnamese. In *Linguistics of Vietnamese: An international survey*, ed D. Hole and E. Löbel, 185–214. Berlin: De Gruyter Mouton.
Hentschel, E. (ed.). 2010. *Deutsche Grammatik.* Berlin: De Gruyter Mouton.
Hirtle, W. H. and C. Bégin. 1991. Can the progressive express a state? *Langues et Linguistique* 17:99–137.
Hogg, R. and D. Denison. 2008. *A history of the English language.* Cambridge: Cambridge University Press.
Huddleston, R. D. and G. K. Pullum. 2002. *The Cambridge grammar of the English language.* Cambridge: Cambridge University Press.
Hundt, M. 2004. Animacy, agentivity, and the spread of the progressive in Modern English. *English Language and Linguistics* 8:47–69.
Iggesen, O. A. 2013. Asymmetrical case-marking. In *The world atlas of language structures online*, ed. M. S. Dryer and M. Haspelmath. Leipzig: Max Planck Institute for Evolutionary Anthropology. http://wals.info/chapter/50 (accessed April 4, 2022).
Jendraschek, G. 2011. A fresh look at the tense-aspect system of Turkish. *Language Research* 47:245–270.
Klein, W. 1994. *Time in language.* London: Routledge.
König, E. and V. Gast. 2018. *Understanding English-German contrasts.* 4th edn. Berlin: Erich Schmidt Verlag.
Kornfilt, J. 2011. Turkish and the Turkic languages. In *The world's major languages*, ed. B. Comrie, 619–644. London: Routledge.
Kranich, S. 2010. *The progressive in modern English: A corpus-based study of grammaticalization and related changes.* Amsterdam/New York: Rodopi.
Lehmann, V. 2013. *Linguistik des Russischen: Grundlagen der formal-funktionalen Beschreibung.* München: Verlag Otto Sagner.

Lewis, G. L. 1967. *Turkish grammar*. Oxford: Oxford University Press.
Mair, C. 2006. *Twentieth century English: History, variation and standardization*. Cambridge: Cambridge University Press.
Miller, G. D. 2012. *External influences on English: From its beginnings to the Renaissance*. Oxford: Oxford University Press.
Ngô, B. N. 2001. The Vietnamese language learning framework. Part one: Linguistics. *Journal of Southeast Asian Language and Teaching* 10:1–23.
Nguyễn, Đ.-H. 1997. *Vietnamese*. Amsterdam: Benjamins.
Nguyễn, Đ.-H. 2011. Vietnamese. In *The world's major languages*, ed. B. Comrie, 777–796. London: Routledge.
Quirk, R., S. Greenbaum, G. Leech, and J. Svartvik. 1985. *A comprehensive grammar of the English language*. London/New York: Longman.
Radden, G. and R. Dirven. 2007. *Cognitive English grammar*. Amsterdam: Benjamins.
Rothstein, S. 2004. *Structuring events: A study in the semantics of lexical aspect*. Oxford: Blackwell.
Siemund, P. 2004. Analytische und synthetische Tendenzen in der Entwicklung des Englischen. In *Die europäischen Sprachen auf dem Wege zum analytischen Sprachtyp*, ed. U. Hinrichs, 169–195. Wiesbaden: Harassowitz.
Siemund, P. 2013. *Varieties of English: A typological approach*. Cambridge: Cambridge University Press.
Slobin, D. I. 2016. Thinking for speaking and the construction of evidentiality in language contact. In *Exploring the Turkish linguistic landscape: Essays in honor of Eser Erguvanlı-Taylan*, ed. M. Güven, D. Akar, B. Öztürk, and M. Kelepir, 105–120. Amsterdam: Benjamins.
Slobin, D. I. and A. A. Aksu. 1982. Tense, aspect and modality in the use of the Turkish evidential. In *Tense and aspect: Between semantics and pragmatics*, ed. P. J. Hopper, 185–200. Amsterdam: Benjamins.
Smith, C. S. 1983. A theory of aspectual choice. *Language* 59:479–501.
Sonnenhauser, B. 2004. Aspect in Russian and Turkish: Semantics and pragmatics of a grammatical category. *Turkic Languages* 8:245–270.
Swan, M. 2005. *Practical English usage*. 3rd edn. Oxford: Oxford University Press.
Tang, G. 2007. Cross-linguistic analysis of Vietnamese and English with implications for Vietnamese language acquisition and maintenance in the United States. *Journal of Southeast Asian American Education and Advancement* 2:1–34.
Taylan, E. E. 2001. Introduction. In *The verb in Turkish*, ed. E. E. Taylan, vii–xvii. Amsterdam: Benjamins.
Thompson, L. C. 1965. *A Vietnamese grammar*. Seattle: University of Washington Press.
van Gelderen, E. 2006. *A history of the English language*. Amsterdam: Benjamins.
Velupillai, V. 2013. *An introduction to linguistic typology*. Amsterdam: Benjamins.
Vendler, Z. 1957. Verbs and times. *Philosophical Review* 66:143–160.
Wade, T. L. B. 2011. *A comprehensive Russian grammar*. Oxford: Blackwell.

5 Acquisition of tense and aspect

5.1 Acquisition of tense and aspect by native speakers of English

Young children who acquire English as their native language typically use verbs without their inflectional endings in the initial stages of language acquisition. This means that in the beginning, they only produce the verb stem (Clark 2009: 180). Examples of inflectional endings omitted initially are the third person singular *–s*, the regular past tense ending *–ed*, as well as irregular past tense forms such as *went* and *gone* of the verb *go*. These and other grammatical morphemes appear in child native speakers at later stages, but still at a very young age, at around one year and eight months, thus, before the age of two (Shirai 2009: 169).

The learning of grammatical morphemes in general seems to follow a sequential pattern, characterized by relative uniformity across individual L1 learners (Meisel 2011: 241). Clark (2009: 182), based on Brown (1973), proposes the acquisitional order of grammatical morphemes in English, which includes, among others, the inflectional endings necessary for tense and aspect distinctions in English (see numbers 1, 5, 7, 9, 10, 11, 12, 13, and 14). The following list (taken from Clark 2009: 182), shows first the rank order followed by the respective morpheme, the meaning of the grammatical morpheme in parenthesis, as well as one example sentence.

1 *–ing* (ongoing process) *He's sitting down.*
2 *in* (containment) *It's in the box.*
3 *on* (support) *It's on the chair.*
4 *–s* [PL] (number) *The dogs bark.*
5 irregular past [e.g., *went*] (earlier in time) *He went home.*
6 *–'s* [POSS] (possession) *The girl's dog ran away.*
7 uncontractible copula [*was, are,* as in questions] (number, earlier in time) *Are they boys?*
8 *a, the* [articles] (nonspecific/specific) *Jan has a book.*
9 *–ed* [regular past] (earlier in time) *He jumped the stream.*

DOI: 10.4324/9781003134336-5

10   *-s* [third person singular regular] (number, earlier in time) *She runs fast.*
11   third person singular irregular [*has, does*] (number, earlier in time) *Does the dog bark?*
12   uncontractible auxiliary verb [*is, were*] (number, earlier in time, ongoing process) *Is he coming? That's Tom, that is.*
13   contractible copula verb (number, earlier in time) *That's a spaniel.*
14   contractible auxiliary verb (number, earlier in time, ongoing process) *They're running fast.*

Following this list, native learners of English acquire the *–ing* form of the verb quite early but typically as a single inflected form without the corresponding auxiliary verb, as auxiliary verbs are acquired relatively late (Clark 2009: 183). Moreover, the third person singular *–s* appears only in the second half of this sequence (rank 10), yet before the irregular forms of *have* and *do* and before the auxiliary verb *be*. Furthermore, the past perfect or combinations of tense and aspect, such as the past or future progressive aspect, are acquired fairly late, at around nine years of age (Clark 2009: 333). This means that children acquire and master compound tenses and aspect successively, possibly due to the complexity of the conceptual load.

In addition, there are other ways of expressing time reference, namely by introducing events in the order of occurrence or by using adverbials. Clark (2009: 334) observes that when children refer to events or a string of events, they first mention them in the actual order of occurrence, and only later are more complex patterns, such as simultaneity, retrospect, anteriority, or prospect, used to structure their speech. To achieve the latter, conjunctions such as *while* or *after* are used, or simple past in opposition to past perfect forms to indicate contrasts (Clark 2009: 334). However, in first language acquisition in general, children appear to make use of grammatical tense and aspect marking first, and lexical means, such as adverbials, start to emerge only later (Shirai 2009: 169).[1]

5.2 Acquisition of tense and aspect by non-native speakers of English

5.2.1 General comments

Like native speakers of English, non-native or foreign language learners of English also rely on the chronological structuring of sequences of events and the use of pragmatic means to establish time reference (Shirai 2009: 168). Yet, what differentiates L2 from L1 learners is that the former have already acquired the concept of time and temporal reference in their native language. Therefore, they can make use of this conceptual knowledge in their second language right from the start (Shirai 2009: 168).

Furthermore, as a second step, L2 learners (here specifically adult L2 learners) typically make use of adverbials to express tense and aspect (Shirai 2009: 169). This is a contrast to L1 learners who were argued to produce adverbials later, after grammatical marking has been developed. Thus, L1 learners use grammatical means early, whereas (adult) second language learners start to use these comparably later, but instead generally prefer to rely on lexical information (Shirai 2009: 169–170).[2]

Without considering L1 influence, there is also the idea that L2 learners of English acquire different morphemes also in a more or less fixed order (Luk 2013: 442). In 1977, Krashen (as cited in Luk 2013: 442) proposed such a universal order consisting of four groups, namely (i) *–ing*, plural *–s*, copula verb; (ii) auxiliary verb, article; (iii) irregular past; and (iv) regular past, third person singular *–s*, possessive *–'s*.[3] Bardovi-Harlig (2013: 6) presented the same order of morpheme acquisition for both adult and child L2 learners of English, i.e., first *–ing*, then irregular past morphemes, and only then the third person singular *–s*. In addition to this acquisition order, the lexical aspect, i.e., the inherent temporal meaning of the verb, governs the distribution of tense and aspect marking, especially in the initial stages of second language acquisition (Bardovi-Harlig 2013: 6). Moreover, the acquisition of complex tenses and aspectual distinctions seem to follow a sequential acquisitional process: verbs first appear with the necessary suffix (e.g., *–ing*) only and then later on also with the required auxiliary (e.g., a form of *be*) (Ellis 2015: 79).

However, given the preceding discussions on influence of previously acquired languages on foreign language acquisition (see Chapter 3), a universal acquisition order of tense and aspect morphemes for all foreign language learners of English seems to be relatively unlikely. In fact, a comprehensive review study of foreign language learners of English with different L1s (i.e., Japanese, Chinese, Korean, and Spanish) demonstrated that the order of morpheme acquisition is by no means universal for all L2 learners (Luk and Shirai 2009: 742). Quite the opposite is true: Luk and Shirai (2009: 742) identified a strong influence from the L1 and they claimed that it is possible to predict, based on the grammatical categories present in the respective L1, the challenges or advantages learners have when acquiring English morphology (Luk and Shirai 2009: 742). Therefore, Section 5.3 zooms in on L1 German, Russian, Turkish, and Vietnamese learners of English, to identify patterns of tense and aspect acquisition, i.e., differences and similarities, based on their L1 background.

In addition, the lexical aspect of the verb influences the acquisition and use of tense and aspect. Bardovi-Harlig and Reynolds (1995) presented evidence that early L2 learners of English tend to use only achievement and accomplishment verbs in past tense contexts. They argued that these verbs are treated as "best case examples of past tense carriers at all levels of proficiency" (Bardovi-Harlig and Reynolds 1995: 118–119). Thus, even at the initial stages of English acquisition, the past tense use of achievement and accomplishment verbs appears to be fairly easy. On the contrary, Bardovi-Harlig and Reynolds (1995: 114) reported lower levels of appropriate simple past uses with activity verbs with less proficient learners of English and only later, at a more advanced level, do such appropriate uses increase. At first, non-native learners of English associate the past tense with punctual events. This distributional restriction stands in contrast to observations of native speakers of English, who are not characterized by such a restrictive use (Bardovi-Harlig and Reynolds 1995: 121).

Furthermore, it was shown that in additional or foreign language acquisition, a new linguistic form appears first in one context or a very limited range of contexts and spreads only later to other contexts (Ellis 2015: 109). Such a development could be visible in a greater number of different verbs that are used in the progressive aspect, to provide just one example. The next section further discusses the progressive aspect, because of its special status in English, especially with respect to foreign language learners.

5.2.2 The English progressive aspect

The English (present) progressive has generally been demonstrated to be a challenging area for learners of English (see, for instance, Bland 1988: 55; Dose-Heidelmayer and Götz 2016). One potential difficulty for non-native learners of English is forming the progressive aspect, since this is a complex form that was argued to be acquired during later stages of acquisition (see Section 5.2.1). Apart from formal issues, this claim can be further substantiated due to the progressive being restricted in its use. This means that it is incompatible with certain verbs, especially verbs expressing states and achievements (Biber et al. 2000: 471–472). In Chapter 4, it was discussed that in the languages that have a grammaticalized progressive aspect (i.e., Russian, Turkish, and to some extent also Vietnamese), there are also usage restrictions. However, these restrictions only partially overlap with the distribution of the progressive aspect in English.

Hence, language teaching material or grammar books typically include non-progressive verbs, such as *believe*, *doubt*, *feel*, to point learners to this difficulty (Swan 2005: 457). As was briefly mentioned in Section 4.2, there is a general trend concerning semantic and contextual expansions of the progressive aspect in Present-Day English (König 1994; Kranich 2010; van Rooy 2014). Furthermore, recent corpus-based analyses investigating the progressive aspect in World Englishes point out that it may be incorrect to claim that there is a definite number of verbs that are never used in the progressive aspect (for an overview of the variation of the progressive in English see, for example, Rautionaho 2014).

Nevertheless, there are specific (or rather untypical) progressive contexts that appear relatively infrequently in the progressive aspect (Fuchs and

Werner 2018b: 198). For instance, stative verbs are not frequently used, but they can still be attested in large corpora such as the *British National Corpus (BNC)* (Davies 2004) or the *Corpus of Contemporary American English (COCA)* (Davies 2008–) (Fuchs and Werner 2018b: 208). However, the combination with dynamic verbs and its use for actions or ongoing situations are still the core functions of the progressive aspect in English (Fuchs and Werner 2018b: 198), whereas states and achievements occur less frequently (especially in direct comparison with activity and accomplishment verbs) (see also Rothstein 2004).

In principle, there are two types of difficulty for non-native learners of English. Non-native English speakers might overuse the progressive aspect in unusual or non-prototypical contexts, whereas it might be underrepresented in prototypical situations. The former, i.e., an overuse of the progressive aspect with stative verbs, has been reported in numerous studies based on (advanced) L2 learners of English (e.g., Dose-Heidelmayer and Götz 2016; Meriläinen, Paulasto, and Rautionaho 2017; see Fuchs and Werner 2018b: 198–200 for a detailed overview).

Yet, Fuchs and Werner (2018b), who extended the previous studies to younger, less advanced learners of English (8- to 19-year-old English users), reported that the overall frequencies of stative verbs used in the progressive aspect were comparably low (Fuchs and Werner 2018b: 212). This finding supports one of the assumptions of the *Aspect Hypothesis*, namely that language learners do not expand the use of the progressive aspect to stative verbs and stative contexts (Fuchs and Werner 2018b: 212–213).[4] Furthermore, and this is even more interesting in the context of the current study, Fuchs and Werner (2018b: 213–214) noticed dissimilar patterns for learners with different L1s. These differences appeared when controlling for languages that have a grammaticalized progressive aspect versus languages that do not.

5.3 Specific foreign language learners of English

The remaining sections of this chapter focus on the acquisition and use of tense and aspect by learners of English, specifically German, Russian, Turkish, and Vietnamese learners of English. The selected studies discussed below will highlight some major patterns of tense and aspect usage identified among these learners whose possible source may be explained by L1 influence.

5.3.1 German learners of English

Section 4.3 discussed, mostly based on König and Gast (2018), differences and similarities between English and German with respect to tense as well as aspect marking and use. It was shown that tenses are formed comparably similarly in both languages, yet that there are clear differences regarding the meaning and use of the different tenses, for instance concerning the simple present and the present perfect. In addition, German does not have a grammaticalized progressive aspect.

Therefore, the discussion in Erling (2002) is particularly interesting for the current study. She specifically focused on German university students (with English as one of their majors) and their use of English in the classroom (Erling 2002: 8). She observed a number of frequently occurring non-target-like English uses, such as incorrect uses of the present tense for situations that started in the past and lead up to the present moment (i.e., a present perfect use would be target-like here), the use of the progressive aspect for stative situations (i.e., simple aspect would be target-like for stative verbs), or the use of the present perfect where a simple past tense form would be target-like (Erling 2002: 11). Initially, she interpreted these uses as indications for crosslinguistic influence from German, or differently put "as a common 'German error'" (Erling 2002: 11). Erling then explained that she started to doubt that these are just German errors, because many of these structures can also be found in other varieties of English, the so-called "New Englishes" (2002: 11). Therefore, she proposed that these non-target-like uses were wrongly classified as crosslinguistic influence from the L1, and that "It is more likely that these common features are actually a symptom of a change in the language which is coming about in non-native contexts" and not just the German context (Erling 2002: 11). She strengthened this claim by describing that the German learners of English she observed are highly proficient in English and frequent users of this language (Erling 2002: 12). She took this as support for a new English variety that deviates from Standard English.

Although this may be a feasible interpretation, alternative explanations merit consideration. First, without weakening Erling's argumentation and without questioning the development of a German-English (this is another problem that will not be further investigated here; however, see again Chapter 2 for a discussion on the status of English in Germany), the observations she made could still be understood as evidence for L1 influence. Since the students in Erling's (2002) study are advanced L2 English speakers, the non-target-like uses that are frequently observed may come from erroneously acquired structures affected by the characteristics of their L1 German that have fossilized by now (see also Hickey 2020; Section 10.3 below). Second, these errors are consistent with the results of the contrastive analysis of English and German (see Sections 4.3 and 4.7). Third, others have also reported similar non-target-like English uses of tense and aspect because of crosslinguistic influence from the L1 German. Swan (2001), for instance, providing an overview of common problematic areas for German learners of English based on teachers' observations, presented findings strikingly similar to Erling's (2002). He also listed the progressive aspect as a challenging category. He further explained that German learners of English may use the present perfect as if it were a narrative past, as is the case in German, and that the simple past or the simple present are used for situations that require a present perfect in English (Swan 2001: 42).[5] Furthermore, he also argued that in order to refer to future events, German learners of English frequently use the simple present tense (Swan 2001: 42). In addition, Swan (2001) identified a number of other common non-target-like English uses by learners with a German background: German lacks an equivalent to the English auxiliary verb *do*, which may result in English questions and negated sentences where this auxiliary verb is omitted, and the German present perfect is formed with a form of *haben* ('have'), like in English, or a form of *sein* ('be') (see again Section 4.3). This may cause German learners of English to also build the present perfect in English with *be* instead of *have*, to name just two of these potential difficulties (Swan 2001: 41).

Davydova (2011: 275), however, made some interesting observations based on intermediate German learners of English when analyzing spontaneous spoken language. Although one could expect that German learners overuse the present perfect in definite past time contexts in English (as the present perfect is frequently used for definite past time reference in German, particularly in spoken discourse), Davydova (2011: 288) only rarely found this in her study. Instead, she observed that the simple past is the default tense when referring to the past. She argued that the reason for this infrequent present perfect usage could be explained by "the semantic mismatch between the German *Perfekt* and the English present perfect" (Davydova 2011: 288). Thus, in order to avoid potential mistakes in English with an inappropriate present perfect use due to insecurity of the learners, this form is replaced by the simple past tense form, almost like a default past tense (Davydova 2011: 289). In addition, Davydova (2011: 280) observed that the present tense – and not the present perfect, as would be target-like in English – is frequently used for "extended-now contexts." As previously mentioned, this can be motivated by transfer from German, since in this context, the simple present would be used, and not a perfect form, as in *Ich warte hier seit drei Stunden* (which would result in the word-by-word translation **I wait here since three hours*, although a more target-like English translation would be *I have waited here for three hours*) (Davydova 2011: 281).

5.3.2 *Russian learners of English*

Recall that Russian has many verb pairs that transmit a different meaning because of their grammatical aspect (either perfective or imperfective). Thus, most English verbs could be translated with two different Russian verb forms, such as *do* may either be translated as Russian imperfective *delat* 'to be doing something' or imperfective *sdelat* 'to have done something' (Pavlenko 2003: 45). Moreover, since Russian has only one past tense form, there are multiple translational equivalents in English (i.e., simple past, present perfect, past perfect) for a Russian past tense verb. One could say that Russian is underspecified here. Consider the following examples, the perfective (1) and imperfective (2) verb of the English equivalent *leave*, provided by Pavlenko (2003: 45):

(1) *ushel* 'left, has left, had left'
(2) *ukhodil* 'was leaving, left several times, used to leave'

Pavlenko (2003: 45) therefore argued that "Russian learners of English find the English tense system challenging" as the English and Russian tense and aspect systems differ considerably. Some support for this observation is offered by Flashner (1989). She reported findings from a study based on oral production in the foreign language English by three Russian native speakers. Flashner (1989: 95) argued for crosslinguistic influence from Russian in the English performance, as she found that prototypical perfective contexts in the English production were expressed with simple past forms and that imperfective situations appeared for the most part in the base form. Flashner (1989: 96) thus argued that the Russian speakers transferred their past/non-past opposition to their oral English production (for a more detailed description of the individual performance of each speaker, see Flashner 1989: 77–95).

Further evidence comes from Monk and Burak (2001) who provide an overview of typical learner mistakes of Russian learners of English. Due to the absence of present perfect or present progressive tenses in Russian, Russian learners may use the simple present in contexts that would require a progressive or perfect form in English, as in **Where you go now?* (instead of *Where are you going now?*) or **How long you are here?* (instead of *How long have you been here?*) (Monk and Burak 2001: 152). The same applies to past tenses, where Russian learners may use the simple past instead of the past perfect or past progressive as in **I read when he came home* (instead of *I was reading when he came home*) (Monk and Burak 2001: 152). This nicely illustrates what Pavlenko (2003: 45) meant by having multiple English translation equivalents for one verb form in Russian. Two further areas of common learner errors are, according to Monk and Burak (2001: 152, 154), the frequent omission of the third person singular *–s* as well as the omission of the copula verb *be* in the present tense. Given what was discussed earlier, the former, however, may be argued to be a general difficulty for learners of English. The latter can be motivated because there is no copula verb in the present tense in Russian (see again Section 4.4). This may lead to mistakes such as **He good boy* (instead of *He is a good boy*) (Monk and Burak 2001: 154).

Davydova (2011), who considered different L2 learners of English, also mentioned some features of intermediate Russian speakers of English (or in her terminology "mesolectal" speakers of English in Russia (Davydova 2011: 15–16)). Like Monk and Burak (2001), she explained that the frequent omission of the copula verb *be* in the present tense, which occurs much less frequently in the past tense, is likely to be a sign of influence from Russian (Davydova 2011: 27–28). Also, the progressive aspect may be overgeneralized to habitual contexts which would require simple aspect in English; or the present perfect may also be used in contexts with explicit reference to a past time event instead of a verb in the simple past (Davydova 2011: 28, 266). What she also observed, however, is that in typical English present perfect contexts, such as "in resultative, experiential and recent past time contexts," the Russian learners do not use the present perfect but rely on the simple past instead (Davydova 2011: 261). Contrary to what she argued for German learners of English (see Section 5.3.1), Davydova (2011: 289–290) submitted that the infrequent use of the present perfect in these contexts as well as for contexts with specific past time reference can be explained with L1 influence (see also Pavlenko 2003: 45). Moreover, she also reported that the present tense may be used for situations that have started in the past but are still relevant at the moment of speaking and which would typically occur with a perfect form as in *I'm studying French for five years* (instead of *I have been studying French for five years*) (Davydova 2011: 28, 261).

5.3.3 Turkish learners of English

Based on the discussion in Section 4.5, several potential difficulties were established with respect to the acquisition and use of tense and aspect for Turkish learners of English. For instance, contrary to English, the Turkish progressive aspect can also be used with verbs expressing stative meanings, and the Turkish past tense suffix is used for contexts that correspond in English to both simple past and present perfect situations.

In a small-scale study using contrastive analysis, Abushihab (2014: 217) found a considerable number of errors (15 percent of the mistakes identified in the students' writings) related to the use of tense and aspect in English. Based on English writings of Turkish university students (n = 20), Abushihab (2014) reported incorrect uses of the present progressive (instead of the target-like simple present form), and the simple present or simple past was erroneously used where a present perfect form should appear in English. More precisely, 26 percent of all tense and aspect errors in the students' English writings pertained to verbs used in the simple past instead of the present perfect. These non-target-like uses can be explained with (negative) transfer effects from Turkish (Abushihab 2014: 213) and can be linked to the previous discussion.

Çakır (2011) took a more educational perspective and focused on teaching the English tense and aspectual system to Turkish learners of English (university level). Çakır (2011: 124–125) analyzed written exams of first year students from various departments (n = 330) and reported the frequent misuse of the present progressive form instead of the simple present form. Especially stative verbs, such as *know*, *believe*, and *like*, which are typically not used with a progressive meaning in English, were used in the progressive aspect by some students (Çakır 2011: 125). Moreover, like Abushihab (2014), Çakır (2011: 125–126) remarked that Turkish learners of English found it particularly difficult to use the present and past perfect correctly and that as a consequence, the simple past was often used in place of the present perfect. In some cases, the present progressive occurred instead of the target-like present perfect (Çakır 2011: 126). Again, this can be explained with interference from the L1 Turkish. Furthermore, another rather common grammatical error, according to Çakır (2011: 126), was the overgeneralization of a past tense form of *be* instead of using the simple past tense of the main verb. This could result in sentences like, **He was study English yesterday* (instead of *He studied English yesterday*) (Çakır 2011: 126). He explained this as a typical developmental process, namely that particularly early learners of English produced such simple past tense forms (Çakır 2011: 126).

In addition, Thompson (2001) reported, similar to what Swan (2001) did for Russian learners of English, typical mistakes of Turkish learners of English as observed by English language teachers. The use of the copula verb *be* appeared to be an area of difficulty and was frequently omitted, presumably because of the lack of a Turkish equivalent (Thompson 2001: 219; see also Section 4.5). Moreover, as also pointed out by Çakır (2011), Turkish learners of English may incorrectly use the progressive aspect with stative verbs or for habitual situations, which could result in non-target-like uses as in **I am knowing her* (instead of *I know her*) or **I am seeing her every day* (instead of *I see her every day*) (Thompson 2001: 220). Furthermore, for situations that have started in the past and are still ongoing, learners with a Turkish L1 may use the present tense and not the target-like present perfect as in **I learn English since three years* (instead of *I have learned English for three years*)[6] (Thompson 2001: 220). Moreover, Thompson (2001: 220) reported that the past perfect may be used for events with a definite reference to a past situation relatively far away from the moment of speaking although in English, the simple past would be target-like, as in **This castle had been built 600 years ago* (instead of *This castle was built 600 years ago*). Finally, the different constructions used to refer to the future in English may constitute another area of confusion. Thompson (2001: 220) mentioned the non-target-like use of the simple present instead of the *will*-future particularly with requests, promises, or for unavoidable outcomes as in **Don't drop it – it breaks!* (instead of *Don't drop it – it will break!*).

5.3.4 Vietnamese learners of English

As detailed in Section 4.6, Vietnamese does not morphologically mark tense and aspect, and often optional tense markers are omitted as the context serves as a cue for temporal distinctions. This is a crucial difference to the previously discussed languages, and this may be reflected in the output of learners of English with Vietnamese as their L1.

In a longitudinal study, Sato (1990) investigated how two young children (10 and 12 years old) with a Vietnamese background acquire English in an American foster family (see also Sato 1988). This sample is based on conversational data recorded over a period of 10 months. Even though this sample is highly context specific and includes only two speakers (Sato 1990: 51–52), some interesting observations relevant for the current study can be extracted. In her analysis of past tense marking, Sato (1990: 66, 84–85) observed overall only few past tense verbs; if a past tense form was used, then it occurred only with lexical verbs (for instance *saw*) and not with the inflectional past tense marker. In addition, there was hardly any increase of past tense forms visible during the 10-month period of the study in the speech of the two L1 Vietnamese learners of English (Sato 1990: 66). Sato (1990: 68) argued that this observation could be attributed to transfer effects from the speakers' L1, as in Vietnamese, consonant clusters do not appear in syllable-final position. A regular past tense form in English, however, has a syllable-final consonant cluster, such as /kt/ in *walked*, the past tense form of *walk*. Producing this in speech may therefore be difficult for these learners of English. Another explanation for the infrequent use of past tense forms may be the lack of morphological tense and aspect marking in Vietnamese, which may have influenced the speech of these two young learners.

This difficulty with past tense morphology finds some support in Schleppegrell and Go (2007). In their study, the written text performance of four young ESL learners (school years five and six), originally from Vietnam, but who had moved to the United States a year earlier, were analyzed (Schleppegrell and Go 2007: 529). For this investigation, the foreign language learners were asked to engage in a typical classroom activity, namely, to narrate a past experience in form of a short text (Schleppegrell and Go 2007: 530). The analysis revealed that "tense marking is not a feature of these writers' grammatical repertoires" (Schleppegrell and Go 2007: 536). One child exclusively relied on present tense verbs even though they occurred in conjunction with past tense adverbials such as *last time*. Moreover, the inconsistent use of past versus present tense verbs in another student's text or the limited use of past tense verbs, as only the irregular verb *said* was used in the text of the third student, also indicated lack of control of using the past tense in English (Schleppegrell and Go 2007: 536). The fourth text, supposedly written by the most advanced user of English, even showed some *–ing* forms, which could be early indications of progressive uses (Schleppegrell and Go 2007: 537). Since the aim of this study was not to investigate the use of tense and aspect, the authors did not elaborate on this further. However, the texts of the four students are available, which makes an additional inspection possible. For the current study, this had been done cursorily. It is quite striking that even though *–ing* forms occur in the fourth text, the auxiliary verb is completely absent, resulting in forms such as **Everybody clapping* or *he playing (Schleppegrell and Go 2007: 534). Furthermore, present and past tense forms are also used inconsistently, and the third person singular *–s* is frequently omitted, as in **he know everything* and

He think (Schleppegrell and Go 2007: 534). Similar learner errors are visible in the other three texts. Here as well, third person singular *–s* is practically completely lacking, and there are also examples where the copula verb is missing, as in **He very kind to the students* and **he very good of this game* (Schleppegrell and Go 2007: 532–533).

The final case study discussed here employs a grammaticality judgment task instead of production data (McDonald 2000: 402). McDonald (2000: 399, 408) investigated how L1 Vietnamese affects the acquisition of English by comparing early learners (age of acquisition at five or younger; *n* = 14) and child learners (age of acquisition at six to ten; *n* = 10) of English.[7] All learners grew up in the United States (they were either born in this country or had relocated at the age of five or earlier) and were between 18 and 24 years old at the time of testing. Their performance was compared to native English speaker responses. The grammaticality judgment task included sentences which tested the formation of the past tense and present progressive, the use of plural and third person singular *–s*, as well as the use of auxiliaries to form tenses, among others (McDonald 2000: 402). The results show that overall, both learner groups (early as well as child learners) scored lower on the grammaticality judgment task in comparison to the English native speakers. The main differences pertained to sentences including inflections (past tense, plural formation, subject-verb agreement), except for the use of auxiliaries (McDonald 2000: 410–413). This lines up with expectations. Considering the features of Vietnamese introduced in Section 4.6, the learners in McDonald's (2000) study were found to have difficulties with inflectional endings, which may be explained by negative transfer from the L1 Vietnamese.

Finally, in line with what has been reported for German, Russian, and Turkish learners of English, a more educational perspective is offered here as well, based on a discussion of difficulties or typical errors of learners of English with a Vietnamese background. Based on a crosslinguistic analysis of Vietnamese and English in addition to occasional anecdotal evidence, Tang (2007) presented potential interactions or contexts of transfer between Vietnamese and English.[8] Clearly in line with the preceding discussion, Tang (2007: 21) identified a number of potential difficulties for English learners at the level of grammar, which may result in the omission of inflectional endings for tense (*–ed*) and subject-verb agreement (*–s*), as well as the omission of auxiliary verbs (*are*, *is*). Thus, Vietnamese learners of English may use a verb in the present tense (i.e., without an inflectional ending) instead of a past tense verb to refer to the past (Tang 2007: 22). This observation was based on the lack of morphological markers for tense in Vietnamese. Finally, Tang (2007: 21) curtailed this list of learner difficulties and maintained that not all L2 learners of English with a Vietnamese background will exhibit all patterns but that, particularly, adult or adolescent learners who study it as a second language may exhibit these features in their language production. Moreover, age of onset, among other learner characteristics, might play a decisive role.

5.4 Summary

This chapter investigated two types of language acquisition, namely first and second language acquisition of English. The preceding discussion has shown, by zooming in on how different learners of English acquire tense and aspect, that there are manifold differences in the acquisition and use of English by those who learn it as a second language. These manifested in distinct patterns of language output which differed from those reported for native speakers of English. In opposition, the section on the acquisition of tense and aspect by native speakers of English was considerably shorter and included several developmental stages which appeared to be relatively stable across all L1 English learners (see, for example, Brown 1973 who suggested an acquisition order of grammatical morphemes). This is in line with Meisel (2011: 241) who pointed out that one characteristic of L1 acquisition is "that children unfailingly attain full knowledge of the grammatical system and that the developmental process exhibits remarkable similarities across individuals and across languages." Thus, even though young children undeniably have different conditions under which they acquire their native language (for instance cognitive, social, or contextual differences), they normally reach a high level of grammatical knowledge after a relatively short amount of time (Meisel 2011: 241–244).[9]

The questions that arise are which ways L2 acquisition differs from L1 acquisition and why the acquisition and use of an L2 is not characterized by full or "successful attainment of native grammatical knowledge" and why there is more variation among L2 speakers (Meisel 2011: 244). Not all of these can be answered in the current study. However, it is noteworthy to point out that one crucial (and thus also the most obvious) difference between L1 and L2 speakers is that the latter have access to more than one language. The previously acquired language influences the acquisition process of the second language, potentially resulting in typical learner errors or non-target-like language production. Some specific examples have been elaborated on in Section 5.3 with respect to the acquisition of tense and aspect by German, Russian, Turkish, and Vietnamese learners of English. Furthermore, L2 learners are by and large an even more heterogeneous group than L1 learners. In addition to the different learning conditions mentioned above for L1 learners (i.e., cognitive, social, or contextual differences), these are further extended for L2 learners, as they may have different ages of onset or different motivations, to name but these two (see Meisel 2011: 8–9; see also Carroll 2001 on further aspects of second language acquisition).

In addition to these distinct acquisitional paths for learners with different L1s, there also seem to be grammatical areas that are particularly difficult for all L2 learners, such as the progressive aspect (see, for example, Bland 1988; see also Mauranen 2017: 239 on the use of the progressive in English as a Lingua Franca (ELF) contexts). However, as Fuchs and Werner (2018b: 213–214) discovered, learners with different L1s showed distinct patterns of progressive uses that could be explained by whether the L1 has a grammaticalized progressive aspect or not. Similarly, Davydova (2011: 289) remarked that the present perfect is arguably a challenging category for any non-native learner, but that it becomes particularly difficult if it is absent in the L1. Finally, the use of the third person singular *–s* was repeatedly mentioned as an especially difficult grammatical concept, frequently resulting in omission of this inflectional ending (see, for example, Bardovi-Harlig 2013; Luk 2013).

Notes

1 For more information on first language acquisition, including but not limited to the acquisition of tense and aspect, see, for example, Clark (2009) and Meisel (2011), or for the development of English verbal morphology based on a case study with one child, see Gülzow (2003).
2 Shirai (2009: 170) proposed that because of the frequently occurring "redundancy in language, often times adults do not have to process grammatical information." Arguably, the lexical means is more salient to the learner vis-à-vis the grammatical means.
3 From today's perspective, this proposal was overoptimistic and modeled on L1 acquisition. Yet, as previous research has shown (see, for example, Chapter 3), L2 acquisition needs to be studied in its own right.
4 More information about the Aspect Hypothesis can be found, for example, in Andersen and Shirai (1994), Bardovi-Harlig (2000), Fuchs and Werner (2018a, 2018b), Li and Shirai (2000), and Shirai (2009).
5 An interesting and perhaps related development can be observed in Australian English. A fairly recent observation shows that there are attested uses of the present perfect tense which occur in typical simple past tense contexts in Australian English (see, for example, Collins and Peters 2004: 597–598; Engel and Ritz 2000: 130–131; Siemund 2019: 616). This may even be an instance of language contact, as there are many German immigrants in Australia (Peter Siemund, p.c.).
6 Here, an additional difficulty arises. Turkish does not have separate words for *since* and *for*, which may result in non-target-like usage of these as visible in this example (Thompson 2001: 220).
7 This study consisted of two experiments. Experiment one included Spanish learners of English and experiment two Vietnamese learners of English. For the current study, only experiment two is considered.
8 Tang (2007) also considered the reverse, i.e., the influence of L1 English on L2 Vietnamese, but this is disregarded in the current study.
9 There are of course children who suffer from specific language impairments, which interfere with the development of language acquisition, and who may

never fully master their native language. Moreover, native speakers also show variation in the acquisition and use of their L1, although L1 acquisition is characterized by more "uniformity" than L2 acquisition (Meisel 2011: 245).

References

Abushihab, I. 2014. An analysis of grammatical errors in writing made by Turkish learners of English as a foreign language. *International Journal of Linguistics* 6:213–223.

Andersen, R. W. and Y. Shirai. 1994. Discourse motivations for some cognitive acquisition principles. *Studies in Second Language Acquisition* 16:133–156.

Bardovi-Harlig, K. 2000. *Tense and aspect in second language acquisition: Form, meaning, and use.* Oxford: Blackwell.

Bardovi-Harlig, K. 2013. Acquisition of tense and aspect. In *The Routledge encyclopedia of second language acquisition*, ed. P. Robinson, 6–8. New York/London: Routledge.

Bardovi-Harlig, K. and D. W. Reynolds. 1995. The role of lexical aspect in the acquisition of tense and aspect. *TESOL Quarterly* 29:107–131.

Biber, D., S. Johannson, G. Leech, S. Conrad, and E. Finegan. 2000. *Longman grammar of spoken and written English.* Harlow, UK: Longman.

Bland, S. K. 1988. The present progressive in discourse: Grammar versus usage revisited. *TESOL Quarterly* 22:53–68.

Brown, R. 1973. *A first language: The early stages.* Cambridge, MA: Harvard University Press.

Çakır, İ. 2011. Problems in teaching tenses to Turkish learners. *Theory and Practice in Language Studies* 1:123–127.

Carroll, S. E. 2001. *Input and evidence: The raw material of second language acquisition.* Amsterdam: Benjamins.

Clark, E. V. 2009. *First language acquisition.* 2nd edn. Cambridge: Cambridge University Press.

Collins, P. and P. Peters. 2004. Australian English: Morphology and syntax. In *A handbook of varieties of English. Volume 2: Morphology and syntax*, ed. B. Kortmann, K. Burridge, R. Mesthrie, E. W. Schneider, and C. Upton, 593–610. Berlin/New York: De Gruyter Mouton.

Davies, M. 2004. *British National Corpus (BNC)* (from Oxford University Press). Available online at www.english-corpora.org/bnc (accessed April 4, 2022).

Davies, M. 2008–. *The Corpus of Contemporary American English (COCA).* Available online at www.english-corpora.org/coca (accessed April 4, 2022).

Davydova, J. 2011. *The present perfect in non-native Englishes: A corpus-based study of variation.* Berlin/Boston: De Gruyter Mouton.

Dose-Heidelmayer, S. and S. Götz. 2016. The progressive in spoken learner language: A corpus-based analysis of use and misuse. *International Review of Applied Linguistics* 54:229–256.

Ellis, R. 2015. *Understanding second language acquisition.* 2nd edn. Oxford: Oxford University Press.

Engel, D. M. and M. E. A. Ritz. 2000. The use of the present perfect in Australian English. *Australian Journal of Linguistics* 20:119–140.

Erling, E. J. 2002. 'I learn English since ten years': The global English debate and the German university classroom. *English Today* 18:8–13.

Flashner, V. E. 1989. Transfer of aspect in the English oral narratives of native Russian speakers. In *Transfer in language production*, ed. H. W. Dechert and M. Raupach, 71–97. Norwood, NJ: Ablex.

Fuchs, R. and V. Werner. 2018a. Tense and aspect in second language acquisition and learner corpus research: Introduction to the special issue. *International Journal of Learner Corpus Research* 4:143–263.

Fuchs, R. and V. Werner. 2018b. The use of stative progressives by school-age learners of English and the importance of the variable context: Myth vs (corpus) reality. *International Journal of Learner Corpus Research* 4:195–224.

Gülzow, I. 2003. Early development of verbal morphology in an English-speaking child. In *Development of verb inflection in first language acquisition: A crosslinguistic perspective*, ed. D. Bittner, W. U. Dressler, and M. Kilani-Schoch, 205–238. Berlin: De Gruyter Mouton.

Hickey, R. 2020. English in the German-speaking world: The nature and scale of language influence. In *English in the German-speaking world*, ed. R. Hickey, 1–10. Cambridge: Cambridge University Press.

König, E. 1994. English. In *The Germanic languages*, ed. E. König and J. van der Auwera, 532–565. London/New York: Routledge.

König, E. and V. Gast. 2018. *Understanding English-German contrasts*. 4th edn. Berlin: Erich Schmidt Verlag.

Kranich, S. 2010. *The progressive in modern English: A corpus-based study of grammaticalization and related changes*. Amsterdam/New York: Rodopi.

Krashen, S. D. 1977. Some issues relating to the monitor model. In *On TESOL'77: Teaching and Learning English as a second language: Trends in research practice*, ed. H. Brown, C. Yorio, and R. Crymes, 144–158. Washington, DC: TESOL.

Li, P. and Y. Shirai. 2000. *The acquisition of lexical and grammatical aspect*. Berlin: De Gruyter Mouton.

Luk, Z. P. 2013. Morpheme acquisition orders. In *The Routledge encyclopedia of second language acquisition*, ed. P. Robinson, 441–443. New York/London: Routledge.

Luk, Z. P. and Y. Shirai. 2009. Is the acquisition order of grammatical morphemes impervious to L1 knowledge? Evidence from the acquisition of plural –s, articles, and possessive 's. *Language Learning* 59:721–754.

Mauranen, A. 2017. A glimpse of ELF. In *Changing English: Global and local perspectives*, ed. M. Filppula, J. Klemola, A. Mauranen, and S. Vetchinnikova, 223–253. Berlin: De Gruyter Mouton.

McDonald, J. 2000. Grammaticality judgments in a second language: Influences of age of acquisition and native language. *Applied Psycholinguistics* 21:395–423.

Meisel, J. M. 2011. *First and second language acquisition: Parallels and differences*. Cambridge: Cambridge University Press.

Meriläinen, L., H. Paulasto, and P. Rautionaho. 2017. Extended uses of the progressive form in inner, outer and expanding circle Englishes. In *Changing English: Global and local perspectives*, ed. M. Filppula, J. Klemola, A. Mauranen, and S. Vetchinnikova, 191–215. Berlin: De Gruyter Mouton.

Monk, B. and A. Burak. 2001. Russian speakers. In *Learner English: A teacher's guide to interference and other problems*, 2nd edn, ed. M. Swan and B. Smith, 145–161. Cambridge: Cambridge University Press.

Pavlenko, A. 2003. "I feel clumsy speaking Russian": L2 influence on L1 in narratives of Russian L2 users of English. In *Effects of the second language on the first*, ed. V. Cook, 32–61. Clevedon: Multilingual Matters.

Rautionaho, P. 2014. *Variation in the progressive: A corpus-based study into world Englishes*. Tampere: Tampere University Press.

Rothstein, S. 2004. *Structuring events: A study in the semantics of lexical aspect*. Oxford: Blackwell.

Sato, C. J. 1988. Origins of complex syntax in interlanguage development. *Studies in Second Language Acquisition* 10:371–395.

Sato, C. J. 1990. *The syntax of conversation in interlanguage development*. Tübingen: Gunter Narr Verlag.

Schleppegrell, M. J. and A. L. Go. 2007. Analyzing the writing of English learners: A functional approach. *Language Arts* 84:529–538.

Shirai, Y. 2009. Temporality in first and second language acquisition. In *The expression of time*, ed. W. Klein and P. Li, 167–194. Berlin: De Gruyter Mouton.

Siemund, P. 2019. Regional varieties of English: Non-standard grammatical features. In *Oxford handbook of English grammar*, ed. B. Aarts, J. Bowie, and G. Popova, 604–629. Oxford: Oxford University Press.

Swan, M. 2001. German speakers. In *Learner English: A teacher's guide to interference and other problems*, 2nd edn, ed. M. Swan and B. Smith, 37–51. Cambridge: Cambridge University Press.

Swan, M. 2005. *Practical English usage*. 3rd edn. Oxford: Oxford University Press.

Tang, G. 2007. Cross-linguistic analysis of Vietnamese and English with implications for Vietnamese language acquisition and maintenance in the United States. *Journal of Southeast Asian American Education and Advancement* 2:1–34.

Thompson, I. 2001. Turkish speakers. In *Learner English: A teacher's guide to interference and other problems*, 2nd edn, ed. M. Swan and B. Smith, 214–227. Cambridge: Cambridge University Press.

van Rooy, B. 2014. Progressive aspect and stative verbs in outer circle varieties. *World Englishes* 33:157–172.

6 English learner corpus based on written and spoken stories

6.1 Research design and data collection

The data used for the current study come from the E-LiPS project carried out between 2009 and 2013 at the University of Hamburg. E-LiPS was part of the English LiMA Panel Study directed by Peter Siemund and Ingrid Gogolin. Most of the data were collected between 2009 and 2013 in Germany, Russia, Turkey, and the UK.[1] Then, in 2016 and 2017, additional data collections were carried out by the author to supplement the original dataset. These additional data collections took place in Hamburg, Germany (2016), with an English native speaker control group, and in Hanoi, Vietnam (2017), with monolingual Vietnamese learners of English. The following sections describe the procedures of the written and oral task and present the contents of the background questionnaire. The written and oral output make up the English learner corpus which is the basis of the subsequent linguistic analysis (Chapter 7). In a second step, the English production and the information from the questionnaire are combined to inform about the effect of social factors on the performance in English (Chapter 8). Even though there was a considerable number of people involved in the data collection process over a long period of time, all researchers and student assistants strictly adhered to a set of defined rules to assure a uniform data collection process. The exact procedure will be explained in the three sections that follow.

6.1.1 Written task

The first tasks the participants had to complete consisted of writing a short narrative based on the picture story *Gut gemeint…* ('Good intentions…') by Erich Ohser (2003). The original cartoon (Figure 6.1) is in black and white, but for the current study, a colored version was used. The participants were seated separately in their classroom, and one interviewer and their teacher were present. They were asked to write at least two sentences for each of the six pictures of the story with a time limit of 30 minutes. To ensure comparability, they were not allowed to use any additional help. This means that they could neither use grammar books

DOI: 10.4324/9781003134336-6

English learner corpus 115

Figure 6.1 Picture story *Gut gemeint...* ('Good intentions...').
Source: Erich Ohser (2003).

or dictionaries, nor were the interviewer or teacher authorized to answer questions related to vocabulary or grammar. If such a question came up, an answer was not provided but the interviewer and teacher were asked to reassure the participant and to motivate him or her to think again and to do the task as best as possible.

During the 30 minutes, the interviewer and the teacher made sure that each participant focused only on their worksheet and did not talk to their neighbors or look at their neighbors' writings. Some students refused to write or gave up writing early. Those who did were kindly encouraged to continue and to try to write down a little more. It was always stressed that they should not be afraid of any negative consequences like getting a bad school grade, and that they should write as freely as possible, i.e., whatever came to their minds in that moment. They were reassured that this was not a graded task.

The main aim of this task was to elicit natural learner language in a guided setting. This may seem at first contradictory, especially when considering the premises for *learner corpus research* and the definition of *naturally occurring language*.[2] However, the advantage of such a directed writing task (and as will become apparent later, this is also true for the oral task) is that all participants have, to a certain extent, the same activity setting (see Coughlan and Duff 1994 for a critical look at learner tasks and replicability). Moreover, by selecting a specific set of pictures, the topic and the potential vocabulary can be manipulated, and the specific context of the writing task is known to the researcher, which facilitates a comparison across different learners (Bardovi-Harlig 2000: 199). Hence, the availability of the task and the exact pictures provides useful guidance for the analysis of the written texts. Therefore, it will be possible to compare the language production of the different groups with this peripheral text type.[3]

In addition, picture descriptions or writing short stories are activities that secondary school students are familiar with, because such tasks are introduced in the English classroom early on (see, for instance, Seidl 2006 as one example of an English workbook, school year five). Using picture stories to elicit written (and spoken) language has proven useful and effective for analyzing a number of linguistic features (Pallotti 2010: 171). Yet, Pallotti (2010: 171) remarks that the analysis of tense and aspect may prove difficult, because using either simple present or simple past would be acceptable, and that with such data one can only analyze "the forms that are used, not those that are missing." Nevertheless, this method of using a picture sequence to elicit written production data seems suitable for comparing learner language.

Furthermore, as a natural consequence, certain vocabulary items or grammatical structures will be triggered because of the story that is portrayed in the pictures. However, even if participants are presented with one and the same task, the results need not necessarily be the same. As Coughlan and Duff (1994: 185) explain, "the basic task can be conceptualized differently by different people." Accordingly, the results must be interpreted carefully, because every task or activity is always part of a specific sociocultural setting, and this context affects the task fulfillment and the outcome (Coughlan and Duff 1994: 190).

6.1.2 *Oral task*

Some of the students not only participated in the written task but were also presented with a second picture sequence they had to retell orally. This picture story was created by Simone Lechner (2013), based on Gagarina et al. (2012), as part of the LiMA project. Like the sequence used for the written task, the second picture sequence also consisted of six individual images, this time, however, featuring a hen, her two chickens, a fox, and a dog. The pictures displayed a hen feeding her chickens. They get attacked by a fox, who in turn gets its tail bitten and is chased away by a dog.

The oral task was conducted after the written task. This way the participants had already met the interviewer and were familiar with him or her and with participating in such a study. This was especially crucial for this oral task, considering it is much more intimidating to be recorded while saying something in a foreign language as compared to completing a writing assignment that is presumably recognizable from the activities of foreign language classes. Therefore, in order to familiarize the students as much as possible, this oral task was scheduled last.

Each student was presented the task individually, with only the interviewer present. The assignment was as follows: *Please tell me what you can see happening in the pictures!* Before the actual recording, the student was given some minutes to have a closer look at the pictures and to think about what he or she could say about them. When the participant was ready, the oral production was recorded. Here again, the interviewer was not allowed to answer any questions related to vocabulary or grammar. Especially during this task, the presence of the interviewer potentially interfered with the performance of the students. Various interviewers were involved in the data collection process and small differences, such as smiling or encouragingly nodding, be it consciously or unconsciously, potentially influences the participants (Coughlan and Duff 1994). Although detailed instructions were given to the interviewers prior to the testing, small effects due to differing test conditions cannot be completely ruled out.

6.1.3 Questionnaire

In addition to describing the two picture stories, the students had to fill in two questionnaires. One was about personal information such as age, native language(s), foreign language(s), years of studying English, profession of mother and father, etc. The second was about their attitudes toward English and situations in which they use English outside of school.

For this task, and this is a difference to the two tasks previously described, the students were allowed to ask content questions and to ask for vocabulary. As an example, the students frequently asked for specific vocabulary regarding the question about the profession of their parents. Here again, if students refused to fill in the questionnaires, or if it seemed as if they had not answered every question, they were gently encouraged to have another look at it and to try their best to provide as much information as possible to help with the study.

The following background variables and questions, taken from the questionnaires the participants had to fill in, were selected for this study:

(1) Age of onset of learning German
(2) School type

118   *English learner corpus*

(3) School grades in German and English
(4) Socio-economic status of mother, father, and Highest Socio-Economic Status Value (HISEI) per family
(5) Number of books per household
(6) Language use at home: language use of parents with each other; language use of participants with mother, father, and sibling(s)
(7) Which statement would you agree with?
   a. English is a difficult language. (Yes/No)
   b. English is a useful language. (Yes/No)

In addition, the interviewer filled in a form for each participant containing the following information:

(1) Age
(2) Gender
(3) Language group

6.2 Corpus data coding scheme

This section briefly comments on the transcription process of the handwritten texts and the oral recordings of the learners of English, and it explains the manual annotation process of the learner corpus. It was necessary to transcribe the handwritten texts and the oral recordings to create a machine-readable learner corpus that can be accessed with concordance programs such as AntConc (Anthony 2016). The texts were copied as accurately as possible; however, if a student crossed out a mistake in his or her writing, this was not marked in the corpus. Hence, a sentence such as example (1) appears as sentence (2) in the E-LiPS learner corpus.

(1)   *A mann catcht a fisch off the water.*
(2)   *A mann catcht a fish off the water.*

If a word or individual letters were illegible, the @-symbol was used; the number of @'s within a word represent the number of letters that were unreadable, and a total of four @@@@-symbols demonstrates that the entire word was not decipherable.

The procedure of the oral data description was slightly different. All grammatical and lexical mistakes were transcribed, although no attention was paid to pronunciation (errors). Hence, a non-target-like pronounced /th/, as in *this*, was transcribed as *this* and not as *dis*. Short pauses up to two seconds within the recordings were marked with square brackets, i.e., [...]. If the pause was longer than two seconds, the approximate duration was included within the square brackets. For example, there appears [...5...] in the text for a pause that lasted approximately five seconds. In addition, incomprehensible words were also marked with @-signs to keep it consistent with the transcripts of the written data.

Some students asked short questions in between the recordings, such as *What does this mean?*, or they used filled pauses (see Götz 2013) such as *ehm* or *mh*. Those cases were marked similarly to pauses in square brackets. Comments made by the interviewer were not transcribed. In most recordings, the interviewer said nothing, or only *Thank you very much!* at the end, and therefore, no comments were transcribed.

Furthermore, the students occasionally repeated single words or groups of words. This sometimes co-occurred with pauses. Cases of such repetition were marked with square brackets, and these words were not included in the analysis, meaning that these words were only counted once. Consider examples (3) and (4). The former consists of eight tokens, the latter of six tokens; the lower number was included in the analysis.

(3)　*The fox **the fox** goes to the chicken.*
(4)　*The fox [**the fox**] goes to the chicken.*

The motivation for this was that later, the total number of words used to describe the pictures was calculated. The use of more words is understood as a sign of higher proficiency;[4] yet, if all repetitions were included, this measure would be distorted. In sum, a learner corpus was compiled that consists of 249 written text files, and 176 files of oral recordings. This adds up to a corpus size of 42,887 tokens, separated into a written section (28,427 tokens) and an oral section (14,460 tokens).

These files were then, in a second step, analyzed and manually coded. It should be noted that the use of an automatic tagger was not suitable for the specific language (learner language) and the specific grammatical category (tense and aspect) analyzed in this study. However, for some frequency measures and for the analysis of the progressive aspect, the concordance program AntConc (Anthony 2016) was used. For the sake of consistency, each text was annotated twice by the author. In a second step, these two rounds of coding were compared, and irregularities were adjusted accordingly.

For the following analysis, a subsample of all coding categories was used. These relevant variables are listed below and the ones that require further explanation are described and exemplified thereafter.

(a)　Number of words
(b)　Number of sentences
(c)　Number of verb tokens
(d)　Number of verb types
(e)　Type-token-ratio verbs
(f)　Number of infinitives, *to*-infinitives, gerunds, progressives, present progressives, past progressives, simple presents, simple pasts,

present perfects, past perfects, *will*-futures, *going-to*-futures, passives, modals, conditionals, imperatives
(g) Number of copula verbs
(h) Number of missing copula verbs
(i) Number of auxiliary verbs
(j) Number of missing auxiliary verbs
(k) Number of required third person singular *–s*
(l) Number of missing third person singular *–s*
(m) Overuse of third person singular *–s*
(n) Correct subject-verb agreement (suppletive verbs)
(o) Incorrect subject-verb agreement (suppletive verbs)
(p) Correct form of progressive aspect
(q) Target-like meaning of progressive aspect
(r) Number of grammatically correct verbs
(s) Number of verbs with target-like meaning
(t) Use of present or past tense
(u) Consistent use of tense or unmotivated switch

In addition to the overall number of words, the numbers of verb tokens and types were counted separately. This differentiation is important, because many students used the same verbs repeatedly, and this type-token ratio of verbs informs about lexical variability within one text. In addition, each verb was labeled according to the (presumed) tense/aspect/function (see (f) above). Examples (5) to (19) represent the available categorizations.

(5) *His Grandpa sugest, that he cut him to death.* (infinitive)
(6) *So they decided to return the fish to its home.* (*to*-infinitive)
(7) *From that day on baby Ron re has stopped eating fish.* (gerund)
(8) *The young boy is looking into the cup.* (present progressive)
(9) *The sun was shining.* (past progressive)
(10) *The boy is happy.* (simple present)
(11) *They waited for hours on end without any results.* (simple past)
(12) *And the son has looked on the fish.* (present perfect)
(13) *Happy about what they had caught Jack and Bob go home.* (past perfect)
(14) *At home Harry will kill the fish for eat.* (*will*-future)
(15) *The cute fish going to die.* (*going-to*-future)
(16) *The fish was put in a bucket of water.* (passive)
(17) *But the fish can't swim away.* (modal)
(18) *But even if he wants to kill him, his son is very sad and tears come from his eyes.* (conditional)
(19) *"Don't kill the fish, Dad."* (imperative)

Moreover, missing verbs were marked. This could be either a copula verb, an auxiliary verb, or a main verb (see (20) to (22)).

(20) *The cute fish ⌀ going to die.* (auxiliary verb missing)
(21) *They ⌀ happy.* (copula missing)
(22) *But Bennie would'nt ⌀ it.* (main verb missing)

Another crucial category is the use of subject-verb agreement. For this purpose, a categorization into grammatical uses of third person singular –*s*, omissions, and overuses (i.e., an –*s* appears but no inflectional ending is required) was employed. Thus, the sum of all grammatical uses plus the non-uses represents the number of third person singular –*s* endings that should have appeared in each text or recording.

To distinguish between regular and irregular verbs, subject-verb agreement of suppletive verbs was considered as a separate category. Hence, a distinction was made between verbs that have the inflectional ending –*s*, and between verbs, such as *be*, that have a more complex verbal paradigm (see (23) to (26)).

(23) *David take a fish and he go_ at home with Bennie.* (third person singular –*s* missing)
(24) *The man and the boy look**s** angry.* (overuse of third person singular –*s*)
(25) *They **are** happy.* (correct subject-verb agreement)
(26) *Both of them **was** happy.* (incorrect subject-verb agreement)

All occurring progressives in the students' writings were counted and classified according to formal correctness and target-like use of the verb (see also Lorenz 2019). Formal correctness relates to spelling mistakes, for example **lauthing* versus *laughing*, and the absence or presence of the auxiliary verb, for example **the boy looking* versus *the boy is looking*. Target-like use denotes that the verb represents a verb that is commonly used in the progressive aspect for the situation portrayed in the picture, i.e., describing an action or ongoing situation, based on the standard reference grammars (Biber et al. 2000; Huddleston and Pullum 2002; Swan 2005), on the *aktionsart* of the verb (Vendler 1957), but also in comparison with the English native speaker control group that was presented with the same task and the same picture story. Examples (27) and (28) demonstrate two grammatically incorrect sentences; yet, they differ in the type of error. Sentence (27) is formally correct, but the use of the verb *see* in this particular meaning 'being able to see someone or something' is non-target-like. The opposite scenario is represented by sentence (28). This sentence is formally incorrect because the auxiliary verb *be* in the correct form is missing. The verb *walk*, however, expresses an activity and it is commonly used in the progressive aspect. Therefore, this sentence is coded as having target-like meaning.

(27) *They **were seeing** a much bigger fish [...].*
(28) *The man and child **walking**.*

Let us briefly consider sentence (27), to motivate the choice to label this as a 'non-target-like progressive'. The expression *were seeing* is a formally correct past progressive form, i.e., the spelling is accurate because of the presence of a form of the verb *be* plus the suffix *–ing*. However, the verb *see* is not commonly used in the progressive aspect in English, and here, in particular, the verb should be in the simple form and not in the progressive to adhere to grammar rules. It is, of course, possible to formulate a sentence with the verb *see* in the progressive aspect, such as *She was seeing a police officer*. Yet, the meaning of this sentence contrasts with the meaning of the simple form *She saw a police officer*. The former describes a situation where a female person was dating a police officer, and in the latter sentence, a woman could simply perceive with her eyes that there was a police officer present (see again Section 4.2 for the use of the English progressive). Of course, it is not easy to state with certainty what the writer of the story wanted to say; however, since the pictures are available and were the basis for the story in the first place, it is possible to make educated guesses of the intended meaning of the verb. Based on this, example (27) is assumed to have the intended meaning of 'to perceive someone or something'.

Several examples that could not be clearly identified or categorized remain. Consider the following examples.

(29) *Children **is** cry*.
(30) *The man **is** throw the fish in river*.
(31) *The child **is** sees fish*.
(32) *They **ayt** a fish in river. Fish was happy*.

The verbal uses in the format *is* and a main verb (see examples (29), (30), and (31)) could be classified either as a form of the progressive, where the *–ing* ending is missing, such as *is throwing*, or it could be a way of trying to use the simple present form of a verb, such as *cries*, but incorrectly formed with a form of *be* and the plain form. Therefore, examples like these were marked as unanalyzable verb forms.[5] The same applies to examples such as (32); the meaning of the verb (*ayt*) can neither be unambiguously identified, nor the form assigned to a specific tense. The final plosive /t/ could indicate that it is a simple past form, and the rest of this text is also mainly written in the simple past, yet it remains unclear.[6]

The analysis follows a *meaning-oriented approach* (Bardovi-Harlig 2000: 22–25) which focuses on the devices and the range of devices that the students used in their written and oral picture descriptions. A *meaning-oriented study* targets (i) how the learners express temporality and aspectuality; (ii) how this temporal reference and aspectual reference change in the course of time; and (iii) the factors that explain a development over time in contrast with the target-like use of the relevant temporal and aspectual devices (Bardovi-Harlig 2000: 23). The following study concentrates on these three questions with an extended focus. The study is not limited to the development over time, but it also relates the performance and the development to the different languages the participants know.

Moreover, tense and aspect can be expressed not only with verbal morphology, as in adding *–ed* to an English verb in the base form. Locative adverbials (i.e., *now, yesterday, afterwards, today*), connectives (i.e., *then, and, meanwhile, after*), specific reference points (i.e., *first of October, Independence Day*), nouns (i.e., *Monday, weekend*), or verbs (i.e., *begin, end*) can also be used to structure a story and to express time reference and aspectual relations (Bardovi-Harlig 2000: 36). This means, that independent of the grammatical system of a language, there is an interplay between several devices to express time, reference, and aspect. Bardovi-Harlig states that "The verbal categories of tense, aspect, and lexical aspect interact with each other and with adverbials, the type of text, and the order of mention" (2000: 36). Furthermore, there is not only an interaction between morphological devices and lexical devices, but studies with adult learners of a second language have shown that the learners are able to convey temporal relations even when the tense and aspect morphology has not yet been acquired (Bardovi-Harlig 2000: chapter 2).

A further point is the differentiation between *form* and *function* (Bardovi-Harlig 1992, 2000). This has already been introduced when discussing the coding of the progressive aspect. According to Bardovi-Harlig (2000: 120), such a two-tier coding system allows the analyst to recognize attempts at producing target-like language, which thus uncovers differences in the level of proficiency between the individual groups. Bardovi-Harlig reports results from cross-sectional studies and describes the usefulness of such an approach because it allows one to detect a development and it does not simply portray the end-state result (2000: 120). The advantage of this two-tier coding scheme can be demonstrated with examples (33) and (34) (the latter is sentence (27) from above, here repeated for reasons of readability).

(33) *[…] they **caugchet** the fish […]*
(34) *They **were seeing** a much bigger fish […]*

(33) is formally inaccurate, yet the use of the simple past is appropriate in this position of the story and represents a target-like use. On the contrary, as was explained above, the use of the progressive aspect for the verb *see* is contextually inappropriate in (34).

Analogously to these two sentences, all verbal uses were coded according to formal correctness and target-like usage (Bardovi-Harlig 1992; see also Lorenz 2019). The former only considers the correct expression of tenses and aspectual distinctions, including the presence of an auxiliary verb, the use of correct inflectional endings, and correct subject-verb agreement, regardless of whether this particular tense was appropriate in that context or not. The latter measure ignores formal errors and targets the assumed tense by distinguishing between target-like or non-target-like meaning. Special attention is paid to consistency. Unmotivated switches between tenses are coded as non-target-like uses. Unmotivated refers, for example, to verbs that are in a different tense than the previous and following verbs. Consider the short passage in (35) as one such example. This story from one of the participants is written in the simple past; however, the verb *throw* appears in the simple present. Hence, this use of *throw* is coded as 'formally correct', but it is also categorized as a 'non-target-like use'.[7] These decisions are based on contextual information (i.e., the picture stories) in addition to consulting standard reference grammars (Biber et al. 2000; Huddleston and Pullum 2002; Swan 2005).

(35) *So father and son went back to the sea. Alex was very proud of his father! They **throw** the fish in the sea. And Alex was very happy.*

The final coding category is related to this last classification in that it is about the main or overall tense (mainly) used throughout each text to assess how consistently they were composed. Three measures are differentiated, namely 'present', 'past', and 'mixed'. If verbs are exclusively used in the present tense, or if no more than three past tense forms appear, the text is classified as 'present'. The same applies to past tense. If there is considerable variation, as in alternating between simple and past tense, or if there are four or more verbs of one tense, and the rest of the verbs are written in another tense, the text is labeled 'mixed'.

6.3 Profile of participants

6.3.1 General

Eight different learner groups participated in the study, i.e., monolingual German, Russian, Turkish, and Vietnamese speakers, Russian-German, Turkish-German, and Vietnamese-German speakers, and an English native speaker control group (Table 6.1). All monolingual learners (except the English native speakers) were raised with one language and these students learn the foreign language English as their second language in school. The bilingual participants are considered heritage speakers, because they immigrated with their families to Germany during their early years or were already born in Germany to parents/one parent who have/has immigrated in the past. These bilinguals speak German, which is the language of the environment and the language of instruction in school, in addition to either Russian, Turkish, or Vietnamese, which is considered their heritage language. They are characterized as unbalanced bilinguals, because German is their majority or dominant language, i.e., the language they are most proficient in and the language they use most frequently in their daily lives. The heritage language is their weaker language, and it is typically only used in the family context (further information at the end of Section 6.3.2).

The native English speakers who function as a control group do not represent monolingual speakers, since they come from international families and are mostly being raised bi- or multilingually, in addition to growing up in Germany and learning other foreign languages at school. However, they all attend a schooling program for native speakers of English in an international school which leads to the International Baccalaureate. Hence, for these students, English is at least one native language. They may have another native language and they study one or more foreign languages in school. The native speaker control group is meant to be a reference group which provides additional information about the foreign language learners' use of English in the form of a baseline reference for English. This is the reason why novice native speakers were chosen. These novice native speakers are also still learners of their native language in a formal school setting, and they are of the same age as the rest of the participants.[8]

In total, the 249 participants are not only divided into eight language groups, but they are split into two age cohorts, namely 12-year-old and 16-year-old students. Ideally, each group should consist of the same number of participants. However, due to the voluntary nature of the data collection process and the large number of different data collection locations, this was not possible. Most strikingly, the group of Turkish monolingual participants is particularly small. A number of participants had to be excluded after data collection, because their English performance consisted of only a few words, sometimes even Turkish instead of English words. Therefore, these texts are not included in the learner corpus to keep a balanced dataset. Moreover, all 249 students participated in the written task but only a subgroup ($n = 176$) took part in the oral task. The English native speaker control group did not participate in the oral task.

6.3.2 Background variables

The social information gathered from the questionnaires is described in some detail below. The respective numeric output including the between group effect reported as η^2 (eta squared) can be found in Table 6.1. Most of the information is only available for the bilinguals and the German monolinguals, i.e., those students who grow up in Germany. In addition, the social variables are partly incomplete due to a considerable number of missing answers (indicated with NA).

6.3.2.1 Gender

There is an almost equal number of females (49 percent) and males (47.4 percent), but the distribution per age cohort and per language

Table 6.1 Descriptive overview (sum, mean, standard deviation) of participants and social variables

Age		RUS-GER		TUR-GER		VIET-GER	
		12	16	12	16	12	16
No. of texts		15	23	20	21	26	22
No. of recordings		12	20	15	17	20	21
Gender	f	9	17	9	14	13	9
	m	6	6	6	6	13	13
	NA	-	-	5	1	-	-
Age of onset of German	mean	2.07	3.79	1.88	3.00	2.36	3.14
	sd	1.64	2.55	1.86	2.38	1.41	1.81
	NA	1	4	4	3	1	-
SES	mean	44.69	48.94	(33.67)	(47.43)	36.90	42.21
	sd	16.88	16.93	(11.71)	(22.92)	11.45	12.29
	NA	2	5	14	14	5	3
Type of school	GY	10	16	9	4	22	10
	other	4	3	8	11	3	7
	NA	1	4	3	6	1	5
School grade German	mean	2.92	2.80	(2.67)	(3.00)	2.48	2.82
	sd	0.59	0.68	(0.82)	(0.76)	0.85	0.71
	NA	1	3	11	14	5	5
School grade English	mean	2.86	2.89	(2.63)	(3.43)	2.14	2.3
	sd	0.64	0.89	(0.70)	(0.50)	0.99	0.82
	NA	1	2	12	14	5	5
No. of books (household)	mean	228.86	279.32	(47.86)	(172.67)	65.48	167.21
	sd	197.36	180.44	(50.67)	(167.16)	59.25	138.93
	NA	1	4	13	18	5	3
English difficult	yes	4	3	8	8	4	7
	no	11	19	11	12	21	14
	NA	-	1	1	1	1	1
English useful	yes	14	23	16	17	25	22
	no	1	-	4	4	1	-
	NA	-	-	-	-	-	-

Abbreviations: ENG = English, f = female, GER = German, GY = Gymnasium (university-bound secondary school type), m = male, NA = not available, RUS = Russian, RUS-GER = Russian-German, sd = standard deviation, SES = socio-economic status, TUR = Turkish, TUR-GER = Turkish-German, VIET = Vietnamese, VIET-GER = Vietnamese-German

Significance codes: *significant at the .05 probability level; **significant at the .01 probability level; ***significant at the .001 probability level

Explanation: Most means and standard deviations of the Turkish-German participants appear in parenthesis, since these are based on extremely low numbers and are thus not representative of this group.

GER		RUS		TUR		VIET		ENG		Total	%	Between group effect (η2)
12	16	12	16	12	16	12	16	12	16			
20	20	10	10	7	5	10	10	15	15	249		
10	11	10	10	6	4	10	10	-	-	176		
9	7	4	2	2	4	2	6	6	9	122	49	
10	11	6	8	5	1	8	4	9	6	118	47.4	
1	2									9	3.6	
										2.75		.102*
										2.03		
										13		
61.92	54.00									46		.212***
14.99	17.92									17.46		
8	6									57		
6	7									84	50.3	
5	6									47	28.1	
9	7									36	21.6	
2.13	2.31									2.34		.139*
0.62	0.46									0.86		
5	4									48		
2.01	2.44									2.82		.169**
0.77	0.93									1.42		
5	4									48		
289.91	316.14									199.36		.288***
194.26	184.74									177.63		
9	6									59		
4	2			-	1	5	1	1	2	50	21.8	
16	18			7	4	5	9	14	13	174	76	
-	-			-	-	-	-	-	-	5	2.2	
17	20			2	2	10	9	14	13	204	89.1	
3	-			5	3	-	1	1	2	25	10.9	
-	-			-	-	-	-	-	-	0	0	

group is not perfectly balanced. There are slightly more females in the older cohort and more males in the younger cohort. In addition, for nine participants (3.61 percent) this information is unknown.

6.3.2.2 Age of onset of German

The bilinguals differ in their age of onset of learning German. Some were born in the foreign country (i.e., Russia, Turkey, or Vietnam) and immigrated to Germany at an older age, while the rest were born in Germany. Table 6.1 shows the respective mean values of the bilinguals' age of onset of learning German, separated into language and age groups. More than two thirds of the participants were three years old or younger

128 English learner corpus

when they moved to Germany and when they were exposed to German for the first time. A considerable number of participants (n = 13) did not indicate their age when they started to learn German. Overall, the 12-year-old participants were younger when they came to Germany in comparison to their older peers. This significant between group effect (η^2 = .10) can be considered medium, following Cohen's (1988) threshold values.[9]

6.3.2.3 Socio-economic status

The socio-economic status (SES) is based on the International Socio-Economic Index of Occupational Status (ISEI) of the family of the participants, which is estimated by using information about the profession of the parents or caretakers (Ehmke and Siegle 2005; Ganzeboom, De Graaf, and Treiman 1992; International Labor Office 2012). For the current study, only the highest ISEI value of the parents or caretakers was selected. These resulting HISEI (Highest International Socio-Economic Index of Occupational Status) values range from low (16) to high values (88), with higher values suggesting a higher social status. The means per language group are given in Table 6.1.

On average, the three bilingual groups have a lower socio-economic status than their German monolingual peers. However, the values of the Turkish-German bilinguals need to be taken with caution, because the means are based on an extremely limited number of participants (12-year-old cohort: n = 6; 16-year-old cohort: n = 7). Overall, the between group effect (η^2 = .212) can be considered large, based on the aforementioned thresholds (Cohen 1988).

6.3.2.4 Type of school

Children in Germany are required to attend a minimum of 9 or 10 years[10] at an educational institution. After primary education (typically after school year four), they can either attend the university-bound school type, called *Gymnasium*, whose completion qualifies students to study at a university, or they attend any of the other secondary schools. Such other school types are, for instance, *Gesamtschule*, *Stadtteilschule*, or *Realschule*. The choice is based on the school grades the children received during their primary education, teacher recommendation, or the decision of the parents (see Kultusministerkonferenz (KMK) 2019; see also Section 2.3). Children who attend a type of school with a higher level of education receive more formal education which should result in a higher proficiency in (all) school subjects (at least on an average level).

This study only differentiates between two categories of school, namely *Gymnasium*, the university-bound school type, and 'other', including all remaining types of secondary school, following Lechner and Siemund (2014) and Maluch and Kempert (2019). Lechner and Siemund (2014: 334) argue that there is an observable gap between students attending a university-bound school as opposed to students attending any of the remaining types of school, with little variation within the latter group. They continue by stressing "that the school forms children attend are a result of social stratification and thus a result of multiple underlying variables" (Lechner and Siemund 2014: 334–335). As such, the type of school itself comprises a variety of factors that can hardly be separated, at least not with the information gathered from the questionnaire the participants had to fill in.

Table 6.1 gives an overview of the bilingual and the monolingual German participants and their respective school type.[11] For a considerable number of students it was again not possible to obtain the relevant data. Yet, the numbers of the complete subject profiles show that the different groups are not equally distributed across the school types. The Vietnamese-German bilinguals, especially the younger cohort, and the Russian-German bilinguals, especially the older cohort, attend a *Gymnasium*, i.e., the university-bound secondary school type, noticeably more frequently as opposed to the other groups of students. The Turkish-German bilinguals show the highest number of students who attend other secondary schools.

6.3.2.5 School grades of German and English

Table 6.1 lists the average grades for the school subjects German and English for the bilingual as well as the monolingual German participants.[12] The German monolinguals received the best scores in German, followed by the younger cohort of the Vietnamese-German bilinguals. All other groups have mean values above 2.5, which would translate into a grade three in the German school system. The between group variation ($\eta^2 = .139$) indicates a moderate effect.

For English, there is interesting variation between and within the groups. Again, the German monolingual students have the best school grades, followed by the Vietnamese-German bilinguals. Here, the difference seems to be only minor because both groups achieved grade two. The Russian-German bilinguals have noticeably lower English grades, and the results of the Turkish-German bilinguals are even lower, especially in the older cohort. In fact, the 16-year-old Turkish-German bilinguals are at the lower end of still receiving grade three. However, these values are again based on less than 50 percent of the participants, due to missing data, and may not be representative. Overall, the between group effect ($\eta^2 = .169$) is larger than for the German school grades, indicating a greater variance across the language groups.

6.3.2.6 Number of books per household

Another variable, which could be understood as being related to the socio-economic status, is the number of books available in the household of the participants. The number of books may be related to the family's educational aspirations. The distribution turns out to be like the socio-economic status (Table 6.1). The German monolinguals and the Russian-German bilinguals have, on average, a higher number of books per household, while the Vietnamese-German bilinguals indicated possession of fewer books. As before, there is barely a clear result for the bilingual Turkish-German participants. The large between group effect across all participants (η^2 = .288) supports the social imbalance across the different groups, which was already mentioned when discussing the socio-economic status.

6.3.2.7 Attitudes toward English: English is a difficult/useful language

Two further variables are included, and these belong to attitudes toward English. The participants were asked (i) whether they found English difficult and (ii) whether they considered English a useful language. They could respond with either 'yes' or 'no'. In contrast to the former variables, the monolingual Turkish and Vietnamese participants' as well as the English native speakers' responses are also known (Table 6.1).

The majority across all participants regards English as a useful language. This may be an approximation of regarding it as important to study English, although this is of course not a perfect equation. The only exceptions are both monolingual Turkish groups. More than half of these students (66 percent) regard English as not useful.[13]

As far as the other variable is concerned, a higher number of the participants shares the view that English is a difficult language, but the majority (75.98 percent) thinks that English is not difficult to learn. There is a fairly similar trend across all language groups, with the Turkish-German bilinguals and the younger Vietnamese monolinguals answering slightly more often that English is difficult.

6.3.2.8 Heritage language use

As previously indicated, bilingual heritage speakers are unbalanced bilinguals whose majority language is German and whose weaker language is the heritage language. This claim needs to be further substantiated by considering the language use and language habits. This will be regarded as a reasonable approximation of defining language dominance, because this dataset lacks other measures of language proficiency as the students did not participate in proficiency tests, assessing their skills in German or the heritage language.

For all students, German is the language of instruction in school, which means that for a large part of the day, this will be the language they are mostly exposed to and are required to use. Regarding language use at home, there is an interesting trend among all bilinguals and their families. The parents only rarely communicate with each other in German at home; in total, only 4 out of 88 parents use German to talk to their spouse (for 39 families, no information is available). Furthermore, there is only a small number of participants who speak German (3.5 percent) or mostly German (3.5 percent) with their parents. Thus, the majority uses the heritage language when talking to their parents at home. The opposite scenario is visible when looking at the language of communication between the participants and their sibling(s). Only few participants indicated that they use mostly Russian, Turkish, or Vietnamese with their brother(s) or sister(s) (5.5 percent), and none of them indicated that they exclusively use the heritage language. This is a remarkable observation and demonstrates that German is not only used outside of the homes but that it plays a significant role within the families among the younger generations, as well. It is also striking that this trend is visible across all three language groups.

This language use profile displays the roles of the two languages in the lives of the bilinguals. Thus, they are treated as German-dominant bilinguals or unbalanced bilinguals because it can be assumed that the skills in their two languages differ considerably, i.e., formal language use learned in an educational setting versus colloquial language use.

6.4 Research objectives and predictions

The main objective of this study is subdivided into several research targets. The learner corpus is used to identify crosslinguistic influence in third language acquisition by unbalanced bilingual heritage speakers who grow up in Germany and study English as an additional language in school. The aim is to determine whether crosslinguistic influence comes from the majority language German, the heritage language, or both languages. Furthermore, this corpus allows for the investigation of whether bilingual heritage speakers enjoy linguistic advantages in further foreign language acquisition vis-à-vis their monolingual peers. In addition, the two different age cohorts provide a quasi-developmental perspective. Thus, it can be investigated how crosslinguistic influence is affected by increasing age and increasing competence in the language currently acquired.

It is expected, based on Kortmann (2005: 158–159) and Jarvis and Pavlenko (2008), to find a considerable amount of individual variation. When analyzing learner language, not every mistake or error can be explained with transfer (Kortmann 2005: 158–159). Hence, contrastive analysis, as a way of identifying crosslinguistic influence, is still a useful "diagnostic tool" which can help to explain errors and language production, despite there being numerous other factors that must be considered as well (Kortmann 2005: 159). In addition, Jarvis and Pavlenko (2008: 13) rightly stress "that CLI [crosslinguistic influence] is a highly complex cognitive phenomenon that is often affected by language users' perceptions, conceptualizations, mental associations, and individual choices." What this assumes is that learners are not *homogeneous* (even if they belong to one group and even if they have similar background variables) and that crosslinguistic influence is not the same for every learner in every situation. Hence, it is unlikely to find homogeneous learner groups whose language background defines the outcome in English. However, with the help of additional personal variables and by focusing on general properties and overall trends, it is expected to discover both differences and similarities across the language groups.

Despite the expected heterogeneity, it will be possible to identify whether crosslinguistic influence comes from the majority language German, the heritage language, or from both languages because of the triangular, cross-sectional setting. This study follows Jarvis (2000) and Jarvis and Pavlenko (2008) who identified three essential types of evidence that are needed to determine crosslinguistic influence. These are (i) *intragroup homogeneity* ("Evidence that the behavior in question is not an isolated incident, but is instead a common tendency of individuals who know the same combination of languages"), (ii) *intergroup heterogeneity* ("Evidence that the behavior in question is not something that all language users do regardless of the combinations of L1s and L2s that they know"), and (iii) *crosslinguistic performance congruity* ("Evidence that a language user's behavior in one language really is motivated by her use (i.e., the way she demonstrates her knowledge) of another language") (Jarvis and Pavlenko 2008: 35).

The bilingual participants may either largely behave like the German monolinguals, or they may resemble the monolingual Russian, Turkish, or Vietnamese speakers. It is also possible that they are somehow in between the two monolingual groups. Figure 6.2 visualizes these possibilities, in addition to another possibility, namely no transfer. First of all, scenario one represents the relations between the individual groups of learners: it connects the bilingual participants with two monolingual learner groups. The German monolinguals are in the center, connected to the three bilingual groups. Without any further additions, this indicates the possibility introduced last, namely that there is no crosslinguistic influence from any of the previously acquired languages, but that all learners show the same learning patterns. This last option is highly unlikely, because most research on second language acquisition agrees that the L1 influences the L2, and that the no-transfer hypothesis is implausible. Therefore, there must at least be some crosslinguistic influence visible in the L2 and the L3 learners (see again Section 3.2). Yet, in theoretical terms, this is in principle possible, hence its addition here. In the remaining scenarios, shared language features in English are represented with a dashed box. In the second scenario, which visualizes crosslinguistic influence from the majority language German, four of the learner groups show corresponding patterns, namely the Russian-German, Turkish-German, Vietnamese-German bilinguals, as well as the German monolinguals. If transfer comes from the heritage language, here seen in the third scenario, then the Turkish-German bilinguals should show the same or at least similar patterns as the Turkish

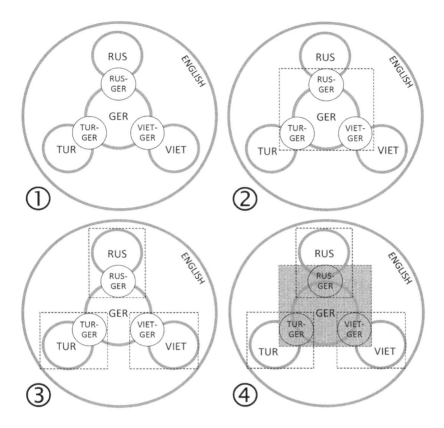

Figure 6.2 Potential patterns of crosslinguistic influence.

monolinguals. The same applies to the Russian-German and Russian participants, respectively, and to the Vietnamese-German and Vietnamese participants. The German monolinguals, however, would differ from the others. The fourth possibility suggests that there are some similarities between the bilinguals and the German monolinguals and that there are also some similarities between the bilinguals and the respective other monolingual language groups.

Among these four possibilities, it is predicted that the results will show that crosslinguistic influence comes from both previously acquired languages (scenario 4). This is based on what was discussed in Sections 3.2 and 3.4. Furthermore, it is predicted that there is both positive as well as negative transfer, and it is anticipated that crosslinguistic influence is different for different grammatical phenomena. This would support the Linguistic Proximity Model proposed by Westergaard et al. (2017). Yet, it is assumed that the principle behind this model is not the only one at work in bilingual heritage speaker contexts, but that typological similarity between German and English and the dominant status of German are additional significant factors. Therefore, crosslinguistic influence from German is presumably proportionally larger than the crosslinguistic influence coming from the heritage language. This means that there is likely more overlap between the bilinguals and the German monolinguals than between the bilinguals and the respective monolingual groups. Therefore, in scenario 4, the grey shading that includes the German monolinguals and the bilinguals is depicted more prominently than the areas that include the languages Russian, Turkish, Vietnamese as well as the respective bilingual combinations. In Chapter 4, the individual tense and aspect systems of the languages present here were compared, and it was noted that there is a lot of conceptual and formal overlap between German and English, more than between English and the other three languages. In addition, German, as the language of instruction and as the majority language of the bilinguals, is the language that they use most frequently, and that they are most proficient in. These two factors taken together in combination with the evidence presented in studies such as Hopp (2019), Fallah and Jabbari (2018), and Siemund, Schröter, and Rahbari (2018), to name but these three, strongly suggests that transfer from German seems to be most influential. Yet, it is not hypothesized that transfer comes exclusively from German, but that heritage language influence is also visible in the bilingual data.

Apart from the language background, further variables are likely to play an important role. The most important ones are presumably the socio-economic status of the families, the type of secondary school the students attend, and the age of onset of learning German. Additional influence may also come from the number of books available in the household, gender, and from attitudes toward learning English.

Another background variable is age. Many previous studies (see, for example, Lorenz et al. 2019; Maluch, Neumann and Kempert 2016; Şahingöz 2014) assigned explanatory power to the age of the participants. These studies reported differences between younger L2 and L3 learners. Yet, these differences were either less pronounced or even disappeared when looking at older L2 and L3 learners. The current participants represent similar age groups to those discussed in Lorenz et al. (2019), Maluch, Neumann and Kempert (2016), and Şahingöz (2014). Based on this, it is feasible to expect more differences in crosslinguistic influence across the younger than across the older participants.

Furthermore, crosslinguistic influence also depends on the type of language competence tested. Grammaticality judgment tasks may lead to different conclusions than when considering production tasks such as sentence repetitions or story telling (see again Section 3.2). Therefore, there may be differences between the oral and the written data. For writing a story, the participants have more time to think, and they may also correct and modify earlier versions. Spoken production, however, is more spontaneous, potentially frightening, and unusual for the participants, and this may have a negative effect on the outcome in English. Frightening and unusual means that secondary school students are quite familiar with writing stories, but they are less familiar with being recorded while telling a story. This may influence the outcome.

Notes

1 The following researchers were also involved in the data collection process: Mark Gerken, Simone Lechner, Anika Lloyd-Smith, Jessica Terese Mueller, and Sharareh Rahbari. In addition, the following student assistants were also involved in the data collection and/or transcription process of the handwritten texts and oral recordings: Perihan Akpinar, Sevilay Arabaci, Aybül Babat, Merve Bas, Julia Benz, Alexij Benz, Can Bilici, Phan-Ngoc Binh, Bartu Bosdurmoz, Philip Braun, Eugenia Budnik, Viktoria Diana Bui, Irem Bulut, Ayregul Cokiroglu, Thi Tan Dang, Halil Demir, Jana Endres, Volker Englich, Onur Gündüz, The Hung Huynh, Anna Kaiser, Sara Kalitina, Tülay Karakaya, Cham Anh Khoung, Lena Knutz, Shari Knutz, Thieu Lien Kong, Sengül Kotan, Viktoria Kronhard, Cem Kücük, Svenja Lubinski, Tarik Meric, Alexander Michaelis, Mehmet Moderba, Olga Neufeld, Tuyet Mai Nguyen, Thi Phuong Hon Nguyen, Efekan Nodasbas, Begüm Oktay, Akin Özbek, Tansel Öztürk, Dao Ngoc Phuong, Ton Kom Phuong, Tran T. Phuong, Süreyya Polat, Martina Ruß, Volka Sacok, Malis Sahmanija, Kathrin Sarudko, Jennifer Schemtschuk, Sophia Spiewok, Inci Toksoy, Maria Tschistjakova, Beyla Urgun, Nadja Victoria, Anna Vinets, Hai-Van Vu, Hoai Nam Vu, Paula Marie Walter, Sophie Wedemeyer, Berfin Yavuz, Mihriban Yavuz, and Merve Yücel. Their help is greatly appreciated.
2 Learner corpora can be defined as collections of texts produced in a (near) natural setting by language learners (Granger 2008: 338; Granger, Gilquin, and Meunier 2015: 1). Naturally occurring language or language produced in a natural surrounding refers to "authentic" language use, i.e., one of the principles in corpus linguistics (Gilquin and Granger 2015: 419). This means that ideally, a corpus should consist of language that was not produced for the sake of corpus compilation but that had a communicative function. However, for learner language, it is not always possible to collect such data, simply because in many contexts, learners who formally acquire a foreign language (as is the case in the current setting) may never actually use this language outside the classroom (Gilquin and Granger 2015: 419). This means that "the criterion of authenticity therefore needs to be relaxed in case of learner corpora" (Gilquin and Granger 2015: 419). Thus, many learner corpora contain essays, a typical classroom activity (Granger, Gilquin, and Meunier 2015: 2). This is in several respects a useful text type, because learners engage quite regularly in essay writing, at least after a certain amount of formal training. Also, essays usually contain not just a few words but a larger number of sentences or even paragraphs, which results in enough production data for a quantitative analysis.
3 Peripheral text type refers to the premises of learner corpus research to use production data from a naturalistic language production context, see note 2.

4 One basic proficiency measure is the number of words that is produced (either in written or in oral performance). Vermeer (2000: 78) argues that the number of sentences and words increases with increasing competence in that language. Furthermore, lexical diversity increases; hence, there are more infrequent words and more overall lexical variety in language use with increasing competence or proficiency (see, for example, Milton 2009: 126). Looking at the number of words produced and including the token frequency is one point of reference when comparing the students.

5 An alternative explanation or classification is offered by García-Mayo, Lázaro Ibarrola, and Liceras (2005). They regard instances of *is* before infinitives/the bare stem of lexical verbs as "placeholders" (447), which function as agreement morphemes (472). Furthermore, they argue against the interpretation that *is* plus lexical verb represents a present progressive (472).

6 It may actually mean *ate*; at least one could infer this meaning if one pronounced the word. However, this is not part of the story (i.e., it is not visualized in the pictures), and the following sentence does not point to the meaning of 'to eat the fish' either.

7 The reverse coding is in principle also possible. It could be assumed that the participant intended to use a simple past form of *throw* as well, in accordance with the other verb forms in the story. Yet, the correct form *threw* may be unknown, or the student may have thought that *throw* is the simple past form. Then, the resulting coding of this verb form would be (i) 'incorrect form', and (ii) 'target-like meaning'. Based on the learner corpus data, this dilemma cannot be solved unambiguously. Therefore, it was decided that the formal cues rank higher, because these are the only items that can be directly assessed. Since this is a formally correct simple present form and not an ill-formed past tense, such as the example *they caugchet* in (33), this verb was coded as 'formally correct' with 'non-target-like meaning'.

8 Instead of relying exclusively on comparisons with reference corpora (such as the *British National Corpus (BNC)* (Davies 2004) and the *Corpus of Contemporary American English (COCA)* (Davies 2008–)), which represent language of academically trained, expert native speakers, some researchers rely on novice writing, i.e., language samples that were produced by younger, novice native speakers, such as students (Granger 2015: 12). The reason is that such language use may better reflect the text type produced by the learners (here picture descriptions) which are otherwise not represented in large corpora (Granger 2015: 17).

9 Cohen's (1988) thresholds of eta squared are the following: small effect ($\eta^2 = 0.01$), medium effect ($\eta^2 = 0.06$), and large effect ($\eta^2 = 0.14$) (see also Adams and Conway 2014; Lakens 2013).

10 In Germany, the responsibility for the education system, including the minimum number of years a student must attend school, lies with the federal states. Therefore, there is also variation concerning school types. *Gymnasium*, the university-bound school type, can be found everywhere; yet the other types of secondary schools differ from state to state (see Kultusministerkonferenz (KMK) 2019; Stanat et al. 2016 for more information).

11 Specific information about the type of school of the monolingual Russian, Turkish, and Vietnamese participants is not considered. The school systems in these countries differ substantially from the German school system.

12 In Germany, the school grades range from 1 to 6, with 1 being the best possible grade and 6 the lowest grade. It is common to use further differentiations between these cardinal numbers, whether the grade leans more toward the higher or the lower grade, i.e., 2+ or 2-. Usually, a grade 1 is obtained for values ranging from 1.0 to 1.5; 1.5 to 2.5 equals grade 2; 2.5 to 3.5 is a grade 3; the same applies to all remaining school grades. However, in this study, only the complete values 1, 2, 3, 4, 5, and 6 are used. In fact, only values from 1 to 4 are included, because none of the students received grades 5 or 6 for either German or English.

13 Note that with this simple yes-or-no question, it is impossible to assess whether someone considers English to be globally useful versus personally useful. Someone might view English as useful in a greater social sense but may not see any personal usefulness in their lives for English.

References

Adams M. A. and T. L. Conway. 2014. Eta Squared. In *Encyclopedia of quality of life and well-being research*, ed. A. C. Michalos, 1965–1966. Dordrecht: Springer.

Anthony, L. 2016. AntConc (Version 3.4.4.0) [Computer Software]. Tokyo: Waseda.

Bardovi-Harlig, K. 1992. The relationship of form and meaning: A cross-sectional study of tense and aspect in the interlanguage of learners of English as a second language. *Applied Psycholinguistics* 13:253–278.

Bardovi-Harlig, K. 2000. *Tense and aspect in second language acquisition: Form, meaning, and use*. Oxford: Blackwell.

Biber, D., S. Johannson, G. Leech, S. Conrad, and E. Finegan. 2000. *Longman grammar of spoken and written English*. Harlow, UK: Longman.

Cohen, J. 1988. *Statistical power analysis for the behavioral sciences*. 2nd edn. New York: Lawrence Erlbaum Associates.

Coughlan, P. and P. Duff. 1994. Same task, different activities: Analysis of a SLA task from an activity theory perspective. In *Vygotskian approaches to second language research*, ed. J. P. Lantolf and G. Appel, 173–193. Norwood, NJ: Ablex.

Davies, M. 2004. *British National Corpus (BNC)* (from Oxford University Press). Available online at www.english-corpora.org/bnc (accessed April 4, 2022).

Davies, M. 2008–. *The corpus of contemporary American English (COCA)*. Available online at www.english-corpora.org/coca (accessed April 4, 2022).

Ehmke, T. and T. Siegle. 2005. ISEI, ISCED, HOMEPOS, ESCS: Indikatoren der sozialen Herkunft bei der Qualifizierung von sozialen Disparitäten. *Zeitschrift für Erziehungswissenschaft* 8:521–539.

Fallah, N. and A. A. Jabbari. 2018. L3 acquisition of English attributive adjectives: Dominant language of communication matters for syntactic cross-linguistic influence. *Linguistic Approaches to Bilingualism* 8:193–216.

Gagarina, N., D. Klop, S. Kunnari, K. Tantele, T. Välimaa, I. Balčiūnienė, U. Bohnacker, and J. Walters. 2012. *MAIN: Multilingual Assessment Instrument for Narratives*. ZAS Papers in Linguistics. Berlin: Zentrum für Allgemeine Sprachwissenschaft.

Ganzeboom, H. B. G., P. M. De Graaf, and D. J. Treiman. 1992. A standard international socio-economic index of occupational status. *Social Science Research* 21:1–56.
García Mayo, M. d. P., A. Lázaro Ibarrola, and J. Liceras. 2005. Placeholders in the English interlanguage of bilingual (Basque-Spanish) children. *Language Learning* 55:445–489.
Gilquin, G. and S. Granger. 2015. Learner Language. In *The Cambridge handbook of English corpus linguistics*, ed. D. Biber and R. Reppen, 418–435. Cambridge: Cambridge University Press.
Götz, S. 2013. *Fluency in native and nonnative English speech*. Amsterdam: Benjamins.
Granger, S. 2008. Learner corpora in foreign language education. In *Encyclopedia of language and education*, 2nd edn, ed. N. Van Deusen-Scholl and N. H. Hornberger, 337–351. New York: Springer.
Granger, S. 2015. Contrastive interlanguage analysis: A reappraisal. *International Journal of Learner Corpus Research* 1:7–24.
Granger, S., G. Gilquin, and F. Meunier. 2015. Introduction: Learner corpus research – past, present and future. In *The Cambridge handbook of learner corpus research*, ed. S. Granger, G. Gilquin, and F Meunier, 1–5. Cambridge: Cambridge University Press.
Hopp, H. 2019. Cross-linguistic influence in the child third language acquisition of grammar: Sentence comprehension and production among Turkish-German and German learners of English. *International Journal of Bilingualism* 23:567–583.
Huddleston, R. D. and G. K. Pullum. 2002. *The Cambridge grammar of the English language*. Cambridge: Cambridge University Press.
International Labour Office. 2012. *International standard classification of occupations. ISCO-08. Volume 1: Structure, group definitions and correspondence tables*. Geneva: ILO.
Jarvis, S. 2000. Methodological rigor in the study of transfer: Identifying L1 influence in the interlanguage lexicon. *Language Learning* 50:245–309.
Jarvis, S. and A. Pavlenko. 2008. *Crosslinguistic influence in language and cognition*. London: Routledge.
Kortmann, B. 2005. *English linguistics: Essentials*. Berlin: Cornelsen.
Kultusministerkonferenz (KMK). 2019. *Das Bildungswesen in der Bundesrepublik Deutschland 2016/2017*. www.kmk.org/fileadmin/Dateien/pdf/Eurydice/Bildungswesen-dt-pdfs/dossier_de_ebook.pdf (accessed April 4, 2022).
Lakens, D. 2013. Calculating and reporting effect sizes to facilitate cumulative science: A practical primer for t-tests and ANOVAs. *Frontiers in Psychology* 4:863. https://doi.org/10.3389/fpsyg.2013.00863
Lechner, S. 2013. *E-LiPS: Fox and chicken instrument [Based on three chicks and one bird]*. Hamburg: LiMA, University of Hamburg.
Lechner, S. and P. Siemund. 2014. The role of language external factors in the acquisition of English as an additional language by bilingual children in Germany. In *Language contacts at the crossroads of disciplines*, ed. H. Paulasto, L. Meriläinen, H. Riionheimo, and M. Kok, 319–345. Newcastle-upon-Tyne: Cambridge Scholars Publishing.
LiMA, Linguistic Diversity Management in Urban Areas-LiPS, LiMA Panel Study. 2009–2013. Projektkoordination LiPS: Prof. Dr. Dr. h. c. Ingrid Gogolin; ©LiMA-LiPS 2013. Hamburg: LiMA, University of Hamburg.

Lorenz, E. 2019. Analysis of verb phrases and the progressive aspect in a learner corpus of L2 and L3 learners of English. In *Widening the scope of learner corpus research: Selected papers from the 4th learner corpus research conference*, ed. A. Abel, A. Glaznieks, V. Lyding, and L. Nicholas, 253–287. Louvain-la-Neuve: Presses Universitaires de Louvain.

Lorenz, E., R. J. Bonnie, K. Feindt, S. Rahbari, and P. Siemund. 2019. Crosslinguistic influence in unbalanced bilingual heritage speakers on subsequent language acquisition: Evidence from pronominal object placement in ditransitive clauses. *International Journal of Bilingualism* 23:1410–1430.

Maluch, J. T. and S. Kempert. 2019. Bilingual profiles and third language learning: The effects of the manner of learning, sequence of bilingual acquisition, and language use practices. *International Journal of Bilingual Education and Bilingualism* 22:870–882.

Maluch, J. T., M. Neumann, and S. Kempert. 2016. Bilingualism as a resource for foreign language learning of language minority students? Empirical evidence from a longitudinal study during primary and secondary school in Germany. *Learning and Individual Differences* 51:111–118.

Milton, J. 2009. *Measuring second language vocabulary acquisition*. Bristol: Multilingual Matters.

Ohser, E. (E. O. Plauen). 2003. *Vater und Sohn: Sämtliche Streiche und Abenteuer* (Schmuckausgabe). Konstanz: Südverlag.

Pallotti, G. 2010. Doing interlanguage analysis in school contexts. In *Communicative proficiency and linguistic development: Intersections between SLA and language testing research*, ed. I. Bartning, M. Martin, and I. Vedder, 159–190. Amsterdam: Eurosla.

Şahingöz, Y. 2014. *Schulische Mehrsprachigkeit bei türkisch-deutsch bilingualen Schülern: Eine Analyse von transferinduzierten Wortstellungsmustern*. PhD diss., University of Hamburg. http://ediss.sub.uni-hamburg.de/volltexte/2018/9128

Seidl, J. 2006. *English G 21 – Ausgabe A/Band 1: 5. Schuljahr – Workbook mit Audio-Materialien*, ed. H. Schwarz and J. Rademacher. Berlin: Cornelsen.

Siemund, P., S. Schröter, and S. Rahbari. 2018. Learning English demonstrative pronouns on bilingual substrate: Evidence from German heritage speakers of Russian, Turkish, and Vietnamese. In *Foreign language education in multilingual classrooms*, ed. A. Bonnet and P. Siemund, 381–405. Amsterdam: Benjamins.

Stanat, P., K. Böhme, S. Schipolowski, and N. Haag (eds.). 2016. *IQB-Bildungstrend 2015: Sprachliche Kompetenzen am Ende der 9. Jahrgangsstufe im zweiten Ländervergleich*. Münster/New York: Waxmann.

Swan, M. 2005. *Practical English usage*. 3rd edn. Oxford: Oxford University Press.

Vendler, Z. 1957. Verbs and times. *Philosophical Review* 66:143–160.

Vermeer, A. 2000. Coming to grips with lexical richness in spontaneous speech data. *Language Testing* 17:65–83.

Westergaard, M., N. Mitrofanova, R. Mykhaylyk, and Y. Rodina. 2017. Crosslinguistic influence in the acquisition of a third language: The linguistic proximity model. *International Journal of Bilingualism* 21:666–682.

7 Use of tense and aspect of monolinguals versus bilinguals

7.1 Frequency overview (written component of the learner corpus)

The following four sections offer a descriptive overview of the written component of the E-LiPS learner corpus. The eight language groups are compared and contrasted with respect to overall text composition, subject-verb agreement, the use of the copula verb *be*, in addition to formal correctness and target-like use of verbs.

7.1.1 Text composition (sentences, words, verbs)

For a general overview of the entire dataset, the numbers of words, sentences, as well as verbs for each individual text of the learner corpus were calculated. Verb forms were differentiated into verb tokens and types to account for variability of different verb uses. In a second step, the verb type-token-ratio (TTR) was calculated for each student.[1] Moreover, the normalized verb tokens and types were calculated to the basis of 100 tokens to account for text length differences. In addition, some verbs, as described in Section 6.2, were left unclassified (i.e., no tense/aspect label was used), because the form could not unambiguously be assigned to one of the given categories.

Table 7.1 provides the absolute and mean values of the respective variables. Notably, the absolute numbers of sentences and words differ across the eight language groups and between the two age cohorts. The task for the students was to write at least two sentences per picture, which should result in 12 sentences per text. The mean numbers of sentences in Table 7.1 demonstrate that the students largely met this requirement (with at least on average 11 sentences per text), except for both cohorts of the Turkish-German bilinguals, as well as the 12-year-old Russian-German bilinguals and the Vietnamese monolinguals (these groups wrote on average fewer than 10 sentences per text).

Differences in the absolute numbers of words can be explained with the differing numbers of students per cohort. This, however, is controlled for when considering the mean values. It can be observed that except

DOI: 10.4324/9781003134336-7

for the Turkish monolinguals, the older cohorts produced on average more words per story than the younger cohorts. This finding is not unexpected and supports the hypothesis that with increasing number of years of studying English, the students have a higher level of proficiency, here demonstrated by a higher number of words per text. Not surprisingly, the native speakers of English wrote on average the highest numbers of words (143 and 173, respectively), except for the 16-year-old Vietnamese monolingual learners of English who wrote on average 182 words. The Turkish monolinguals, the 12-year-old monolingual speakers of Russian, the Turkish-German bilinguals, as well as the 12-year-old Vietnamese monolinguals wrote on average the shortest English texts (below 90 words). The performance of the German, Russian-German, Vietnamese-German, and the 16-year-old Russian monolingual students is somewhere in the middle: the means range between 90 and 140 words per text.

Arguably, the six images of the picture story trigger specific vocabulary items, including verbs such as *fish*, *go*, *walk*, or *catch*. Yet, it could be anticipated that with increasing English proficiency, students would use a greater variety of verbs. Like Vermeer's (2000) argument that the number of words grows with increasing competence, it can be examined whether this applies to the number of verb tokens and types as well. Previous studies analyzing and measuring lexical diversity (see, for example, Crossley and McNamara 2012; Jarvis 2002; Yu 2009) observed that greater lexical diversity and fewer overlap repetitions seem to correlate with higher proficiency. When considering the verb tokens (mean values), an increase from the younger to the older cohorts within each language group can be observed, except for the Turkish monolinguals and the English native speaker control group (the increase in the latter group is merely marginal). The picture remains largely the same for verb types (mean values). There is an increase from the 12-year-old to the 16-year-old students except for the Turkish monolinguals.

Furthermore, a comparison of the normalized verb tokens and types across the language groups yields slightly different results. The mean values across all learner groups are now much more similar than the absolute values. Hence, the relatively large differences previously observed were mainly caused by the overall length differences. Moreover, it can be noticed that for five of the eight groups, the older cohorts display lower numbers of normalized verb tokens. This appears plausible, as it can be assumed that the more proficient a student is, the more complex the sentence structures he or she produces. More complex sentence structures could mean that additional words such as adverbials or connectors are more frequently used. This potentially decreases the number of verbs per 100 words. In addition, the differences in normalized verb types between the two age cohorts per language group as well as across the eight language groups are relatively minor (range between 8.5 and 13.2 verb types per 100 words).

142 *Tense and aspect: mono- vs. bilinguals*

Table 7.1 Frequency overview: absolute numbers, mean values (with standard deviations in parenthesis), normalized mean values per 100 words (with standard deviations in parenthesis) of sentences, words, and verbs per text

Language group	Age	No. of sentences	Mean no. of sentences per text	No. of words	Mean no. of words per text	V tokens
ENG	12	233	15.53 (8.57)	2321	143.73 (34.48)	435
	16	210	14.00 (7.80)	2609	173.93 (87.39)	439
GER	12	227	11.35 (2.25)	1825	91.25 (26.77)	280
	16	241	12.05 (5.46)	2739	136.95 (64.31)	433
RUS	12	124	12.40 (1.65)	789	78.90 (25.28)	153
	16	121	12.10 (1.66)	1031	103.10 (33.60)	180
RUS-GER	12	157	10.47 (3.70)	1611	107.40 (41.68)	272
	16	265	11.52 (4.07)	3214	139.74 (40.95)	533
TUR	12	77	11.00 (1.91)	440	62.86 (13.24)	73
	16	59	11.80 (1.30)	292	58.40 (10.67)	51
TUR-GER	12	195	9.75 (2.02)	1615	80.75 (21.06)	257
	16	186	8.86 (2.95)	1863	88.71 (34.49)	306
VIET	12	82	8.20 (3.74)	840	84.00 (33.72)	156
	16	152	15.20 (3.22)	1821	182.10 (63.62)	283
VIET-GER	12	297	11.42 (2.73)	2480	95.38 (20.83)	432
	16	245	11.14 (4.28)	2937	133.50 (50.62)	463
Total		2,871	11.53 (4.51)	28427	114.16 (54.44)	4,746

Abbreviations: no. = number, V = verb.

Finally, even though the number of Turkish monolingual participants is the lowest (*n* = 12), most unanalyzable verbs can be found in this group, i.e., 15.3 percent of all verb tokens in the texts of the Turkish monolinguals were marked as formally unanalyzable. In general, the overall performance of the Turkish monolingual group is intriguing. Not only is the length difference striking, but also, when analyzing the texts composed by the Turkish students, a distinct difference is observable in comparison to all other texts.[2] The Turkish monolingual participants rarely produced long sentences or complete stories, and they often used Turkish words within their English texts.

7.1.2 Subject-verb agreement

This section zooms in on subject-verb agreement (SVA) in the present tense of lexical verbs (affixal SVA) and SVA in the present and past tense of suppletive verbs (*be*, *have*). The latter also includes passive forms as well as progressive forms. This distinction is important, since in English,

Tense and aspect: mono- vs. bilinguals 143

Mean no. of V tokens per text	Mean no. of V tokens per text (normalized)	V types	Mean no. of V types per text	Mean no. of V types per text (normalized)	V type-token-ratio	No. of unanalyzable Vs
29.00 (10.03)	18.65 (3.36)	267	17.80 (4.42)	11.60 (2.05)	0.61	0
29.27 (15.92)	16.74 (1.91)	314	20.93 (11.00)	12.17 (2.17)	0.72	0
14.00 (3.42)	15.57 (1.91)	166	8.30 (2.41)	9.47 (2.47)	0.59	0
21.65 (9.98)	16.09 (1.80)	277	13.85 (6.12)	10.31 (2.44)	0.64	0
15.30 (5.62)	19.31 (3.03)	102	10.20 (3.28)	13.17 (2.87)	0.67	1
18.00 (6.15)	17.46 (1.79)	125	12.50 (3.67)	12.44 (2.39)	0.69	2
18.13 (6.77)	17.42 (4.21)	168	11.20 (4.61)	10.82 (3.19)	0.62	5
23.17 (6.77)	16.66 (1.89)	363	15.78 (4.93)	11.32 (1.81)	0.68	2
10.43 (2.72)	16.46 (1.80)	41	5.86 (2.23)	9.01 (1.73)	0.56	10
10.20 (4.79)	16.62 (7.52)	26	5.20 (2.56)	8.46 (3.60)	0.51	9
12.85 (3.28)	16.10 (2.02)	168	8.40 (2.31)	10.87 (2.89)	0.65	6
14.57 (4.50)	17.31 (3.39)	205	9.76 (3.13)	11.98 (3.73)	0.67	4
15.60 (8.51)	18.08 (2.78)	102	10.20 (3.57)	12.37 (1.33)	0.65	9
28.30 (7.84)	16.20 (2.73)	201	20.10 (6.30)	11.33 (1.66)	0.71	1
16.62 (3.95)	17.53 (2.29)	264	10.15 (2.26)	11.02 (3.15)	0.61	4
21.05 (8.05)	15.91 (2.24)	307	13.95 (6.24)	10.45 (2.66)	0.66	1
19.06 (9.32)	16.91 (2.92)	3,096	12.43 (6.38)	11.08 (2.84)	0.65	54

lexical verbs do not inflect in the simple past tense. However, several students' texts are composed in the simple past.

The data were coded for required/present/missing/overuse of the third person singular –s (affixal SVA), and correct/incorrect SVA of suppletive verbs. The respective absolute numbers as well as percentages per language group and age cohort can be found in Table 7.2. Presence of the third person singular –s represents target-like usage, and absence or overuse refer to non-target-like uses. The number of missing –s morphemes is relatively high, especially compared to the number of third person singular –s endings that are present (across the entire sample, approximately 55 percent of third person singular –s morphemes are missing). Yet, there is an overall improvement from the younger to the older cohorts, visible in the decreasing error rates within all language groups apart from the Turkish monolingual students. Moreover, overuse of third person singular –s is a relatively infrequent phenomenon, since there are only 26 suffixes in total that appear on verbs where no inflectional endings are required. This occurs, for example, in combination with a modal or

Table 7.2 Affixal and suppletive SVA: absolute frequencies and percentages

Language group	Age	Required 3rd sg –s	Present 3rd sg –s	Missing 3rd sg –s	Overuse of 3rd sg –s	% missing 3rd sg –s	Correct suppletive SVA	Incorrect suppletive SVA	% incorrect suppletive SVA
ENG	12	24	24	0	1	0.00	111	2	1.77
	16	51	51	0	0	0.00	110	0	0.00
GER	12	69	27	42	4	60.87	76	3	3.80
	16	71	52	19	1	26.76	112	0	0.00
RUS	12	16	0	16	0	100.00	24	1	4.00
	16	26	5	21	2	80.77	44	5	10.20
RUS-GER	12	51	10	41	1	80.39	56	12	17.65
	16	82	34	48	2	58.54	103	8	7.21
TUR	12	11	0	11	2	100.00	39	3	7.14
	16	13	0	13	0	100.00	34	2	5.56
TUR-GER	12	74	35	39	3	52.70	66	11	14.29
	16	67	41	26	3	38.81	75	12	13.79
VIET	12	36	0	36	0	100.00	38	8	17.39
	16	15	7	8	0	53.33	65	0	0.00
VIET-GER	12	134	30	104	5	77.61	114	12	9.52
	16	113	68	45	2	39.82	116	6	4.92
Total		853	384	469	26	54.98	1,183	85	6.70

Abbreviations: 3rd sg –s = third person singular –s; SVA = subject-verb agreement.

auxiliary verb (1) or with a plural subject (2). In these cases, no third person singular –s is required in English.

(1) *The Father will this Fish **cuts**.* (Turkish-German student, 12 years old)
(2) *Son and Father **goes** at home and son looks in the bucket with the Fish.* (Turkish-German student, 16 years old)

Whereas many lexical verbs are formed incorrectly in the third person singular, the opposite is visible for the distribution within the second SVA category. For SVA agreement of suppletive verbs the reverse pattern emerges, namely few incorrect and many correct forms (across the entire sample, only approximately 7 percent incorrect SVA agreement with suppletive verbs). Thus, the error rates are comparably lower, with 17.7 percent being the highest rate of incorrect SVA among the 12-year-old Russian-German bilinguals. Moreover, a general learner improvement also becomes apparent, which manifests in lower error rates among the older students, except for the groups of Russian and Turkish monolinguals. In addition, there are also comparably more instances of SVA with *be* or *have*. As indicated above, this is largely due to many past tense as well as progressive uses, plus the overall high frequency of copula verbs, both in the present and past tense.

Initially, one hypothesis was that the Vietnamese monolinguals in particular might have difficulties with morphological tense formation because Vietnamese is an isolating language (see Chapters 4 and 5). Yet, this cannot be (completely) corroborated. Even though the 12-year-old Vietnamese monolingual participants are indeed at the lower end of all students (both for affixal and suppletive SVA), the Turkish monolinguals as well as the younger cohort of the Russian monolinguals also did not produce any third person singular –s morphemes, and the error rates for suppletive verbs of the 12-year-old Russian-German and Turkish-German bilinguals are comparably high.

To assess the significance of these observations, Pearson's chi-squared tests were performed by considering the age cohorts individually, limited to the non-native learners (i.e., the English native speaker control group is excluded). All following analyses were performed in R (Version 4.0.2; R Core Team 2020). The differences between present versus missing third person singular –s reach statistical significance for both the 12-year-old ($x^2(6) = 47.65$, $p < .001$) and 16-year-old ($x^2(6) = 70.88$, $p < .001$) participants. Among the younger participants, the German monolinguals and the Turkish-German bilinguals have a significantly lower rate of missing third person singular –s inflections, whereas the Russian, Turkish, as well as Vietnamese monolinguals omitted the third person singular –s significantly more frequently. Almost the same is true for the older participants. Again, the German monolinguals as well as the Turkish-German bilinguals have the lowest proportions of missing affixal SVA. Here, however, the Russian and Turkish monolinguals and the Vietnamese-German bilinguals produced significantly fewer third person singular –s morphemes.

The differences between the foreign language learner groups observed for suppletive SVA only reach statistical significance among the older participants ($x^2(6) = 23.88$, $p < .001$), yet not among the younger ones ($x^2(6) = 12.37$, $p = .054$). Among the 16-year-old students, the German monolinguals and the Vietnamese-German bilinguals have the lowest and the Turkish-German bilinguals the highest error rates.

Overall, the observed differences between affixal and suppletive SVA correspond to findings from other studies focusing on L2 learners. For example, Ionin and Wexler (2002) demonstrated that L2 learners make fewer mistakes with suppletive agreement than with affixal agreement. They argued that the acquisition of certain inflectional endings, such as the third person singular –s, is proportionally more difficult. First, L2 learners acquire SVA with the verb *be*, and only later with lexical verbs (Ionin and Wexler 2002: 128–129).

7.1.3 Copula verb be

Since Russian, Turkish, and Vietnamese are languages which frequently allow the omission of a copula verb where in English or in German a copula verb is required (see again Chapter 4), it was assumed that learners with a Russian, Turkish, or Vietnamese background would have more difficulties with the use of the copula verb *be* in English. For example, the following two sentences (taken from the E-LiPS corpus) are contexts where the use of the copula *be* is required in English, but in Russian this sentence is target-like without the use of a copula verb (see Section 4.4).

(3) *They Ø very happy.* (Russian monolingual student, 12 years old)
(4) *Fish Ø in net.* (Russian monolingual student, 16 years old)

The analysis of the copula verbs in the E-LiPS corpus yields interesting observations. The corresponding overview of the uses (required and missing) of the copula verb *be* can be found in Table 7.3. Noticeably, the Russian, Turkish, and Vietnamese monolinguals (in particular the younger cohort of the latter group) show comparably high numbers of missing copula verbs (highlighted in bold). Since the number of students per group differs, the percentages of missing copulas per language group as well as the percentages of students who omitted at least one copula verb are indicated as well. Crucially, less than 50 percent of the monolingual Russian, Turkish, or Vietnamese students omitted one or more copula verbs. This shows that not all but only some of the respective participants have difficulties with using copula verbs in English. However, these numbers are still higher than the remaining learner groups.

Two chi-squared tests (for each age cohort separately and with the English native speaker group excluded from the analysis) confirm

Table 7.3 Absolute frequencies and percentages of required and missing copula verbs

Language group	Age	N	Required copula be	Missing copula be	% of missing copula be	No. of students who omitted at least 1 copula be	% of students who omitted at least 1 copula be
ENG	12	15	60	0	0.00	0	0.00
	16	15	47	0	0.00	0	0.00
GER	12	20	63	1	1.59	1	5.00
	16	20	68	1	1.47	1	5.00
RUS	12	10	32	10	31.25	3	30.00
	16	10	35	8	22.86	4	40.00
RUS-GER	12	15	47	0	0.00	0	0.00
	16	23	85	1	1.18	1	4.35
TUR	12	7	32	8	25.00	2	28.57
	16	5	24	3	12.50	2	40.00
TUR-GER	12	20	52	0	0.00	0	0.00
	16	21	60	1	1.67	1	4.76
VIET	12	10	22	8	36.36	4	40.00
	16	10	38	1	2.63	1	10.00
VIET-GER	12	26	84	1	1.19	1	3.85
	16	22	72	0	0.00	0	0.00
Total		249	821	43	5.24	21	8.43

Abbreviation: N = number of students per language group.

that the observed differences are statistically significant (12-year-old students: $x^2(6) = 73.82$, $p < .001$; 16-year-old students: $x^2(6) = 44.64$, $p < .001$). The residuals substantiate that for the younger cohorts, the Russian, Turkish, and Vietnamese monolingual students show more absent copula verbs than expected. Slightly different are the results for the older participants. Here, only the Russian and Turkish monolinguals have a higher number of absent forms of *be*. The Vietnamese monolinguals perform like the other groups and show more present copula verbs than expected, i.e., fewer missing forms of *be*.[3]

Furthermore, separate chi-squared tests were run for the number of students who omitted at least one copula verb. Again, the obtained p-values are lower than 0.05, suggesting that the null hypothesis of no difference can be rejected (12-year-old cohorts: $x^2(6) = 22.30$, $p = .001$; 16-year-old cohorts: $x^2(6) = 21.23$, $p = .002$). The residuals of both chi-squared tests confirm that for the monolingual Russian and Turkish groups, the number of students who omitted (a) copula verb(s) is higher than expected. The same is true for the monolingual Vietnamese students, however only among the 12-year-old students.

148 *Tense and aspect: mono- vs. bilinguals*

Overall, these results indicate that the previous expectation is largely met. The high number of missing copula verbs for the Russian, Turkish, as well as the younger Vietnamese monolingual participants could be explained by (negative) crosslinguistic influence from the respective native languages. Striking, however, is the observation that the Russian-German, Turkish-German, and Vietnamese-German bilinguals do not show negative crosslinguistic influence from their heritage language but rather perform like the German monolingual students.

7.1.4 Formal correctness and target-like meaning of verbs

The following analysis investigates the overall formal correctness and target-like meaning of verbs. Formal correctness only considers the form of the verb but disregards whether this particular tense or aspect form fits into the concrete context. This stands in opposition to target-like use of verbs that regards whether the verb represents a target-like English use, i.e., a suitable choice of tense and aspect, irrespective of the form. Table 7.4 presents the absolute numbers and proportions of formally (in)correct verbs and (non-)target-like meaning of verbs.

The data in Table 7.4 reveal that there are more formally incorrect verbs (n = 1,156) than verbs with non-target-like meaning (n = 630). Also, the variation across the groups is larger for formal correctness (range between 44 and 99 percent of formally correct verbs) than for target-like meaning (range between 79 and 97 percent of verbs with target-like meaning). In addition, there is an increase in the rates of both formal correctness and target-like meaning from the younger to the older participants. As before, this trend is not visible in the Turkish monolingual group, underlining that this group appears to be less proficient than the other 16-year-old foreign language learners of English. The second exception is the older cohort of the Vietnamese monolinguals. These participants seem to be relatively more proficient in English in comparison to their peers, which is particularly visible for formal correctness (approximately 93 percent of the verbs are formally correct).

To assess whether the observed differences in the proportions of formally correct verbs and verbs with target-like meaning across the groups reach statistical significance, an analysis of variance was conducted (again, without the English native speaker control group). The data showed some violations in terms of normal distribution. But since the variance was homoscedastic, Kruskal-Wallis one-way ANOVAs could be employed (see Levshina 2015: 176–179). Only one ANOVA reports a statistically significant difference, namely among the 16-year-old participants when comparing the proportions of formally correct verbs ($H(6)$ = 27.44, p < .001). As previously mentioned, two groups perform comparably differently among the older cohorts, namely the Turkish monolinguals (relatively low proportions of formally correct verbs) and the Vietnamese monolinguals (relatively high proportions of formally correct verbs). The

Table 7.4 Absolute frequencies and proportions (with standard deviations in parenthesis) of formally (in)correct verbs and (non-)target-like meaning of verbs per learner group

Language group	Age	Absolute number of Vs	Correct form of Vs	Incorrect form of Vs	Proportion of formally correct Vs (sd)	Target-like meaning of Vs	Non-target-like meaning of Vs	Proportion of target-like meaning of Vs (sd)
ENG	12	435	408	27	0.94 (0.06)	424	11	0.97 (0.04)
	16	439	432	7	0.99 (0.03)	428	11	0.97 (0.06)
GER	12	280	195	85	0.65 (0.27)	236	44	0.84 (0.13)
	16	433	360	73	0.78 (0.25)	375	58	0.85 (0.13)
RUS	12	153	104	49	0.60 (0.23)	120	33	0.79 (0.14)
	16	180	123	57	0.64 (0.26)	155	25	0.83 (0.15)
RUS-GER	12	272	166	106	0.55 (0.24)	192	80	0.70 (0.19)
	16	533	435	98	0.80 (0.15)	468	65	0.87 (0.15)
TUR	12	73	42	31	0.58 (0.22)	61	12	0.85 (0.14)
	16	51	27	24	0.44 (0.24)	41	10	0.84 (0.11)
TUR-GER	12	257	150	107	0.56 (0.19)	204	53	0.79 (0.12)
	16	306	192	114	0.58 (0.25)	260	46	0.83 (0.12)
VIET	12	156	72	84	0.49 (0.15)	126	30	0.86 (0.15)
	16	283	263	20	0.92 (0.08)	260	23	0.91 (0.05)
VIET-GER	12	432	264	168	0.62 (0.19)	366	66	0.86 (0.13)
	16	463	357	106	0.74 (0.25)	400	63	0.87 (0.10)
Total		4,746	3,590	1,156	0.69 (0.25)	4,116	630	0.85 (0.14)

Abbreviations: sd = standard deviation; Vs = verbs.

150 *Tense and aspect: mono- vs. bilinguals*

variances across the other groups do not differ to a statistically significant extent.

7.2 Progressive aspect (written component of the learner corpus)

For the analysis of the progressive aspect, the concordance program AntConc (Anthony 2016) was used to obtain all relevant progressive tokens. First, all word forms with the suffix *–ing* were extracted, and in a second step, the dataset was cleaned by excluding all non-progressives such as gerunds or nouns. As detailed in Section 6.2, all remaining *–ing*-forms were counted and classified according to formal correctness and target-like use of the verb (see also Bardovi-Harlig 1992, 2000). One additional variable relevant here is the absence or presence of the auxiliary verb. This is strictly speaking a subcategory of formal correctness, because all formally correct tokens are automatically coded 'auxiliary verb present'. Progressives that are coded as being formally incorrect, however, do not necessarily imply that the auxiliary is absent, because the main verb could be misspelled or the form of *be* could be incorrect.

The numeric overview in Table 7.5 shows that overall, the progressive aspect was used relatively infrequently. In total, there appear only 356 uses of the progressive aspect in the E-LiPS corpus stemming from a total of 259 transcripts.

The English native speaker control groups achieve the highest rates of formal correctness as well as target-like meaning, and the lowest rates of missing auxiliaries. The results for the foreign language learners are more differentiated. Concerning the target-like meaning of the progressive aspect, the monolingual Turkish and Russian speakers use (almost) all progressives correctly. Yet, these proportions are based on few examples, especially for the two monolingual Turkish groups (i.e., 13 and 5 uses of the progressive aspect, respectively). This high rate of target-like meaning contrasts with the comparably low ratios of formally correct progressives for the same two groups, particularly among the 12-year-old participants, with less than 50 percent of formally correct progressive uses. In addition, the Turkish-German and Vietnamese monolingual students show low proportions of formal correctness as well (between 40 and 54 percent of formally correct progressives).

Furthermore, the ratios of formal correctness and target-like meaning show an increase from the younger to the older cohorts. Exceptions are the native speakers of English for formal correctness, and the German monolinguals for target-like meaning. Moreover, there is only a fairly minor increase of formally correct progressives among the Turkish-German bilinguals.

When comparing the two categories, the generally higher rates of target-like meanings of the progressive aspect demonstrate that the form of the progressive aspect appears to be more difficult than context-specific

Table 7.5 Overview of formal correctness and target-like usage of the progressive aspect, absence of auxiliary verb

Language group	Age	Progressive aspect tokens N	Progressive aspect types N	Formally correct progressive aspect N	%	Target-like meaning of progressive aspect N	%	Auxiliary missing N	%	state	achievement	activity	accomplishment
ENG	12	20	17	19	95.00	19	95.00	-	0.00	1	-	12	7
	16	37	23	34	91.89	37	100.00	2	5.41	-	4	25	8
GER	12	19	10	8	42.11	17	89.47	11	57.89	-	2	5	12
	16	40	16	25	62.50	33	82.50	8	20.00	5	6	19	10
RUS	12	6	3	2	33.33	6	100.00	4	66.67	1	-	4	1
	16	22	13	11	50.00	21	95.45	8	36.36	-	1	11	10
RUS-GER	12	18	7	8	44.44	14	77.78	8	44.44	3	-	7	8
	16	19	10	10	52.63	18	94.74	8	42.11	2	-	10	7
TUR	12	13	7	6	46.15	13	100.00	7	53.85	-	-	7	6
	16	5	5	5	100.00	5	100.00	-	0.00	-	-	3	2
TUR-GER	12	20	12	8	40.00	15	75.00	12	60.00	1	4	3	12
	16	32	13	13	40.63	27	84.38	16	50.00	2	3	16	11
VIET	12	16	10	7	43.75	14	87.50	6	37.50	1	-	6	9
	16	13	13	7	53.85	12	92.31	1	7.69	-	-	10	3
VIET-GER	12	34	12	18	52.94	30	88.24	14	41.18	2	4	15	13
	16	42	20	31	73.81	37	88.10	7	16.67	3	3	16	20
Total		356	67	212	59.55	318	89.33	112	31.46	21	27	169	139

Abbreviation: N = absolute frequency.

usage. Formal correctness could signal difficulties of using the correct form of the auxiliary verb *be*. Yet, the findings in Section 7.1.2 have shown that subject-verb agreement with suppletive verbs has mostly been used correctly. Therefore, and this is confirmed by the numbers in Table 7.5, the low ratios of formally correct progressive forms seem to be related to the omission of the auxiliary verb. This confirms one of the claims presented in Chapter 5, namely that complex tenses and aspectual distinctions, here shown with the progressive aspect, are used without the auxiliary verb in an early acquisitional phase (see also Ellis 2015: 79).

Moreover, as lexical variation may increase with increasing competence in a language, it could be assumed that the variety of verbs that is used in the progressive aspect correlates with higher proficiency. Thus, it is likely that during earlier acquisitional stages, only a limited number of verbs is used with the *–ing* suffix, but that with increasing knowledge of English, the types of verb used in the progressive rise. The number of different verbs occurring in the progressive aspect per language group and age cohort is reported in Table 7.5 (progressive aspect types). Overall, there is an increase in progressive verb types with increasing age, except for the Turkish monolingual participants. Among the most frequently occurring verbs are *go* ($n = 60$), *fish* ($n = 52$), *cry* ($n = 30$), and *look* ($n = 25$). This is not much of a surprise, considering these verbs were particularly triggered by the plot of the story and, in addition, these are typical activity verbs, hence, verbs that commonly occur in the progressive aspect in English. Together, they make up roughly 50 percent of all verbs that were used. Other verbs that appeared less frequently (but that were also triggered by the story plot or at least related to it) are, for instance, *catch* ($n = 19$), *walk* ($n = 16$), *eat* ($n = 15$), *shine* ($n = 10$), *watch* ($n = 10$), *kill* ($n = 9$), *stand* ($n = 8$), *come* ($n = 8$), and *swim* ($n = 6$).

Finally, the distribution of lexical aspect is investigated (see also Table 7.5). Activity and accomplishment verbs should appear most frequently in the progressive, and achievement and state verbs should be used less frequently. Generally, this trend is visible across all groups. Achievement (8 percent) and state (6 percent) verbs occur indeed relatively rarely, compared to the high frequencies of activity (47 percent) as well as accomplishment (39 percent) verbs. This is in accordance with the findings reported in Fuchs and Werner (2018), in that (young) foreign language learners do not overextend the progressive aspect to stative contexts but that the frequencies of stative progressives in learner language are in fact very low (Fuchs and Werner 2018: 212).

7.3 Present versus past time reference (written component of the learner corpus)

Across the written component of the learner corpus, the variation that occurs is mainly between simple present (approximately 46 percent) and simple past (approximately 28 percent). For most groups (except the older cohorts of the Russian and Vietnamese monolinguals) more than 70 percent of the story is written in either the simple past or simple present tense. In addition, there are several *to*-infinitive forms (approximately 10 percent), progressives (approximately 8 percent), and modal/conditional forms (approximately 4 percent), whilst present perfect (approximately 1 percent) or past prefect (approximately 0.01 percent), *will*-future (approximately 1.5 percent) or *going-to*-future (approximately 1 percent) appear only rarely.

Due to this distribution, this section focuses on the use of present and past time reference, in addition to discussing past tense reference in more detail. This approach may allow some insights into the developmental stages of the different learner groups. When learning a foreign language, learners first acquire present tense (or bare) forms and second, they start to use past tense(s) (see again Chapter 5).

Table 7.6 provides an overview of the absolute frequencies of simple present, simple past, present perfect, and past perfect verbs. Clearly, the latter two tenses occur particularly infrequently and there are nearly twice as many simple present tense forms than simple past tense forms.

For most learners who used at least some simple past verbs (i.e., all except for the Turkish monolinguals), there is an increase of past tense and a decrease of present tense from the younger to the older cohorts.

Table 7.6 Overview of tenses (absolute frequencies and percentages)

Language group	Age	No. of simple present	% of simple present	No. of simple past	% of simple past	No. of present perfect	% of present perfect	No. of past perfect	% of past perfect	Total
ENG	12	119	29.60	180	44.78	3	0.75	2	0.50	304
	16	131	31.64	168	40.58	3	0.72	5	1.21	307
GER	12	178	65.93	43	15.93	3	1.11	0	0.00	224
	16	154	37.65	136	33.25	4	0.98	3	0.73	297
RUS	12	39	26.53	79	53.74	0	0.00	0	0.00	118
	16	84	48.28	31	17.82	3	1.72	3	1.72	121
RUS-GER	12	117	46.99	72	28.92	3	1.20	2	0.80	194
	16	187	36.03	200	38.54	4	0.77	2	0.39	393
TUR	12	49	77.78	0	0.00	0	0.00	0	0.00	49
	16	37	88.10	0	0.00	0	0.00	0	0.00	37
TUR-GER	12	143	58.61	43	17.62	9	3.69	0	0.00	195
	16	173	59.86	32	11.07	4	1.38	1	0.35	210
VIET	12	94	69.63	9	6.67	2	1.48	0	0.00	105
	16	56	21.71	119	46.12	3	1.16	7	2.71	185
VIET-GER	12	274	66.02	55	13.25	5	1.20	1	0.24	335
	16	221	49.66	100	22.47	4	0.90	3	0.67	328
Total		2,056	45.94	1,267	28.31	50	1.11	29	0.01	3,402

Note: The percentages are based on the overall tense classification of 4,475 verbs (including progressives, modal and conditional verbs, *will*-future, *going-to*-future, infinitives; excluding passives, imperatives, non-English verbs, unclassified verbs).

Intriguingly, the only groups that differ are the English native speakers, the Russian monolinguals, and the Turkish-German bilinguals. The proportions for present and past tense are nearly identical for the two English native speaker groups, potentially attributable to comparable proficiency levels among the native speakers. The 12-year-old Russian monolinguals used relatively high proportions of past tense, whilst the opposite is the case for the 16-year-old students. The Turkish-German bilinguals use few past tense forms overall, the older even fewer than the younger students. Furthermore, the 12-year-old Russian monolinguals, both English native speaker groups, as well as the 16-year-old Vietnamese monolinguals show the highest frequencies of past tense uses.

Some of these observations seem to be in line with what has previously been noted. The English native speakers were reported as performing at ceiling (which is of course to be expected) and they used a relatively high number of simple past tense verbs (approximately 40 percent of all verbs). The 16-year-old Vietnamese monolinguals were also identified as presumably having a higher proficiency in English than their same-age peers. This was reinforced by the high percentage of simple past tense verbs (approximately 46 percent). Moreover, the Turkish monolinguals were pointed out to have a comparably low English proficiency, which may be an explanation for not having used any past tense verbs when composing the English texts. They largely relied on simple present tense forms.[4]

The next step is to investigate whether the observed frequency differences are statistically significant. Two Pearson's chi-squared tests were performed, based on the absolute frequencies of simple present and simple past tense forms, separately for the two age cohorts and excluding the English native speaker control group. Both for the 12-year-old as well as the 16-year-old participants, the two chi-squared tests prove to be highly significant (12-year-old cohorts: $x^2(6) = 174.01, p < .001$; 16-year-old cohorts: $x^2(6) = 178.34, p < .001$). The residuals underline what was noticed from the proportional differences: among the younger cohorts, the Russian monolinguals and the Russian-German monolinguals are reported as using more past tense forms than expected. Conversely, the Turkish-German, Vietnamese-German, as well as the German, Turkish, and Vietnamese monolingual students produce significantly fewer past tense forms than expected. For the 16-year-old students, though, the residuals reveal that the Russian-German bilinguals as well as the German and Vietnamese monolinguals show higher rates of past tense verbs than expected, whereas past tense verbs are underrepresented in the texts of the Russian and Turkish monolinguals in addition to those of the Turkish-German and Vietnamese-German bilinguals.

7.4 Written versus spoken production

The final results section of the in-depth linguistic analysis provides a comparison between the written and spoken component of the E-LiPS learner corpus. As was mentioned in Chapter 6, not all students participated in both the oral and the written tasks, but only a subgroup took part in the oral exercise. Thus, the spoken component of the learner corpus contains fewer transcripts than the written section. To ensure comparability in this section, the written component of the learner corpus was reduced so that only those written text samples are included that also have a spoken counterpart. This minimizes the dataset to a total number of 176 students (see Table 7.7), which makes up a learner corpus that includes 352 individual files and consists of 33,759 word tokens. All foreign language learner groups are included, whilst the English native speakers are not, because none of the English native speakers participated in the oral task.

7.4.1 Frequency overview: written texts versus oral recordings

The frequency overview reported in Table 7.7 compares the number of words written/spoken as well as the normalized mean number of verb tokens and types in the students' texts and recordings.

The 12-year-old cohorts produced approximately between 55 and 62 words per oral recording. Noticeably different are the German monolinguals (98.5 words on average) and the Turkish monolinguals (77.76 words on average). The average frequencies of the 16-year-old participants are higher (except for the monolingual Turkish learners) which shows that there is an overall increase in the length of the oral recordings with increasing age.

In comparison to the written texts, it can be observed that on average, the students produced longer written texts (apart from the 12-year-old German and Turkish monolinguals). Moreover, a comparison across the learner groups reveals that the German monolinguals, the Russian-German and Vietnamese-German bilinguals, as well as the 16-year-old Vietnamese monolinguals have slightly higher mean values than the other monolinguals and the Turkish-German bilinguals. This trend is visible for both the spoken and written transcripts and has already been discussed in the previous sections. Hence, the same trends can be observed across the written and spoken sections of the learner corpus.

Moreover, a correlation analysis visualized in R, using the package *lattice* (Sarkar 2008) and following Schweinberger (2021), reveals that across the individual language groups there are significant associations between the written and spoken words (see Figure 7.1). All Pearson's correlations are moderately positive and significant, except for the Turkish monolinguals.

Furthermore, when looking at the mean frequencies of verb tokens in both the written as well as the spoken part of the learner corpus, the differences both across the language groups and within each language group are very small (Table 7.7). This finding is similar to what was presented in Section 7.1.1, where only the written texts were investigated. In addition, the same trend can be observed for the normalized mean

156 *Tense and aspect: mono- vs. bilinguals*

Table 7.7 Frequency overview of written and spoken component of the learner corpus; absolute numbers and means (with standard deviations in parenthesis)

Language group	Age	N	No. of words w	No. of words s	Mean no. of words per text/recording w	Mean no. of words per text/recording s	Mean no. of V tokens (normalized) w	Mean no. of V tokens (normalized) s	Mean no. of V types (normalized) w	Mean no. of V types (normalized) s
GER	12	10	874	985	87.40 (22.21)	98.50 (43.11)	15.46 (1.99)	14.89 (3.90)	9.91 (2.76)	10.19 (2.97)
	16	11	1,699	1,350	154.45 (72.95)	122.73 (66.32)	15.86 (2.10)	13.89 (2.71)	10.06 (2.90)	11.07 (3.58)
RUS	12	10	789	555	78.90 (26.65)	55.50 (18.10)	19.31 (3.19)	19.16 (5.27)	13.17 (3.03)	12.49 (3.89)
	16	10	1,031	856	103.10 (35.42)	85.60 (51.96)	17.46 (1.89)	17.11 (3.32)	12.44 (2.52)	10.58 (2.97)
RUS-GER	12	12	1,283	747	106.92 (44.74)	62.25 (25.29)	16.97 (4.80)	14.99 (1.65)	11.03 (3.67)	11.68 (2.14)
	16	20	2,835	1,942	141.75 (43.57)	97.10 (25.55)	16.55 (1.96)	15.58 (2.37)	11.36 (1.85)	11.54 (2.05)
TUR	12	6	368	466	61.33 (15.03)	77.67 (25.72)	16.43 (2.13)	13.72 (6.01)	9.12 (2.02)	7.39 (3.62)
	16	4	250	248	62.50 (8.81)	62.00 (23.05)	20.18 (3.13)	19.79 (2.69)	9.98 (2.49)	8.91 (1.73)
TUR-GER	12	15	1,234	856	82.27 (18.96)	57.07 (18.59)	16.01 (2.36)	16.47 (2.80)	10.58 (2.94)	12.41 (2.68)
	16	17	1,624	1,468	95.53 (34.87)	86.35 (46.94)	16.56 (3.07)	14.49 (3.51)	11.18 (3.67)	9.85 (3.25)
VIET	12	10	840	602	84.00 (35.54)	60.20 (16.54)	18.08 (2.93)	17.63 (2.45)	12.37 (1.40)	13.41 (3.59)
	16	10	1,821	1,209	182.10 (67.06)	120.90 (42.96)	16.20 (2.88)	17.51 (3.56)	11.33 (1.75)	12.29 (3.08)
VIET-GER	12	20	1,943	1,337	97.15 (20.56)	66.85 (25.24)	17.37 (2.27)	17.94 (3.67)	10.65 (2.46)	12.61 (3.12)
	16	21	2,708	1,839	128.95 (48.38)	87.57 (40.05)	16.03 (2.28)	16.57 (3.00)	10.45 (2.79)	11.98 (3.77)
Total		176	19,299	14,460	109.65 (49.64)	82.16 (40.67)	16.81 (2.78)	16.30 (3.58)	11.01 (2.77)	11.48 (3.27)

Abbreviations: N = number of students per language group; s = spoken; V = verb; w = written.

Tense and aspect: mono- vs. bilinguals 157

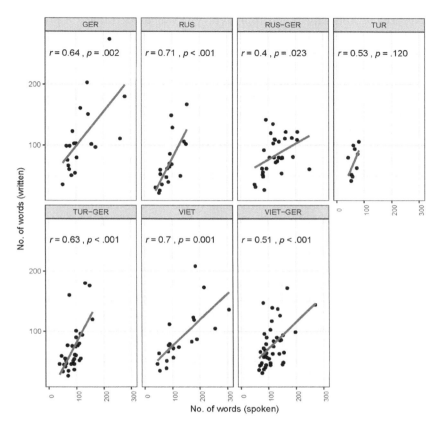

Figure 7.1 Pearson's correlations between number of words written and spoken per language group.

frequencies of verb types. For both categories, no clear age-specific or group-specific differences are visible. However, the mean frequencies of verb types are lower than those of the verb tokens. Thus, in general, all foreign language learners use a comparable number of verb tokens and types. This is a crucial result and confirms that in terms of quantity, the learners are clearly comparable. Whereas there are frequency differences in terms of overall word frequency (i.e., more words used in the written task), there seems to be a parallel performance for verb types and tokens when controlled for frequency differences (i.e., normalized mean frequencies).

7.4.2 Subject-verb agreement

For the comparison between SVA in the written and oral production, the same differentiation between SVA of lexical verbs (i.e., affixal SVA), which is realized with the third person singular –s morpheme, and SVA of the verbs be and have (i.e., suppletive SVA) was used. Table 7.8 presents the frequency overview of the spoken component of the learner corpus (absolute frequencies and percentages) in addition to the percentages of correct SVA of the written component.

The overall distribution of SVA in the written texts and oral recordings is relatively similar. There are generally high proportions of missing third person singular –s morphemes across all language groups. This is especially visible in the monolingual Russian, Turkish, and Vietnamese, as well as the Turkish-German bilingual cohorts, with more than 75 percent of missing third person singular –s morphemes per language group in the oral recordings. The other three groups show relatively more target-like uses (less than 75 percent missing –s morphemes). Noteworthy, however, are the differences observed in the data of the Turkish-German bilinguals and Vietnamese monolinguals. Whereas the error rates of the former are much lower in the written texts than in the spoken data (approximately 40 percent of missing –s morphemes versus approximately 80 percent), the opposite is true for the 16-year-old Vietnamese monolinguals. While only around 50 percent of third person singular –s morphemes were omitted in the written task, almost all (97 percent) were omitted in the oral task. In addition, the 16-year-old monolingual German students show the lowest proportions of missing third person singular –s morphemes in both the texts as well as recordings.

In accordance with what was shown in Section 7.1.2, the error rates for suppletive SVA are generally much lower in the oral data as well. Yet, whereas in the written data, SVA agreement with suppletive verbs was overall more frequent than with lexical verbs, the reverse is visible in the oral data. By and large, there are few incorrect forms of be or have in the learner corpus (only approximately 8 percent), with slightly higher error rates in the oral data of the 12-year-old German monolinguals and Russian monolinguals. Note, however, that in the latter group, only a total number of four uses of suppletive verbs occurred in the oral data. In the remaining learner groups, the distribution between correct and incorrect SVA with suppletive verbs is highly similar.

Thus, it can be argued that for both the written and oral production, the same general trends can be observed: the third person singular –s is frequently omitted (in total, 70 percent in the oral and 61 percent in the written data), whereas the students make few mistakes with SVA of suppletive verbs (less than 10 percent incorrect forms in both corpus sections).

7.4.3 Copula verb be

Table 7.9 presents the absolute numbers of required and missing copula verbs, as well as the respective percentages. As was done in Section 7.1.3, separate columns include the number of students (as well as percentages)

Table 7.8 Affixal and suppletive SVA: absolute frequencies and percentages of spoken and percentages of written corpus component

Language group	Age	Required 3rd sg –s (s)	Present 3rd sg –s (s)	Missing 3rd sg –s (s)	Overuse of 3rd sg –s (s)	% missing 3rd sg –s (s)	% missing 3rd sg –s (w)	Correct suppletive SVA (s)	Incorrect suppletive SVA (s)	% incorrect suppletive SVA (s)	% incorrect suppletive SVA (w)
GER	12	62	20	42	0	67.74	74.07	20	6	23.08	4.26
	16	34	28	6	0	17.65	26.19	58	0	0.00	0.00
RUS	12	41	0	41	0	100.00	100.00	2	2	50.00	4.00
	16	43	2	41	1	95.35	80.77	24	1	4.00	10.20
RUS-GER	12	56	23	33	0	58.93	76.19	13	3	18.75	15.38
	16	105	43	62	3	59.05	60.27	44	3	6.38	5.43
TUR	12	13	3	10	3	76.92	100.00	31	1	3.13	9.09
	16	7	1	6	0	85.71	100.00	21	2	8.70	5.56
TUR-GER	12	54	10	44	2	81.48	41.18	20	3	13.04	12.90
	16	54	13	41	0	75.93	38.89	42	5	10.64	11.90
VIET	12	43	9	34	0	79.07	100.00	32	3	8.57	17.39
	16	32	1	31	1	96.88	53.33	53	6	10.17	0.00
VIET-GER	12	121	32	89	0	73.55	79.41	33	3	8.33	11.65
	16	98	46	52	3	53.06	39.82	50	4	7.41	5.17
Total		763	231	532	13	69.72	61.13	443	42	8.66	7.99

Abbreviations: 3rd sg –s = third person singular –s; s = spoken; SVA = subject-verb agreement; w = written.

160 Tense and aspect: mono- vs. bilinguals

Table 7.9 Absolute frequencies and percentages of required and missing copula verbs of spoken and percentages of written corpus component

Language group	Age	Required copula be	Missing copula be	% of missing copula be		No. of students who omitted at least 1 be		% of students who omitted at least 1 be	
		s	s	s	w	s	w	s	w
GER	12	14	0	0.00	2.78	0	0	0.00	0.00
	16	20	0	0.00	2.86	0	1	0.00	9.09
RUS	12	3	0	0.00	31.25	0	3	0.00	30.00
	16	19	6	31.58	22.86	4	4	40.00	40.00
RUS-GER	12	11	1	9.09	0.00	1	0	8.33	0.00
	16	24	0	0.00	1.43	0	1	0.00	5.00
TUR	12	16	2	12.50	29.63	1	2	16.67	33.33
	16	16	3	18.75	4.55	1	1	25.00	25.00
TUR-GER	12	16	0	0.00	0.00	0	0	0.00	0.00
	16	18	1	5.56	1.67	1	1	5.88	5.88
VIET	12	15	1	6.67	36.36	1	4	10.00	40.00
	16	29	1	3.45	2.63	1	1	10.00	10.00
VIET-GER	12	22	1	4.55	1.45	1	1	5.00	5.00
	16	37	0	0.00	0.00	0	0	0.00	0.00
Total		260	16	6.15	6.91	11	19	6.25	10.80

Abbreviations: s = spoken; w = written.

who omitted at least one copula verb, to put these numbers of missing copula uses into perspective.

Intriguingly, there are considerably fewer absent copula uses in the oral recordings (*n* = 16) compared to the absent copula verbs in the reduced part of the written corpus (*n* = 41). However, in the written texts, there are 593 contexts where a copula verb would be required, whereas in the oral recordings, there are only 260 forms of the copula verb that are necessary. Thus, in the oral picture descriptions, there are markedly fewer contexts that require a copula verb. These low numbers of absent copula verbs (particularly in the oral recordings) are difficult to interpret, and this must be kept in mind in the following paragraph.

Yet, qualitatively, it can be observed that the oral recordings and written texts appear to be rather comparable. It remains true that the Russian, Turkish, and Vietnamese monolinguals show relatively higher rates of copula omissions, compared to the bilinguals and the German monolinguals. However, none of the 12-year-old Russian monolinguals omitted a copula (but note that there are only three copulas required in the recordings). Moreover, the overall number of students who omitted at least one copula verb is quite low, with 11 and 19 out of 176 students in the spoken and the written section of the corpus, respectively. The number is presumably lower in the spoken component, as there are overall fewer copula uses that are required. Yet, as mentioned, it is difficult to make any general statements because of these low frequencies. A larger corpus sample would be needed to substantiate these initial trends.

7.4.4 Formal correctness and target-like meaning of verbs

For the comparison of formal correctness and target-like meaning of verbs, there is one important difference between the oral and the written data. In the oral recordings, formal correctness does not, of course, refer to spelling mistakes, but rather to grammatical mistakes, such as missing third person singular *–s* morphemes (see Section 7.4.2), or incorrectly formed past tense verbs, such as *catched* instead of *caught*. The absolute frequencies as well as mean proportions of formally correct verbs and verbs used in target-like contexts of the spoken data and the proportions of the written data can be found in Table 7.10.

The overall trend of formal correctness in the oral data is that the younger cohorts have proportionally more formally incorrect verbs than the respective older cohorts. Similar to what was reported about the written data in Section 7.1.4, the Turkish monolinguals are an exception, because in this group, this age-related improvement does not hold. In addition, they show the weakest performance of all groups. Furthermore, the comparably high frequency of formally correct verbs of the 16-year-old German monolinguals is remarkable (85 percent). This aligns with the former analysis of subject-verb agreement, where these learners were presented as having few omitted third person singular *–s* morphemes per recording and as always correctly using the forms of *be* and *have*. Since subject-verb agreement is a subcategory of formal correctness, this overlap between Section 7.4.2 and the current analysis is motivated. In addition, in all groups, except the 16-year-old German monolinguals, the students have higher mean proportions of formal correctness in the written texts in comparison to the oral recordings.

The findings for target-like versus non-target-like meaning of verbs are different. Overall, the ratios of verbs with target-like meaning are higher (approximately 80 percent in both the oral as well as the written data) than for formally correct verbs. Moreover, there are only minor differences across the groups as well as between the oral and written language production. Slightly lower are the rates for verbs with target-like meaning in the groups of the Turkish monolinguals and the 12-year-old Turkish-German monolinguals (oral data) and the 12-year-old Russian-German bilinguals (written data). However, the proportions of verbs with target-like meaning are still higher than 70 percent, apart from the older Turkish monolinguals. In this latter group, there are on average only 38 percent of verbs used in target-like contexts. Furthermore, there is a small increase of target-like meaning with increasing age, true for both subparts of the corpus. The only groups that diverge are the Turkish

Table 7.10 Absolute frequencies and proportions (with standard deviations in parenthesis) of formally (in)correct verbs and (non-)target-like meaning of spoken and proportions of written corpus component

Language group	Age	Correct form of Vs		Incorrect form of Vs		Proportion of formally correct Vs (sd)		Target-like meaning of Vs		Non-target-like meaning of Vs		Proportion of target-like meaning of Vs (sd)	
		s		s		s	w	s		s		s	w
GER	12	78		63		0.48 (0.28)	0.60 (0.21)	120		21		0.84 (0.11)	0.80 (0.12)
	16	163		19		0.85 (0.25)	0.77 (0.24)	171		11		0.91 (0.16)	0.84 (0.15)
RUS	12	50		50		0.47 (0.23)	0.60 (0.24)	71		29		0.73 (0.20)	0.79 (0.15)
	16	90		56		0.55 (0.27)	0.64 (0.28)	121		25		0.82 (0.23)	0.83 (0.17)
RUS-GER	12	67		45		0.51 (0.31)	0.55 (0.25)	92		20		0.81 (0.13)	0.72 (0.21)
	16	215		87		0.70 (0.25)	0.78 (0.15)	262		40		0.87 (0.16)	0.86 (0.16)
TUR	12	27		35		0.39 (0.28)	0.55 (0.22)	42		20		0.72 (0.24)	0.87 (0.16)
	16	23		27		0.37 (0.28)	0.55 (0.14)	24		26		0.38 (0.33)	0.80 (0.10)
TUR-GER	12	57		79		0.43 (0.29)	0.59 (0.17)	103		33		0.75 (0.19)	0.80 (0.13)
	16	130		65		0.59 (0.31)	0.64 (0.20)	169		26		0.86 (0.13)	0.82 (0.12)
VIET	12	52		55		0.47 (0.18)	0.49 (0.16)	92		15		0.86 (0.10)	0.86 (0.16)
	16	157		46		0.76 (0.23)	0.92 (0.09)	178		25		0.90 (0.13)	0.91 (0.06)
VIET-GER	12	118		115		0.48 (0.28)	0.63 (0.21)	196		37		0.83 (0.13)	0.85 (0.14)
	16	227		66		0.75 (0.18)	0.73 (0.26)	242		51		0.82 (0.19)	0.87 (0.11)
Total		1,454		808		0.58 (0.29)	0.66 (0.23)	1,883		379		0.82 (0.18)	0.83 (0.14)

Abbreviations: s = spoken; sd = standard deviation; Vs = verbs; w = written.

monolinguals (here target-like meaning is lower in the data of the older participants) as well as the Vietnamese-German bilinguals (in the oral data, the rate of target-like meaning is on average slightly lower).

7.4.5 Use of tenses and the progressive aspect

The final analysis zooms in on the use of tenses and the progressive aspect across the two components of the learner corpus. Table 7.11 includes the percentages for each language group and age cohort. Similar to what was presented for the written texts in Section 7.3, the simple present is the majority tense across the entire corpus. Percentage rates are even higher in the oral recordings. In nearly all groups, approximately 50 percent or more of the verbs occur in the simple present. Only the 16-year-old German and Vietnamese monolinguals use the simple present less frequently. Moreover, except for the Turkish monolinguals and the 16-year-old Turkish-German and Vietnamese-German bilinguals, the overall frequencies of simple present tense are higher in the oral recordings in comparison to the written texts.

The opposite can be observed for the use of the simple past tense. The proportions of the simple past are higher in the written texts, apart from the Turkish monolinguals (remember that they did not use the simple past in their writings; however, three simple past verbs occurred in the oral recordings) as well as the Vietnamese-German bilinguals (the simple past rates are almost identical in both corpus sections). The present perfect and past perfect occur equally infrequently and make up less than 1 percent each in both the oral and written data.

The use of the progressive aspect yields some interesting observations. First, the Russian-German and Turkish-German, as well as the Turkish and Vietnamese monolinguals use the progressive aspect more frequently in speech then in writing. The same is true for the 12-year-old German monolinguals. This group, together with the 12-year-old Turkish monolinguals, shows the highest rates of progressive uses (approximately 30 percent of all verbs). Only the Russian monolinguals, Vietnamese-German bilinguals, as well as the 12-year-old German monolinguals use the progressive less frequently in the oral data.

The frequencies of modal verbs and conditional verb uses are relatively low in both parts of the E-LiPS corpus. However, by and large, the proportions are either higher or almost alike in the spoken part. The only groups that did not make use of any modal or conditional forms are the 12-year-old Russian monolinguals and both groups of the Turkish monolinguals. Finally, there are few uses of *will-* or *going-to-*future verbs. This finding, however, is not too surprising, as the tasks involved retelling a story, and these settings did not particularly trigger future time reference, but clearly justify the use of present and past tenses.

This general overview of tense and aspect usage has revealed three main trends, although no absolute patterns could be detected as there are

164 *Tense and aspect: mono- vs. bilinguals*

Table 7.11 Overview of tenses in the oral recordings and written texts (absolute frequencies and percentages)

Language Group	Age	% simple present s	% simple present w	% simple past s	% simple past w	% present perfect s	% present perfect w	% past perfect s	% past perfect w	% progressive s	% progressive w	% modal conditional s	% modal conditional w	% will-future s	% will-future w	% going-to-future s	% going-to-future w	% to-infinitive s	% to-infinitive w	Absolute number of verb tokens s	Absolute number of verb tokens w
GER	12	68.79	62.12	6.38	13.64	1.42	0.76	0.00	0.00	7.09	11.36	2.13	2.27	2.13	2.27	0.71	0.00	5.67	2.27	141	132
	16	34.62	31.32	13.19	33.96	0.55	1.13	0.55	0.75	29.12	10.57	10.99	4.53	0.00	0.00	0.00	1.13	9.34	11.32	182	265
RUS	12	51.00	25.49	32.00	51.63	1.00	0.00	0.00	0.00	0.00	3.92	0.00	1.31	0.00	0.00	0.00	0.65	15.00	13.07	100	153
	16	56.16	46.67	10.96	17.22	1.37	1.67	0.68	1.67	6.16	12.22	4.11	3.89	0.00	0.00	2.74	2.22	17.81	11.11	146	180
RUS-GER	12	65.18	46.41	6.25	23.92	0.89	1.44	0.00	0.96	8.04	6.70	6.25	2.87	4.46	2.87	0.00	0.48	8.04	5.26	112	209
	16	48.01	33.33	18.21	39.10	0.00	0.85	0.66	0.43	6.29	3.63	7.28	5.77	0.33	0.00	0.00	0.00	14.57	14.10	302	468
TUR	12	50.00	68.85	3.23	0.00	0.00	0.00	0.00	0.00	32.26	18.03	0.00	0.00	0.00	0.00	0.00	0.00	14.57	1.64	62	61
	16	48.00	72.00	2.00	0.00	0.00	0.00	0.00	0.00	16.00	10.00	0.00	0.00	0.00	0.00	0.00	0.00	0.00	0.00	50	50
TUR-GER	12	56.62	54.87	8.82	20.00	0.74	4.10	0.74	0.00	11.03	6.67	5.15	4.62	5.88	2.56	0.00	0.00	2.94	2.05	136	195
	16	49.23	59.69	5.13	8.14	1.54	1.55	0.00	0.00	12.82	11.63	13.85	5.81	4.10	1.94	2.05	1.55	4.62	4.26	195	258
VIET	12	63.55	60.26	0.93	5.77	0.00	1.28	0.00	0.00	14.02	9.62	0.93	0.64	1.87	2.56	0.00	0.00	7.48	6.41	107	156
	16	23.15	19.79	32.51	42.05	0.49	1.06	1.48	2.47	14.78	4.95	3.45	3.89	0.99	1.06	0.99	1.41	18.72	14.49	203	283
VIET-GER	12	65.67	60.83	7.30	15.13	0.43	1.48	0.00	0.30	2.58	7.12	6.01	1.48	2.58	2.08	0.00	0.00	10.73	6.82	233	337
	16	47.44	50.93	17.75	18.06	0.34	0.93	0.00	0.46	6.48	9.03	5.80	2.78	0.68	0.46	1.02	1.16	18.43	12.27	293	432
Total		50.66	45.77	13.44	24.16	0.62	1.26	0.35	0.60	10.52	7.96	5.79	3.46	1.64	1.10	0.62	0.69	11.36	9.22	2,262	3,179

Abbreviations: s = spoken, w = written.

Note: The percentages per language mode are based on the overall tense classification of 2,262 verbs (oral recordings) and 3,179 verbs (written texts). The percentages do not add up to 100%, as the frequencies of passives, imperatives, non-English verbs, and unclassified verbs are excluded in this table.

always some learner groups that deviate. First, the most frequent tenses used in both the oral recordings as well as the written texts are the simple present and the simple past. Second, there are comparably higher rates of simple present tense uses in the oral recordings, and, conversely, comparably higher rates of simple past tense uses in the written texts.[5] Third, in nine out of the fourteen groups, the progressive aspect is used more frequently in the oral task than in the written task. This is in line with what was presented in Section 4.2, namely that the progressive occurs more often in speech than in writing (see Aarts, Close, and Wallis 2010: 158).

7.5 Summary

This chapter set out to investigate the use of tense and aspect in the E-LiPS learner corpus. First, a thorough analysis of the written data was provided, followed by a less detailed comparison of the written and oral transcripts of the learner corpus. The aim was to identify differences and similarities across the native speakers of English and the foreign language learners, exclusively motivated by language group membership and age. Based on the preceding discussion of the results, some interesting findings which are partly in line with the points established in Chapters 4 and 5 could be identified.

First, the native speakers of English perform at ceiling, both in terms of quantity (comparably longer text production) as well as quality (overall high rates of correct or target-like performance). All foreign language learners show a generally weaker performance when compared to the native speakers of English, with some noticeable exceptions of the 16-year-old Vietnamese monolingual learners (quantity and quality of the texts).

Second, there is a general trend of more target-like performance with increasing age. Thus, the older participants show an overall better performance than their younger peers. The only learner group that deviates is the Turkish monolinguals. This group is the smallest in size and shows a generally weaker performance altogether, most likely due to an overall lower proficiency in English.

Third, the simple present turned out to be the most frequently used tense, followed by uses of the simple past. Together, these two tenses make up approximately three quarters of the written component of the learner corpus. Yet, some learner groups show a slightly different distribution. The native speakers of English, the 16-year-old Russian-German and monolingual Vietnamese speakers, as well as the 12-year-old Russian monolinguals produce higher proportions of the simple past than the simple present, whereas the Turkish monolinguals do not use any simple past tense forms in the writing task.

Fourth, some areas of difficulty could be singled out. With respect to SVA, it could be noticed that affixal SVA is overall more challenging than suppletive SVA. Also, to produce correct forms of the progressive aspect is by and large more difficult than target-like usage. It could be shown that the major challenge is to use both forms, i.e., a form of *be* as well as the *–ing* form of the verb, with the former being frequently omitted. The same trend, namely that form is more difficult than correct use, could also be identified for all verbs in general.

Fifth, the main verbs used in the progressive aspect are activity and accomplishment verbs. An overuse of state or achievement verbs could not be noticed.

Sixth, the comparison of the spoken and written data revealed that the overall use of tense and aspect is rather comparable between the two language modes. On average, though, the learners produce more words in the written task, whereas in the oral recordings, the proportions of the simple present are on average slightly higher. Moreover, the frequency of progressive aspect is higher in the spoken task.

Finally, seventh, several instances of crosslinguistic influence could be recognized. Noticeably, the Russian and Turkish monolinguals use the progressive aspect (almost) exclusively in target-like contexts (but show considerably lower rates of formal correctness). It could be argued that these learners profit from positive crosslinguistic influence from Russian and Turkish. Noteworthy, however, is that the bilingual Russian-German or Turkish-German participants do not show equally high rates of target-like progressive uses but rather perform similarly than their German monolingual peers. Moreover, the Russian, Turkish, and Vietnamese monolingual learners show relatively high rates of missing copula verbs (note that this does not apply to the 16-year-old Vietnamese monolinguals). Again, this could be explained with negative crosslinguistic influence from their L1s, which lack copula verbs in contexts where they are obligatory in English. Yet again, the bilingual cohorts perform just like the monolingual German participants, that is, they barely omit the copula verb *be*. Surprisingly, the Vietnamese monolinguals do not have more difficulties with subject-verb agreement than their peers with different L1s. The 12-year-old Vietnamese monolinguals do not use any third person singular *–s* morphemes, but neither do the Russian and Turkish monolinguals, although their L1s are characterized by complex verbal morphologies. Moreover, the other foreign language learner groups also show relatively high rates of missing third person singular *–s* morphemes. Hence, it cannot be substantiated that speakers of an L1 without verbal morphology have more difficulties with acquiring the English verbal morphology.

The following chapter extends this analysis by including a number of social variables to investigate whether the variation identified within the E-LiPS corpus can be better explained with further variables in addition to language group membership and age.

Notes

1 This measure is not uncontroversial. TTRs may not be reliable measures for lexical richness or the quality of a text (see Jarvis 2002; Larsen-Freeman 2006;

Vermeer 2000), because with differing text length, the TTR cannot simply be compared. Since in the current study, the texts distinctively vary in length, this measure is not further considered in the remaining analysis, but only included, for illustrative purposes, in Table 7.1. Text length alone, however, can be seen as a first point of reference. As discussed in Section 6.2, the number of words increases with increasing proficiency (Vermeer 2000: 78). Therefore, the number of words used for describing the picture story should correlate with the overall performance: the longer the texts the better the student performance, and the shorter the texts the less advanced the students are.

2 Recall that some texts had to be removed from the study due to the quality being so low that they could not be considered here. The remaining texts also seem to be different in quality. The following analyses need to assess to what extent this group is representative or whether the students may simply have a lower proficiency than the rest of the participants and therefore may be an unfavorable control group.

3 Noticeably, the 16-year-old Vietnamese monolinguals are also outstanding (to the opposite degree from the Turkish monolingual students, see Sections 7.1.1 and 7.1.2), as they seem to be comparably more proficient in English than the other 16-year-old learners of English.

4 Or to be more precise, mainly bare verbs appeared, which were classified as simple present tense forms that lack the third person singular –*s* morpheme.

5 The high rates of simple present in the oral recordings may also be psychologically motivated. Talking about a story may lend itself more to framing it in the present because the talking is also something that is occurring in the present.

References

Aarts, B., J. Close, and S. Wallis. 2010. Recent changes in the use of the progressive construction in English. In *Distinctions in English grammar: Offered to Renaat Declerck*, ed. B. Cappelle and N. Wada, 148–168. Tokyo: Kaitakusha.

Anthony, L. 2016. AntConc (Version 3.4.4.0) [Computer Software]. Tokyo: Waseda.

Bardovi-Harlig, K. 1992. The relationship of form and meaning: A cross-sectional study of tense and aspect in the interlanguage of learners of English as a second language. *Applied Psycholinguistics* 13:253–278.

Bardovi-Harlig, K. 2000. *Tense and aspect in second language acquisition: Form, meaning, and use*. Oxford: Blackwell.

Crossley, S. A. and D. S. McNamara. 2012. Predicting second language writing proficiency: The roles of cohesion and linguistic sophistication. *Journal of Research in Reading* 35:115–135.

Ellis, R. 2015. *Understanding second language acquisition*. 2nd edn. Oxford: Oxford University Press.

Fuchs, R. and V. Werner. 2018. The use of stative progressives by school-age learners of English and the importance of the variable context: Myth vs (corpus) reality. *International Journal of Learner Corpus Research* 4:195–224.

Ionin, T. and K. Wexler. 2002. Why is 'is' easier than '-s'?: Acquisition of tense/agreement morphology by child second language learners of English. *Second Language Research* 18:95–136.

Jarvis, S. 2002. Short texts, best-fitting curves and new measures of lexical diversity. *Language Testing* 19:57–84.

Larsen-Freeman, D. 2006. The emergence of complexity, fluency, and accuracy in the oral and written production of five Chinese learners of English. *Applied Linguistics* 27:590–619.

Levshina, N. 2015. *How to do linguistics with R. Data exploration and statistical analysis*. Amsterdam: Benjamins.

R Core Team. 2020. *R: A language and environment for statistical computing*. R foundation for statistical computing, Vienna, Austria. Available at www.R-project.org

Sarkar, D. 2008. *Lattice: Multivariate data visualization with R*. New York: Springer.

Schweinberger, M. 2021. *Data Visualization with R*. Brisbane: University of Queensland. https://slcladal.github.io/dviz.html (Version 2021.03.22) (accessed April 1, 2021).

Vermeer, A. 2000. Coming to grips with lexical richness in spontaneous speech data. *Language Testing* 17:65–83.

Yu, G. 2009. Lexical diversity in writing and speaking task performances. *Applied Linguistics* 31:236–259.

8 Use of tense and aspect versus social variables

8.1 Formal correctness and target-like meaning of verbs

The following two sections zoom in on the formal correctness (Section 8.1.1) and target-like meaning (Section 8.1.2) of verb forms. In addition, subject-verb agreement (SVA) – a subcategory of formal correctness – is investigated separately (Section 8.1.3). A distinction is made between affixal SVA (i.e., third person singular –s morpheme) and SVA of suppletive verbs (i.e., the verbs *be* and *have*). In contrast to Chapter 7, all social background variables of the different language groups are taken into consideration (in addition to differentiating between language background and age). For all analyses, normalized frequencies to the basis of 100 words are used to ensure comparability.

8.1.1 Formal correctness

Formal correctness was coded as a binary response variable. This means that a verb form can be either formally correct or incorrect (see again Section 6.2). In total, 1,458 verb forms (normalized frequency to the basis of 100 words, calculated for each student individually) are considered, out of which 951 (65 percent) verbs are formally correct (coded as 'true') and 507 (35 percent) are formally incorrect (coded as 'false'). Note that only those students with complete background variables are included in the following regression analysis (see Section 8.5 for more information). A binary logistic regression was run to predict the response variable (formal correctness 'true' or 'false'). This and all following analyses were conducted in R (Version 4.0.2; R Core Team 2020). In addition, for all regression analyses, the package *car* (Fox and Weisberg 2019) in R was used. The explanatory variables listed in (1) were included in the regression analysis to explain the variance in the response variable.

(1) language group (German monolingual, Russian-German, Turkish-German, Vietnamese-German); age (12- and 16-year-old students); age of onset of acquiring German (between age zero (= birth) and age seven); gender (female, male); English perceived as a difficult

DOI: 10.4324/9781003134336-8

language (yes, no); English perceived as a useful language (yes, no); number of books per household (between five and 500); socio-economic status (operationalized as HISEI, between 16 and 88); type of school (*Gymnasium*, other)

Prior to the model selection procedure, the data were checked for normality and some variable refinement was performed. Age was recoded as a binary variable (factor) because there are only two levels ('age 12' and 'age 16'). In addition, the number of books was included as a logged value (to improve normality). The final regression model was obtained via stepwise backward model selection (see Gries 2021). The maximum model, including all main effects as well as all two-way interactions, was the starting model.

The final model encompasses the following variables (main effects and interactions), specified in (2). Note that all main effects were retained in the model, but that several interactions had to be removed as they did not add statistically significantly to explaining the variance. Interactions are listed using the asterisk (*).

(2) language group, age, age of onset of acquiring German, gender, English useful, English difficult, number of books per household, socio-economic status, type of school, group*books, group*school, age*age of onset, age*English difficult, age*books, age of onset*English difficult, age of onset*school, gender*socio-economic status, gender*school

The final model is overall significant (*LR*-statistic = 245.75, *df* = 24, *p* < .001), yet the R^2, which represents the model fit, is relatively low (0.214). The exact binary logistic regression output (logged odds, predicting the second level of the response variable, i.e., formal correctness 'true'; for more information on regressions see Gries 2021) can be found in Table 8.1.

The most important and interesting significant observations resulting from the binary logistic regression are visualized in five effects plots (Figure 8.1) with the help of the package *effects* (Fox 2003; Fox and Weisberg 2019) in R. These effects plots are based on predicted probabilities, again predicting the second level of the response variable (i.e., formal correctness 'true'). What this means is that if the predicted probability is below 0.5, the model predicts formal correctness 'false' (i.e., formally incorrect verb forms), and if the predicted probability is above 0.5, the model predicts formal correctness 'true' (i.e., formally correct verb forms) (see Gries 2021: Section 5.3).

Language group as a main effect does not show up as a significant predictor. However, there are significant interactions of language group and number of books per household and type of school. All four language groups show an increase in predicted probabilities of formally correct verbs with increasing number of books (remember that this graph depicts

Tense and aspect: social variables 171

Table 8.1 Binary logistic regression of formal correctness of verbs (predicting 'true')

	Estimate	2.50%	97.50%	Standard error	p-value	
(Intercept)	−2.01605	−4.88078	0.8031	1.447556	.163702	ns
Group (RUS-GER)	3.027962	0.108542	5.999678	1.500338	.043572	*
Group (TUR-GER)	3.465569	−0.26984	7.241025	1.913041	.070056	ns
Group (VIET-GER)	4.035099	1.181652	6.946444	1.467966	.005982	**
Age (16)	−2.07242	−3.15031	−1.00973	0.545301	<.001	***
Age of onset German	−0.25709	−0.41113	−0.10697	0.077474	<.001	***
Gender (male)	−0.32676	−1.19573	0.543276	0.443242	.461001	ns
English useful (yes)	−0.78914	−1.50268	−0.07666	0.362863	.029647	*
English difficult (yes)	−1.97628	−2.65169	−1.31851	0.339502	<.001	***
Number of books per household	0.715265	0.256185	1.185902	0.236725	.002515	**
Socio-economic status (= HISEI)	−0.00189	−0.01569	0.012079	0.007076	.789837	ns
School type (other)	0.231854	−0.66425	1.151181	0.462306	.616008	ns
Group (RUS-GER) * books	−0.46226	−0.96174	0.029009	0.252348	.066979	ns
Group (TUR-GER) * books	−0.76963	−1.5695	0.034024	0.407874	.059169	ns
Group (VIET-GER) * books	−0.72175	−1.21616	−0.23705	0.24938	.003801	**
Group (RUS-GER) * school (other)	−2.73492	−3.97994	−1.52054	0.626523	<.001	***
Group (TUR-GER) * school (other)	−1.68084	−3.12679	−0.27329	0.726229	.020641	*
Group (VIET-GER) * school (other)	−1.60842	−2.95025	−0.27794	0.680957	.018177	*
Age (16) * age of onset German	0.313866	0.155473	0.474668	0.081351	<.001	***
Age (16) * English difficult (yes)	−0.41924	−1.1958	0.351817	0.394298	.287664	ns
Age (16) * books	0.442119	0.252491	0.634532	0.097332	<.001	***
Age of onset * English difficult (yes)	0.782608	0.528587	1.04458	0.131486	<.001	***
Age of onset * school (other)	0.514618	0.211303	0.822907	0.155814	<.001	***
Gender (male) * HISEI	0.001003	−0.01666	0.018539	0.00897	.910959	ns
Gender (male) * school (other)	−0.11047	−0.79509	0.56549	0.346678	.749889	ns

Note: *Cells list variables (main effects and two-way-interactions) with reference levels in parenthesis, coefficients, confidence intervals, standard errors, and p-values with significance levels.*

Significance codes: ⁿˢ = not significant; * significant at the .05 probability level; ** significant at the .01 probability level; *** significant at the .001 probability level.

172 *Tense and aspect: social variables*

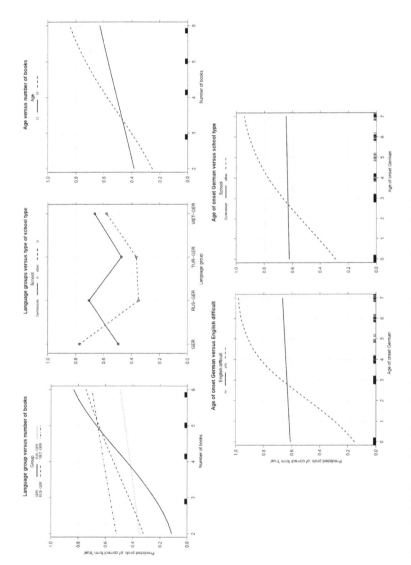

Figure 8.1 Effects plots binary logistic regression of correct form of verbs.

the logged values of number of books per household, ranging between 2 and 6). Yet, the slopes differ for each language group. The German monolingual students start out with the lowest predicted probability of formally incorrect verb forms relative to the number of books (0.11) and show the highest predicted probability of formally correct verbs with the highest number of books per household (0.83). Even though there is an increase for the Turkish-German participants, none of the predicted probabilities reaches the threshold of 0.5 (the highest is still below, i.e., 0.49). This means that the model does not predict formally correct verb forms for the Turkish-German participants, irrespective of the number of books per household. The Russian-German bilinguals start out with a lower predicted probability (0.32) than the Vietnamese-German participants (0.52), but they reach nearly the same predicted probabilities with the highest number of books per household (Russian-German: 0.74; Vietnamese-German: 0.70).

Interestingly, type of school plays out fundamentally differently across the four language groups. For the German monolingual group, attending other types of secondary school results in a higher predicted probability of formally correct verbs (0.77) and attending *Gymnasium* results in a lower predicted probability (0.49) not even reaching the 0.5 threshold. For the bilingual students, the reverse is true. The model predicts the highest probabilities for the Russian-German (0.70) and Vietnamese-German (0.67) students attending the university-bound secondary school type *Gymnasium*, and the lowest for the Russian-German (0.35) and Turkish-German (0.37) students attending other types of school. The Vietnamese-German students are above the 0.5-threshold in both school types, that is, also for other types of school (0.58), and the Turkish-German students remain below the threshold in both school types, i.e., also in the university-bound secondary school type *Gymnasium* (0.47).

There is also a significant interaction between the age of the participants and the number of books per household. As before, there is an increase of predicted probabilities of formally correct verbs with increasing number of books. The effects plot, however, shows that it is additionally contingent on the age of the participants. In general, the 12-year-old cohort has a higher predicted probability (0.38) than their older peers (0.25) when having only few books per household. Yet, both remain below the 0.5 threshold. This pattern reverses with increasing number of books until the younger students (0.63) show a lower predicted probability than their 16-year-old peers (0.84) with the highest number of books per household.

For those students who do not consider English a difficult language to learn, all predicted probabilities are above the 0.5 threshold (which means that the model always predicts formally correct verb forms) regardless of the age of onset of acquiring German. This is different for those who think that English is a difficult language. Here, an increase of predicted probabilities with increasing age of onset (from 0.15 to 0.98) can be seen.

174 *Tense and aspect: social variables*

Finally, the last effects plot replicates the same pattern as before. For students attending the university-bound secondary school type *Gymnasium*, the predicted probabilities are above 0.5 (with a small upturn from 0.62 to 0.64 with increasing age of onset of acquiring German). For those who attend other school types, a significant increase (from 0.29 to 0.94) can be observed with growing age of onset of acquiring German.

8.1.2 Target-like meaning

Like formal correctness, target-like meaning was also coded as a binary response variable. Thus, in addition to considering its form, a verb can also be used in either target-like or non-target-like contexts (see again Section 6.2). 1,452 verb forms (normalized) are analyzed; 1,177 are used in a target-like manner (coded as target-like meaning 'true') and 275 are not used target-like (coded as target-like meaning 'false').[1] Overall, most verbs occur in target-like contexts (81 percent), and only approximately 19 percent are used in non-target-like contexts. Again, only those students with complete background variables are included in the following binary logistic regression analysis. The same explanatory variables as for formal correctness (see Section 8.1.1) were used to predict the binary response variable target-like meaning 'true' or 'false'.

As before, the data were checked for normality prior to model selection, which resulted in using the logged number of books per household. In addition, age was included as a binary factor ('age 12' and 'age 16'). Model selection followed the same stepwise backward procedure, and the maximum model included all main effects as well as all two-way interactions. The variables of the resulting final model are listed in (3). Note that one main effect, namely English perceived as a useful language, was removed; all other main effects remained in the model.

(3) language group, age, age of onset of acquiring German, gender, English difficult, number of books per household, socio-economic status, type of school, group*age, group*books, age*gender, age*English difficult, age*socio-economic status, age of onset*English difficult, age of onset*books, gender*English difficult, English difficult*socio-economic status, English difficult*school

The final model is overall significant (LR-statistic = 126.39, df = 24, $p < .001$), yet the model fit R^2 (0.134) is even lower than for the previous logistic regression, showing that the model predicts only 13.4 percent of the variance. The exact binary logistic regression output (logged odds, predicting the second level of the response variable, i.e., target-like meaning 'true') can be found in Table 8.2.

Figure 8.2 visualizes the most important and interesting significant effects resulting from the binary logistic regression. Again, the package *effects* (Fox 2003; Fox and Weisberg 2019) in R was used to generate

Table 8.2 Binary logistic regression of target-like meaning of verbs (predicting 'true')

	Estimate	2.50%	97.50%	Standard error	p-value	
(Intercept)	1.005165	−1.38471677	3.4429585	1.228189	.413121	ns
Group (RUS-GER)	−2.4206	−5.43680888	0.55906555	1.526964	.112912	ns
Group (TUR-GER)	−5.167887	−10.75983969	−0.41258369	2.596942	.046592	*
Group (VIET-GER)	−0.64885	−3.38110728	2.05436941	1.383428	.639058	ns
Age (16)	−1.35662	−2.75050175	0.01016922	0.703285	.053734	ns
Age of onset German	0.234407	−0.1834012	0.63521659	0.208085	.259957	ns
Gender (male)	0.526316	0.11792228	0.94221753	0.209919	.012168	*
English difficult (yes)	3.689425	1.04886801	6.41631104	1.361025	.006713	**
Number of books per household	0.015709	−0.39123646	0.41905785	0.206165	.939263	ns
Socio-economic status (= HISEI)	0.001938	−0.01147318	0.01564134	0.006902	.778939	ns
School type (other)	−0.448683	−0.85689112	−0.03652206	0.20899	.0318	*
Group (RUS-GER) * age (16)	0.521925	−0.32962774	1.37853696	0.435073	.230284	ns
Group (TUR-GER) * age (16)	1.351185	−0.46420818	3.51061164	0.98169	.168702	ns
Group (VIET-GER) * age (16)	0.956523	0.01771134	1.91885495	0.484043	.048142	*
Group (RUS-GER) * books	0.434812	−0.11592645	0.99280178	0.282447	.123696	ns
Group (TUR-GER) * books	1.599855	0.35873718	3.25174564	0.717364	.025735	*
Group (VIET-GER) * books	0.262228	−0.25003092	0.77738498	0.261627	.316201	ns
Age (16) * gender (male)	−0.199993	−0.87486542	0.47476878	0.343875	.560845	ns
Age (16) * English difficult (yes)	−2.622295	−4.20832731	−1.28872208	0.729325	<.001	***
Age (16) * HISEI	0.031447	0.01040473	0.053317751	0.010893	.00389	**
Age of onset * English difficult (yes)	1.452502	0.89489028	2.16213876	0.317706	<.001	***
Age of onset * books	−0.059466	−0.14065476	0.0241371	0.041912	.155948	ns
Gender (male) * English difficult (yes)	−5.272087	−7.62411782	−3.3210104	1.07951	<.001	***
English difficult (yes) * HISEI	−0.119895	−0.18435451	−0.05775955	0.032058	<.001	***
English difficult (yes) * school (other)	3.551565	2.20872275	5.14062765	0.734146	<.001	***

Note: Cells list variables (main effects and two-way-interactions) with reference levels in parenthesis, coefficients, confidence intervals, standard errors, and p-values with significance levels.
Significance codes: ns = not significant; * significant at the .05 probability level; ** significant at the .01 probability level; *** significant at the .001 probability level.

176 *Tense and aspect: social variables*

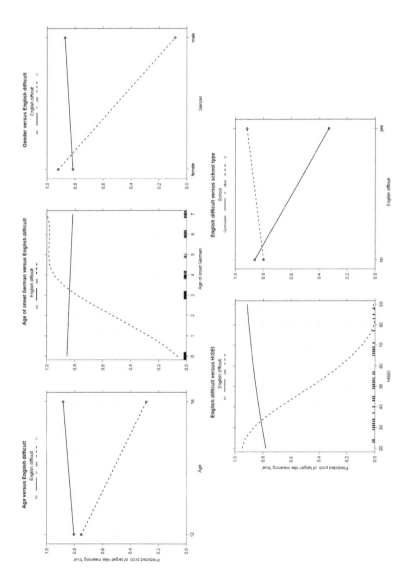

Figure 8.2 Effects plots binary logistic regression of target-like meaning of verbs. *Abbreviation: HISEI = socio-economic status.*

these and all subsequent effects plots. The same logic behind the output of these plots, as explained in the previous section, remains. The plots are based on predicted probabilities. If the value is below 0.5, the model predicts target-like meaning 'false' (i.e., non-target-like verb forms) and if the predicted probability is above 0.5, the model predicts target-like meaning 'true' (i.e., target-like verb forms).

Other than for formal correctness, language group does not appear as a significant main effect or as part of an interaction with another variable when target-like meaning is considered. In addition, all significant interactions include the variable 'English difficult'.

For students who think that English is not a difficult language, the predicted probabilities are high, regardless of the age of the students, their age of onset of acquiring German, gender, socio-economic status, or school type. Thus, the model predicts target-like meaning for both 12-year-old (0.80) as well as 16-year-old (0.88) students, for all ages of onset of learning German (with a small decrease from 0.86 to 0.82), for both female (0.82) as well as male (0.87) students, for all socio-economic status values (with a small increase from 0.78 to 0.92 with increasing socio-economic status, operationalized as HISEI values), and for both types of school (*Gymnasium*: 0.86; other: 0.80).

This is different for those students who answered that English is a difficult language to learn. Here, the predicted probabilities are high for the 12-year-old students (0.75) but low for the 16-year-old students (0.29) (i.e., predicting target-like meaning 'false' for the latter). There is also a sharp increase with increasing age of onset of German (i.e., the predicted probabilities increase from 0.06 to 0.99), and the predicted probabilities are very high for female students (0.92) and very low for male students (0.08). Surprisingly, a steep decrease can be observed with increasing socio-economic status (predicted probabilities decrease from 0.95, i.e., predicting target-like meaning 'true', to 0.01, predicting target-like meaning 'false'). Moreover, the predicted probability for students attending the university-bound secondary school type *Gymnasium* is surprisingly low (0.33) but very high for those attending other secondary schools (0.92).

8.1.3 Subject-verb agreement

Subject-verb agreement (SVA) is a subcategory of formal correctness, because it also considers the form of the verb. It disregards misspellings or other ill-formed verbs (such as *caugchet* instead of *caught*, the correct past form of *catch*) and is exclusively concerned with the correct verbal agreement. Most verbs in English show agreement only in the third person singular form in the present tense by adding the inflectional ending –*s* to the verb (see again Section 4.2). This is called affixal SVA and will be discussed first. The second type is called suppletive SVA and is discussed thereafter. The irregular verb *be* shows agreement in both the present and past tense and not only in the third person singular form. The verb *have* is also included in this category.

8.1.3.1 Affixal SVA

Affixal SVA was coded as a binary response variable, namely singular *–s* 'present' or 'missing'. Overuse of *–s* was excluded from the analysis because there was only a total of 21 such uses in the written part of the learner corpus (see Section 7.1.2). The following analysis relies on normalized frequencies (to the basis of 100 words) to ensure comparability. Overall, there are 169 verbs where the third person singular *–s* was present (47 percent) and 189 verbs where it was missing (53 percent). First, a binary logistic regression was run, similar to those for formal correctness and target-like meaning (see Sections 8.1.1 and 8.1.2). Again, this analysis was based on students with complete background variables. The variables included (both as main effects and as two-way interactions) are the same as in the previous two analyses (see Section 8.1.1).

However, the resulting binary logistic regression model did not produce any meaningful or interpretable output. Therefore, a conditional inference tree was fit to the data. Conditional inference trees are "a method for regression and classification based on binary recursive partitioning" (Levshina 2015: 291). It is an alternative to regression modelling when there are complex interactions present in the data, or when there are not enough data points for each variable. Furthermore, it is a non-parametric method, which does not rely on distributional assumptions such as normality (Levshina 2015: 292).

The same explanatory variables (main effects only) as introduced in Section 8.1.1 feature in the conditional inference tree to predict the binary response variable third person singular *–s* 'present' or 'missing'. The resulting tree structure, created with the package *party* and the function *ctree* (Hothorn, Hornik, and Zeileis 2006) in R, is visualized in Figure 8.3. Overall, the tree has a *classification accuracy* of 0.6955, which means that the model correctly predicts 70 percent of the data. This is an improvement of nearly 17 percent when compared to the baseline model. Without any variables, the model would always predict third person singular *–s* 'missing', as this is the most frequent category (i.e., the mode), which results in a *baseline accuracy* of 0.5279 (i.e., 53 percent correct predictions).

Two additional measures are important, namely *precision* and *recall*. Precision indicates how often the model was right when it predicted either third person singular *–s* 'present' or 'missing', and recall states how many of the actual third person singular *–s* 'present' or 'missing' cases the model found (Gries 2021: 325). Precision equals 0.8224 for 'present', and 0.5820 for 'missing'. Recall is 0.6376 for 'present' and equals 0.7857 for 'missing'. Note that precision for third person singular *–s* 'missing' is comparably low.

Tense and aspect: social variables 179

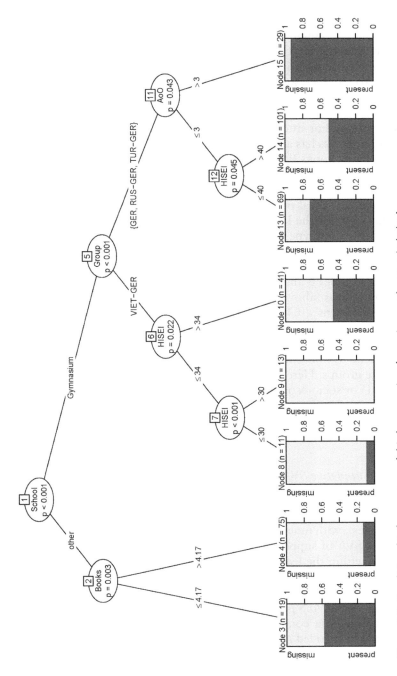

Figure 8.3 Conditional inference tree of third person singular –s 'present' versus 'missing'.
Abbreviations: AoO = age of onset of acquiring German; HISEI = socio-economic status.

180   *Tense and aspect: social variables*

The conditional inference tree (see Figure 8.3) shows the following: five out of the nine variables that were originally included produce a significant partitioning of the dataset. These are type of school, number of books per household, language group, socio-economic status (HISEI), and age of onset of acquiring German. Like the effects plots of the binary logistic regressions discussed in Sections 8.1.1 and 8.1.2, the output of the tree shows probabilities, and the threshold is 0.5. Only if the predicted probability is above 0.5 does the model predict the respective category.

The highest order split (node 1) of the conditional inference tree is the type of school. For students who attend other secondary school types, the number of books has a significant effect (node 2). For those students with 4.17 or fewer books (logged values, see Section 8.1.1 for an explanation) the probability of third person singular –*s* 'present' (0.579) is higher than for those with more books per household (0.133). This means that the model predicts third person singular –*s* 'present' for the former students and 'missing' for the latter. For students attending the university-bound secondary school type *Gymnasium*, the model separates the Vietnamese-German bilinguals from the other three language groups (node 5). Socio-economic status (HISEI) has an effect for the Vietnamese-German bilinguals (nodes 6 and 7). However, even though having a higher socio-economic status (above 34) increases the probability of third person singular –*s* 'present' (0.463), it remains below the threshold of 0.5. This means that regardless of socio-economic status, the model always predicts third person singular –*s* 'missing' for the Vietnamese-German bilinguals who attend *Gymnasium*. The opposite is true for the remaining three language groups. Here, irrespective of age of onset of acquiring German (node 11) or socio-economic status (node 12), the model always predicts third person singular –*s* 'present', albeit the strength of the predictions differs (for example, very high predictive probability for age of onset above three with 0.931).

8.1.3.2 Suppletive SVA

Suppletive SVA was also coded as a binary response variable, namely 'correct' versus 'incorrect'. In total, there are 715 observations (normalized frequencies), with more than 90 percent of correct forms ($n = 646$). Thus, incorrect SVA of suppletive verbs is a relatively infrequent phenomenon ($n = 69$) within the learner corpus. This is crucially different to the previous section discussing affixal SVA. In principle, any model trying to predict suppletive SVA 'correct' versus 'incorrect' would already have an accuracy rate of 90.3 percent (= baseline model). Therefore, the data were only analyzed via conditional inference tree modelling to investigate if any variable included increased this baseline accuracy. The package *party* and function *ctree* (Hothorn, Hornik, and Zeileis 2006) in R were used for this and all subsequent conditional inference trees.

The conditional inference tree predicting SVA was based on the same variables (main effects) as listed in (1) (see Section 8.1.1). The resulting tree produces a significant split at language group level (Russian- and Turkish-German bilinguals in one group, German monolinguals and Vietnamese-German bilinguals in the other). However, it predicts correct SVA in all cases, albeit with slightly differing probabilities. The predicted probability for correct SVA for the former group is 0.847, and for the latter 0.986. Even though the predicted probability of correct SVA is marginally higher for the German monolinguals and the Vietnamese-German bilinguals, the model prediction remains the same for the other two groups. Thus, the conditional inference tree predicting suppletive SVA is not significantly better than the baseline model. This means that none of the variables considered add to explaining the (generally relatively small) variance observed. It can be said that most of the students excel at using the correct verbal form of *be* and *have*. This could be due to the fact that these are very frequent verbs, practiced over and over again in school.

8.2 Progressive aspect

The following two sections zoom in on the progressive aspect. First, formal correctness is considered, and second, target-like meaning of the progressive aspect is analyzed. For all analyses, normalized frequencies to the basis of 100 words were used.

8.2.1 Formal correctness

Just as for formal correctness of verbs, formal correctness of the progressive aspect was also coded as a binary variable with either formally correct or incorrect progressive forms. Overall, there are 223 progressive uses, out of which 121 are formally correct (54 percent) and 102 are formally incorrect (46 percent). First, a binary logistic regression predicting 'correct' versus 'incorrect' was fit. The model included all main effects as well as two-way interactions of the variables used in the preceding analyses (see Section 8.1.1). A number of regressions were run; however, none of them returned any significant main effects or interactions, but all effects had overlapping confidence intervals and the confidence intervals included zero. Thus, none of the models was a good fit.

Therefore, in a second step, a conditional inference tree was fit with the same response variables. The final tree includes only one predictor, namely school type (node 1); no other predictors reached statistical significance (see Figure 8.4). The cut-off point for predicting either 'correct' or 'incorrect' is 0.5. Thus, for students who attend the university-bound secondary school type *Gymnasium*, the tree predicts formally correct progressives (predictive probability of 0.654), and for participants who attend other school types, the model predicts formally incorrect progressives (predictive probability of 0.754).

182 *Tense and aspect: social variables*

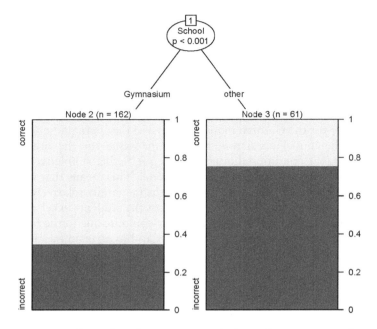

Figure 8.4 Conditional inference tree of formally correct and incorrect progressives.

Overall, the tree has a classification accuracy of 68.2 percent (i.e., the overall number of correct predictions, with $n = 152$ correct predictions). Thus, the model offers some improvement to the baseline model, which always predicts formally correct progressive uses and has a classification accuracy of 54.3 percent. In addition, precision and recall are calculated for correct form and incorrect form separately. As a reminder, precision informs about how often the model predicts what it is supposed to predict, and recall shows how many times the model prediction is correct when it should be (see also Section 8.1.3). Precision is relatively low for predicting formally incorrect progressives (45.1 percent), but it is higher for predicting formally correct progressives (87.6 percent). Recall is highest for formally incorrect progressives (75.4 percent) and a bit lower for formally correct progressives (65.4 percent).

8.2.2 Target-like meaning

The same methodology as for formal correctness of progressives was repeated for target-like meaning. However, overall, there are only 33 (15 percent) non-target-like progressives and 190 (85 percent) target-like progressives. The baseline model already has a classification accuracy of 85.2 percent when only predicting target-like meaning 'true'. A resulting conditional inference tree did not identify any other predictor variables that increased this classification accuracy. Prior to this, a binomial logistic regression did not show any significant main effects or interactions either. In conclusion, the students of this study (of those who used the progressive aspect) nearly always (i.e., in 85.2 percent of all uses) used the progressive aspect in target-like contexts and no relevant or statistically significant differences could be identified based on their social background (see also Section 7.2).

8.3 Present versus past time reference

This section considers the main tense used in the students' writing. Each text was coded as mainly being written in the present tense ($n = 120$, 71.9 percent), past tense ($n = 31$, 18.6 percent), or with mixed tenses ($n = 16$, 9.6 percent) (see again Section 6.2). The frequency distribution shows that most of the students relied largely on the present tense when composing their stories.

A conditional inference tree, based on the main tense of the students' texts, was fit. The first tree included tense as a categorical variable with three levels ('present', 'past', and 'mixed'). The resulting tree only predicted present tense and had a classification accuracy of 71.9 percent, which is essentially the baseline model. None of the predictor variables used (language group, age, age of onset of acquiring German, gender, English difficulty, English usefulness, number of books per household, socio-economic status, and type of school; see Section 8.1.1) remained in the model to improve its classification accuracy. This means, the baseline model is the best model. The issue for this tree was that one of the three levels (i.e., 'present') was so frequent, whereas the frequency of the other two levels was comparably low.

Therefore, a second tree was fit, based on a refined version of the variable main tense. The former categorical variable was recoded as a binary one. The two remaining levels are 'present' ($n = 120$, 71.9 percent) and 'other' ($n = 47$, 28.1 percent). All remaining predictor variables stayed the same. The resulting conditional inference tree can be found in Figure 8.5. The classification accuracy of this tree is 74.9 percent, which is higher than the baseline accuracy (71.9 percent), but the increase is really small. This means that this tree, which includes one predictor (number of books per household), is marginally better than the baseline model (with a 3 percent improvement). Note that for this analysis, the actual number of books per household (and not the logged values) were used, which range between 5 and 500. The conditional inference tree predicts 'present' as the main tense used for writing the story (0.764) for students with 350 or fewer books per household. For students with more than 350 books at home, the model predicts 'other' (0.632), i.e., either mixed or past tense use. Note, however, that the second group is comparably small ($n = 19$; node 3).

184 *Tense and aspect: social variables*

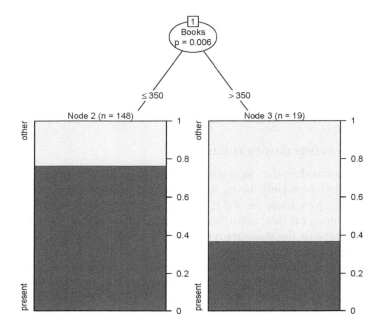

Figure 8.5 Conditional inference tree of main tense used in the written story ('present' versus 'other').

As pointed out, the overall classification accuracy of this tree is 74.9 percent. Precision for predicting 'present' is very good (0.9417), yet comparably weak for predicting 'other' (0.2553). This means that the model was correct in only 25.5 percent of the cases when it predicted this level. Recall is relatively high for both 'present' (0.7635) and 'other' (0.6315), which means that the model correctly classified 76.3 percent of all present tense texts and 63.2 percent of all texts written in mixed or the past tense.

8.4 Written versus spoken production

The subsequent three sections are based on the written and spoken parts of the learner corpus. In total, 126 students participated in both the written as well as the oral task. This means that fewer students per group are considered in the following analyses. However, for each student, two different tasks are analyzed. The participating students wrote 14,200 word tokens and uttered 10,524 word tokens (see Section 7.4.1). Formal correctness, target-like meaning of verb forms, and SVA are analyzed in turn. Similar to the preceding investigations, normalized frequencies to the basis of 100 words are considered to ensure comparability. Essentially, the methodological procedure presented in Section 8.1 is replicated here.

Tense and aspect: social variables 185

The only difference is that one additional variable is included, namely mode ('written' or 'spoken').

8.4.1 Formal correctness

For formal correctness, 2,448 (normalized) verb forms are considered, coded as either formally correct 'true' (*n* = 1,590, 65 percent) or formally correct 'false' (*n* = 858, 35 percent). Only students without missing background data were included in the binary logistic regression analysis. The binary logistic regression predicts the response variable correct form 'true' versus 'false'. All previously used predictor variables were included again, in addition to the mode, that is, 'written' versus 'spoken'. All predictor variables are listed in (4).

(4) language group (German monolingual, Russian-German, Turkish-German, Vietnamese-German); age (12- and 16-year-old students); age of onset of acquiring German (between age zero (= birth) and age seven); gender (female, male); English perceived as a difficult language (yes, no); English perceived as a useful language (yes, no); number of books per household (between five and 500); socio-economic status (operationalized as HISEI, between 16 and 88); type of school (*Gymnasium*, other); mode (spoken, written)

The same model selection procedure as described in Section 8.1.1 was followed (see also Gries 2021). The start was the maximum model, which included all main effects as well as two-way interactions. Via stepwise backward model selection, all variables that did not contribute statistically significantly to explaining the variance in the response variable were removed. Prior to this, the data were checked for normality. Therefore, the logged number of books per household was used, and age was recoded as a binary variable (two factor levels, 'age 12' and 'age 16'). The final model includes the variables (main effects and two-way interactions) specified in (5):

(5) language group, age, age of onset of acquiring German, gender, English difficult, mode, number of books per household, socio-economic status, type of school, group*gender, group*English difficult, group*socio-economic status, age*age of onset, age*English difficult, age*mode, age*books, age*socio-economic status, age of onset*books, age of onset*school, gender*English difficult, gender*socio-economic status, English difficult*books, English difficult*socio-economic status, English difficult*school, socio-economic status*school

Overall, this binary logistic regression model is significant (*LR*-statistic = 461.07, *df* = 33, *p* < .001). The model fit R^2 is relatively low

186   *Tense and aspect: social variables*

(0.236), which means that only approximately 24 percent of the variance in the dataset can be explained. The exact binary logistic regression output (logged odds, predicting the second level of the response variable, i.e., formal correctness 'true') can be found in Table 8.3.

As before, the most important and interesting significant observations resulting from the regression analysis are shown in the effects plots (see Figure 8.6). These plots visualize the predicted probabilities of formally correct verbs. This means that if the predicted probability is below 0.5, the model predicts formal correctness 'false' (i.e., formally incorrect verbs) and if the predicted probability is above 0.5, the model predicts formal correctness 'true'. All nine effects plots are discussed in turn.

The first observation when looking at Figure 8.6 is that mode ('spoken' versus 'written') is neither a main effect nor among the significant interactions. This means that there is no statistically significant difference with respect to the mode. Moreover, language group appears twice, indicating that there are indeed some differences related to the language background of the students. For all four language groups, the predicted probability of correct form increases with increasing socio-economic status, yet only for the German monolinguals, as well as the Turkish-German and Vietnamese-German bilinguals, are the values above the 0.5 threshold. This means that the model always predicts formally correct 'true', regardless of the students' socio-economic status. The slopes, however, differ, and the German monolinguals have overall very high predictions (from 0.891 to 0.945). The predicted probabilities for the Russian-German bilinguals are below 0.5 for a socio-economic status of 30 and below and reach high probabilities for a high socio-economic status (general increase from 0.316 to 0.978).

The second significant interaction concerns age and age of onset of acquiring German. For the 16-year-old participants, the predicted probabilities are quite high and increase from 0.729 to 0.933 with increasing age of onset. The reverse is true for the younger students. Their predicted probabilities decrease from 0.722 to 0.326. This means that at an age of onset of four and older, the model predicts formally correct 'false'. The third interaction is between language group and English difficulty. For students who think that English is not a difficult language to learn, the model returns predicted probabilities above 0.5, ranging from 0.547 for the Turkish-German up to 0.762 for the German monolingual students. The Russian-German (0.692) and Vietnamese-German (0.614) bilinguals are in-between. Whereas the predicted probabilities are in fact higher for the German monolinguals (0.999), the Russian-German (0.725), and the Turkish-German (0.983) bilinguals, they are lower for the Vietnamese-German (0.458) students and do not reach the 0.5 cut-off point.

In the fourth effects plot, one can see that the model always predicts the correct verbal form for both school types and all ages of onset of acquiring German, except for students attending other types of school and who started acquiring German from birth onwards. For this group

Tense and aspect: social variables 187

Table 8.3 Binary logistic regression of formal correctness of verbs (predicting 'true') in the spoken and written data

	Estimate	2.50%	97.50%	Standard error	p-value	
(Intercept)	-0.331713	-1.81444194	1.12727441	0.74956	.658096	ns
Group (RUS-GER)	-1.722007	-2.96338429	-0.48273365	0.632047	.00644	**
Group (TUR-GER)	-1.124975	-2.90585606	0.65777616	0.90778	.215249	ns
Group (VIET-GER)	0.842166	-0.40851135	2.09803749	0.638784	.187373	ns
Age (16)	-1.791023	-2.86323941	-0.72327183	0.545615	.001029	**
Age of onset German	-0.151562	-0.41121153	0.10757152	0.132206	.251628	ns
Gender (male)	3.30273	2.11204103	4.52366022	0.614462	<.001	***
English difficult (yes)	4.948121	0.8871867	8.6501224	1.965148	.011804	*
Mode (written)	0.470773	0.23083912	0.71222927	0.122761	<.001	***
Number of books per household	0.295288	0.12580076	0.46709113	0.086979	<.001	***
Socio-economic status (= HISEI)	-0.007157	-0.02953378	0.01529188	0.011423	.530948	ns
School type (other)	-1.327243	-2.21641959	-0.44954095	0.450319	.003205	**
Group (RUS-GER) * gender (male)	-2.100478	-2.8498311	-1.36518559	0.378336	<.001	***
Group (TUR-GER) * gender (male)	-1.436186	-2.44805134	-0.43411964	0.512987	.005116	**
Group (VIET-GER) * gender (male)	-2.743342	-3.47025458	-2.03245327	0.366475	<.001	***
Group (RUS-GER) * English difficult (yes)	-7.262045	-9.54035894	-5.07894526	1.134915	<.001	***
Group (TUR-GER) * English difficult (yes)	-3.555972	-6.01318227	-1.0748464	1.255324	.004615	**
Group (VIET-GER) * English difficult (yes)	-8.048631	-11.23455472	-5.06654021	1.564008	<.001	***
Group (RUS-GER) * HISEI	0.054588	0.03108233	0.07860291	0.012103	<.001	***
Group (RUS-GER) * HISEI	0.01972	-0.01695076	0.057075	0.018837	.29514	ns
Group (RUS-GER) * HISEI	-0.003197	-0.02394554	0.01762347	0.010592	.762748	ns
Age (16) * age of onset German	0.4763	0.31379816	0.64068231	0.083328	<.001	***
Age (16) * English difficult (yes)	2.650628	1.31308711	4.09873417	0.704328	<.001	***
Age (16) * mode (written)	-0.462833	-0.83646904	-0.09012804	0.190336	.01503	*
Age (16) * books	0.059346	-0.10951586	0.2279445	0.086043	.490368	ns
Age (16) * HISEI	0.030521	0.01394253	0.04723195	0.008487	<.001	***

(continued)

Table 8.3 Cont.

	Estimate	2.50%	97.50%	Standard error	p-value	
Age of onset * books	-0.051796	-0.11485094	0.01066364	0.031995	.105478	ns
Age of onset * school (other)	0.55744	0.38690768	0.72989244	0.087442	<.001	***
Gender (male) * English difficult (yes)	5.431133	3.52770254	7.44227691	0.993918	<.001	***
Gender (male) * HISEI	-0.041376	-0.06044424	-0.02251038	0.009667	<.001	***
English difficult (yes) * books	-1.384137	-1.81173024	-0.97203875	0.213512	<.001	***
English difficult (yes) * HISEI	0.13909	0.06099423	0.23246715	0.043295	.001316	**
English difficult (yes) * school (other)	-6.250222	-8.23292433	-4.37191389	0.981387	<.001	***
HISEI * school (other)	0.006055	-0.01070387	0.02294731	0.008578	.480284	ns

Note: Cells list variables (main effects and two-way interactions) with reference levels in parenthesis, coefficients, confidence intervals, standard errors, and p-values with significance levels.

Significance codes: ns = not significant; * significant at the .05 probability level; ** significant at the .01 probability level; *** significant at the .001 probability level.

Tense and aspect: social variables 189

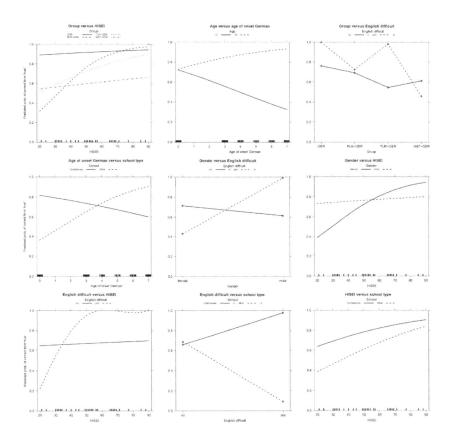

Figure 8.6 Effects plots binary logistic regression of correct form of verbs in the spoken and written data.

Abbreviation: HISEI = socio-economic status.

of students, the predicted probability is relatively low (0.361). Plot five visualizes the interaction between gender and English difficulty. Female students who think that English is a difficult language to learn have a low predicted probability of correct form (0.432), which means that the model predicts formally incorrect verb forms. The same effect cannot be observed for their male peers or for both genders when English is not considered to be a difficult language. The sixth effects plot juxtaposes gender and socio-economic status. For both males and females, the model predicts an increase in probabilities with increasing socio-economic status. Yet, for the male students, the values are always above the 0.5 threshold (from 0.735 to 0.803), and for the female students, the predicted probabilities are only higher than 0.5 for socio-economic status values above 30. Below 30, the model predicts formally correct 'false'.

190 *Tense and aspect: social variables*

Effects plot seven shows an interesting interaction between English difficulty and socio-economic status. For students who think that English is not difficult, the predicted probabilities remain almost the same, with a very small increase from 0.647 to 0.698 with increasing socio-economic status. There is also an increase in probabilities with increasing socio-economic status for students who think that English is difficult. However, this increase is a lot steeper and starts out lower (from 0.222 to 0.999). This means that for low socio-economic values, the model predicts formally incorrect verbs. The next effects plot shows the interaction of English difficulty and type of school. For students attending the university-bound secondary school type *Gymnasium*, the model predicts probabilities of 0.658 and 0.979, for English difficult 'yes' and 'no', respectively. For students attending other types of school, the model returns a relatively high probability of 0.687 for those who think that English is not difficult, and a very low probability of 0.092 for correct form for those who think that English is a difficult language. Finally, the last effects plot depicts the interaction between socio-economic status and type of school. There is an increase in probabilities visible with increasing socio-economic status. However, for students attending *Gymnasium*, the probabilities are comparably high (from 0.639 to 0.906), whereas for students attending other school types, the probabilities are below 0.5 for low socio-economic values (from 0.386 to 0.460) and are only higher than 0.5 for socio-economic status values of 40 and above (from 0.610 to 0.840).

8.4.2 *Target-like meaning*

For target-like meaning, 2,427 verb forms are considered, coded as either target-like meaning 'true' ($n = 1,977$, 81 percent) or target-like meaning 'false' ($n = 450$, 19 percent).[2] Again, these numbers are based only on students who have complete background variables. Crucially, the ratio of target-like meaning versus non-target-like meaning mirrors the ratio reported in Section 8.1.2, where only the written texts were considered, and it is quite different from what was previously reported for formal correctness. There are considerably fewer verb forms that were used in non-target-like contexts. For the binary logistic regression predicting the binary response variable target-like meaning 'true' versus 'false', the same predictor variables as for formal correctness (see (4) in Section 8.4.1) were considered, including age as a factor and the logged number of books per household. Via stepwise backward model selection from the maximum model with all main effects as well as two-way interactions, the following variables were retained in the final model (6).

(6) language group, age, age of onset of acquiring German, gender, English difficult, mode, number of books per household, socio-economic status, type of school, group*gender, group*mode,

group*books, group*school, age*age of onset German, age*English difficult, age*school, age of onset*English difficult, age of onset*mode, age of onset*school, gender*English difficult, gender*books, English difficult*books, books*socio-economic status, books*school

This model is significant (LR-statistic = 235.83, df = 34, p < .001), yet the R^2 (0.150), i.e., the model fit, is relatively low. The complete binary logistic regression output (logged odds, predicting the second level of the response variable, i.e., target-like meaning 'true') can be found in Table 8.4.

Three significant effects plots result from this binary logistic regression and can be assessed in Figure 8.7. These plots can be interpreted as follows (see also Section 8.1, or Section 8.4.1): if the predicted probability is below 0.5, the model predicts target-like meaning 'false' (i.e., non-target-like verb forms) and if the predicted probability is above 0.5, the model predicts target-like meaning 'true'.

There are two significant interactions that include language group. For the German monolinguals as well as the Turkish-German and Vietnamese-German bilinguals, the regression always predicts target-like meaning regardless of the number of books per household, albeit with different slopes. Whereas there is an increase visible for the two bilingual groups (from 0.574 to 0.850 for the Turkish-German students, and from 0.912 to 0.941 for the Vietnamese-German bilinguals) with increasing number of books, the opposite is true for the German monolingual students (decrease from 0.898 to 0.597). For the Russian-German bilinguals, there is also an increase with increasing numbers of books (from 0.144 to 0.840), yet the predicted probability is only higher than 0.5 above four books (logged numbers). Below that number, the model predicts that verbs are used in non-target-like contexts.

Interestingly, students who attend the university-bound secondary school type *Gymnasium* have predicted probabilities above 0.5 (from 0.727 to 0.877), irrespective of the language group to which they belong. For those who attend other school types, the model predicts non-target-like meaning for the German (0.176) as well as the Russian-German students (0.129), and target-like meaning for the Turkish-German (0.859) as well as the Vietnamese-German students (0.994). Lastly, the third significant interaction includes type of school and age of onset of acquiring German. There is little variability among the students who attend *Gymnasium* (with a small increase from 0.796 to 0.888 with increasing age of onset). However, probabilities decrease with increasing age of onset for students attending other school types (from 0.966 to 0.059). Crucially, none of the effects plots includes mode ('written' versus 'spoken'), which suggests that the mode does not have a statistically significant effect in explaining the variance in the response variable target-like meaning 'true' versus 'false'. This is the same observation as for formal correctness (see Section 8.4.1).

192 *Tense and aspect: social variables*

Table 8.4 Binary logistic regression of target-like meaning of verbs (predicting 'true') in the spoken and written data

	Estimate	2.50%	97.50%	Standard error	p-value	
(Intercept)	9.53542	5.08856303	14.27390971	2.34038	<.001	***
Group (RUS-GER)	−6.55186	−10.81478817	−2.62828675	2.08243	.001654	**
Group (TUR-GER)	−4.98423	−9.51524863	−0.67698267	2.2486	.026651	*
Group (VIET-GER)	−2.42302	−6.50636581	1.26341102	1.97389	.219622	ns
Age (16)	0.81258	0.35169549	1.28256497	0.23707	<.001	***
Age of onset German	−0.01046	−0.16497131	0.1410077	0.07797	.893264	ns
Gender (male)	−2.20366	−3.83738774	−0.59983995	0.82521	.007575	**
English difficult (yes)	3.6619	1.59099457	5.98569132	1.10572	<.001	***
Mode (written)	−0.40415	−0.90451815	0.08620887	0.25208	.108879	ns
Number of books per household	−1.78599	−2.64805418	−0.96780967	0.42854	<.001	***
Socio-economic status (= HISEI)	−0.09326	−0.13870875	−0.04858061	0.02293	<.001	***
School type (other)	−4.57622	−7.93648754	−1.58055065	1.62467	.004852	**
Group (RUS-GER) * gender (male)	0.50841	−0.27787916	1.3166825	0.40581	.210263	ns
Group (TUR-GER) * gender (male)	−0.38354	−2.00039068	1.22406071	0.81894	.639544	ns
Group (VIET-GER) * gender (male)	−0.60095	−1.3935688	0.19620581	0.40502	.137876	ns
Group (RUS-GER) * mode (written)	−0.76404	−1.50205546	−0.02981791	0.37513	.041679	*
Group (TUR-GER) * mode (written)	1.14289	0.22218219	2.08940084	0.47468	.016053	*
Group (VIET-GER) * mode (written)	0.09154	−0.63006468	0.8163225	0.36864	.803888	ns
Group (RUS-GER) * books	1.30523	0.62310748	2.03525153	0.35946	<.001	***
Group (TUR-GER) * books	0.80422	0.01201753	1.62117362	0.40974	.049677	*
Group (VIET-GER) * books	0.55028	−0.0823387	1.24050429	0.33618	.101662	ns
Group (RUS-GER) * school type (other)	0.46444	−0.54613154	1.50049898	0.52079	.372501	ns
Group (TUR-GER) * school type (other)	4.34049	1.51183757	7.43784163	1.50954	.004035	**
Group (VIET-GER) * school type (other)	6.80825	2.92218629	11.24188245	2.12807	.001378	**
Age (16) * age of onset German	−0.20741	−0.34739065	−0.06860758	0.07106	.003513	**

Age (16) * English difficult (yes)	−2.02866	−3.10029637	−1.02000376	0.52744	<.001 ***
Age (16) * school type (other)	−0.85059	−1.54101493	−0.17798267	0.34731	.014322 *
Age of onset * English difficult (yes)	0.62867	0.2664707	1.04804308	0.19627	.00136 **
Age of onset * mode (written)	0.21669	0.08161542	0.35355878	0.06928	.001763 **
Age of onset * school type (other)	−0.97566	−1.63307179	−0.37652106	0.321	.00237 **
Gender (male) * English difficult (yes)	−2.42373	−3.79565547	−1.32231825	0.61763	<.001 ***
Gender (male) * books	0.51187	0.22421925	0.80900241	0.14906	<.001 ***
English difficult (yes) * books	−0.82629	−1.30458221	−0.40445471	0.22621	<.001 ***
Books * HISEI	0.02257	0.01358877	0.03181972	0.00464	<.001 ***
Books * school type (other)	0.7936	0.26607648	1.37971026	0.28539	.005423 **

Note: Cells list variables (main effects and two-way-interactions) with reference levels in parenthesis, coefficients, confidence intervals, standard errors, and p-values with significance levels.

Significance codes: ⁿˢ = not significant; * significant at the .05 probability level; ** significant at the .01 probability level; *** significant at the .001 probability level.

194 *Tense and aspect: social variables*

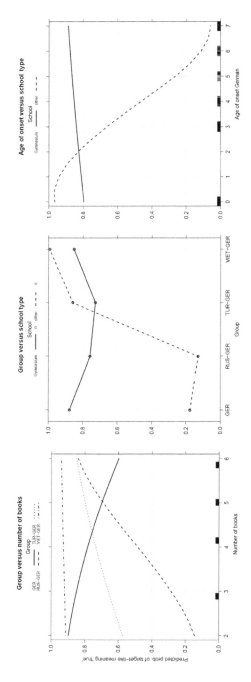

Figure 8.7 Effects plots binary logistic regression of target-like meaning of verbs in the spoken and written data.

8.4.3 Subject-verb agreement

The analysis of SVA in the written and spoken sections of the learner corpus is exclusively based on affixal SVA, that is, the presence or absence of the third person singular *–s* morpheme. The analysis of suppletive SVA in Section 8.1.3 did not produce any meaningful or significant output, because the correctness rate was simply too high. In Section 7.4.2, where SVA was analyzed without considering any social background variables except for age or language group of the participants, it was reported that incorrect SVA with suppletive verbs was also a relatively infrequent phenomenon. Thus, most of the students considered in the current study used *be* and *have* formally correctly. The opposite is true for the third person singular *–s*.

Again, affixal SVA was coded as a binary variable, that is, third person singular *–s* morpheme 'present' versus 'missing'. In total, there are 802 verb forms, out of which 286 (36 percent) represent third person singular *–s* 'present' and 516 (64 percent) 'missing'. Therefore, the baseline model, which always predicts third person singular *–s* 'missing', has a classification accuracy of 64.3 percent. A conditional inference tree predicting this binary response variable was fit, based on the same predictor variables (main effects only) as stated in (4) (see Section 8.4.1), to investigate whether this classification accuracy can be improved. The resulting conditional inference tree (see Figure 8.8) shows an improvement of 10 percent. This means that when the number of books per household, socio-economic status, age, age of onset of acquiring German, language group, school type, and English difficulty are considered, the tree makes correct predictions for 74.1 percent of all verb forms. Precision of predicting third person singular *–s* 'present' is comparably low (0.5734), and the tree performs better with predicting third person singular *–s* 'missing' (0.8333). Recall of 'present' equals 0.6560, and of 'missing' 0.7790.

The significant highest order variable is the number of books per household (node 1). The tree splits the dataset into students with 2.322 or fewer books (logged values) and more than 2.322 books. For the former, the predicted probabilities of third person singular *–s* 'missing' is very high (0.912). For the latter, the tree suggests a significant split depending on the socio-economic status (node 3). A socio-economic status of 50 or below, in addition to 'age 16' (node 4), having acquired German from birth onwards (node 5), and belonging to the German monolingual group predicts third person singular *–s* 'present', with a predicted probability of above 0.5 (0.556). Belonging to the Russian-German bilingual group has the opposite effect. Here the model predicts third person singular *–s* 'missing' (0.878), when all other conditions are also met. This is different for students with the same socio-economic values and age but with an age of onset after birth. For these students, the model predicts third person singular *–s* 'present' (0.587). Node 10 represents those who have

196 *Tense and aspect: social variables*

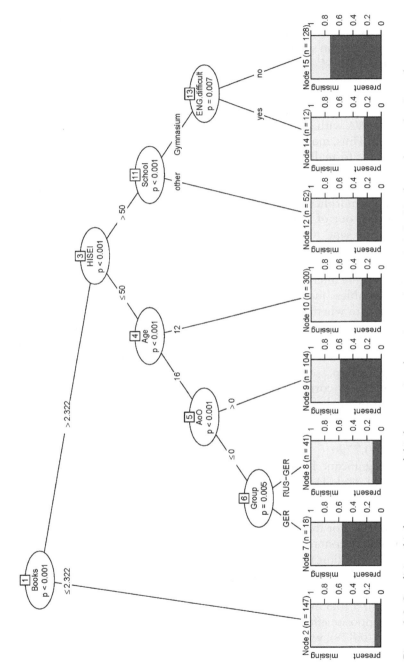

Figure 8.8 Conditional inference tree of third person singular –s 'present' versus 'missing' in the spoken and written data.
Abbreviations: AoO = age of onset of acquiring German; ENG.difficult = English difficult; HISEI = socio-economic status.

more books than 2.322 (logged values), a socio-economic status of 50 or below and are at the age of 12. The predicted probability of third person singular –s 'missing' is relatively high (0.723). The third main branch includes students who have more than 2.322 books per household (logged values) and whose socio-economic status is above 50. The tree makes a significant difference between students attending the university-bound secondary school type *Gymnasium* and those attending other school types (node 11). For the latter, the model predicts third person singular –s 'missing' (0.654). The same prediction, albeit with a higher probability (0.750), is true for students attending *Gymnasium* who additionally consider English a difficult language (node 14). Attending *Gymnasium* and thinking that English is not a difficult language (node 15) results in a prediction of third person singular –s 'present' (0.727).

Interestingly, language group membership is only significant in one out of seven splits (node 6), and there is only a difference between German monolinguals as well as Russian-German bilinguals. Additionally, the mode, i.e., 'written' versus 'spoken', does not appear as a significant predictor variable.

8.5 Limitations

This study is of course not without limitations. The main shortcomings regarding the analysis presented in this chapter are briefly addressed in the current section. Initially, it was intended to include student as a random factor to account for the fact that the participants were not, and – to be precise – cannot be, randomly assigned to one of the four language groups, or school types, etc. (see also Llanes and Cots 2020: 9). However, due to convergence issues, it was not possible to add student as a random factor. Therefore, none of the regression analyses or conditional inference trees considers the individual student as a separate variable. Essentially, this means that any underlying dependence of the individual data points is ignored in the regression and tree models (Levshina 2020: 622). Only language group belonging is factored in, as well as the remaining social variables.

Furthermore, the school grades for German and English (as introduced in Section 6.3.2) were not used in the analyses. It is unclear how well the grades reflect the actual proficiency level of the students. This is particularly crucial since two different types of secondary school are included in this study, the university-bound secondary school type *Gymnasium* and other types of school. Receiving a very good (1) or good grade (2) in *Gymnasium* underlies a different performance assessment than is used in other school types.[3] Therefore, it was eventually decided to refrain from using this measure. Unfortunately, no other proficiency measures, neither for German or English nor for the heritage languages Russian, Turkish, or Vietnamese were collected within this project.

Moreover, part of the reason why the models presented above have comparably low explanatory power and score poorly at times with respect to recall and precision may be because cognitive ability was not included in the project either. Previous research has shown that cognitive ability is a strong predictor for English proficiency, particularly in heritage speaker contexts comparable to the present setting (see, for example, Lorenz, Toprak, and Siemund 2021; Lorenz, Toprak-Yildiz, and Siemund 2022). In a follow-up study, cognitive ability, as well as proficiency in all languages of the participants' repertoires, would need to be included in order to obtain better results and more predictive power in the statistical analyses.

Finally, unfortunately, for a number of students, the background variables were partially incomplete. Imputation of missing cases was not performed, because the data were most likely not missing completely at random (see also Lorenz, Toprak, and Siemund 2021; Lorenz, Toprak-Yildiz, and Siemund 2022). To successfully conduct the regression as well as conditional inference tree analyses, only those students could be included who had complete sets of background variables. This considerably reduced the dataset. Overall, the reduction of the written learner corpus accounted for approximately 40 percent ($n = 69$). The cleaned dataset included 23 German monolingual (out of 40), 27 Russian-German (out of 38), 13 Turkish-German (out of 41), and 35 Vietnamese-German (out of 48) students, resulting in a total number of 98 students (out of 167). The reduction was particularly high for the Turkish-German group. For the analysis of the spoken and written data, 38 percent ($n = 48$) of the students had to be excluded due to missing data. The final data used for these analyses contained 17 German monolingual (out of 21), 21 Russian-German (out of 32), 8 Turkish-German (out of 32), and 32 Vietnamese-German (out of 41) students, resulting in a total number of 78 students (out of 126) whose written and spoken production ($n = 156$) was contrasted. Again, the Turkish-German group had the lowest number of participants.

8.6 Summary

This chapter looked at the students' performance in both the written as well as the spoken task with respect to formal correctness, and target-like meaning, as well as subject-verb agreement (SVA) as a subcategory of formal correctness. In addition, the use of the progressive aspect, considering both formal correctness and target-like use, as well as present versus past time reference were exclusively analyzed in the written part of the learner corpus. Four learner groups were differentiated, namely German monolingual students, and their bilingual peers with a Russian-German, Turkish-German, and Vietnamese-German background. All students were raised in Germany and attended one of two secondary school types at the time of testing. Additional background variables controlled for were age, age of onset of acquiring German, socio-economic status, number of books per household, English difficulty, English usefulness, and, if applicable, the mode of the task.

Several interesting conclusions can be drawn from the preceding sections. They are briefly summarized here, before being taken up again in the following two discussion chapters, Chapters 9 and 10. First of all, the mode, i.e., 'spoken' versus 'written', did not appear as a significant predictor variable, neither as a main effect nor as part of an interaction. Thus, there is no statistically significant difference with respect to formal correctness (including SVA) or target-like meaning when comparing the written with the spoken English production of the learners examined here. Language group membership appeared among the significant predictors. Interestingly, however, it did not surface as a main effect but only in interactions. This shows that language group alone is not a good predictor of any of the tense and aspect categories investigated in the current study, but in relation to other social variables, language group significantly adds to explaining the variance. Most significant interactions are related to formal correctness (formal correctness of verbs or affixal SVA). Notably, there is no clear-cut finding that is repeated in all analyses, ascribing one or more language groups an advantage over their peers. However, more often than not, the German monolinguals are on par with those bilinguals scoring highest, or they even perform better. See, for instance, Figures 8.3 and 8.8, visualizing affixal SVA, or Figures 8.1 and 8.6, displaying formal correctness of verbs.

Furthermore, a strong influence, both as main effects and as part of interactions, can be attributed to school type and number of books. In addition, socio-economic status frequently appears among the interactions. Typically, attending the university-bound secondary school type *Gymnasium* increases the likelihood of formal correctness (Figure 8.1), and formally correct SVA (Figures 8.3 and 8.8) or positively impacts target-like meaning of verbs (Figure 8.7), often additionally contingent on socio-economic status (Figures 8.3, 8.6, and 8.8) or also on number of books per household (Figure 8.8). In addition, the students appear to self-assess their English skills relatively well. Generally, perceiving English as a difficult language results in lower predictive probabilities of formal correctness or target-like meaning for one level of the respective interactions (Figures 8.2, 8.6, and 8.8). This pattern, however, is not always true; see, for example, the interactions with age of onset (Figures 8.1 and 8.2) or with socio-economic status (Figure 8.6). The age of the participants (12-year-old versus 16-year-old students) also appears to have some significant effects. Often, the probabilities are as expected, namely lower performance of the younger cohort (Figures 8.6 and 8.8). Yet, this trend is not always categorical (see Figures 8.1, 8.2, and 8.6) and clearly depends on other social variables (age of onset of acquiring German, number of books, socio-economic status, and English difficulty).

Finally, none of the background variables returned any significant effects with respect to target-like meaning of the progressive aspect and suppletive SVA. It appears that all students barely misused the progressive aspect or used an incorrect form of the verbs *be* and *have*. The little variance noticed could at least not be explained based on the variables included in this study. Moreover, most of the students used the simple present tense to write their stories. Few relied on the simple past or mixed tenses within one story.

Notes

1 Note that the number of considered verb forms differs slightly from the one reported in Section 8.1.1, where formal correctness was discussed, due to the use of normalized data (frequency per 100 words) and rounding to integers.
2 Note that these numbers differ slightly from those reported in Section 8.4.1, where formal correctness was discussed, due to the use of normalized data (frequency per 100 words) and rounding to integers.
3 In addition, the specific grading scheme not only differs across school types, but each individual school may use its own assessment scale. Even though the school grades unanimously range from one to six, the respective percentages of correct responses may show contrasts.

References

Fox, J. 2003. Effect displays in R for generalised linear models. *Journal of Statistical Software* 8:1–27.

Fox, J. and S. Weisberg. 2019. *An R companion to applied regression.* 3rd edn. Thousand Oaks, CA: Sage Publications.

Gries, S. Th. 2021. *Statistics for linguistics with R: A practical introduction.* 3rd edn. Berlin: De Gruyter Mouton.

Hothorn, T., K. Hornik, and A. Zeileis. 2006. Unbiased recursive partitioning: A conditional inference framework. *Journal of Computational and Graphical Statistics* 15:651–674.

Levshina, N. 2015. *How to do linguistics with R: Data exploration and statistical analysis.* Amsterdam: Benjamins.

Levshina, N. 2020. Conditional inference trees and random forests. In *A practical handbook of corpus linguistics*, ed. M. Paquot and S. Th. Gries, 611–643. Cham: Springer.

Llanes, À. and J. M. Cots. 2020. Measuring the impact of translanguaging in TESOL: A plurilingual approach to ESP. *International Journal of Multilingualism.* https://doi.org/10.1080/14790718.2020.1753749

Lorenz, E., T. E. Toprak, and P. Siemund. 2021. English L3 acquisition in heritage contexts: Modelling a path through the bilingualism controversy. *Poznan Studies in Contemporary Linguistics* 57:273–298.

Lorenz, E., T. E. Toprak-Yildiz, and P. Siemund. 2022. Why are they so similar? The interplay of linguistic and extra-linguistic variables in monolingual and bilingual learners of English. *Pedagogical Linguistics*. https://doi.org/10.1075/pl.21016.lor

R Core Team. 2020. *R: A language and environment for statistical computing*. R Foundation for Statistical Computing, Vienna, Austria. Available at www.R-project.org

9 Crosslinguistic influence in heritage speakers' L3 production

9.1 Crosslinguistic influence in third language acquisition

The first section relates the findings reported in Chapters 7 and 8 to the previously introduced transfer scenarios in third language acquisition (Section 6.4; see also Section 3.2). The main aim is to identify which of the previously acquired languages of the bilingual learners affects the acquisition of the additional language English. For second language learners, there is only one potential source, namely the respective first language. For bilingual learners, however, there are two languages that might transfer to the currently acquired foreign language and influence the acquisition process.

Crucially, among the Russian, Turkish, and Vietnamese monolinguals, specifically the 12-year-old cohorts, the copula verb *be* was omitted comparably frequently, most notably in the written task (see Section 7.1.3). This is arguably negative crosslinguistic influence from the corresponding background languages. In Russian, Turkish, and Vietnamese, there are numerous contexts where no copula verb is required, whereas in English as well as in German, omitting the copula verb would result in an ungrammatical construction (see Chapter 4). Intriguingly, among all three bilingual groups, the rate of copula verb omission was as low as among the German monolinguals (mirroring the English native speakers). This indicates that both the bilingual as well as the monolingual German students show positive transfer from German in their English production in that they use the copula verb in contexts that require such uses. No negative transfer from the heritage languages Russian, Turkish, or Vietnamese could be identified in the bilinguals' English production. This might be interpreted as an advantage for the bilinguals, at least in comparison to the monolingual Russian, Turkish, and Vietnamese learners of English (see also Section 10.1).

Furthermore, it is quite striking that the Russian as well as Turkish monolingual students showed proportionally high rates of target-like uses of the progressive aspect, just as did the English native speaker control group (see Section 7.2). None of the other foreign language learners reached comparably high correctness rates, even though all

DOI: 10.4324/9781003134336-9

learners displayed more target-like used progressive forms than formally correct uses of the progressive aspect. It could be argued that the high rates of target-like meaning of the progressive aspect among the Russian and Turkish learners of English are evidence for positive crosslinguistic influence from their native languages. As before, the same could not be observed among the bilinguals. Instead, the three bilingual groups exhibited a comparable performance to their monolingual German peers. This is reinforced by the conditional inference tree analysis (Section 8.2) that returned no statistically significant differences between the monolingual and bilingual participants for the use of the progressive aspect, even when additional background variables were controlled for. The only exception was the type of school, which was revealed to have a significant impact regarding formal correctness of the progressive aspect (see Section 9.3.1).

Moreover, in Chapter 8, which narrowed down the focus and exclusively compared the English performance of the three bilingual cohorts and their monolingual German peers, language group did not show up as a main effect when explaining the variance found in the students' data. However, in several analyses, language group was among the significant interactions. This demonstrates that being a monolingual or bilingual learner of English alone is no significant predictor for explaining performance or crosslinguistic influence in the foreign language English. Instead, the influence resulting from the language background is contingent on additional background variables such as school type, socio-economic status, attitudes toward English, number of books per household, or age (see Section 9.3).

This finding, namely that crosslinguistic influence in the bilingual heritage speakers comes from German and not from their heritage language, would in principle be in line with the L2 Status Factor (Bardel and Falk 2007, 2012; see also Williams and Hammarberg 1998; Hammarberg 2009). Bardel and Falk (2007, 2012) argued that crosslinguistic influence in third language acquisition comes from the L2, which functions as a filter and makes the L1 inaccessible. However, as pointed out in Chapter 3, it is unclear whether this hypothesis is applicable in the current context because the bilinguals of the present study are not classic L2 learners who study a foreign language, as alluded to by the L2 Status Factor (see also Bardel and Falk 2012: 69–70, where the authors discuss this point themselves). Instead, German, even though acquired as the consecutively second language,[1] should be considered at least a second L1, owing to the fact that it is their dominant language (see Hopp 2019; Lorenz et al. 2019). This view is in line with Wiese et al. (2022: 16) who argue that heritage bilinguals are "native speakers of both their languages" (see also Aalberse, Backus, and Muysken 2019). In addition, Flynn, Foley, and Vinnitskaya's (2004) Cumulative Enhancement Model proposed that crosslinguistic influence is possible from both languages, but that it is never impeding and always facilitative. If this model were true, positive transfer should be visible from Russian and Turkish in the bilinguals' English production, noticeably in a more target-like performance in the use of the progressive aspect when compared to their German monolingual peers. Yet, the results returned an equal performance of the monolingual German and the bilingual students and no crosslinguistic influence from Russian or Turkish was visible (but arguably negative crosslinguistic influence from German). This is evidence for rejecting the Cumulative Enhancement Model, at least in this strong sense of positive influence only. Moreover, there should be no doubt that exclusive influence from the L1, as claimed by Na Ranong and Leung (2009) or Hermas (2014), needs to be discarded as well. It certainly is not transfer from Russian, Turkish, or Vietnamese that governs the bilinguals' acquisition of English.

Rothman's (2011) Typological Primacy Model, which predicts wholesale transfer from the language that is typologically closest to the language currently being acquired, would strictly speaking be in line with the results of the current study. Out of all the languages considered, German is typologically closest to English, and the results presented in Chapters 7 and 8 have demonstrated that it is indeed German that is being transferred. However, Rothman's (2011) model was based on the initial stages, and the learners considered in the current study are beyond the initial stage of acquiring English.

Two further L3 models, the Linguistic Proximity Model (Westergaard et al. 2017) and the Scalpel Model (Slabakova 2017), argued that crosslinguistic influence is selective and not wholesale as proposed by Rothman (2011). The idea is that it is either the L1 or the L2 that is being transferred, depending on the linguistic similarity for each specific grammatical phenomenon (Westergaard et al. 2017). What this means is that for property A transfer may come from the L1, because this grammatical structure is similar to the structure in the language currently acquired, and that for property B, it is the L2 that acts as the source for crosslinguistic influence due to linguistic proximity between the L2 and the L3 in this context.

As demonstrated, the current study did not identify differences between the bilingual participants and their monolingual German peers that can be explained by their different language repertoires. Nevertheless, for the use of the copula verb *be*, transfer from German is certainly in line with the Linguistic Proximity Model (Westergaard et al. 2017), because German and English share this feature, which motivates (positive) crosslinguistic influence from German. Furthermore, even though the monolingual Russian and Turkish learners displayed some positive influence from their L1 with respect to the use of the progressive aspect, the same positive transfer was not visible among the Russian-German or Turkish-German bilingual learners. Based on the Linguistic Proximity Model, it could have been anticipated that the bilinguals make use of their knowledge of Russian or Turkish. However, the fact that there is no crosslinguistic influence from Russian or Turkish does not imply that the Linguistic Proximity Model is not applicable. Instead, it may be that the underlying grammatical similarity that linguists identify (namely that Russian and Turkish possess grammatical aspect, which is – on a conceptual level – comparable to the English progressive aspect; see Section 4.7), might not be transparent enough for the young foreign language learners. In addition, it cannot be ruled out – based on the data available in the current study – that the students may show a different or "divergent attainment" of the respective grammatical properties in their heritage language (Polinsky 2018: 24; see also Puig-Mayenco, González Alonso, and Rothman 2020; Section 9.4 below).

Hence, it seems difficult to clearly argue for (or against) the Linguistic Proximity Model (Westergaard et al. 2017) due to the lack of evidence of transfer from the heritage languages. Nevertheless, it needs to be kept in mind that property-by-property transfer does not mean that crosslinguistic influence from both languages needs to be found within the confines of one study. The reason for this is that the Linguistic Proximity Model should rather be understood as "transfer potential" (Westergaard 2021a, 2021b; see also Section 3.2.2). Overall, the Linguistic Proximity Model is extremely plausible, particularly given the number of recent studies convincingly arguing for selective (positive and negative) crosslinguistic influence (see, for example, Flynn and Berkes 2017; Jensen et al. 2021; Kolb, Mitrofanova, and Westergaard 2022; Lorenz et al. 2019; Sokolova and Plisov 2019; Wrembel 2021).

In addition, even though Rothman (2011) defended wholesale transfer in the initial stages of third language acquisition, in a more recent publication, Rothman, González Alonso, and Puig-Mayenco (2019: 150) pointed out that during the developmental processes of acquiring a third language, the learners may also transfer properties from the other language, but simply not during the initial stages. What this means is that "the TPM [Typological Primacy Model] is compatible with arguments from the LPM [Linguistic Proximity Model]/Scalpel Model in many aspects, except for one crucial, nontrivial point: the claimed completeness of transfer from a single source as the initial L3 interlanguage grammar" (Rothman, González Alonso, and Puig-Mayenco 2019: 156; see also Archibald 2022).

Clearly, in order to argue for property-by-property transfer, different features need to be tested among the same language learners (Rothman, González Alonso, and Puig-Mayenco 2019).[2] Even though several features were investigated in the current study, they may either be structurally too similar, or it may simply be that the selected properties all work the same. So, in a sense, not finding transfer from the heritage language does not exclude its possibility altogether. Proof of transfer from the heritage language comes from several studies that have discovered differences between heritage bilinguals and their monolingual peers, even if these appeared to be relatively small (Lloyd-Smith, Gyllstad, and

Kupisch 2017; Lloyd-Smith et al. 2018; Lorenz et al. 2019; Siemund and Lechner 2015; Siemund, Schröter, and Rahbari 2018; see Section 3.4).

This, however, also means that based on the evidence presented in Chapters 7 and 8, namely that transfer comes from the majority language German, this study is also in line with Hopp (2019) and Fallah and Jabbari (2018) who argued that it is exclusively the dominant language that is being transferred in third language acquisition (see also Lechner 2016; Lechner and Siemund 2014). Fallah and Jabbari (2018: 209) could clearly demonstrate that typological similarity did not play a role, because neither of the two languages (i.e., neither Mazandarani nor Persian) is typologically related to English. Hopp (2019), however, admitted that he could not distinguish between language dominance and typological similarity, because German pertains to both categories, i.e., it is typologically closer to English (than Turkish), and it is the dominant language of the students. This last point applies to the current study as well: language dominance (see also Section 9.2) and typological similarity cannot be considered separately, because both categories are overlapping (and perhaps reinforce each other). Therefore, the current study supports Hopp's (2019) and Fallah and Jabbari's (2018) findings, i.e., that transfer comes exclusively from the majority language German. At the same time, however, it does not argue against the Linguistic Proximity Model (Westergaard et al. 2017), the Scalpel Model (Slabakova 2017), or the Typological Primacy Model (Rothman 2011), as the current findings are also in line with these three L3 models.[3]

In conclusion, it can be maintained that in the current context, where bilingual heritage speakers with a Russian-, Turkish-, or Vietnamese-German background grow up in Germany and study English as a foreign language in a German school, language dominance as well as typological similarity or linguistic proximity are the core effects that govern crosslinguistic influence. The order of acquisition of the two previously acquired languages seems to be negligible, yet the status of the languages may additionally further this development. Cabrelli et al. (2020) noticed that in L3 acquisition, transfer from the L1 is more difficult to overcome than from the L2 (see also Section 3.2.2). The heritage language of the bilinguals, even though technically the L1, does not behave as a typical L1 but may be demoted to a secondary status.[4] Instead, German, acquired either simultaneously or consecutively, takes over the role of the L1 (see also the following Section 9.2). Thus, inhibition of a heritage language may be less difficult compared to a dominant language (see Cabrelli et al. 2020: 27) which may additionally explain the current findings, i.e., transfer from the majority language German instead of the heritage languages Russian, Turkish, or Vietnamese.

In addition, the regression and conditional inference tree analyses (see Chapter 8) revealed that there are differences among these learners. These, however, cannot be explained based on language group belonging alone but are due to other (social) background variables (see also Lorenz et al. 2022), at times interacting with language background. This supports the view that third language acquisition is a highly complex phenomenon (Cenoz 2013; Slabakova 2017). The most important factors seem to be the type of school the students attend, their socio-economic status, the number of books per household, their age as well as age of onset of acquiring German, in addition to attitudes toward learning English. These effects will be discussed in Section 9.3. Moreover, finding exclusive transfer from German, and thus a comparable English performance of the monolingual and bilingual learners of English, could also be related to the largely monolingual German syllabus and teaching style followed in German secondary schools (this will be addressed in some detail in Section 10.3; see also Chapter 2). Before discussing these effects, the role of German as the dominant language of the heritage bilinguals will be further elaborated.

9.2 Language dominance

Bilingualism was introduced as a gradable category, contingent (at least) on proficiency and language status (Berthele 2021; see Section 3.3). Moreover, heritage bilinguals were presented as one specific type, who are typically dominant in the official language of the country of residence (= majority or dominant language) and have limited skills in their heritage or family language (Pascual y Cabo and Rothman 2012; Montrul 2016; Montrul and Polinsky 2021). The heritage language is commonly used in specific situations, confined to the home and family context. Yet, even at home, the use of the majority language increases over time, as Brehmer and Mehlhorn (2017) showed in a study investigating the role of the heritage language among Russian-German as well as Polish-German students. In addition, siblings typically resorted to German as their main medium of communication and only rarely used Russian or Polish; parents even reported that they noticed a loss of their own competences due to a relative infrequency of use (Brehmer and Mehlhorn 2017). This means that in many families, the heritage language is often marginalized and over time less commonly used. The language of the speech community is slowly taking over and could perhaps be considered a second L1 for heritage bilinguals, or it may even become the de facto L1 because of its dominant status (Hopp 2019; see also Wiese et al. 2022). It goes without saying that this may not be true for every family with an immigrant background or every heritage speaker, but this is the trend that has been frequently observed among young heritage speakers and their families in Germany (see Gogolin 2021; Lorenz et al. 2020).

This scenario clearly applies to the current bilingual heritage speaker population. German was established as their dominant and frequently used language, in addition to being the language of instruction in school.

Russian, Turkish, or Vietnamese are less frequently used and could be considered minority languages. Most participants' parents reported using the heritage language as their medium of communication among each other, whereas fewer participants use the heritage language when talking to their parents and even less frequently with their siblings (see Section 6.3.2; see also Lorenz 2019: 211). German is the language they use most often, both with their peers and in school.

Based on their language use behavior, it appears plausible that their proficiency in German is higher than in the heritage language, even though no proficiency measure of the heritage languages was included in the current study. This may in turn make the availability or accessibility of the heritage language less likely when acquiring English and the influence of German potentially stronger (see also Cabrelli et al. 2020; Hopp 2019; Lorenz et al. 2019; Lorenz, Hasai, and Siemund 2021). Even though the bilingual heritage speakers are not equally proficient in German and their heritage language, the latter may still have an influence on further language acquisition. This finds support at least in several studies investigating similar heritage bilinguals (Lloyd-Smith, Gyllstad, and Kupisch 2017; Lloyd-Smith et al. 2018; Lorenz et al. 2019; Siemund and Lechner 2015; Siemund, Schröter, and Rahbari 2018) and it also relates to a striking claim by Franceschini (2016). She argued that even languages acquired via "unfocused language acquisition" may have an impact on further foreign language acquisition (Franceschini 2016: 102–105).[5] Of course, the heritage languages were shown to play an active role in the lives of the bilinguals of the current study (even if they are comparably less active than the majority language German) and are therefore different than unfocused languages. However, if a language that a speaker has barely any competences in can impact the learning of additional languages, one could expect to find at least some influence of the heritage language on the performance in English.

Yet, given that theoretically all previously acquired languages, even if they have been acquired in an unfocused setting (Franceschini 2016), have the potential to transfer to the language currently acquired (Westergaard et al. 2017), it appears still plausible that it is the dominant language that is mainly being transferred (Hopp 2019; Fallah and Jabbari 2018). This is particularly so because the dominant language, i.e., the most frequently activated language, is the typologically closest language to the one currently being acquired (Rothman 2011) and the language of instruction in school (see Section 10.3). This explains why language background alone did not account for any statistically significant differences between the heritage bilinguals and their monolingual German peers in the current study. German, the dominant language, was established to be the source of crosslinguistic influence for both the monolingual as well as the bilingual learners. Notwithstanding, some differences could be identified. These relate to additional background variables and will be discussed in the following sections.

9.3 Influence of (social) background variables

As was demonstrated, no statistically significant differences between the monolingual and bilingual participants with respect to crosslinguistic influence could be reported. This, however, does not mean that there are no observable differences in the learners' performance in English. In fact, the opposite is the case: several interesting effects were detected, which reveals the importance of including additional background variables when investigating crosslinguistic influence in third language acquisition (see also Lorenz et al. 2022). Each variable will be discussed in turn. All following sections are exclusively based on the monolingual German students and the Russian-German, Turkish-German, and Vietnamese-German bilingual students. Reference to all learners considered in the current study will only feature when discussing age.

9.3.1 Type of school

The participants of the present investigation are 12- and 16-year-old secondary school students. In Germany, there are several types of secondary school. For this study, two types were considered, namely the university-bound secondary school type *Gymnasium* and all other types comprised within one category (see Section 6.3.2). This choice was made because students attending the former school type show, on average, a higher overall performance in school (Lorenz et al. 2022), which may potentially be tied to additional social factors, motivation, or cognitive skills (Lechner and Siemund 2014; see also Maluch and Kempert 2019). For example, previous research on lexical transfer found that students attending *Gymnasium* had lower ratios of lexical transfer in their foreign language English production than their peers attending other secondary schools (Lorenz, Hasai and Siemund 2021). It is therefore not too surprising that type of school turned out to be an important predictor for both the written and the oral production in the E-LiPS corpus.

It was shown that the participants of the current study are not equally distributed between the two school types (see Table 6.1). Overall, more students attend *Gymnasium* (n = 84), and fewer students attend other institutions (n = 47).[6] Moreover, the Russian-German and Vietnamese-German bilinguals in particular attend the university-bound secondary school type *Gymnasium* comparably more frequently. The reverse is true for the Turkish-German bilinguals; the German monolinguals nearly equally attend either *Gymnasium* or other school types. These patterns are intriguing and indicate that school type and socio-economic status are not necessarily correlated, because the German monolinguals have on average a higher socio-economic status, yet they do not attend *Gymnasium* more frequently than their Russian- or Vietnamese-German bilingual peers (see also Section 9.3.2).

As shown in Chapter 8, school type featured both as a main effect (use of the progressive aspect) as well as within interactions (correct form and target-like-meaning of verbs; affixal subject-verb agreement (SVA)). The university-bound school type *Gymnasium* was mostly associated with more target-like use or more formal correctness (for example use of the progressive aspect), and on average, less variability was observed within this type of school and the interacting variables. Nevertheless, the predicted probabilities for formal correctness of verbs were lower among the German monolinguals attending *Gymnasium* compared to students of this language group attending other types of school (see Figure 8.1). This selective feature exemplifies that it was typically not school type alone that returned a statistically significant effect. Instead, the influence of school type is further contingent on the socio-economic status or the number of books per household. What this means is that in general, attending *Gymnasium*, in addition to possessing a high number of books and having a high socio-economic status, presents a favorable context for learning and using the foreign language English (see also Sections 9.3.2 and 9.3.3). This is true for bilingual and monolingual students alike.

9.3.2 Socio-economic status

The socio-economic status values used in the current study are based on the occupation and income of the participants' caretakers, operationalized as HISEI values, ranging from low (16) to high scores (88) (Ehmke and Siegle 2005; Ganzeboom, De Graaf, and Treiman 1992; International Labor Office 2012). The current dataset reflects common statistics about the younger population in Germany and their respective socio-economic status in relation to being first, second, or third generation immigrants. On average, adolescents from immigrant families have a lower socio-economic status than their peers growing up in a monolingual German household (see, for example, Kempert et al. 2016; Stanat et al. 2016). Overall, the German monolinguals of the present study have higher HISEI values than the bilingual students. Note, however, that for some students this information is not available (see Table 6.1), and the proportion of missing values is particularly high for the Turkish-German bilinguals (see also Lorenz 2019).

Previous research often reports that socio-economic status influences the acquisition of a foreign language (see, for example, Cenoz 2013; Franceschini 2016; Lechner and Siemund 2014; Lorenz, Hasai, and Siemund 2021). However, this is not always the case, considering research that found no differences with respect to socio-economic status has also been put forward (Hopp 2019; Lorenz et al. 2020; see also Lorenz et al. 2022).

As demonstrated in Chapter 8, HISEI appears in numerous interactions with other background variables, yet never as a main effect. This means that the socio-economic status is dependent on further social factors

Crosslinguistic influence in heritage speakers' 211

such as language group, gender, type of school, attitudes toward English, number of books, as well as age, and age of onset of acquiring German. The general trend is that with increasing HISEI values, the predicted probabilities of formal correctness and target-like meaning rise (see, for example, Figures 8.2, 8.3, 8.6). This result finds support in studies that identified an effect of socio-economic status (see, for example, Cenoz 2013), namely that a higher socio-economic status is associated with a better performance in the foreign language. A notable exception is visible in the effects plot showing an interaction between English difficulty and HISEI regarding the target-like meaning of verbs (Figure 8.2). This interaction demonstrates that the predicted probability of target-like meaning decreases with increasing socio-economic status, at least for students who think that English is a difficult language. In summary, having a higher socio-economic status (in addition to other social variables) presents a more beneficial condition for foreign language acquisition. This means that the German monolingual students of the present study have, per se, an advantage over their bilingual peers, simply because the former come from families whose HISEI values are on average higher.

9.3.3 *Number of books per household*

The number of books per household was collected within the present study to assess whether the educational aspirations or general literacy interests of the families have a measurable impact on the acquisition of the foreign language English. This variable could be understood as a supplementary measure related to the socio-economic status of the participants' families, but it may also provide an additional explanatory value that is not captured by socio-economic status alone. Overall, the distribution of the number of books seems to resemble the socio-economic status to a certain extent (see Table 6.1). There is considerable variability among the participants, and the German monolingual groups have, on average, a higher number of books in their homes. Particularly low are the numbers of books in the households of the Vietnamese-German and the Turkish-German bilinguals, whereas the Russian-German bilinguals reported to have only somewhat fewer books than their monolingual German peers.

If the number of books represents the caretakers' educational aspirations, if not de facto level, which in turn indicates higher educational aspirations and possibly higher educational success of their children, a higher number should theoretically correspond to higher rates of correct form and target-like performance in English.

This assumption can largely be substantiated. The analysis in Chapter 8 even returned one main effect: students whose families have a lower number of books per household used the present tense when writing their picture stories, whereas those with more than 350 books either composed their stories in the simple past or they mixed tenses (see Figure 8.5). With respect to the correct form of verbs, the predicted probabilities increased with increasing number of books per household, irrespective of the age of the participants or their language group (see Figure 8.1). Even though the slopes for the 12- and 16-year-old students as well as the four language groups differed slightly, they all indicated an increase. Similarly, low numbers of books predicted a high probability of third person singular *–s* 'missing' (see Figure 8.8). For higher numbers of books per household, however, the predicted probabilities interacted with socio-economic status, age, age of onset of acquiring German, language group, school type, and English difficulty, suggesting a rather complex underlying dependency. Moreover, regarding target-like meaning of verbs (see Figure 8.7), the predicted probabilities showed an increase for the three bilingual groups but a small decrease for the German monolinguals. Note, however, that the predicted probabilities remain above 0.5, which means that the binary logistic regression model nevertheless predicted target-like meaning for this group. Overall, the number of books offers some explanatory value, mostly in the direction of having more books being related to a more target-like performance in English. Again, this suggests a principal advantage for the German monolingual participants, as their families possess comparably more books.

9.3.4 Age

Two different age cohorts, i.e., 12- and 16-year-old participants, representing two acquisitional stages, were compared in the current study. The former comprise initial or intermediate third language learners, whereas the latter can be considered more advanced learners with four more years of formal English tuition. Generally, crosslinguistic influence becomes smaller over time, meaning that foreign language learners should show more and more target-like performance with increasing age. This means that with increasing proficiency, the influence from the background language(s) is inhibited (see, for example, Lorenz et al. 2019; Lorenz, Hasai, and Siemund 2021; Siemund, Schröter, and Rahbari 2018) and the interlanguage approximates the target language (Cenoz, Hufeisen, and Jessner 2001; Cenoz 2003; De Angelis 2007). At some point, language learners should converge on a common target (at least in an idealized scenario, if a language is fully acquired).

The target or baseline comparison of the current study are the two English native speaker control groups, in addition to monolingual Russian, Turkish, and Vietnamese second language learners of English. Interestingly, practically no developmental progress was observable among the English native speakers (see Chapter 7). This indicates that with respect to verbal use and usage of tense and aspect, the 12- and 16-year-old English native speakers are comparable to one another. This is different when considering the other seven learner groups. Based on age and language group alone, i.e., disregarding social background variables, there is indeed an overall trend of more target-like or better performance with increasing age. One such example is affixal SVA. All learner groups omitted fewer third person singular –s morphemes with increasing age (yet even among the older students, the error rate remained relatively high). The only exception is the Turkish monolingual participants. This group clearly deviated from the remaining participants and appeared to have an overall lower proficiency in English. Furthermore, a development is also observable with respect to the omission of the copula verb *be*. The Russian, Turkish, and Vietnamese L2 learners of English omitted the copula verb comparably frequently, but fewer omissions could be found among the 16-year-old cohorts. Hence, overall, crosslinguistic influence decreases over time and the target-like performance in English increases.

In conjunction with the remaining social background variables, this age factor persisted. Yet, and this is a crucial finding, only in some analyses did age appear to have a significant impact. In Chapter 8, which is exclusively based on the three bilingual groups as well as the German monolinguals, the general trend of lower performance at a younger age was visible. However, the participants' age did not feature in all analyses, and when it did, it interacted with other variables, for example the number of books (see Section 9.3.3) or the age of onset of acquiring German (see Section 9.3.6) and was not always a categorical factor.

Given the analyses included in Chapter 8, it may not be so surprising that the differences with respect to age featured less prominently when considering additional social factors. Several studies proposed that, as argued at the beginning of this section, the differences between foreign language learners diminish over time (see also Maluch, Neumann, and Kempert 2016). The results reported in Chapter 8 may thus be contingent on the feature choice: affixal SVA agreement was generally shown to be a problematic area for all learners, both the younger as well as the older cohorts,[7] and suppletive SVA was arguably not challenging anymore, not even for the youngest learners. The same can be said about the progressive aspect. Using the correct form was demanding for all four learner groups, irrespective of their age, and using the progressive aspect in target-like contexts was less difficult. In conclusion, learner age is a significant factor in the current study, but other variables, among others school type and socio-economic status, appear to have more explanatory power.

9.3.5 Language task assessment: written versus spoken

Two different production tasks, namely a written and an oral task, were employed in the present investigation. The main focus lay on the written task, because all students wrote a descriptive text to a picture story, while only a subsample ($n = 176$, 70.7 percent) participated in the oral description task. On average, the students used fewer word tokens when orally describing the story in comparison to writing a text (see Section 7.4.1). A simple explanation may be that because of the time limit of 30 minutes in the written task (see Section 6.1.1), the students had more time, which they used to compose longer stories. In the oral task, they were also given some time before the actual recording started (see Section 6.1.2), but it is undeniably different to sit in a room with fellow students while writing a text versus sitting in a room with one interviewer while thinking about what to say about a specific picture story. Moreover, the stories itself could have triggered these quantity differences. This cannot be excluded, because each picture sequence was only used once, either in the written or the oral task but not alternated, and randomly assigned to the students.

In addition, there was a positive correlation between the number of words written and spoken for each individual language group (see Figure 7.1). This indicates that those who used more words in their text composition also used more words when orally retelling a story. Only for the Turkish monolinguals did this positive correlation not reach statistical significance.

Finally, the analyses in Section 8.4 demonstrated that the mode, i.e., spoken versus written, had no statistically significant effect with respect to formal correctness, target-like meaning, SVA, or the use of the progressive aspect. Thus, in terms of quality, there is no grammatical difference between the written and spoken data. However, in terms of quantity, a disparity between the texts and recordings was observable.

9.3.6 *Age of onset of acquiring German*

All bilingual participants in the current study are heritage speakers, but they differ in their age of onset of acquiring German. This means that some are simultaneous (acquired German from birth onwards), whereas others are sequential bilinguals (age of acquisition of German before age seven or after). In Section 6.3.2, it was established that a considerable number of the bilinguals were either born in Germany ($n = 30$) or started to acquire German at the age of three or younger ($n = 62$), whereas approximately one third of all bilinguals came to Germany at a later age (see also Lorenz 2019). Thus, the majority can be considered early bilinguals (age of onset at the age of three or younger). Moreover, the age of onset of acquiring German of the younger cohorts is on average lower compared to their 16-year-old peers (see Table 6.1). Needless to say, all German monolinguals acquired German from birth onwards.

In the current study, several interesting trends could be observed, which stand in opposition to what was reported in Lechner and Siemund (2014: 336), because in their investigation, no differences could be ascribed to the age of onset of the participants. In the present analyses, however, the age of onset returned some significant effects in interactions with type of school, English difficulty, and language group. Intriguingly, in most interactions, the predicted probability of correct form, including correct SVA, and target-like meaning increased with increasing age of onset of acquiring German (see, for example, Figures 8.1, 8.2, 8.3, and 8.8). The steepness of the slopes varied to a certain extent, but the upward trend remained for both types of school and for students perceiving English either as a difficult language or not. Yet, for example with respect to formal correctness, the opposite was true for the 12-year-old students; here, a decrease of predicted probabilities with increasing age of onset was reported (Figure 8.6).

This means that, by and large, it is not the early bilinguals who show an advantage, but rather those participants who acquired German at a later age seem to have a more target-like and formally correct English production. Note that this puts the bilinguals technically in an advantageous position. However, it should be kept in mind that the conditional inference trees pointed out that age of onset interacted with numerous other variables, i.e., school type, language group, socio-economic status, number of books, and age (see Figures 8.3 and 8.8).

A possible interpretation of this overall trend should be taken cautiously and needs to be understood as somewhat speculative. All bilinguals have a high level or native-like level of German, no matter at which age they started to acquire this language, and attend German secondary schools. A late(r) age of onset could in principle imply that these bilinguals have higher proficiency levels in their heritage language, which may in turn be helpful for acquiring English (Cummins 1976, 1979, 1996). This, however, cannot be proven based on the current dataset, because proficiency in the heritage language (or any of the languages in the students' repertoires for that matter) was not measured (see Section 9.4).

9.3.7 Attitudes toward learning English

Two different attitudes toward English were assessed within the current study, namely whether English was regarded as a useful or difficult language or not. Both represent binary variables, i.e., the students could respond with either 'yes' or 'no'. This certainly is a limitation and did not give the students an opportunity to negotiate or grade their answers. Nevertheless, the general assumption is that perceived difficulty as well as usefulness could affect the motivation to learn this foreign language. To be more precise, lower motivation might result in less effort and lower success in acquiring a second or foreign language (see, for example, Dörnyei 1998, 2005; Dörnyei and Csizér 1998; Gardner 1985; Zafar and Meenakshi 2012).

Almost 90 percent of the participants think that English is a useful language. This clearly corroborates the view that young people are aware of the important and useful role that English plays or will play in their future (see also Section 2.1). Furthermore, slightly over 20 percent consider English to be a difficult language, and the remaining 76 percent feel it is not (2 percent did not indicate a response).

Not surprisingly, the variable English usefulness did not show up as a significant predictor. Since most students agreed that English is indeed a useful language, this variable lacks statistical power. However, several interesting findings pertain to the variable English difficulty, because it appeared as a statistically significant predictor in some interactions. Overall, agreeing that English is a difficult language was mostly shown to be associated with lower formal correctness as well as target-like use of verbs, or with relative variability, interacting, for example, with age, age of onset, gender, socio-economic status, and school type (see Figures 8.1, 8.2, and 8.8). Interestingly, for students who did not regard English as a difficult language to learn, the respective interactions were mostly stable across the different levels. This means, for instance, that irrespective of gender, socio-economic status, age of onset, or age, the predicted probabilities of target-like verbs remained high for negating that English is difficult (Figure 8.2). Note that none of the significant interactions included language group, demonstrating that across the four language groups, this variable did not behave statistically significantly differently. In general, the results should not be overinterpreted given that only two yes-or-no statements were included. Nevertheless, they provide some compelling insights, which are to be further investigated in future research (see Section 11.2).

9.4 Shortcomings and limitations

The current study provides a detailed description of the oral and written use of tense and aspect of monolingual and bilingual learners of English. With this, it adds to the understanding of how third language acquisition works in unbalanced bilingual heritage speakers growing up in Germany. Yet, there are several limitations that must be mentioned. These are briefly addressed in the following paragraphs.

The main shortcoming is that the proficiencies of the heritage languages Russian, Turkish, or Vietnamese, as well as German and English, were not systematically assessed by using, for example, C-tests, cloze-tests, or reading comprehension tests, as employed in other studies (see, for example, Brehmer and Mehlhorn 2015; Gogolin et al. 2017; Maluch, Neumann, and Kempert 2016). Based on self-reported language use, it is still possible to estimate that the heritage language is the weaker language of the bilinguals participating in the current study. Yet, no other information is available, which means that it remains to a certain extent unclear whether the relevant grammatical properties assessed in English, i.e., tense and aspect, have also been acquired in the heritage languages in a native-like manner, specifically whether they match the respective baseline standards (Putnam, Schwarz, and Hofman 2021; Puig-Mayenco, González Alonso, and Rothman 2020). Investigations of heritage morphology have shown that tense appears to be a relatively salient functional category, whereas more variability or restructuring can be found with respect to aspect (for a topical overview see Putnam, Schwarz, and Hofman 2021; see also Polinsky 2018), additionally contingent on the level of proficiency in the heritage language (Montrul 2016: 61–63, 65–66). But even without knowing these specific details of the current speaker population, the respective heritage bilinguals can be assumed to be representative of young, bilingual heritage speakers growing up in Germany, underlining the importance of the current findings.[8] Furthermore, since all bilingual students attended secondary schools in Germany at the time of testing, a certain level of German can be assumed. Moreover, the amount of English exposure of those participants who grow up in Germany is comparable within the two age cohorts. However, some differences are to be expected based on the type of school the students attend, even though this was controlled for by differentiating the university-bound secondary school type *Gymnasium* from all other secondary schools. Information about additional internal variability is, however, not available in the current study.

Moreover, the present investigation is interested in a developmental perspective by comparing foreign language learners at two different points in time, i.e., more initial or intermediate (12-year-old students) versus more advanced (16-year-old students) learners of English. Ideally, this would have been done with a longitudinal study (see, for example, Gogolin et al. 2017) instead of using a cross-sectional design, as was done in the present study. The former is to be preferred as it controls for interfering social variables. Nevertheless, by including several background variables like age of onset, school type, or socio-economic status in the statistical analyses of the present study, several influencing factors were controlled for. Controlling for social background is particularly relevant for the type of data considered here. Ideally, a learner corpus should consist of carefully balanced background variables, which was impossible to achieve given the social realities found in Germany. By and large, adolescents growing up in immigrant families have on average a lower socio-economic status than their peers growing up in non-immigrant families (Kempert et al. 2016; Stanat et al. 2016). The data of the present study clearly reflect this social asymmetry and it is therefore not a balanced data set.

Furthermore, as has been pointed out multiple times, for some of the participants the background information is partly incomplete. Even though the overall number of participants is moderately high (n = 249), this reduces some of the groups, especially the Turkish-German bilinguals, to a relatively low number. For the linguistic analysis presented in Chapter 7, the written and oral data of all participants could be used. However, for the sociolinguistic analysis discussed in Chapter 8, a smaller dataset, relying on complete datasets only, had to be employed. This considerably scaled down the number of texts and oral recordings (see also Section 8.5).

Notes

1 It needs to be pointed out that for some bilinguals, German is strictly speaking not even the second language, because the heritage language and German were acquired simultaneously (see also Sections 6.3.2 and 9.3.6).

2 Note that particularly non-facilitative transfer evidenced on two distinct features would be needed to prove property-by-property transfer and to distinguish it from target language performance (see Rothman, González Alonso, and Puig-Mayenco 2019: 152).
3 Interestingly, Ramos Feijoo and García Mayo (2021: 24) argue against "clear evidence supporting any of the L3 models" but maintain that it is a multitude of different factors (instead of one single factor) that determines crosslinguistic influence in third language acquisition. Note, however, that their study, albeit investigating dominant bilinguals, is not part of a bilingual heritage speaker context but set in the Basque Autonomous Country in Spain.
4 The heritage language is not only confined to limited communicative situations, but a potential assimilation pressure or desire to be seen as a German native speaker may additionally influence this development.
5 Unfocused language acquisition should not be understood as implicit language learning. According to Franceschini (2016: 102), it means that the respective languages have not been consciously or explicitly learned, but that they have merely been overheard or absorbed via recurring exposure in, for example, someone's neighborhood or social surroundings.
6 Note that for 36 students (21.6 percent) this information is unknown.
7 Note that age was a statistically significant factor explaining the variance in third person singular –*s* 'present' versus 'missing' (see Figure 8.8), although it interacted with additional social variables.
8 This could be understood as a comparable situation to what Vallerossa et al. (2021: 14) refer to as "ecological validity," i.e., "the real composition of multilingual students' background languages in the current context."

References

Aalberse, S., A. Backus, and P. Muysken. 2019. *Heritage languages: A language contact approach*. Amsterdam: Benjamins.

Archibald, J. 2022. Phonological parsing via an integrated I-language: The emergence of property-by-property transfer effects in L3 phonology. *Linguistic Approaches to Bilingualism*. https://doi.org/10.1075/lab.21017.arc

Bardel, C. and Y. Falk. 2007. The role of the second language in third language acquisition: The case of Germanic syntax. *Second Language Research* 23:459–484.

Bardel, C. and Y. Falk. 2012. The L2 status factor and the declarative/procedural distinction. In *Third language acquisition in adulthood*, ed. J. Cabrelli Amaro, S. Flynn, and J. Rothman, 61–78. Amsterdam: Benjamins.

Berthele, R. 2021. The extraordinary ordinary: Re-engineering multilingualism as a natural category. *Language Learning* 71:80–120.

Brehmer, B. and G. Mehlhorn. 2015. Russisch als Herkunftssprache in Deutschland: Ein holistischer Ansatz zur Erforschung des Potenzials von Herkunftssprachen. *Zeitschrift für Fremdsprachenforschung* 26:85–123.

Brehmer, B. and G. Mehlhorn. 2017. Biliteralität in russisch- und polnischen Familien in Deutschland: Ein Vergleich. Conference *Biliteralität zwischen Mündlichkeit und Schriftlichkeit*, March 24–25, 2017, University of Hamburg.

Cabrelli, J., M. Iverson, D. Giancaspro and B. Halloran González. 2020. The roles of L1 Spanish versus L2 Spanish in L3 Portuguese morphosyntactic development. In *Linguistic approaches to Portuguese as an additional language*, ed. K. V. Molsing, C. Becker Lopes Perna, and A. M. Tramunt Ibaños, 11–33. Amsterdam: Benjamins.

Cenoz, J. 2003. The additive effect of bilingualism on third language acquisition: A review. *International Journal of Bilingualism* 7:71–87.

Cenoz, J. 2013. The Influence of bilingualism on third language acquisition: Focus on multilingualism. *Language Teaching* 46:71–86.

Cenoz, J., B. Hufeisen, and U. Jessner (eds.). 2001. *Cross-linguistic influence in third language acquisition: Psycholinguistic perspective*. Clevedon: Multilingual Matters.

Cummins, J. 1976. The influence of bilingualism on cognitive growth: A synthesis of research findings and explanatory hypothesis. *Working Papers on Bilingualism* 9:1–43.

Cummins, J. 1979. Linguistic interdependence and the educational development of bilingual children. *Review of Educational Research* 49:222–251.

Cummins, J. 1996. *Negotiating identities: Education for empowerment in a diverse society*. Ontario: California Association for Bilingual Education.

De Angelis, G. 2007. *Third or additional language acquisition*. Clevedon: Multilingual Matters.

Dörnyei, Z. 1998. Motivation in second and foreign language learning. *Language Teaching* 31:117–135.

Dörnyei, Z. 2005. *The psychology of the language learner: Individual differences in second language acquisition*. Mahwah, NJ: Lawrence Erlbaum.

Dörnyei, Z. and K. Csizér. 1998. Ten commandments for motivating language learners: Results of an empirical study. *Language Teaching Research* 2:203–229.

Ehmke, T. and T. Siegle. 2005. ISEI, ISCED, HOMEPOS, ESCS: Indikatoren der sozialen Herkunft bei der Qualifizierung von sozialen Disparitäten. *Zeitschrift für Erziehungswissenschaft* 8:521–539.

Fallah, N. and A. A. Jabbari. 2018. L3 acquisition of English attributive adjectives: Dominant language of communication matters for syntactic cross-linguistic influence. *Linguistic Approaches to Bilingualism* 8:193–216.

Flynn, S. and É. Berkes. 2017. Toward a new understanding of syntactic CLI: Evidence from L2 and L3 acquisition. In *L3 syntactic transfer: Models, new developments and implications*, ed. T. Angelovska and A. Hahn, 35–61. Amsterdam: Benjamins.

Flynn, S., C. Foley, and I. Vinnitskaya. 2004. The cumulative-enhancement model for language acquisition: Comparing adults' and children's patterns of development in first, second and third language acquisition of relative clauses. *International Journal of Multilingualism* 1:3–16.

Franceschini, R. 2016. Multilingualism research. In *The Cambridge handbook of linguistic multi-competence*, ed. V. Cook and Li Wei, 97–124. Cambridge: Cambridge University Press.

Ganzeboom, H. B. G., P. M. De Graaf, and D. J. Treiman. 1992. A standard international socio-economic index of occupational status. *Social Science Research* 21:1–56.

Gardner, R. C. 1985. *Social psychology and second language learning: The role of attitudes and motivation*. London: Edward Arnold.

Gogolin, I. 2021. Multilingualism: A threat to public education or a resource in public education? – European histories and realities. *European Educational Research Journal* 20:297–310.

Gogolin, I., T. Klinger, M. Lagemann, B. Schnoor, in collaboration with C. Gabriel, M. Knigge, M. Krause, and P. Siemund. 2017. *Indikation, Konzeption und Untersuchungsdesign des Projekts Mehrsprachigkeitsentwicklung im Zeitverlauf (MEZ)*. MEZ Arbeitspapier Nr. 1. Hamburg (University of Hamburg). www.pedocs.de/frontdoor.php?source_opus=14825 (accessed April 4, 2022).

Hammarberg, B. (ed.). 2009. *Processes in third language acquisition*. Edinburgh: Edinburgh University Press.

Hermas, A. 2014. Multilingual transfer: L1 morphosyntax in L3 English. *International Journal of Language Studies* 8:1–24.

Hopp, H. 2019. Cross-linguistic influence in the child third language acquisition of grammar: Sentence comprehension and production among Turkish-German and German learners of English. *International Journal of Bilingualism* 23:567–583.

International Labour Office. 2012. *International standard classification of occupations. ISCO-08. Volume 1: Structure, group definitions and correspondence tables*. Geneva: ILO.

Jensen, I. N., N. Mitrofanova, M. Anderssen, Y. Rodina, R. Slabakova, and M. Westergaard. 2021. Crosslinguistic influence in L3 acquisition across linguistic modules. *International Journal of Multilingualism*. https://doi.org/10.1080/14790718.2021.1985127

Kempert, S., A. Edele, D. Rauch, K. Wolf, J. Paetsch, A. Darsow, J. Maluch, and P. Stanat. 2016. Die Rolle der Sprache für zuwanderungsbezogene Ungleichheiten im Bildungserfolg. In *Ethnische Ungleichheiten im Bildungsverlauf: Mechanismen, Befunde, Debatten*, ed. C. Diehl, C. Hunkler, and C. Kristen, 157–241. Wiesbaden: Springer.

Kolb, N., N. Mitrofanova, and M. Westergaard. 2022. Crosslinguistic influence in child L3 English: An empirical study on Russian-German heritage bilinguals. *International Journal of Bilingualism* 26:476–501.

Lechner, S. 2016. Literale Fähigkeiten als Ressource beim Erwerb von Fremdsprachen in mehrsprachigen Kontexten. In *Mehrsprachigkeit als Ressource in der Schriftlichkeit*, ed. P. Rosenberg, and C. Schröder, 113–131. Berlin: De Gruyter Mouton.

Lechner, S. and P. Siemund. 2014. The role of language external factors in the acquisition of English as an additional language by bilingual children in Germany. In *Language contacts at the crossroads of disciplines*, ed. H. Paulasto, L. Meriläinen, H. Riionheimo, and M. Kok, 319–345. Newcastle-upon-Tyne: Cambridge Scholars Publishing.

Lloyd-Smith, A., H. Gyllstad, and T. Kupisch. 2017. Transfer into L3 English: Global accent in German-dominant heritage speakers of Turkish. *Linguistic Approaches to Bilingualism* 2:131–162.

Lloyd-Smith, A., H. Gyllstad, T. Kupisch, and S. Quaglia. 2018. Heritage language proficiency does not predict syntactic CLI into L3 English. *International Journal of Bilingual Education and Bilingualism* 24:435–451.

Lorenz, E. 2019. *The use of tense and aspect in the additional language English by monolingual speakers and bilingual heritage speakers*. PhD diss., University of Hamburg. https://ediss.sub.uni-hamburg.de/handle/ediss/6317

Lorenz, E., R. J. Bonnie, K. Feindt, S. Rahbari, and P. Siemund. 2019. Crosslinguistic influence in unbalanced bilingual heritage speakers on subsequent language acquisition: Evidence from pronominal object placement in ditransitive clauses. *International Journal of Bilingualism* 23:1410–1430.

Lorenz, E., K. Feindt, S. Rahbari, and P. Siemund. 2022. The influence of extra-linguistic variables on cross-linguistic influence – Case studies of bilingual heritage speakers. In *Language development in diverse settings: Interdisziplinäre Ergebnisse aus dem Projekt Mehrsprachigkeitsentwicklung im Zeitverlauf (MEZ)*, ed. H. Brandt, M. Krause, and I. Usanova, 305–338. Westport, CT: Springer.
Lorenz, E., Y. Hasai, and P. Siemund. 2021. Multilingual lexical transfer challenges monolingual educational norms: Not quite! *Multilingua* 40:791–813.
Lorenz, E., S. Rahbari, U. Schackow, and P. Siemund. 2020. Does bilingualism correlate with or predict higher proficiency in L3 English? A contrastive study of monolingual and bilingual learners. *Journal of Multilingual Theories and Practices* 1:185–217.
Maluch, J. T. and S. Kempert. 2019. Bilingual profiles and third language learning: The effects of the manner of learning, sequence of bilingual acquisition, and language use practices. *International Journal of Bilingual Education and Bilingualism* 22:870–882.
Maluch, J. T., M. Neumann, and S. Kempert. 2016. Bilingualism as a resource for foreign language learning of language minority students? Empirical evidence from a longitudinal study during primary and secondary school in Germany. *Language and Individual Differences* 51:111–118.
Montrul, S. 2016. *The acquisition of heritage languages*. Cambridge: Cambridge University Press.
Montrul, S. and M. Polinsky (eds.). 2021. *The Cambridge handbook of heritage languages and linguistics*. Cambridge: Cambridge University Press.
Na Ranong, S. and I. Leung. 2009. Null objects in L1 Thai-L2 English-L3 Chinese: An empiricist take on a theoretical problem. In *Third language acquisition and universal grammar*, ed. I. Leung, 162–191. Bristol: Multilingual Matters.
Pascual y Cabo, D. and J. Rothman. 2012. The (il)logical problem of heritage speaker bilingualism and incomplete acquisition. *Applied Linguistics* 33:450–455.
Polinsky, M. 2018. *Heritage languages and their speakers*. Cambridge: Cambridge University Press.
Puig-Mayenco, E., J. González Alonso, and J. Rothman. 2020. A systematic review of transfer studies in third language acquisition. *Second Language Research* 36:31–64.
Putnam, M. T., L. Schwarz, and A. D. Hoffman. 2021. Morphology of heritage languages. In *The Cambridge handbook of heritage languages and linguistics*, ed. S. Montrul and M. Polinsky, 613–643. Cambridge: Cambridge University Press.
Ramos Feijoo, J. and M. d. P. García Mayo. 2021. The acquisition of relative clauses by Spanish-Basque learners of L3 English: Does dominance play a role? *International Review of Applied Linguistics in Language Teaching*. https://doi.org/10.1515/iral-2021-0054
Rothman, J. 2011. L3 syntactic transfer selectivity and typological determinacy: The typological primacy model. *Second Language Research* 27:107–127.
Rothman, J., J. González Alonso, and E. Puig-Mayenco. 2019. *Third language acquisition and linguistic transfer*. Cambridge: Cambridge University Press.
Siemund, P. and S. Lechner. 2015. Transfer effects in the acquisition of English as an additional language by bilingual children in Germany. In *Transfer*

effects in multilingual language development, ed. H. Peukert, 147–160. Amsterdam: Benjamins.

Siemund, P., S. Schröter, and S. Rahbari. 2018. Learning English demonstrative pronouns on bilingual substrate: Evidence from German heritage speakers of Russian, Turkish, and Vietnamese. In *Foreign language education in multilingual classrooms*, ed. A. Bonnet and P. Siemund, 381–405. Amsterdam: Benjamins.

Slabakova, R. 2017. The scalpel model of third language acquisition. *International Journal of Bilingualism* 21:651–665.

Sokolova M. and E. Plisov. 2019. Cross-linguistic transfer classroom L3 acquisition in university setting. *Vestnik of Minin University* 7. https://doi.org/10.26795/2307-1281-2019-7-1-6

Stanat, P., K. Böhme, S. Schipolowski, and N. Haag (eds.). 2016. *IQB-Bildungstrend 2015: Sprachliche Kompetenzen am Ende der 9. Jahrgangsstufe im zweiten Ländervergleich*. Münster/New York: Waxmann.

Vallerossa, F., A. Gudmundson, A. Bergström, and C. Bardel. 2021. Learning aspect in Italian as additional language: The role of second languages. *International Review of Applied Linguistics in Language Teaching*. https://doi.org/10.1515/iral-2021-0033

Westergaard, M. 2021a. Microvariation in multilingual situations: The importance of property-by-property acquisition. *Second Language Research* 37:379–407.

Westergaard, M. 2021b. The plausibility of wholesale vs property-by-property transfer in L3 acquisition. *Linguistic Approaches to Bilingualism* 11:103–108.

Westergaard, M., N. Mitrofanova, R. Mykhaylyk, and Y. Rodina. 2017. Crosslinguistic influence in the acquisition of a third language: The linguistic proximity model. *International Journal of Bilingualism* 21:666–682.

Wiese, H., A. Alexiadou, S. Allen, O. Bunk, N. Gagarina, K. Iefremenko, M. Martynova, T. Pashkova, V. Rizou, C. Schroeder, A. Shadrova, L. Szucsich, R. Tracy, W. Tsehaye, S. Zerbian, and Y. Zuban. 2022. Heritage speakers as part of the native language continuum. *Frontiers in Psychology* 12:717973.

Williams, S. and B. Hammarberg. 1998. Language switches in L3 production: Implications of a polyglot speaking model. *Applied Linguistics* 19:295–333.

Wrembel, M. 2021. Multilingual acquisition property by property: A view from a wider perspective. *Second Language Research* 37:441–447.

Zafar, S. and K. Meenakshi. 2012. Individual learner differences and second language acquisition: A review. *Journal of Language Teaching and Research* 3:639–646.

10 Bi-/multilingual advantages of heritage speakers

10.1 Advantages in foreign language acquisition?

Advantages in additional language acquisition, often referred to as *bi- or multilingual advantages*, is a hotly debated topic (see, for example, Siemund 2023 for a recent overview). In contexts where balanced bilinguals acquire a foreign language and are compared to monolingual learners of that foreign language, a learning advantage of the former is often reported (see, for example, Agustín-Llach 2019; Cenoz and Valencia 1994; Sanz 2000). However, bilinguals are not always (nearly) equally proficient in their two languages, and Cummins (1976) pointed out relatively early that there seems to be a connection between the status of being a balanced bilingual and resulting learning advantages (see also Siemund and Lorenz 2023).

The bilinguals of the current context are not balanced bilinguals but unbalanced bilingual heritage speakers, which means that they are more proficient in German, the official language of the speech community of their country of residence, and less proficient in their heritage language (either Russian, Turkish, or Vietnamese). In such heritage speaker contexts, evidence is relatively inconclusive (see Section 3.6). Some studies provided clear indications that bilinguals have an advantage in additional foreign language acquisition when compared to their monolingual peers (e.g., Hesse, Göbel, and Hartig 2008; Maluch and Kempert 2019; Maluch et al. 2015). Here, one could argue that bilingual advantages indeed extend to heritage speaker contexts. Other studies, however, presented select advantages only for specific bilingual subgroups (Hopp et al. 2019; Maluch, Neumann, and Kempert 2016; Rauch, Naumann, and Jude 2012). Moreover, there are also several studies that did not find a bilingual advantage but reported a comparable foreign language performance of monolinguals and bilinguals (Hopp 2019; Lechner and Siemund 2014; Lorenz et al. 2020; Sanders and Meijers 1995).

It goes without saying that when a person has access to more than one language, even if the proficiency level is relatively low, the linguistic repertoire at their disposal is greater than that of a monolingual person. As a necessary consequence, a larger repertoire allows access to more speech

DOI: 10.4324/9781003134336-10

communities and enlarges the speaker groups one can communicate with. In a sense, languages can be seen as collective or "hypercollective goods": the more languages a person speaks, the higher is the cultural capital of this person (de Swaan 2001: chapter 2). This can be understood as a communicative advantage (see also Siemund and Mueller 2020). Hence, this study does not claim that being a bilingual speaker does not have certain advantages. It seems, however, that on a purely grammatical level, here specifically focusing on the use of tense and aspect, heritage bilinguals may not necessarily have an advantage over their monolingual peers when acquiring the foreign language English.

With this, the current study seems to be in line with what was argued in Section 3.6, namely that additional language acquisition is highly complex and that because of the different types of bilinguals, a general bilingual advantage cannot be identified. It seems that there is an interaction between type of bilingualism (i.e., balanced versus unbalanced) and language knowledge tested (Siemund 2023; Siemund and Lorenz 2023). This may explain why some studies, even in heritage speaker contexts, identify bilingual advantages in foreign language acquisition, particularly those assessing general language skills (for example Hesse, Göbel and Hartig 2008), whereas others, i.e., those focusing on more specific grammatical features such as the current study, do not.

This necessarily leads back to the definition of bilingualism and the view of it being a gradable phenomenon (Berthele 2021; Bonfieni 2018; see Section 3.3). Bilingual heritage speakers in general as well as those considered in the current study are dominant in the official language of the (new) speech community. This means that their majority language and the only native language of their monolingual peers is the same. On a conceptual level, such heritage speakers are located on a continuum closer to the position of monolinguals than that of balanced bilinguals. Therefore, it appears plausible that this equally extends to the acquisition of further foreign languages: when acquiring a foreign language in an instructed setting in school, the process or outcome may not be the same as what one would find among balanced bilingual learners but appears to be rather comparable to that of monolingual learners. Two supporting explanations for this must be mentioned (and will be further elaborated on in the following sections). On the one hand, because of the relatively limited skills in one of their native languages, the heritage bilinguals may in fact not possess heightened metalinguistic awareness, at least not to a statistically significant or measurable degree (see Section 10.2). On the other hand, and this is assumed to have an additional suppressing impact on the degree of metalinguistic awareness, the learning environment of German secondary schools does not (currently) regularly or systematically include multilingual pedagogies. Instead, English is taught from a monolingual perspective to German-speaking learners (see Section 10.3). These conditions, in addition to German being typologically closer to English, make crosslinguistic influence from the heritage languages highly unlikely (see Chapter 9), which restrains any potential advantages of the bilinguals and leads to a development one could classify as a monolingual acquisition path (Siemund and Lorenz 2023).

Further evidence can be found in studies showing that some initial advantages of bilinguals over their monolingual peers diminish over time (Maluch, Neumann, and Kempert 2016; Siemund and Lechner 2015). Hopp et al. (2019: 107) specifically noticed that "advantages of the bilingual students attrite in the course of foreign language acquisition" because of the way foreign languages are taught in German schools (see also Agustín-Llach 2019 for a similar argument in the Spanish context). Identifying no differences or advantages in the current study, not even among the younger cohorts, may indicate that the learners have already passed this phase of initial advantages. Furthermore, referring to the successful use of copula verbs in English, one could indeed argue for an advantage of the bilinguals, however not in comparison to the monolingual German students, but instead when compared to the monolingual Russian, Turkish, and Vietnamese learners of English. The bilinguals did not show negative crosslinguistic influence from their heritage language but arguably positive influence from German. This, however, lends additional support to the similar processes happening in the monolingual and bilingual learners when acquiring English.

Finally, only advantages of bilinguals or no differences to monolinguals have been pointed out so far. Therefore, the results reported by van Gelderen et al. (2003) may also be interesting in this regard, because they noticed a weaker foreign language English performance of the heritage bilinguals in comparison to monolingual learners. However – and this is perhaps the crucial point – they admitted that they did not include information pertaining to the social background of the learners and pointed out that their findings may actually be related to the learners' socio-economic status (van Gelderen et al. 2003). This underlines once again the importance of controlling for background variables when comparing L2 and L3 learners. In the current study, a number of favorable preconditions or home conditions have been taken into account (see Section 9.3). In principle, this may put the German monolingual learners of English in an advantageous position, at least with respect to socio-economic status and number of books per household. The Russian-German and Vietnamese-German bilingual students, however, were shown to attend the university-bound secondary school type comparably more frequently, which was presented as another beneficial variable.

In summary, the bottom line is that heritage bilingualism does not entail foreign language acquisition advantages per se. This means that a bilingual advantage does not develop unconditionally (see Berthele and Udry 2022; Maluch and Kempert 2019) but that certain conditions need to be met for bilingualism to be potentially favorable (see Blanco-Elorrieta and Pylkkänen 2018; Şahingöz 2014, who specifically argue for high proficiency, active use of and frequent switching between both languages as prerequisites for a bilingual advantage). Specifically, with respect to the use of tense and aspect, the bilinguals of the present investigation did not outperform their monolingual peers, although they did not underperform either. One could argue that in terms of acquiring a foreign language, the bilinguals of the current study are highly similar to their monolingual peers (see also Siemund and Lorenz 2023), which explains why no differences among the various learner groups could be found. Crosslinguistic influence from German determines the acquisitional trajectories of the German monolinguals and their bilingual peers likewise (see Sections 9.1 and 9.2). Moreover, metalinguistic awareness, often argued to be the reason for advantages in foreign language acquisition, may not necessarily be heightened in heritage bilinguals as this may not happen automatically (see Section 10.2). Since the foreign language English classroom in Germany does not seem to foster heritage languages, these languages may not be accessible for the bilinguals when studying a foreign language in school (see Section 10.3).

10.2 Metalinguistic awareness

The present investigation did not identify advantages of the bilingual participants over their monolingual peers with respect to the use of tense and aspect. Advantages could be expected, because of the assumed heightened metalinguistic awareness in bi- or multilinguals (see, for example, Bialystok 2001; Jessner 2006, 2008; Lasagabaster 1998). Metalinguistic awareness was defined as the ability to think abstractly or theoretically about language as an object (see, for example, Jessner 2006; Section 3.5). In theory, it seems plausible that knowing more than one language results in heightened metalinguistic awareness that could be helpful in further language acquisition. Cenoz (2013) explicitly related advantages of bilinguals to their enhanced experience as language learners. She specifically mentioned "a wider range of language strategies" (Cenoz 2013: 76), which learners can then make use of in additional language acquisition. Arguably, this might apply less to heritage speakers and more to language learners who have acquired their second language as a foreign language in a tutored context, simply because metalinguistic awareness may particularly develop in instructional settings. Thomas (1988: 240) highlighted "the importance of formal instruction" and argued that "Bilingual students who have acquired two language systems in a natural setting do not necessarily develop the skills called upon to perform the kind of linguistic gymnastics required of them in foreign language-learning classrooms" (see also De Angelis 2007: 122–123; Bono 2011).

Even though there is attestation that bilinguals show more metalinguistic awareness than their monolingual peers (see, for example, Cabrelli et al. 2020), the equation [bilingual] = [heightened metalinguistic awareness] may be a simplification that does not do justice to the

Advantages of heritage speakers 227

complexity of bilingualism (see Section 3.3). An interesting study in this respect is Lasagabaster (1998). He argued that "bilinguals' better results at learning an L3 ... [are] caused by their more developed metalinguistic awareness" (Lasagabaster 1998: 77), and claimed that modal verbs such as *can*, *could*, or *may* are not needed, but that a definite statement can be formulated. When having a closer look at the participants of his study, and particularly those defined as monolinguals, it appears that they may actually not be monolinguals in the strict sense. Lasagabaster (1998) compared three groups of foreign language learners, namely group A (Spanish dominant students with a low level of competence in Basque), group B (high proficiency Spanish, intermediate proficiency in Basque), and group D (high proficiency in Spanish and Basque).[1] Interestingly, he defined the group A students "as monolinguals with a certain (rather poor in fact) knowledge of Basque" (Lasagabaster 1998: 70), and the students of group D to be "closer to balanced bilingualism" (Lasagabaster 1998: 71). Hence, it is noteworthy that the monolinguals in Lasagabaster's (1998) study belong to what has been defined as unbalanced bilinguals in the present investigation. The results reported in Lasagabaster (1998) acknowledge that the bilinguals (groups B and D) have on average greater metalinguistic awareness gains, visible in higher scores in both the English tests and the metalinguistic awareness test, than the monolinguals (or rather the unbalanced bilinguals; group A). These results are crucial for the current study as these may relate to what was argued in the preceding section, namely that bilinguals with limited skills in one of their native languages are on a conceptual level with monolinguals, particularly so when considering foreign language acquisition (see Section 10.1).

Additional evidence for the claim that metalinguistic awareness may not necessarily be greater in unbalanced bilingual heritage speakers compared to monolinguals can be found in a study by Spellerberg (2016). She investigated the relationship between metalinguistic awareness and academic achievement by comparing three types of young English learners in Denmark: one monolingual group (L1 Danish) and two bi- and multi-lingual groups (one group used Danish at home, the other did not). The bi- or multilinguals, albeit not referred to as heritage speakers, correspond to the definition of unbalanced bilingual heritage speakers used in the current study. Overall, Spellerberg found that the scores achieved in the metalinguistic awareness test positively correlated with the school exam scores, i.e., with the academic achievement of the students. This was true for all learners. Strikingly, however, the bi- or multilingual participants did not score higher in the metalinguistic awareness test than the mono-lingual participants. Instead, Spellerberg reported that the monolinguals outperformed the bi- and multilingual students.[2] Moreover, she noticed that socio-economic status affected the metalinguistic awareness scores. Socio-economic status was assessed at class level (instead of individu-ally assessing each student's socio-economic background), and the bi- and multilingual students who did not use Danish at home had both the lowest socio-economic status as well as the lowest metalinguistic awareness scores (Spellerberg 2016). Once again, it appears that (i) bi- or multilinguals do not necessarily have a higher level of metalinguistic awareness, and (ii) foreign language acquisition is a complex process additionally affected by other intervening variables, such as the socio-economic background or the learning context (for the latter, see Section 10.3).

These last two arguments seem to be in line with the results reported in the current study. The bilingual students did not differ to a statistically significant degree from their monolingual peers. Even though metalinguistic awareness was not tested as part of the present investigation, there is suggestive evidence (see, for example, Lasagabaster 1998; Spellerberg 2016) that metalinguistic awareness may not be heightened in unbalanced bilingual heritage speakers when compared to their monolingual peers. This may then in turn explain why no bilingual advantages were found. One confounding factor may be the socio-economic status of the participants, although this was controlled for. On average, the monolinguals were shown to have a higher socio-economic status than the bilinguals, which may further impact metalinguistic awareness. Moreover, it needs to be acknowledged that not only bi- or multilinguals can be multicompetent or "flexible speaker[s]" (Franceschini 2016: 106), but that being able to use one language flexibly in various communicative contexts is a property that monolinguals can also possess (Franceschini 2016: 109). In addition, the monolingual learners of English of the current study may also show higher metalinguistic awareness simply because they are foreign language learners which makes them increasingly developing bilinguals (see also Hopp et al. 2019: 107). Finally, since in Germany, the foreign language English is typically taught from a monolingual perspective without making reference to other languages such as the heritage languages, increased metalinguistic awareness and access to the heritage languages appear to be highly unlikely. This latter point is addressed in the following section.

10.3 Learning environment in the English classroom in Germany

Several different variables, such as the role of the previously acquired languages, age, or social background, have been shown to impact the acquisition of a foreign language by monolingual and bilingual heritage speakers. However, the specific foreign language learning context has so far not been sufficiently addressed. All participants of the current study are learners of English in a secondary school setting (in Germany, Russia, Turkey, or Vietnam). Typically, the learners receive target-language input for a few hours per week, which presents a stark contrast to acquiring a language in "the host environment with access to the target-language community" (Bardovi-Harlig 1992: 272). Whereas input outside of the classroom, for instance via TV, radio, or the internet, particularly via social media, is in principle feasible (see Section 2.1), the participants of the current study seem to be comparable to Spellerberg's (2016) participants who were shown to barely be in contact with English outside of the foreign language classroom. Investigating older learners, for instance university-aged students, might result in input differences compared to the 12- and 16-year-old secondary school students considered here (see Davydova 2020; Erling 2002). Therefore, the instructional school setting can be ascribed a major role and will be discussed in the following paragraphs. The discussion zooms in on the heritage bilinguals and their monolingual peers growing up in Germany.

The findings of the current study have shown that crosslinguistic influence comes from the dominant language German and that the bilingual participants do not have an advantage in foreign language acquisition and use. This is (at least partly) related to metalinguistic awareness not being necessarily heightened in the bilingual learner population investigated here.[3] This, however, arguably goes hand in hand with the role of German in the lives of the heritage speakers. German is the institutional language, i.e., the language of schooling, in addition to being the majority language of society at large. What this means is that the reason why the heritage bilinguals were shown to be, by and large, comparable to their monolingual German peers is bolstered by German's institutional status (see also Efeoglu and Schroeder 2021). Furthermore, Russian, Turkish, and Vietnamese are not major languages omnipresent in this society, which might explain why the bilinguals do not draw on these languages when learning the foreign language English. More so, because these languages do not play an institutional role and only German is the prestigious language in the educational setting (Aalberse 2020; Bonnet and Siemund 2018). Wiese et al. (2017:199) observed that heritage languages are often far from being encouraged in the school context, meaning that "migrants of heritage languages other than German are expected to suppress or conceal their linguistic background" (see also Fuller 2020). Moreover, Gogolin quite critically pointed out that "Speaking a language other than German at home was, and often still is, presented as the most important risk factor for educational success" (2021: 302). Such disallowing attitudes toward languages other than German are certainly not a welcoming atmosphere that fosters diversity (see also Siemund and Lorenz 2023). The heritage bilinguals may not even be aware of their additional linguistic resources or potential.[4]

What seems to be the prevailing atmosphere in educational institutions in general can also be found in the English and other foreign language classrooms, namely that other languages than the target are often not encouraged (see also Section 2.3). Interestingly, however, a number of recent studies, not only in Germany, but situated in other European countries such as Finland and Norway, have shown that foreign language teachers usually show positive attitudes toward multilingualism (see, for example, Alisaari et al. 2019; Haukås 2016; Heyder and Schädlich 2014;

Lorenz, Krulatz, and Torgersen 2021). Moreover, teachers also seem to agree that the integration of multilingual teaching approaches can support the learning of a foreign language, but a systematic application of multilingual practices can rarely be found (Heyder and Schädlich 2014). This final point needs to be differentiated, because language comparisons, although typically ad hoc, are integrated but these are largely confined to contrasts and similarities between the majority language (i.e., German) and the respective foreign language (Heyder and Schädlich 2014). Reference to other languages such as heritage languages to reflect the multilingual and diverse realities found in Germany's foreign language classrooms is largely absent (Bonnet and Siemund 2018; Heyder and Schädlich 2014). Even though the implementation and understanding of multilingualism as a resource in the foreign language classroom has seen an increased research interest, such transfer to the teaching practice of foreign languages is largely missing (Jakisch, Hopp, and Thoma 2021). Instead, English and other (foreign) languages are typically taught as separate school subjects following a monolingual teaching approach (Jakisch 2015; see also Cenoz and Gorter 2022). Such a "monolingual habitus" (Gogolin 1994) has a long tradition and appears difficult to overcome. To change this, a transformation needs to happen in teacher education (Cantone 2020; see also Section 10.4 for implications for foreign language education).

By and large, educational institutions in general and the foreign language classroom in particular do not seem sufficiently equipped and prepared to deal with the linguistic and social realities and diversity present in current society (Wiese et al. 2017; see also Busse, McLaren, and Dahm 2021). The prominent role of German in the lives of the heritage bilinguals and monolingual German students in addition to its institutional support and the lack of institutional support of the heritage languages make crosslinguistic influence from the heritage languages highly unlikely. Particularly so because, as argued in Section 10.2, metalinguistic awareness may not develop automatically but may profit especially from formal instruction (see Thomas 1988). Learners might need to be explicitly made aware of similarities and differences between all languages in their repertoires and the new foreign language English (beyond references to the majority language German) in order to access this kind of knowledge. Pedagogical translanguaging seems to have the potential to offer a way forward (Cenoz and Gorter 2021, 2022; see also Section 10.4).

Finally, influence can be argued to come not only from the instructional context per se, but additionally from the English of the teachers, who typically pass on "non-native-like features" – with respect to both phonology and morphosyntax – to the learners (Hickey 2020a; see also Hickey 2020b who discussed persistent pronunciation features in Germany). Although teachers were not in focus in the present investigation, their role should not be discounted (see Section 11.2 for future research directions involving foreign language teachers).

10.4 Implications for foreign language education

Cenoz and Gorter (2022: 2), among others (e.g., Jakisch, Hopp, and Thoma 2021; Martinez 2015; May 2013; Melo-Pfeifer 2018), argued that foreign language learning "can be enhanced when hard boundaries that isolate languages are replaced by soft and permeable boundaries so that students can use their prior knowledge when teaching and learning a second or additional language" (see also Section 2.3). They specifically focused on the role of pedagogical translanguaging and how it can be applied in foreign language classrooms with linguistically heterogeneous and diverse student populations. This is particularly topical in the context of the current study, as the student population investigated here represents a linguistically diverse group (see, for example, Section 6.3). Pedagogical translanguaging in the classroom, that is, the active use of and alternation between different languages, both in input as well as output (i.e., employed by teachers and learners alike), has the potential to develop and foster multilingualism (Cenoz and Gorter 2022; see also Cenoz 2017; Cenoz and Gorter 2020, 2021; see also Section 2.3). Specifically, and this relates back to Section 10.2., the use of pedagogical translanguaging activities is understood to enhance and promote metalinguistic awareness (Cenoz and Gorter 2021, 2022). A similar approach can be found in Cummins, who claimed that it is "reasonable to argue that learning efficiencies can be achieved if teachers explicitly draw students' attention to similarities and differences between their languages and reinforce effective learning strategies in a coordinated way across languages" (2013: 298).

Crucially, the main aim of the English language classroom should be to teach English (the same also applies to other foreign languages). Melo-Pfeifer (2018: 207) maintained that "pedagogical approaches that actively engage with linguistic and cultural diversity do not dismiss the value of language learning as a discipline at school, but instead aspire to bringing languages at school and lived multilingualism closer together." This means that instead of following a teaching approach that allows English only or limits language comparisons to the majority language of the speech community, a more dynamic and open approach that relies on additional (language) resources is to be favored. The activation of all languages may allow the students to access their full linguistic potential. Bilinguals may simply not be aware of their potential resources, especially if their proficiency in the heritage language is comparably low. A systematic inclusion could direct the attention of the students not only to German (which is of course useful, especially given that English and German share numerous grammatical features) but also to their heritage language. The activation of prior language knowledge, hence, the use of the entire linguistic repertoire, i.e., both the heritage and the majority language, could significantly improve the language skills of the bilinguals (Cenoz and Gorter 2017; see also Martinez 2015).

A clear pedagogical significance can be derived from this line of argumentation (see also Siemund and Lorenz 2023). In order for bilingualism to be beneficial, especially in heritage speaker contexts as discussed in the present study, additional language support in the English language classroom is desirable. Hopp et al. (2019: 108) remarked that the course material used for foreign language teaching in German schools is largely designed for monolingual German students. The needs of the bilingual students are not sufficiently addressed. Furthermore, multilingual teaching approaches may also serve both monolingual and bilingual students. This is crucial, as the teaching approach should cater to all students. Positive evidence comes from two intervention studies conducted in German primary schools with monolingual and bilingual students (see Hopp et al. 2020; Hopp and Thoma 2021). Two English teaching settings were contrasted, an experimental group (multilingual/plurilingual teaching approach)[5] and a control group (regular English teaching approach). Approximately 20 percent of the experimental group's English lessons included multilingual elements pertaining to vocabulary, grammar, and phonological awareness (Hopp et al. 2020). Notably, both studies reported selective advantages of the experimental group in comparison to the control group. Moreover, two additional findings are of importance: (i) in both studies, no differences between the monolingual students and their bilingual peers were observed; and (ii) even though less time was devoted to teaching English in the experimental group, these students did not appear to have lower general English skills (Hopp et al. 2020: 158; Hopp and Thoma 2021: 480).[6]

The selective advantages reported in these two studies suggest that multilingual pedagogies may not work wonders (see also Berthele and Udry 2022), simply because other intervening factors influence foreign language acquisition (e.g., cognition, motivation, social background, etc.). However, such positive results as reported in Hopp et al. (2020) or Hopp and Thoma (2021) nevertheless indicate the potential of further investigating the impact of multilingual teaching approaches that employ pedagogical translanguaging (see also Busse, McLaren, and Dahm 2021 for similar promising results). Even if this is not the only explanation, teachers doubtless play a critical role in supporting the acquisition of foreign languages and thus the multilingual development of all students. Acknowledging and incorporating the diverse linguistic backgrounds of all students has the potential to support their learning (Alisaari et al. 2019; Krulatz, Dahl, and Flognfeldt 2018; see also Section 11.2). Clearly, this should not be understood as an easy task, especially since multiple languages may be present in the classroom that the teachers are not familiar with themselves (Busse, McLaren, and Dahm 2021).[7] Elsner refers to the increasingly linguistically diverse and multilingual student cohorts as "challenges and opportunities" (2018: 36) and "new challenges" (2018: 37), acknowledging that this puts additional pressure on teachers and therefore, likewise, on teacher education or professional development of in-service English teachers (or teachers of other languages) (see also Franceschini 2009; Martinez 2015; Schroedler 2021; Wernicke et al. 2021). The crucial undertaking is to address how to implement multilingual teaching practices and how to work with linguistically heterogeneous learners in the foreign language classroom during teacher education as well as professional development of in-service teachers (see Lorenz, Krulatz, and Torgersen 2021). Future research on changes in teacher education, professional development, and the implementation of multilingual pedagogies is needed to assess its effect and potential in the multilingual classroom (see Section 11.2).

Notes

1 In a sense, this is in line with what Berthele (2021) asked for, namely that instead of comparing the binary variable monolingualism versus bilingualism, a graded category should be used.
2 Note, however, that the metalinguistic awareness test was administered in Danish, which may have put the non-native speakers of Danish at a disadvantage (Spellerberg 2016: 37).
3 It may also be due to the specific grammatical phenomenon considered in the present study. But see, for example, Lorenz et al. (2020), Lorenz, Hasai, and Siemund (2021), and Lorenz, Toprak, and Siemund (2021), who also argue against a bi- or multilingual advantage in further foreign language acquisition.
4 Instead, they might (sub)consciously view them as something negative due to negative stereotypes about their language or family's migration background.
5 In Hopp and Thoma (2021), the term plurilingual teaching is used instead of multilingual teaching.
6 See also Leonet, Cenoz, and Gorter (2020) for similar promising findings concerning the application of pedagogical translanguaging and multilingual teaching pedagogies in the Basque Autonomous Country (Spain). The context differs, because all English learners are speakers of Basque and Spanish, even though their proficiency levels vary.
7 Even without considering linguistic diversity, student cohorts already present heterogeneous groups, with differing social backgrounds, cognitive abilities, etc. Thus, linguistic heterogeneity adds an additional level of diversity to an already diverse group (see also Section 2.2).

References

Aalberse, S. 2020. Bilingual optimization strategies and code copy theory: Social predictors of lexical transfer. Workshop des Forschungsschwerpunkts Sprachliche Bildung und Mehrsprachigkeit: Educational Linguistics, January 23–24, 2020, University of Hamburg.

Agustín-Llach, M. d. P. 2019. The impact of bilingualism on the acquisition of an additional language: Evidence from lexical knowledge, lexical fluency, and (lexical) cross-linguistic influence. *International Journal of Bilingualism* 23:888–900.

Alisaari, J., L. M. Heikkola, N. Commins, and E. O. Acquah. 2019. Monolingual ideologies confronting multilingual realities: Finnish teachers' beliefs about linguistic diversity. *Teaching and Teacher Education* 80:48–58.

Bardovi-Harlig, K. 1992. The relationship of form and meaning: A cross-sectional study of tense and aspect in the interlanguage of learners of English as a second language. *Applied Psycholinguistics* 13:253–278.

Berthele, R. 2021. The extraordinary ordinary: Re-engineering multilingualism as a natural category. *Language Learning* 71:80–120.

Berthele, R. and I. Udry. 2022. Multilingual boost vs. cognitive abilities: Testing two theories of multilingual language learning in a primary school context. *International Journal of Multilingualism* 19:142–161.

Bialystok, E. 2001. *Bilingualism in development: Language, literacy, and cognition*. Cambridge: Cambridge University Press.

Blanco-Elorrieta, E. and L. Pylkkänen. 2018. Ecological validity in bilingualism research and the bilingual advantage. *Trends in Cognitive Sciences* 22:1117–1126.

Bonfieni, M. 2018. *The bilingual continuum: Mutual effects of language and cognition*. PhD diss., University of Edinburgh. http://hdl.handle.net/1842/31365

Bonnet, A. and P. Siemund (eds.). 2018. *Foreign language education in multilingual classrooms*. Amsterdam: Benjamins.

Bono, M. 2011. Crosslinguistic interaction and metalinguistic awareness in third language acquisition. In *New trends in crosslinguistic influence and multilingualism research*, ed. G. De Angelis and J.-M. Dewaele, 25–52. Clevedon: Multilingual Matters.

Busse, V., L.-M. McLaren, and A. Dahm. 2021. Responding to migration-related diversity in the classroom: A comparison of diversity-sensitive approaches to stimulate word acquisition in early FL teaching. *Journal of Multilingual and Multicultural Development*. https://doi.org/10.1080/01434632.2021.2005611

Cabrelli, J., M. Iverson, D. Giancaspro, and B. Halloran González. 2020. The roles of L1 Spanish versus L2 Spanish in L3 Portuguese morphosyntactic development. In *Linguistic approaches to Portuguese as an additional language*, ed. K. V. Molsing, C. Becker Lopes Perna, and A. M. Tramunt Ibaños, 11–33. Amsterdam: Benjamins.

Cantone, K. F. 2020. Immigrant minority language maintenance in Europe: Focusing on language education policy and teacher-training. *International Multilingual Research Journal* 14:100–113.

Cenoz, J. 2013. The influence of bilingualism on third language acquisition: Focus on multilingualism. *Language Teaching* 46:71–86.

Cenoz, J. 2017. Translanguaging in school context: International perspectives. *Journal of Language, Identity and Education* 16:193–198.

Cenoz, J. and D. Gorter. 2017. Minority languages and sustainable translanguaging: Threat or opportunity? *Journal of Multilingual and Multicultural Development* 38:901–912.

Cenoz, J. and D. Gorter. 2020. Teaching English through pedagogical translanguaging. *World Englishes* 39:300–311.

Cenoz, J. and D. Gorter. 2021. *Pedagogical translanguaging*. Cambridge: Cambridge University Press.

Cenoz, J. and D. Gorter. 2022. Pedagogical translanguaging and its application to language classes. *RELC Journal* 53:342–354.
Cenoz, J. and J. Valencia. 1994. Additive trilingualism: Evidence from the Basque Country. *Applied Psycholinguistics* 15:195–207.
Cummins, J. 1976. The influence of bilingualism on cognitive growth: A synthesis of research findings and explanatory hypotheses. *Working Papers on Bilingualism* 9:1–43.
Cummins, J. 2013. Implications for language teaching policy and practice. In *Multilingualism and language diversity in urban areas: Acquisition, identities, space, education*, ed. P. Siemund, I. Gogolin, M. E. Schulz, and J. Davydova, 289–304. Amsterdam: Benjamins.
Davydova, J. 2020. English in Germany: Evidence from domains of use and attitudes. *Russian Journal of Linguistics* 24:687–702.
De Angelis, G. 2007. *Third or additional language acquisition*. Clevedon: Multilingual Matters.
de Swaan, A. 2001. *Words of the world: The global language system*. Cambridge: Polity Press.
Efeoglu, G. and C. Schroeder. 2021. Acquisition of object pronouns in EFL in Germany by heritage speakers of Turkish. *Sustainable Multilingualism* 18:71–84.
Elsner, D. 2018. Institutional foreign language learning – Teaching English at different levels. In *Teaching English as a foreign language: An introduction*, ed. C. Surkamp and B. Viebrock, 17–37. Stuttgart: J. B. Metzler.
Erling, E. J. 2002. 'I learn English since ten years': The global English debate and the German university classroom. *English Today* 18:8–13.
Franceschini, R. 2009. Mehrsprachigkeit als Ziel: Didaktische Herausforderungen und Forschungsperspektiven. *Forum Sprache* 1:62–67.
Franceschini, R. 2016. Multilingualism research. In *The Cambridge handbook of linguistic multi-competence*, ed. V. Cook and Li Wei, 97–124. Cambridge: Cambridge University Press.
Fuller, J. M. 2020. English in the German-speaking world: Immigration and integration. In *English in the German-speaking world*, ed. R. Hickey, 165–184. Cambridge: Cambridge University Press.
Gogolin, I. 1994. *Der monolinguale Habitus der multilingualen Schule*. Münster: Waxmann.
Gogolin, I. 2021. Multilingualism: A threat to public education or a resource in public education? – European histories and realities. *European Educational Research Journal* 20:297–310.
Haukås, Å. 2016. Teachers' beliefs about multilingualism and a multilingual pedagogical approach. *International Journal of Multilingualism* 13:1–18.
Hesse, H. G., K Göbel, and J. Hartig. 2008. Sprachliche Kompetenzen von mehrsprachigen Jugendlichen und Jugendlichen nicht-deutscher Erstsprache. In *Unterricht und Kompetenzerwerb in Deutsch und Englisch: Ergebnisse der DESI-Studie*, ed. DESI-Konsortium, 208–230. Weinheim: Beltz.
Heyder, K. and B. Schädlich. 2014. Mehrsprachigkeit und Mehrkulturalität – eine Umfrage unter Fremdsprachenlehrkräften in Niedersachsen. *Zeitschrift für Interkulturellen Fremdsprachenunterricht* 19:183–201.
Hickey, R. 2020a. English in the German-speaking world: The nature and scale of language influence. In *English in the German-speaking world*, ed. R. Hickey, 1–10. Cambridge: Cambridge University Press.

Hickey, R. 2020b. Persistent features in the English of German speakers. In *English in the German-speaking world*, ed. R. Hickey, 208–228. Cambridge: Cambridge University Press.

Hopp, H. 2019. Cross-linguistic influence in the child third language acquisition of grammar: Sentence comprehension and production among Turkish-German and German learners of English. *International Journal of Bilingualism* 23:567–583.

Hopp, H., J. Jakisch, S. Sturm, C. Becker, and D. Thoma. 2020. Integrating multilingualism into the early foreign language classroom: Empirical and teaching perspectives. *International Multilingual Research Journal* 14:146–162.

Hopp, H. and D. Thoma. 2021. Effects of plurilingual teaching on grammatical development in early foreign-language learning. *Modern Language Journal* 105:464–483.

Hopp, H., M. Vogelbacher, T. Kieseier, and D. Thoma. 2019. Bilingual advantages in early foreign language learning: Effects of the minority and the majority language. *Learning and Instruction* 61:99–110.

Jakisch, J. 2015. Zur Einführung in den Themenschwerpunkt. *Fremdsprachen Lehren und Lernen* (FLuL) 44:3–6.

Jakisch, J., H. Hopp., and D. Thoma. 2021. Möglichkeiten und Grenzen von Mehrsprachigkeitsdidaktik im frühen Fremdsprachenunterricht – Spannungsfelder in der schulischen Praxis. *Zeitschrift für Fremdsprachenforschung* 32:253–275.

Jessner, U. 2006. *Linguistic awareness in multilinguals: English as a third language*. Edinburgh: Edinburgh University Press.

Jessner, U. 2008. A DST model of multilingualism and the role of metalinguistic awareness. *Modern Language Journal* 92:270–283.

Krulatz, A., A. Dahl, and M. E. Flognfeldt. 2018. *Enacting multilingualism: From research to teaching practice in the English classroom*. Oslo: Cappelen Damm Adademisk.

Lasagabaster, D. 1998. Metalinguistic awareness in the learning of English as an L3. *Atlantis* 20:69–79.

Lechner, S. and P. Siemund. 2014. The role of language external factors in the acquisition of English as an additional language by bilingual children in Germany. In *Language contacts at the crossroads of disciplines*, ed H. Paulasto, L. Meriläinen, H. Riionheimo, and M. Kok, 319–345. Newcastle-upon-Tyne: Cambridge Scholars Publishing.

Leonet, O., J. Cenoz, and D. Gorter. 2020. Developing morphological awareness across languages: Translanguaging pedagogies in third language acquisition. *Language Awareness* 29:41–59.

Lorenz, E., Y. Hasai, and P. Siemund. 2021. Multilingual lexical transfer challenges monolingual educational norms: Not quite! *Multilingua* 40:791–813.

Lorenz, E., A. Krulatz, and E. N. Torgersen. 2021. Embracing linguistic and cultural diversity in multilingual EAL classrooms: The impact of professional development on teacher beliefs and practice. *Teaching and Teacher Education* 105:103428. https://doi.org/10.1016/j.tate.2021.103428

Lorenz, E., S. Rahbari, U. Schackow, and P. Siemund. 2020. Does bilingualism correlate with or predict higher proficiency in L3 English? A contrastive study of monolingual and bilingual learners. *Journal of Multilingual Theories and Practices* 1:185–217.

Lorenz, E., T. E. Toprak, and P. Siemund. 2021. English L3 acquisition in heritage contexts: Modelling a path through the bilingualism controversy. *Poznan Studies in Contemporary Linguistics* 57:273–298.

Maluch, J. T. and S. Kempert. 2019. Bilingual profiles and third language learning: The effects of the manner of learning, sequence of bilingual acquisition, and language use practices. *International Journal of Bilingual Education and Bilingualism* 22:870–882.

Maluch, J. T., S. Kempert, M. Neumann, and P. Stanat. 2015. The effect of speaking a minority language at home on foreign language learning. *Learning and Instruction* 36:76–85.

Maluch, J. T., M. Neumann, and S. Kempert. 2016. Bilingualism as a resource for foreign language learning of language minority students? Empirical evidence from a longitudinal study during primary and secondary school in Germany. *Learning and Individual Differences* 51:111–118.

Martinez, H. 2015. Mehrsprachigkeitsdidaktik: Aufgaben, Potenziale und Herausforderungen. *Fremdsprachen Lehren und Lernen (FLuL)* 44:7–19.

May, S. (ed.). 2013. *The multilingual turn: Implications for SLA, TESOL, and bilingual education*. New York: Routledge.

Melo-Pfeifer, S. 2018. The multilingual turn in foreign language education: Facts and fallacies. In *Foreign language education in multilingual classrooms*, ed. A. Bonnet and P. Siemund, 191–212. Amsterdam: Benjamins.

Rauch, D. P., J. Naumann, and N. Jude. 2012. Metalinguistic awareness mediates effects of full biliteracy on third-language reading proficiency in Turkish-German bilinguals. *International Journal of Bilingualism* 16:402–418.

Şahingöz, Y. 2014. *Schulische Mehrsprachigkeit bei türkisch-deutsch bilingualen Schülern: Eine Analyse von transferinduzierten Wortstellungsmustern*. PhD diss., University of Hamburg. http://ediss.sub.uni-hamburg.de/volltexte/2018/9128

Sanders, M. and G. Meijers. 1995. English as L3 in the elementary school. *ITL: Review of Applied Linguistics* 107:59–78.

Sanz, C. 2000. Bilingual education enhances third language acquisition: Evidence from Catalonia. *Applied Psycholinguistics* 21:23–44.

Schroedler, T. 2021. What is multilingualism? Towards an inclusive understanding. In *Preparing teachers to work with multilingual learners*, ed. M. Wernicke, S. Hammer, A. Hansen, and T. Schroedler, 17–37. Bristol: Multilingual Matters.

Siemund, P. 2023. *Multilingual development: English in a global context*. Cambridge: Cambridge University Press.

Siemund, P. and S. Lechner. 2015. Transfer effects in the acquisition of English as an additional language by bilingual children in Germany. In *Transfer effects in multilingual language development*, ed. H. Peukert, 147–160. Amsterdam: Benjamins.

Siemund, P. and E. Lorenz. 2023. Multilingual advantages: On the relationship between type of bilingualism and language proficiency. In *Multifaceted Multilingualism*, ed. K. Grohmann. Amsterdam: Benjamins.

Siemund, P. and J. T. Mueller. 2020. Are multilinguals the better academic ELF users? Evidence from a questionnaire study measuring self-assessed proficiencies. In *Language change: The impact of English as a lingua franca*, ed. A. Mauranen and S. Vetchinnikova, 234–266. Cambridge: Cambridge University Press.

Spellerberg, S. M. 2016. Metalinguistic awareness and academic achievement in a linguistically diverse school setting: A study of lower secondary pupils in Denmark. *International Journal of Multilingualism* 13:19–39.

Thomas, J. 1988. The role played by metalinguistic awareness in second and third language learning. *Journal of Multilingual and Multicultural Development* 9:235–246.

van Gelderen, A., R. Schoonen, K. de Glopper, J. Hulstijn, P. Snellings, A. Simis, and M. Stevenson. 2003. Roles of linguistic knowledge, metacognitive knowledge and processing speed in L3, L2 and L1 reading comprehension: A structural equation modelling approach. *International Journal of Bilingualism* 7:7–25.

Wernicke, M., S. Hammer, A. Hansen, and T. Schroedler (eds.). 2021. *Preparing teachers to work with multilingual learners*. Bristol: Multilingual Matters.

Wiese, W., K. Mayr, P. Krämer, P. Seeger, H.-G. Müller, and V. Mezger. 2017. Changing teachers' attitudes towards linguistic diversity: Effects of an antibias programme. *International Journal of Applied Linguistics* 27:198–220.

11 Conclusion and outlook

11.1 Summary of findings

The current study addressed two highly debated topics, namely crosslinguistic influence in (second and) third language acquisition and bi- or multilingual advantages in further foreign language acquisition. Both topics were approached from a theoretical perspective and ultimately empirically investigated by analyzing a written and spoken learner corpus collected from seven distinct groups of monolingual and bilingual English learners. The present investigation zoomed in on a population of bilinguals who can frequently be encountered in countries such as Germany or other Western European countries and beyond: unbalanced bilingual heritage speakers (see Chapters 2 and 3). The current country of residence of such bilinguals may either be their place of birth, or they immigrated to this country with their families at a relatively young age. In addition to growing up with the respective official societal language, they are raised with another native language, their so-called heritage or family language. This language is typically the less dominant and less proficient language of heritage speakers, at least after having spent some time in the new community and after having been part of the education system for some years. This was shown to be true for the bilingual speakers investigated in the current study.

Three different groups of heritage speakers were considered, namely Russian-, Turkish-, and Vietnamese-German bilinguals growing up in Germany. The remaining learners of English served as control groups. These were German, Russian, Turkish, and Vietnamese L2 learners of English growing up in their respective native countries in addition to L1 English speakers. Moreover, two different age cohorts were studied, i.e., 12- and 16-year-old secondary school students, in order to approximate a developmental perspective. This triangular, cross-sectional design made it possible to compare different monolingual and bilingual learners of English as well as English native speakers and to assess the source of crosslinguistic influence in the bilingual cohorts. The grammatical area of interest was the use of tense and aspect (see Chapters 4 and 5) in a written and spoken picture description task (see Chapter 6).

DOI: 10.4324/9781003134336-11

Chapter 3 established that there are two potential sources for crosslinguistic influence in third language acquisition. Most previous research on crosslinguistic influence in third language acquisition relied on L3 learners who study this additional foreign language as (young) adults after they have already learned one foreign language (their L2) in an educational setting and who have grown up with one language (L1). Recently, investigations of L3 acquisition have also extended to heritage speaker contexts, many of which were also conducted in Germany. Heritage speaker contexts differ considerably from the learner populations in the former studies where there is a clear difference between the L1 (native language) and the L2 (foreign language). Heritage speakers were demonstrated to have two native languages. The language they started to acquire either simultaneously with their heritage language or at the latest when entering school typically develops into their dominant language throughout their educational journey. Thus, these two languages are conceptually different from the two languages of a monolingually raised person who acquired a first foreign language during secondary schooling. Moreover, most of the L3 models put forward to explain crosslinguistic influence in L3 acquisition proposed that the order of the previously acquired languages determines the source of crosslinguistic influence. Arguably, this is difficult to test in heritage bilinguals, which is the reason why the focus of the present study was not on the order but rather on the status of the two languages, i.e., the majority language (German) and the less dominant heritage language (Russian, Turkish, or Vietnamese). For the current setting, this means that crosslinguistic influence might either come from the majority language German, the heritage language (Russian, Turkish, or Vietnamese, respectively), or both languages.

In addition to language group (monolingual versus bilingual) and age (12- and 16-year-old learners), further background variables were controlled for. These were, for instance, age of onset of acquiring German, type of school, socio-economic status, number of books per household, as well as attitudes toward English (English difficulty, English usefulness). Furthermore, the current study design allowed for examining whether bilingual heritage speakers show advantages in additional foreign language acquisition when compared to their monolingual peers (see Chapters 3 and 6). Bilinguals have a larger linguistic repertoire than monolinguals which may be helpful or favorable for the former in additional language acquisition. An advantage in the current study would be visible in a more target-like use of tense and aspect (both with respect to form as well as appropriateness of using the respective tense or aspect) in the written and spoken task.

The results reported in Chapters 7 and 8 clearly demonstrated that, contrary to the prediction in Section 6.4, the bilingual heritage speakers did not show crosslinguistic influence from both of their previously acquired languages, i.e., German and either Russian, Turkish, or Vietnamese, in their spoken and written English production. If this were to be the case, they should be in-between their respective monolingual peers, that is the German monolinguals and one of the other monolingual English learner groups. However, with respect to tense and aspect, more precisely formal correctness and target-like use of verbs, subject-verb agreement, present versus past tense use, and the use of the progressive aspect, the bilingual heritage speakers were comparable to the monolingual German students. Differences could be observed in the production data of the Russian, Turkish, and Vietnamese English learners that can be explained with crosslinguistic influence from the respective languages, but similar patterns did not show up in the bilingual data. Thus, it can be argued that it is influence from German that governs the acquisition and use of English of the bilingual populations (just as of the German monolingual learners) considered in the present investigation.

The strongest claim explaining these findings involved the status of the two previously acquired languages of the bilinguals in combination with the structural and typological similarity between English and German (see Chapter 9). Even though the bilinguals' two languages can be considered native languages, German, which is the majority language of their country of residence and the language of instruction in school, is their stronger or more dominant language. Therefore, there are more communicative opportunities in and more input from German when compared to the relatively restricted use of and input from the heritage language. Arguably, even more important than the sheer presence of German in the lives of the heritage bilinguals is the influence of the educational context and with this the way English is taught and learned in Germany (see Chapters 2 and 10). It was shown that English is largely taught from a monolingual German perspective to an assumed monolingual German audience, disregarding the multilingual realities present in Germany's secondary school foreign language classrooms. Moreover, German shares many similarities with English and it is typologically closer to this language compared to Russian, Turkish, or Vietnamese (see Chapter 4). Even though it was established that the latter three languages share some features with English, it is certainly appropriate – both from a learner as well as teacher perspective – to rely heavily on German when teaching and learning English. However, being able to make use of some grammatical features from the heritage language (e.g., aspect) might be beneficial for acquiring and using some properties of English (e.g., the progressive aspect). Yet, it seems that the heritage bilinguals may not be able to access their enlarged linguistic repertoire without it being specifically mentioned in the English language classroom and without multilingual pedagogies receiving space during foreign language acquisition.

In addition, since no statistically significant differences between the German monolingual and bilingual learners' English were found, the idea of a bilingual advantage could not be upheld (see Chapter 10).[1] This is certainly related to the previously introduced argument, namely that the current English teaching realities do not support multilingual learners in making use of all their linguistic resources. Therefore, by and large, the bilingual heritage speakers and their monolingual German peers were presented as exhibiting a similar developmental foreign language acquisition process. For the additional resources of bilingual heritage speakers to have a positive effect on further language acquisition, certain conditions in the language learning context would need to be achieved. These, however, are currently not satisfactorily incorporated into the English language classroom.

In addition to such "an integrated view of multilingualism" in the educational context (Cantone 2020: 109; see also Schroedler 2021; Wernicke et al. 2021 with views on integrating multilingualism in teacher education in Europe and beyond), Cantone not only argues for overcoming the monolingual habitus of the German foreign language classroom, but she additionally argues for the systematic inclusion and development of heritage language instruction[2] in order to ensure that heritage languages are used and maintained (see also Franceschini 2009). In Section 10.4, it was stressed that the increasingly linguistically diverse and heterogeneous student population within one foreign language classroom presents an additional challenge for teachers. Even more so, because, as Franceschini (2009: 64) rightly points out: "Mehrsprachigkeit ist ein Ziel für alle."[3] In a sense, multilingualism is relevant not only to those who are already bilingual, but also to those who grow up with one language only. She additionally claims that "Modern societies struggle with managing issues emergent from the realities of multiple languages which cross institutions and the lives of many individuals" (Franceschini 2009: 62). She therefore formulates what didactics has to achieve with respect to fostering and developing multilingualism among all learners without singling out those who already know more than one language when starting school; most importantly, these individual processes need to be interconnected (Franceschini 2009: 63):

1. Entwicklung und Erhalt der Zwei-, beziehungsweise Mehrsprachigkeit von Migranten(kindern);
2. Entwicklung und Erhalt der Erst-, beziehungsweise Mehrsprachigkeit von Sprach minderheiten;
3. Entwicklung von Fremdsprachenkenntnissen in monolingual Aufwachsenden;
4. Entwicklung von Fremdsprachenkenntnissen (oder Zweit- und Drittsprachen kenntnissen) in allen Gruppen;
5. Lebenslanges Lernen.[4]

Learning and speaking multiple languages certainly implies a lot of hard work and dedication. The school context has the responsibility to foster and develop multilingualism and can support young learners. However, it does not seem to be the case that by simply being a bilingual heritage speaker one is automatically better at learning and using foreign languages. This claim seems to be too simplistic and idealized. Finally, it needs to be kept in mind that all students deserve to be supported in the best possible way for them to reach their full potential. Metalinguistic awareness might play a decisive role in the context of foreign language learning, meaning that raising the metalinguistic awareness of all students could be beneficial for the entire student population, monolinguals and bilinguals alike.

Moreover, several additional variables (such as type of school, number of books per household, socio-economic status) were shown to influence performance in the foreign language English (see Chapter 8). Most importantly, these interacted with each other and occasionally also with the variable 'language group'. A number of favorable conditions for more formally correct and target-like use of tense and aspect in both the written and oral task were identified. Attending the university-bound secondary school type (*Gymnasium*), having a higher socio-economic status, or possessing more books in the household were shown to positively influence English performance. Note that the German monolingual students were reported to come from families with an overall higher socio-economic status. Moreover, for some of the analyses, the older students also showed on average a better performance compared to the younger students. In addition, the age of onset of acquiring German also added some explanatory power to the statistical analyses. A later age of onset yielded a better performance of the bilinguals for some of the analyses. Age of onset is assumed to correlate with proficiency in the heritage language (later age of onset of German might indicate a higher proficiency level in the heritage language). Yet it was not possible to assess heritage language proficiency in the current study, so this claim needs to be investigated in further studies (see also Section 11.2).

A final remark concerning the overall importance of English is in order. Most young people growing up these days, be it in Germany or in another country in Europe and beyond, are aware of the ubiquitous role and general importance of English. Certain advantages are associated with being a fluent or competent user of English, and not only because it enlarges the number of people one can communicate with globally, but it also offers prospective job opportunities or potentially even upward mobility. In addition, English is present nearly everywhere, and even more so on the internet or in social media. This arguably has a huge influence particularly on younger generations. English is an obligatory school subject in most parts of the world, and it certainly has an important role in Germany's education system (see Chapter 2). Most students of the current study agreed that English is a useful language, and many also felt that it was not a difficult language to learn. Nevertheless, most people would perhaps agree that learning and mastering any foreign language is challenging and implies a lot of work, diligence, and dedication. Therefore, students should be supported in the best possible way to become competent and proficient users of English. In our current global times, many English learners are equipped with knowledge of additional languages that can eventually be helpful and turn into resources when studying English. Languages should not be understood as separate, compartmentalized entities. The role of the English classroom is to help students see these connections to their previously acquired languages in order to support the acquisition of English and also other foreign languages.

11.2 Future directions of further research

Even though this study was able to find answers to a number of questions, new issues and questions were raised that present themselves as further research potential. Several such promising future research directions will be pointed out in what follows. These are neither complete nor exhaustive but should simply be understood as selective points of departure for follow-up studies.

Most importantly, the current investigation has shown how essential it is to have information of all previously acquired languages of the English learners. Having access to the proficiency levels in all previously acquired languages might help to identify whether, for instance, higher proficiency in the heritage language has a positive effect on the acquisition of English. Furthermore, beyond general language proficiency tests such as C-tests (see, for example, Klein-Braley and Raatz 1984; Grotjahn and Drackert 2020) or vocabulary tests (for example the British Picture and Vocabulary Scale, BPVS 3, developed by Dunn et al. 2009), the grammatical properties under investigation should ideally be tested in all languages to ensure target-like performance in the two native languages of the heritage bilinguals and to be able to clearly disentangle or exclude crosslinguistic influence from the background languages. For example, if an assumed grammatical property differs in the heritage language of the bilinguals in comparison to an assumed baseline or target-like performance as one would expect in monolingual native speakers, crosslinguistic influence in additional language acquisition should then also be different in these learners. Therefore, it is imperative to test all learners to establish individual baselines for the respective groups investigated in a study (see also González Alonso et al. 2021 for a study that tested the grammatical properties in all languages and found divergence to an assumed native speaker baseline in the native languages of the bilinguals). Thus, it would be equally interesting to compare not only the performance in the written and spoken picture descriptions in English, but to also have access to the same two tasks completed in all languages available to the learners. Then, instead of relying on a contrastive analysis of the English data (see Section 6.4; Kortmann 2005; see also Granger 2015 on Contrastive Interlanguage Analysis), a different approach could be employed, namely the Integrated Contrastive Model (Gilquin and Granger 2015). Contrastive analysis compares different learner populations with various native languages and tries to recognize patterns of non-target-like language use that can be explained with crosslinguistic influence from their native language(s). The Integrated Contrastive Model, however, would go beyond comparing the English learner language, and a corpus-based analysis of the previously acquired language(s) would be included (Gilquin and Granger 2015: 426).

Moreover, using different tasks to elicit the English language production might also be a worthwhile extension. Instead of relying on written and oral picture descriptions, reading comprehension, sentence completion or ordering, and grammaticality judgment tasks may also provide further insights into third language acquisition of bilingual heritage speakers. Even though the current study demonstrated that (i) there were no statistically significant differences between the monolingual and bilingual learners based on the two tasks employed, and (ii) there were no qualitative differences between the two tasks, this might have been different if other English language skills had been tested (i.e., listening comprehension, reading). In Chapters 7 and 8, it was reported that the students rarely used other tenses than the simple present and the simple past. Part of this might be attributed to the specific tasks the students had to perform. They were free to choose verbs and verb forms and had no obligation to vary. Another setting might yield different results, e.g., a more experimental test battery consisting of a grammaticality judgment or a sentence completion task. It may turn out that differences in crosslinguistic influence between monolinguals and bilingual heritage speakers or advantages of heritage bilinguals are attestable in different tasks, perhaps related to comprehension rather than production.

Furthermore, even though metalinguistic awareness was presented as a crucial factor in additional language acquisition, within the confines of the current study, metalinguistic awareness could not be directly assessed. Hence, in addition to testing language proficiency and the use of tense and aspect, an additional measure could be to investigate the learners' levels of metalinguistic awareness to find answers to the questions of whether bilinguals are more metalinguistically aware then monolinguals, or whether higher metalinguistic awareness is helpful in further foreign language acquisition and positively correlates with English performance. One such test that could be employed is the metalinguistic awareness test developed by Pinto, Titone, and Trusso (1999).

In addition, it was pointed out that bilingual advantages might prevail in the initial phases of formal language acquisition but diminish with increasing proficiency in the foreign language English. Hence, including younger participants might provide a more comprehensive picture of the developmental process of acquiring a foreign language in a bilingual heritage context. There might be differences in crosslinguistic influence in the initial stages of English acquisition and potential advantages for the bilingual heritage speakers might still be detectable. At the time of testing, however, the youngest participants of the current study were already 12 years old and might have already been too advanced in English. Moreover, the present investigation employed a cross-sectional study design. In addition to extending the current dataset to younger learners, a longitudinal study design might provide an even more appropriate context of studying the development of the foreign language English. It goes without saying that even though longitudinal studies might have certain advantages over cross-sectional ones, these are also typically costly and time-consuming, and there is the risk that participants might drop out during the course of the study period.

Another point worth investigating is the attitudinal level. The individual attitudes of the students, toward both learning and using English, but also toward their previously acquired languages, might provide additional insights into how perceived importance or usefulness affects the acquisition of a foreign language. Rather than simple yes-or-no statements like the ones used in the current investigation (English is difficult, English is useful), gradable and more fine-grained agreement statements for perceived difficulty and importance would be desirable. Furthermore, instead of limiting these to English only, the students' attitudes toward their previously acquired languages should equally be surveyed. The latter would provide an additional perspective of how the bilingual heritage speakers characterize and value their two native languages.

Finally, instead of exclusively focusing on the learners and their foreign language performance, a follow-up study might additionally target the learning environment and the teachers (including their English usage; see Hickey 2020). With this, it would be possible to directly assess how the teaching methods used in the English language classroom and how acknowledging and incorporating the diverse linguistic backgrounds of all students affect the acquisition and use of the foreign language English. A more comprehensive perspective including teachers and students alike is certainly not an easy endeavor. However, intervention studies implementing translanguaging practices in the English language classroom have the potential to control for additional variables, namely the teaching strategies and thus the learning context (see, for example, Hopp et al. 2020; Leonet, Cenoz, and Gorter 2020).

A final word of caution: it is unlikely that any study will be able to control for all possible confounding factors and to include every single aspect that might play a role in third or additional language acquisition. Nevertheless, each study will eventually add a puzzle piece to the larger picture and increase our understanding of how crosslinguistic influence works in third or additional language acquisition. Any new study zooming in on at least one of the aspects outlined above is highly welcome!

Notes

1 Remember, however, that the German monolingual learners were often shown to be among those learners who had comparatively high rates of correct SVA, formal correctness, and target-like use of verbs or scored even higher (see

Chapters 7 and 8). If at all, this could be understood as a German monolingual advantage, presumably because of their, on average, higher socio-economic status, which was identified as a beneficial condition for foreign language acquisition (see Chapter 9).
2 Cantone (2020: 100) uses the term "mother-tongue instruction" for what has been called heritage language instruction here.
3 "Multilingualism is a goal for everyone" (my translation).
4 1. Development and maintenance of the bilingualism or multilingualism of immigrants (immigrant children); 2. Development and maintenance of the first language or heritage languages of minorities; 3. Development of foreign language competences in monolinguals; 4. Development of foreign language competences (or second and third language competences) in all groups; 5. Lifelong learning (my translation).

References

Cantone, K. F. 2020. Immigrant minority language maintenance in Europe: Focusing on language education policy and teacher-training. *International Multilingual Research Journal* 14:100–113.
Dunn, L. M., D. M. Dunn, B. Styles, and J. Sewell. 2009. *British picture vocabulary scale: BPVS-III*. London: GL Assessment.
Franceschini, R. 2009. Mehrsprachigkeit als Ziel: Didaktische Herausforderungen und Forschungsperspektiven. *Forum Sprache* 1:62–67.
Gilquin, G. and S. Granger. 2015. Learner language. In *The Cambridge handbook of English corpus linguistics*, ed. D. Biber and R. Reppen, 418–435. Cambridge: Cambridge University Press.
González Alonso, J., E. Puig-Mayenco, A. Fábregas, and J. Rothman. 2021. On the status of transfer in adult third language acquisition of early bilinguals. *PLoS ONE* 16:e0247976. https://doi.org/10.1371/journal.pone.0247976
Granger, S. 2015. Contrastive interlanguage analysis : A reappraisal. *International Journal of Learner Corpus Research* 1:7–24.
Grotjahn, R. and A. Drackert. 2020. *The electronic c-test bibliography: Version October 2020*. www.c-test.de, www.ruhr-uni-bochum.de/sprachetesten/index.html.de (accessed April 4, 2022).
Hickey, R. 2020. English in the German-speaking world: The nature and scale of language influence. In *English in the German-speaking world*, ed. R. Hickey, 1–10. Cambridge: Cambridge University Press.
Hopp, H., J. Jakisch, S. Sturm, C. Becker, and D. Thoma. 2020. Integrating multilingualism into the early foreign language classroom: Empirical and teaching perspectives. *International Multilingual Research Journal* 14:146–162.
Klein-Braley, C. and U. Raatz. 1984. A survey of research on the c-test. *Language Testing* 1:134–146.
Kortmann, B. 2005. *English linguistics: Essentials*. Berlin: Cornelsen.
Leonet, O., J. Cenoz, and D. Gorter. 2020. Developing morphological awareness across languages: Translanguaging pedagogies in third language acquisition. *Language Awareness* 29:41–59.
Pinto, M. A., R. Titone, and F. Trusso. 1999. *Metalinguistic awareness: Theory, development and measurement instruments*. Pisa/Rome: Istituti editoriali e poligrafici internazionali.

Schroedler, T. 2021. What is multilingualism? Towards an inclusive understanding. In *Preparing teachers to work with multilingual learners*, ed. M. Wernicke, S. Hammer, A. Hansen, and T. Schroedler, 17–37. Bristol: Multilingual Matters.

Wernicke, M., S. Hammer, A. Hansen, and T. Schroedler (eds.). 2021. *Preparing teachers to work with multilingual learners*. Bristol: Multilingual Matters.

Index

Note: Page numbers in *italics* indicate a figure and page numbers in **bold** indicate a table on the corresponding page.

academic achievement 227
acquisition: additional language acquisition 5–6, 10–11, 33–4, 100, 202, 223, 226, 240, 244–6; adult language acquisition 3–4, 6–7, 41–3, 46, 99, 108, 110n2, 123, 240; child language acquisition 3–4, 6–7, 36, 42–3, 45, 51, 97–9, 106, 108–9, 110n1, 110n9; first language/L1 acquisition 3–6, 36, 98, 109, 110n1, 110n3, 223; foreign language acquisition 3–5, 9–12, 25, 48, 50, 53–8, 94, 99–100, 131, 208, 210–11, 223–9, 232, 233n3, 240–2, 244–6, 247n1; (foreign) language learning 33–4, 53, 58, 218n5, 226, 228, 231, 242–3; formal language acquisition 135, 245; multiple language acquisition 3; second language/L2 acquisition 3–6, 8, 10–12, 33–6, 40, 42, 45, 58n5, 99, 109, 110n3, 132, 239; third language/L3 acquisition 3–8, 9, 10–12, 31, 33–8, 40–3, 46, 49–50, 52, 57–8, 131, 202–3, 205–7, 209, 216, 218n3, 239–40, 245; unfocused language acquisition 208, 218n5; universal acquisition order of tense and aspect 99;
see also age of acquisition, English, foreign language, native, non-native
advantage: bilingual advantage 9, 11–12, 48, 53–8, 202, 215, 223–6, 228–9, 233n3, 239–41, 245; bilingual benefit 10; bilingual effects 48, 54–5, 57; bilingual superiority 54; communicative advantage 224;

linguistic advantage 9, 11, 48, 53, 55–8, 99, 116, 131, 199, 202, 211–12, 215, 223–6, 232, 240; monolingual advantage 247n1; multilingual advantage 11–12, 54–6, 223, 233n3, 239; positive effect 9, 54–5, 57, 242, 244
age 4, 10–12, 19–22, 32, 41, 44–5, 47–8, 50–1, 54, 57, 97–8, 108, 117–18, 125, **126**, 127, 131, 134, 140–1, **142**, 143, **144**, 145–6, **147**, **149**, **151**, **152**, **153**, 154–4, **156**, 157, **159**, **160**, 161, **162**, 163, **164**, 165–6, 169–70, **171**, 173–4, **175**, 177, *179*, 180, 183, 185–6, **187**, 190–1, **192**–**3**, 195, *196*, 197, 199, 203, 207, 209, 211–17, 218n7, 228, 239–40, 243
age of acquisition 44, 108, 214; *see also* age of onset
age of onset 11, 47, 58n6, 109, 117, **126**, 127–8, 134, 169–70, **171**, 173–4, **175**, 177, *179*, 180, 183, 185–6, **187**–**8**, 190–1, **192**–**3**, 195, *196*, 199, 207, 211–17, 240, 243; *see also* age of acquisition
agreement: affixal subject-verb agreement 142–3, **144**, 145–6, 157, **159**, 165, 169, 177–80, 195, 199, 210, 213; subject-verb agreement 47–8, 108, 121, 123, 140, 142, 146, 157–8, 161, 165–6, 169, 177, 184, 195, 198–9, 214, 241; suppletive subject-verb agreement 120–1, 142–3, **144**, 145–6, 152, 158, **159**, 165, 169, 177, 180–1, 195, 200, 213

250 Index

aktionsart 12, 68, 70–1, 74–5, 121; accomplishment 70–1, 74–5, 99–101, **151**, 152, 166; achievement 70–1, 74–5, 99–101, **151**, 152, 166; activity 70–1, 74–5, 100–1, 121, **151**, 152, 166; state 70–2, 74–6, 85, 90, 93, 100–2, 105–6, **151**, 152, 166; *see also* aspect
analytic marking 72, 92, **93**
Arabic 3, 36–7, 42
aspect 7–8, 10–12, 47, 69–73, 75–6, 79–83, 85–7, 89, 91, 92, **93**, 94n2, 97–9, 101–7, 109, 116, 122–3, 134, 140, 148, 212, 216, 224, 226, 239–41, 245; aorist/dispositive aspect 86–7; Aspect Hypothesis 101, 110n4; imperfective aspect 70, 80–1, 85–7, 93, 103–4; lexical aspect 70, 99, 123, **151**, 152 (*see also aktionsart*); perfective aspect 70, 80–2, 85–6, 93, 103–4; progressive aspect 70–1, 75–6, 79, 81, 85, 90, 93, 94n2, 98, 100–2, 104–8, 110, 119–23, 142, 145, 150–3, 163–6, 181–3, 198, 200, 202–5, 210, 213–14, 241
attitude 24, 58n6, 117, 130, 134, 203, 207, 211, 215–16, 229, 240, 246
Austro-Asiatic language 88

background variables 11–12, 55, 117–18, 125–32, 134, 169, 174, 178, 190, 195, 198–200, 203, 207–17, 225, 240
Bardel, C. 36–8, 41, 43, 47–9, 51, 203
Bardovi-Harlig, K. 99–100, 110, 116, 122–3, 150, 228
baseline 125, 178, 180–3, 195, 212, 216, 244
Basque 55, 227, 223n6; Basque Autonomous Country (Spain) 24, 55, 218n3, 233n6
Berthele, R. 9, 43–5, 58n6, 207, 224–5, 232, 233n1
Bialystok, E. 9, 54–5, 59n9, 226
bilingual: active bilingual 59n7; adult bilingual 7; balanced bilingual 44–5, 223–4; bilingual community 6; bilingual experience 57; bilingual immersion program 56; bilingual schoolchildren 46; covert simultaneous bilingual 45; developing bilingual 228; early bilingual 7, 214–15; heritage bilingual 12, 32–3, 43, 45–6, 48, 50–1, 55, 203, 205, 207–8, 217, 224–6, 229–30, 240–1, 244–5; immigrant bilingual 57; late bilingual 7; officially bilingual region 55; regular bilingual 44; sequential bilingual 45, 56, 214; simultaneous bilingual 44, 56; unbalanced bilingual 32, 124, 130–1, 227; (unbalanced) bilingual heritage speaker 11–12, 33, 45–6, 56, 58, 130–1, 134, 203, 206–8, 216–17, 218n3, 223–4, 227–8, 239–42, 245–6; *see also* advantage, bilingualism
bilingualism 5, 33–4, 43–6, 54–5, 57–8, 58n6, 207, 224–5, 227, 232, 233n1, 247n4; adult bilingualism 5; balanced bilingualism 227; early bilingualism 4, 6; elite bilingualism 23; heritage bilingualism 225; late bilingualism 4–6; multidimensional representation of bilingualism 58n6; *see also* bilingual
biliteracy/biscriptuality 48
brain degeneration 54

capital: cultural capital 23, 224; social capital 17
Catalan 55
Cenoz, J. 4–5, 9, 24, 26n12, 34–5, 43, 53–5, 57, 59n7, 207, 210–12, 223, 226, 230–2, 233n6, 246
challenge 22, 24, 56, 99–100, 102, 104, 110, 165–6, 213, 232–3, 242–3
Chinese 36, 42, 99
citizenship 21, 25n4
classroom 13, 20–5, 26n12, 33, 59n7, 72, 102, 107, 114, 116, 135n2, 226, 228–33, 241–2, 244, 246; *see also* English
coding scheme 118, 123
cognition 54, 232; cognitive ability 52, 198, 233n7; cognitive reserve 54; cognitive skill 57, 209
Common European Framework of Reference (CEFR) 23, 45, 59n8
community 6, 13n1, 32–3, 43, 49, 53, 207, 223, 224, 228, 231, 239
competence 1, 4, 6, 8, 10, 21, 23, 24, 31, 34, 45, 53, 131, 134, 136n4, 141, 152, 207, 208, 227, 247n4; passive competence 45; *see also* proficiency

Index

conditional inference tree 178–84, 195–8, 203, 206, 215
continuum 21, 44–5, 92, 224
contrastive linguistics 12, 91; contrastive analysis 72, 91, 102, 105, 131, 244; contrastive interlanguage analysis 244; integrated contrastive model 244–5
Cook, V. 3, 10, 24, 34–5, 53
copula *see* verb
corpus 100–1, 118–19, 131, 135n2, 136n8, 146, 150, 158, **159–60**, 161, **162**, 163, 166, 209, 245; *see also* learner corpus
correlation 155, *157*, 214
cross-language effect *see* crosslinguistic influence
crosslinguistic influence 5–8, 10–12, 33–41, 43, 47–52, 57, 102, 104, 131–2, *133*, 134, 148, 166, 202–6, 208–9, 212–13, 218n3, 224–6, 229–30, 239–40, 244–6; facilitative crosslinguistic influence 38–9, 203; influence from the heritage language 10, 148, 224–5, 230; influence from the L1 36–7, 99, 102, 166, 204; influence from the L2 36–7; influence from the majority language 132; negative (crosslinguistic) influence 11, 148, 166, 202, 204–5, 225; non-facilitative crosslinguistic influence 38–9; phonological crosslinguistic influence 50; positive (crosslinguistic) influence 11, 36–7, 39, 52, 166, 203–5, 225, 243; *see also* third language acquisition models, transfer
cross-sectional 11, 123, 132, 217, 239, 246
C-test 216, 244
Cummins, J. 215, 223, 231

Danish 18–19, 20, 227, 223n2
De Angelis, G. 1, 5, 31, 34, 212, 226
dementia 54
Denmark 19, 227
dialect 2, 44, 94n7
diversity 2, 20–1, 34, 46, 136n4, 141, 229–31, 233n7
Dutch 18, 36, 42

education 17, 22, 23; education policy 22; education system 22–3, 26n10, 136n10, 239, 243; educational aspiration 130, 211; educational context 3, 241–2; educational focus 25; educational framework 22; educational institution 128, 229–30; educational journey 240; educational perspective 105, 108; educational setting 131, 229, 240; educational success 211, 229; formal education 32, 42, 55, 128; primary education 22, 128; school education 22, 32; secondary education 22–3, 25; teacher education 23, 230, 233, 242; university education 31, 36; *see also* foreign language, teaching
E-LiPS project 46, 48, 114, 118, 140, 146, 150, 154, 163, 165–6, 209
English: acquisition of English 3, 11, 17–25, 46, 55, 94, 108–9, 204, 244; Australian English 110n5; British English 23; English in Germany 3, 11, 17–25, 102; English language classroom 23–4, 72, 231–2, 241–2, 246; English as a lingua franca (*see* lingua franca); English native speaker 12, 37, 97–8, 100, 108–9, 114, 121, 124–5, 130, 141, 145–6, 148, 150, 154–5, 165, 202, 212, 239; new English variety 102; Present-Day English 72, 100; Standard English 102; varieties of English 18, 102; World Englishes 18, 25n1, 100; *see also* classroom
Eurobarometer 18–19
executive function 9, 54–5
extra-linguistic 12, 52

Falk, Y. 36–8, 41, 43, 47–9, 51, 203
Finland 229
Flanker task 54, 59n9
Flynn, S. 5, 37–8, 40–3, 49–50, 203, 205
foreign language: additional/further foreign language 5, 9, 11, 34, 36, 48, 52–3, 55–8, 100, 208, 233n3, 240, 244; first foreign language 3, 5, 21–2, 35–6, 43, 45, 240; foreign language class(room) 13, 20–5, 26n12, 33, 59n7, 117, 226, 229–31, 233, 241–2; foreign language education 13, 22, 230–3; foreign language learner/user 5, 18, 51, 59n7, 98–101, 107, 125, 146, 148, 150, 152–3, 155, 157, 165–6, 202, 205, 212–13, 217, 227–8; foreign

language teacher 229, 231; foreign language teaching 20, 22–5, 91, 232; second foreign language 3; *see also* acquisition, teaching
formal correctness 121, 123, 140, 148–50, **151**, 152, 161–3, 166, 169–70, **171**, 174, 177–8, 181–2, 184–6, **187**, 190–1, 198–9, 200n1, 200n2, 203, 210–11, 214–16, 241, 246n1
Franceschini, R. 1, 32, 44, 45, 53, 59n7, 208, 210, 218n5, 228, 233, 242
French 4, 22, 36–7, 42, 105
frequency overview 140–50, 155–8
Full Transfer/Full Access Model 35, 38
Full Transfer Potential 39

gender 47, 82, 118, 125, 127, 134, 169–71, 174–5, 177, 183, 185, **187–8**, 189–91; **192–3**, 211, 216; female 122, 125, 127, 169, 177, 185, 189; male 125, 127, 169, **171**, 175, 177, 185, **187–8**, 189, **192–3**
generation 19, 21, 25n5, 131, 210, 243
Germanic 42, 72, 76
Germany 2–4, 11–12, 17–25, 33, 43, 46, 55–6, 71–2, 74, 83, 102, 114, 124–5, 127–8, 131, 136n10, 137n12, 198, 206–7, 209–10, 214, 216–17, 226, 228–31, 239–41, 243
global 17–18, 22, 50, 243
globalization 3, 6, 21, 33
Gogolin, I. 20–1, 23, 46, 114, 207, 216–17, 229–30

Hamburg 20–1, 25n4, 46, 114
Hammarberg, B. 1, 31, 36, 38, 203
heritage speaker *see* bilingual heritage speaker
Hermas, A. 5–6, 36–8, 41–3, 204
heterogeneity 23, 45, 57, 132, 233n7
heterogeneous 20–1, 23, 25, 109, 231, 233, 233n7, 242
homogeneity 132
homogeneous 6, 57, 70–1, 131–2
Hopp, H. 7, 24, 32–3, 43, 45–6, 49–52, 55–6, 134, 203, 206–8, 210, 223, 225, 228, 230–2, 233n5, 246

identity 17, 19
immigration 6, 20–1; immigrant 2–3, 20–1, 25n4, 25n5, 32, 57, 110n5, 207, 210, 217, 247n4; *see also* migration
Indo-European language family 72, 76, 79, 92
inflectional affix/ending/suffix/marking 47, 68, 72–3, 76, 82, 88, 91–2, 97, 107–8, 110
inhibition 59n9, 206
initial state 42, 51, 58n5; initial stages 36, 38, 42, 50, 58n5, 97, 99, 204–5, 245
input 20, 24, 26n12, 38, 45, 91, 228–9, 231, 241
instruction: English tuition 55, 212; formal instruction 4, 33, 226, 230; heritage language instruction 242, 247n2; heritage language tuition 32; instruction of English 20, 23; instruction at school 20, 23; instructional (school) setting/ context 226, 229–30; language instruction 10, 33; language of instruction 32, 46, 49, 124, 130, 134, 207–8, 241; mother-tongue instruction 247n2; systematic instruction 23; *see also* teaching
interference 8, 35, 106
inversion 39, 51
investment 17
Italian 37–8, 42, 51

Japanese 37, 99
Jessner, U. 5, 10, 31, 34–5, 52–3, 55, 212, 226

Kazakh 37, 42
Korean 99

language: additional language 7, 18, 21, 23, 31, 34, 54–5, 131, 231–2, 244; analytic language 76; dominant language 32–3, 40–1, 44–6, 48–50, 52, 124, 134, 203, 206–8, 224, 229, 239–41; established language 2; first language (L1) 4, 6, 8–9, 17–18, 31–40, 42–3, 49–51, 58n5, 97–9, 101–2, 105–10, 110n8, 111, 166, 132, 202–4, 206–7, 227, 239–40, 247n4; fusional language 76, 79, 92; heritage language 10–11, 21, 23–4, 32–3, 43, 45–6, 48–9, 52, 124–5, 130–2, 134, 148, 197, 202–3, 205–8, 215–16, 217n1, 218n4, 223–6, 228–31, 239–44, 247n2, 247n4;

Index 253

inflecting language 76; interlanguage 205, 212, 244; isolating language 47, 76, 88, 91–2, 145, 231; language dominance 31, 45, 49, 130, 206–8; language shift 18, 32; language status 2, 17–20, 22, 25, 33, 43–6, 49, 51, 100, 102, 134, 206–7, 240–1; learner language 116, 119, 131, 135n2, 152, 245; majority language 4, 13n1, 32, 45–8, 50, 52, 57–8, 124, 130–2, 134, 206–8, 224, 229–32, 240–1; minority language 2, 32, 45, 208; (non-) target language 7, 8, 38, 58n2, 212, 218n2, 228–9; official language 2, 22, 32–3, 207, 223–4, 239; second language (L2) 3–10, 13n1, 18–19, 23, 31–2, 34–40, 42–3, 45–9, 51, 58n5, 59n7, 98–9, 101–2, 104, 108–10, 123–4, 132, 134, 146, 202–4, 206, 212–13, 215, 217n1, 225–6, 231, 239–40; target variety 23; third language (L3) 5–10, 23, 31–2, 35–9, 41–3, 46, 51–2, 55–7, 58n5, 132, 134, 204–5, 212, 225, 227, 240; *see also* acquisition, bilingual, foreign language, instruction, native, non-native
learner corpus 11, 114, 116, 118–19, 125, 131, 135, 135n2, 135n3, 136n7, 136n8, 140, 150, 152, 154–5, **156**, 158, 163, 165, 178, 180, 184, 195, 198, 217, 239; *see also* corpus
learning environment 4, 13, 22–5, 42, 224, 228–31, 246
lexical diversity *see* diversity
lexical similarity 39
limitation 12, 19, 197–8, 215–17
lingua franca 2, 18–19, 110
linguistic proximity 39, 204, 206; *see also* third language acquisition models
linguistic repertoire *see* repertoire
linguistic system 5–6, 53
literacy 24, 48, 52, 211
longitudinal 46, 106, 217, 246

Mazandarani 40, 42, 206
meaning-oriented approach 122
M-effect 10; *see also* metalinguistic awareness
metalinguistic awareness 10–12, 26n13, 52–3, 58, 224, 226–31, 233n2, 243, 245

migration 2, 3, 45, 233n4; migrant 229; *see also* immigration
mixed results 50, 54–6
mode (spoken, written) 164, 178, 185–6, **187**, 190–1, **192–3**, 197, 199, 214; *see also* oral data, spoken data, written data
Mon-Khmer language 88
monocultural ideology 23
monolingual: monolingual acquisition path 225; monolingual beliefs 24; monolingual country 2; monolingual family 45; monolingual habitus 23, 25, 230, 242; monolingual household 210; monolingual ideology 23; monolingual perspective 224, 228, 241; monolingual syllabus 22; *see also* advantage, monolingualism, teaching
monolingualism 44, 233n1; *see also* monolingual
Montrul, S. 20–1, 32–3, 45, 207, 216
morphological typology 91–2; *see also* typology
motivation 42, 109, 209, 215, 232
multi-competence 10, 53; *see also* metalinguistic awareness
multilingual: late multilingual 45, 59n7; multilingual activity 24; multilingual awareness 53; multilingual behavior 34; multilingual children 21; multilingual class 22; multilingual competence 24; multilingual context 40; multilingual country 2; multilingual development 46, 232; multilingual element 232; multilingual group 227; multilingual learner 34, 53, 241; multilingual mind 24; multilingual participant 227; multilingual person 31; multilingual perspective 22; multilingual practice 230; multilingual reality 20, 22, 230, 241; multilingual region 2; multilingual society 1, 3; multilingual space 20; multilingual speaker 9, 21, 35, 52–4, 58, 226–8; multilingual student 24, 218n8, 227, 232; *see also* advantage, multilingualism, teaching
multilingualism 1–2, 5–6, 11–12, 20, 23, 25n8, 34, 53–4, 229–31, 242, 247n3, 247n4; *see also* multilingual

Na Ranong, S. 36, 41–3, 204
native: native acquisition 12; native grammatical knowledge 109; native country 239; native language 2–4, 11, 17–18, 31, 34, 43, 97–8, 109, 111n9, 117, 125, 148, 203, 224, 227, 239–41, 244–6; native learner 98; native-like 44, 215; native proficiency 21; native speaker 4, 12, 18, 36–7, 50, 97, 100, 104, 108–9, 111n9, 114, 121, 124–5, 130, 141, 145–6, 148, 150, 154–5, 165, 202–3, 212, 218n4, 239, 244; native speaker baseline 244; native tongue 3; novice native speaker 125, 136n8
the Netherlands 11, 18–19, 79
non-native: non-native acquisition 3, 12, 34; non-native context 102; non-native language 4, 7, 34; non-native learner 98, 100–1, 110, 145; non-native linguistic knowledge 34; non-native speaker 18, 98, 101, 233n2; non-native-like features 230
North Frisian 2
Norway 11, 24, 229
Norwegian 39, 42
number of books 118, 129–30, 134, 170, **171**, 173–4, **175**, 180, 183, 185, **187**, 190–1, **192**, 195, 199–200, 203, 207, 210–13, 215, 225, 240, 243

omission 47, 104, 108, 110, 121, 146, 152, 160, 202, 213
oral data 12, 118, 134, 158, 161, 163, 217; oral comprehension 59; oral output 114; oral picture description 7, 122, 160, 213, 245; oral production 10–11, 23, 36, 59, 104, 117, 157–8, 161, 209; oral recording 10, 117–19, 121, **126**, 155, **156**, 158, 160–1, 163, **164**, 165–6, 167n5, 214, 217; oral task 10, 114, 116–17, 125, 155, 158, 165, 184, 213–14, 243; *see also* mode, spoken data, transcript
oral interaction 59n8
overuse 101, 103, 120–1, 143, **144**, **159**, 166, 178

performance 7, 9–10, 24, 37, 39, 47–8, 50, 54–6, 104, 107–8, 114, 117, 123, 125, 132, 136n4, 141–2, 157, 161, 165, 167n1, 197–9, 203–4, 207–9, 211, 212–13, 218n2, 223, 225, 243–6
Persian 40, 42, 206
perspective: contrastive linguistic perspective 12, 91; developmental perspective 11, 38, 131, 217, 239; educational perspective 105, 108; German perspective 23, 241; longitudinal perspective 46; monolingual perspective 224, 228; multilingual perspective 22; national perspective 18–19; teacher perspective 241; theoretical perspective 11, 239; typological perspective 12
phonological awareness 232
picture story 49, 114, 116, 121–2, 136n1, 141, 167n1, 213–14
policy 17, 22
Portuguese 38, 42
principle of economy 38
professional development 233
proficiency 19, 21, 31–2, 44–5, 50–1, 56, 59n8, 99, 119, 123, 128, 130, 136n4, 141, 152, 154, 165, 167, 197, 198, 207–8, 212–13, 215–16, 223, 225, 227, 231, 233n6, 243–5; *see also* competence
psychotypology *see* typology

questionnaire 114, 117, 125, 129

register 44, 76
repertoire 8–9, 26n12, 33, 39, 42, 53–4, 107, 198, 204, 215, 223, 230, 240–1
representational level 8
resource 26n12, 229–31, 242, 244
Romance 38, 42
Rothman, J. 3–8, 35–8, 40–3, 45, 47, 50–2, 57, 58n3, 58n5, 204–8, 216, 218n2
Russia 21, 104, 114, 127, 228

Saterfrisian 3
school: *Gymnasium* 22, **126**, 128–9, 136n10, 170, 173–4, 177, 180–1, 185, 190–1, 197, 199, 209–10, 217, 243; primary school 20, 23, 42, 46, 49, 55–6, 232; school-aged 10, 19–20, 40, 50–1; school grade 115, 118, **126**, 128–9, 137n12, 197, 200n3, 215, n33n1; school system 22, 129, 136n11; secondary school 11, 20–1, 23, 42, 128–9, 134,

Index 255

136n10, 173, 177, 180, 197–9, 207, 209, 215, 217, 224, 228, 240–1; secondary school student 19–20, 25, 46, 56, 116, 135, 209, 229, 239; type of school 10–11, 22, 47, 117, **126**, 128–9, 136n10, 136n11, 170, **171**, 173–4, **175**, 177, 180–1, 183, 185–6, **187**, 190–1, **192**–3, 195, 197, 199, 200n3, 203, 207, 209–17, 240, 243; university-bound secondary school **126**, 128–9, 136n10, 173–4, 177, 180–1, 190–1, 197, 199, 209–10, 217, 225, 243; *see also* education
Siemund, P. 7–9, 17–19, 21–4, 26n9, 26n13, 41, 46–9, 51–2, 55–7, 69–70, 76, 91–2, 110n5, 114, 128–9, 134, 198, 206, 208–10, 212, 214, 223–6, 229–30, 232, 233n3
Simon task 54, 59n9
Slabakova, R. 6, 36, 38, 40, 42, 50, 52, 204, 206, 207
Slavonic branch 79
socio-economic background/status 21, 47–8, 52, 55, 57, 118, **126**, 128–30, 134, 170, **171**, 174, **175**, *176*, 177, *179*, 180, 183, 185–6, **187**, *189*, 190–1, **192**, 195, *196*, 197, 199–200, 203, 207, 209–13, 215–17, 225, 227–8, 240, 243, 247n1
Sorbian 3
Spanish 4, 37–8, 42, 55, 99, 110n7, 225, 227, 233n6
spoken conversation 18, 85, 107
spoken data 48–9, 158, 161, 166, **187**, *189*, **192**, *194*, *196*, 198, 214; spoken component 154–5, **156**, 158, **159–60**, 161, **162**; spoken picture description 239, 244; spoken production 134, 154, 184, 198–9, 240; spoken task 198, 213, 240; *see also* mode, oral data, transcript
spoken discourse 77, 103
Stroop task 54, 59n9
subject-verb agreement *see* agreement
success 53, 109, 211, 215, 225, 229
Swedish 36

target-like: non-target-like 36, 47, 102–3, 105–6, 109, 110n6, 118, 121–2, 124, 136n7, 143, 161, 174, 177, 182, 190–1, 244; target-like context 161, 166, 174, 183, 213; target-like language 123; target-like meaning 120–1, 136n7, 148, **149**, 150, 161, **162**, 163, 169, 174–8, 181–4, 190–4, 199–200, 203, 210–12, 214; target-like performance 9, 165, 204, 211–13, 244; target-like translation 103; target-like usage 123, 143, **151**, 165; target-like use 47, 102, 121–3, 140, 150, 158, 166, 198, 202, 210, 216, 240–1, 243, 246n1; target-like word order 56; *see also* progressive aspect
teacher 22–5, 102, 106, 114–15, 229–33, 242, 246; in-service teacher 233; teacher action 26n12; teacher assessment 22; teacher education 23, 230, 233, 242; teacher perspective 241; teacher recommendation 128; teacher training 23; *see also* teaching
teaching: English teaching 22, 105, 232, 241, 246; monolingual teaching approach/principle/style 23–4, 207, 230–1; multilingual pedagogy 224, 232–3, 241; multilingual/plurilingual teaching approach 24, 230–2, 233n5; teaching material 100, 232; teaching practice 23–4, 230, 233; teaching reality 20, 22, 241; *see also* education, foreign language, instruction, multilingual, teacher
tense: complex tense 79, 99, 152; conditional form 82, 87, 120, 153, 163, **164**; future perfect 72, 78–9; future tense 68, 72–82, 84–5, 87, 90, 92–4, 103, 106, 120, 153, 163, **164**; imperfective future 82; past perfect 72, 75, 78, 92, 94n2, 98, 103–4, 106, 120, 153, 163, **164**; mixed tense 124, 183–4, 200, 211; past tense/simple past 68–9, 72–4, 76–8, 80–5, 87–9, 92, 94n3, 97–100, 102–8, 110n5, 116, 119–20, 122–4, 136n7, 142–3, 145, 152–4, 161, 163, **164**, 165, 177–8, 183–4, 198, 200, 211, 241–5; periphrastic tense 72, 82; present perfect 72, 74, 76–8, 84, 92, 94n2, 102–6, 110, 120, 153, 163, **164**; present tense/simple present 69, 72–7, 80–5, 87, 92–3, 102–8, 116, 119–20, 122, 124, 136n7,

142, 145, 152–4, 163, **164**, 165–6, 167n4, 167n5, 177, 183–4, 198, 200, 211, 241, 245; simple tense 75; zero marking 84–5
text composition 140–2, 214
Thai 36, 42
third language acquisition models 32–4, 40–1, 43, 46, 49, 57, 204, 206, 218n3, 240; Cumulative Enhancement Model 37–8, 40, 49–50, 203–4; L2 Status Factor 36–8, 43, 47–9, 51, 203; Linguistic Proximity Model 39–41, 47–52, 133, 204–6; Scalpel Model 40–1, 50, 52, 204–6; Typological Primacy Model 38, 40, 42, 47, 50–1, 204–6; *see also* crosslinguistic influence, linguistic proximity, transfer, typology
transcript 119, 150, 155, 165; transcription 118, 135n1; *see also* mode, oral data, spoken data, written data
transfer: facilitative transfer 35, 37–9, 50; heritage language transfer 49, 132, 134, 205; holistic transfer 38–9, 58n4; L1 transfer 36, 39, 43, 49, 107–8, 204, 206; L2 transfer 36, 39, 204; lexical transfer 8, 56, 209; majority/dominant language transfer 48, 50, 52, 134, 206, 208; morphosyntactic transfer 5; negative (crosslinguistic) transfer 35–7, 39, 48–9, 105, 108, 133, 202; no transfer 131–2, 202, 204–5; non-facilitative transfer 35, 37–9, 50, 218n2; positive (crosslinguistic) transfer 35, 39, 133, 202, 204; property-by-property transfer 38–40, 48, 204–5, 218n2; selective transfer 40–1, 50–1; systemic transfer 58n4; transfer effect 36, 105, 107; transfer potential 39, 205; transfer scenarios 35, 37, 47, 132–4, 202; wholesale (transfer) 40, 58, 204–5; *see also* crosslinguistic influence, third language acquisition models
translanguaging 246; pedagogical translanguaging 24, 26n12, 230, 231–2, 233n6
trilingual 6
Turkey 21, 114, 127, 228
Turkic language 84

typology 38, 45, 91–2; typological similarity/proximity 38–40, 48–9, 52, 58n3, 134, 206, 241; *see also* morphological typology, third language acquisition models

university student 20, 41, 102, 105, 229

variability 120, 140, 191, 210–11, 216–17
verb: auxiliary verb 72, 74, 77–8, 82, 88, 90, 92, **93**, 94n4, 94n7, 98–9, 103, 104, 108, 120–1, 123, 145, 150, **151**, 152; copula verb 82–3, 87, 91, **93**, 97–9, 104, 106, 108, 120–1, 140, 145–8, 158–61, 166, 202, 204, 213, 225; irregular verb 73, 98, 107, 121, 177; lexical verb 72–4, 104, 136n5, 142–3, 145–6, 157–8; modal verb 120, 143, 153, 163, **164**, 227; regular verb 73, 121; suppletive verb 120–1, 142–3, 145, 152, 158, 169, 180, 195; unanalyzable/unclassified verb 122, 140, 142, **143**, **153**, **164**
Vietnam 107, 114, 127, 228
vocabulary 7, 23, 55, 56, 115–17, 141, 232; vocabulary test 244
vowel harmony 84, 94n5

Westergaard, M. 7–8, 39–43, 47–52, 58n5, 133, 204–6, 208
written data 12, 48, 119, 134, 158, 161, 163, 165–6, **187**, **189**, **192**, *194*, *196*, 198, 214, 217; written component 140, 150, 152, 154–5, **156**, 158, **159–60**, **162**, 165; written performance 56, 136n4; written picture description 112, 239, 244–5; written production 10–11, 47, 59n8, 76, 116, 154, 157–8, 161, 184, 198–9, 209, 240; written story 122, 124, 134, 167n1, 183, *184*, 213; written task 114–17, 125, 155, 157–8, 165–6, 184, 198, 202, 213–14, 240, 243; written text 10, 77, 107, 116, 119, 158, 160–1, 163, **164**, 165, 184, 190; *see also* mode, transcript
written exam 105, 227
written interaction 59n8
word order 50, 56, 88